Mrs. Hale

The Letters of Madame de Sevigne to her Daughter and Friends

Mrs. Hale

The Letters of Madame de Sevigne to her Daughter and Friends

ISBN/EAN: 9783337134921

Printed in Europe, USA, Canada, Australia, Japan

Cover: Foto ©ninafisch / pixelio.de

More available books at **www.hansebooks.com**

THE LETTERS

OF

MADAME DE SÉVIGNÉ

TO

HER DAUGHTER AND FRIENDS.

EDITED BY

MRS. HALE,

AUTHORESS OF "WOMAN'S RECORD," "NORTHWOOD," "VIGIL OF LOVE,"
"MANNERS," ETC.

> "There is none
> In all this cold and hollow world, no fount
> Of deep, strong, deathless love, save that within
> A mother's heart." — MRS. HEMANS.

REVISED EDITION.

BOSTON:
ROBERTS BROTHERS.
1878.

PREFACE TO THE REVISED EDITION.

THE Editress has set forth so fully, in the introductory sketch of Madame de Sévigné's Life and Times, her object in offering this book to the American public, that any further prologue may seem superfluous; yet there are one or two things to be said which seem to find their most proper expression in a Preface. Since the date of the first edition, the changes in the manners and feelings of the time have been rapid and continuous; and they have operated in a twofold manner.

In the first place, we have become as a nation more thoroughly acquainted with French literature, and better able to appreciate that world of the past in which the great letter-writer lived. Madame de Sévigné was a woman who lived in and for others, — for her daughter, her friends, and, at a greater distance, for the brilliant circle of distinguished men and women of which she herself was so important a figure. Her letters are made up of incident, of meetings, of conversations: they are full of references to the topics then uppermost; they draw half their charm from the personality of the writer. Literature of this sort cannot stand alone. To enjoy it to the full we must know with some minuteness the history of the times in which it was written, and of the people to whom it was written. The knowledge of these things is now spreading wider every year, as we become familiar, through originals or translations, with the masterpieces of foreign languages. For instance, probably the best French sketch of Madame de Sévigné is from the pen of M. Sainte-Beuve, the great critic whom Mr. Arnold acknowledges for his master. This sketch has been translated by Miss Preston, and published within the last year.* Our limits forbid quotation; but to every one who can enjoy a criticism at once delicate and profound, we recommend this incomparable study.

Again, the times themselves in which we live call for the exercise of just such an influence upon the mind and style as might be wielded by these letters. We in America are almost all educated up to a certain point; few of us, unfortunately, are educated beyond it. The national character is pushing, energetic, ambitious; setting great value upon money and material luxuries, but without appreciation of the refined enjoyments that consist with a moderate purse, or the delicacy of feeling that marks a sensitive but well-balanced mind. The vortex of politics or of business draws into it all our energies; we have nothing to spare for reflection, for the observances of friendship, for the amenities of social intercourse. A life so vulgarizing alike to the mind and to the style, finds its best antidote in the letters of Madame de Sévigné. Here is a beautiful existence centred in home and friends; here are thoughts occupied by love for the dear ones around, and by sympathy with their joys and sorrows. The tumult of the outer world is heard faintly. The writer's mind is busied in a calmer sphere, and the exquisite tenderness of her heart gives that transparent grace to her style that has been the wonder and the despair of two centuries.

We are a letter-writing people; and no better models for letters exist than Madame de Sévigné's. We are a practical and energetic people; and no better complement to such virtues can be found than the tender affection and delicate refinement of Madame de Sévigné.

PHILADELPHIA, Nov. 26, 1868.

---

* Sainte-Beuve's Portraits of Celebrated Women.

MADAME DE SÉVIGNÉ AND HER TIMES.

An honorable celebrity has been universally accorded to Madame de Sévigné. For nearly two centuries her "Letters" have been the admiration of all lovers of elegant literature. The natural grace, the "*curiosa felicitas*" of these epistles have rendered them remarkable as to style, and the artist-like pictures of manners, the lively accounts of cotemporaneous incidents give them very great value as aids to the study of history. Then they are trustworthy documents; every word, every circumstance is read with particular satisfaction, because the character and position of the writer assure us of her perfect intent to communicate truth.

Madame de Sévigné lived in what the French consider their Augustan Age. Great men in arts, in arms, in literature gave glory to the most splendid monarch that ever sat on the throne of France. At the same time the position of women was both active and brilliant. The social existence of the women of the higher classes was one that gave scope to talent and opportunity to energy. In those days the great dame was occupied with the administration of her property and the exaltation of her family. Far from being absorbed in a narrow routine of personality, she considered the sacrifice of private feelings to family greatness a positive duty, and the sacrifice of family greatness to the king—that is, the state—a still more imperative obligation.

As our views of moral responsibility extend, the intellectual horizon enlarges. The woman who was accustomed to dwell upon considerations beyond mere fireside comforts or fashionable display; who went from the individual to the family, and from the family to the state, must of necessity have enlarged her understanding in proportion to the elevation and extent of her views. It is only by a just development of the intellectual faculties that the heart can be properly regulated, and nowhere is this truth more strikingly illustrated than in the life of Madame de Sévigné.

Her passionate love for her daughter was always made to yield to the dictates of a wise prudence and just propriety. Though born with excessive sensibility, great vivacity, amiable instincts, and warm imagination, that is to say, with the qualities and feelings most likely to lead their possessor astray or into indiscretions, yet this youthful widow managed her estate and her children with admirable wisdom, and so regulated her own conduct as to be above the slightest censure in a court of relaxed morals and of many temptations. This was accomplished because her brilliant qualities rested on the solid basis of serious and valuable acquirements, a practical knowledge of business, and a trusting and sincere piety.

To make the example of this excellent woman more widely and familiarly known in America is the main object of this volume. As a model in private life, her conduct and character deserve to be studied. Her "Letters" are referred to by the best authorities, as the most charming specimens of epistolary art extant, yet no edition has ever been issued in this country. Nor would one be profitable, because the complete work is too large. Still it is desirable to have access to this treasury of beautiful sentiments and entertaining sketches; and we have here selected such portions of her correspondence as will make her virtues known and give those lessons of practical goodness her life so happily illustrated.

In order to do this we have arranged the correspondence on a new plan. Hitherto the "Letters" have been thrown together according to date, and the reader was compelled to change from one correspondent to another, even on the same page, often finding similar details in several consecutive epistles. In this volume each person addressed has his or her own department—thus the Letters to Madame de Grignan, the soul of the correspondence, form one unbroken series. Much care has been taken to keep the fine and often sparkling threads of narrative inwoven in the Letters continuous, and errors in the only English translation we have seen (published in London, in 1811) have been corrected by comparing it with the best French editions of the

"Letters."* And now we will endeavor to sketch the life of this lovely and lovable woman, though the events are in no wise remarkable, and the truest portrait of her character and genius must be sought in her letters.

MARIE DE RABUTIN-CHANTAL

was born February 5th, 1627, in the ancestral château of Bourbilly, between Samur and Epoisses. Her father was Celse-Bénigne de Rabutin, Baron of Chantal; her mother, Marie de Coulanges, was daughter of a Secretary of State, and belonged to a family celebrated for wit, and, generally, remarkable for integrity. The baron was slain during the siege of Rochelle, fighting against the English in their descent on the island of Rhé; and it was thought he was killed by the hand of Cromwell. The little Marie was then but eighteen months old, and soon afterward was, by the death of her mother, left an orphan indeed. The Baroness de Chantal, her grandmother, seemed the person naturally destined to have the guardianship of the child, but that lady was occupied in religious duties (she was afterward a canonized saint, and known as the "Blessed Mother of Chantal," and seems to have deserved the distinction, according to the feeling of those days, as she founded eighty-seven religious houses), and, therefore, permitted her granddaughter to pass into the hands of her mother's relations. She was first taken by her grandfather, M. de Coulanges; when he died, shortly afterward, the orphan, then about nine years of age, passed into the family of her uncle, Christophe de Coulanges, Abbé de Livry. This was a fortunate event for the young girl. She was brought up and educated with her cousin, Philippe Emanuel de Coulanges, enjoying the advantages of the most intellectual society of the age; her learned uncle was her companion, and encouraged her to cultivate her talents. This last advantage can hardly be estimated now, when feminine education is common and popular; but then the instruction of young ladies was usually limited to the accomplishments of reading, writing, dancing, and embroidery. Marie de Rabutin had the *entrée* to her uncle's

---

* The explanatory notes, which afford useful particulars concerning personages and events mentioned in the Letters, are partly from the French, and partly by the English translator and the present Editor.

library and his encouragement, if not personal instruction, in her literary pursuits. She was taught Latin, Italian, and Spanish; her instructors were Menage and Chapelain, and other professors of polite literature. The result is before the world—that the woman's mind is as susceptible of cultivation as that of the man's, and that she is made happier, better, more lovely, and more capable of doing good by a liberal and careful cultivation of her intellectual powers.

In person and manners Mademoiselle de Rabutin is represented as very attractive, if not positively beautiful. M. Ph. A Grouville, her French biographer, thus describes her:

"An exact portrait of her person would savor of romance, and would be out of place; we may, however, represent the young Rabutin to our imagination as a truly handsome woman, with more character of countenance than beauty; with features more expressive than commanding; an easy figure, a stature rather tall than short, a redundancy of fine light hair, excellent health, a fine color, a brilliant complexion, eyes, the vivacity of which gave additional animation to her language and agility to her movements, a pleasing voice, as much knowledge of music as existed in those days, and of dancing, in which she excelled for the times. This is the idea that her portraits, her friends, or herself give of her. And certainly her nose, tending a little toward the square, which she herself ridicules, could not spoil her whole appearance as much as the age of eighteen embellished it, when, in 1644, she married Henry, Marquis de Sévigné, of an ancient family of Brittany. To this appendage of merit and charms she added a dower of a hundred thousand crowns, which, at that period, were not of less value than seven hundred thousand francs."

The Marquis de Sévigné was also rich, moreover he was young, handsome, and gay. Her good uncle doubtless believed he had secured the happiness of his niece by this connection; but the sequel proved otherwise. The marquis soon showed himself to be weak, vain, extravagant, and, finally, a profligate. Though he always admitted the charms and merits of his wife, yet, after a year or two, he began to neglect her for unworthy associates. The siren of that age, Ninon de l'Enclos, drew him to her side, and for that wanton the happiness of his home was sacrificed.

Bussy de Rabutin, cousin of Madame de Sévigné's father, an

unprincipled man, but distinguished for wit and talent, had always admired and loved, or pretended to be in love with his fascinating cousin, and she had always laughed at his flattery and rejected his suit. He took advantage of her husband's infidelity to offer an insulting proposal, that she should take her revenge. He was reproved in such terms of cold and calm severity as put a final repulse to his gallantry toward her. Though their intercourse continued friendly through life, yet, judging from the tone of her letters to him, always constrained, and confined chiefly to his own affairs, we feel that, though she acknowledged their relationship, she never esteemed the man.

Her husband was killed in a duel, about seven years after marriage, and Madame de Sévigné, at the age of twenty-five, was left a widow, with two children, the eldest, her son, the youngest, that idolized daughter, who made the light of her mother's life.

In spite of the faults and vices of the Marquis de Sévigné, his sudden and shocking death greatly afflicted his wife. She was, for a time, nearly overwhelmed with sorrow, but soon found devolving upon her the hard and painful duty of endeavoring to extricate her estate from utter ruin. The follies and waste of her husband came near making her and the children penniless. She retired to the country, and, aided by the counsel and encouragement of her uncle the abbé, entered on her new duties. We quote from one of her French biographers, who seems to have searched out her history with great care:

"Madame de Sévigné's good sense, natural rectitude, and laudable pride, gave her a taste for economy, and the advice of her uncle taught her to understand it. Her mind, notwithstanding the habit of sacrificing to the Graces, had no repugnance to business. She well knew how to sell or let estates, receive her rents, direct her workmen, etc. She did not trust to her beauty alone for gaining law-suits. Ménage relates, that one day, recommending an affair with great ease and simplicity to the President de Bellièvre, she felt herself at last a little embarrassed with the terms to be used, when she said, 'At least, sir, I know the air perfectly, but I forget the words.'

"With regard to education, not only do the merit of her son and daughter, as well as their virtues, show the extent of her capacity in this respect, but it would be easy to extract from her letters a series of maxims upon the subject, by which it would be seen that, far from adhering to the false methods in vogue in her days, she had foretold many of the improvements of which we are justly vain in ours."

Though she devoted herself sedulously to the duties of her family, yet Madame de Sévigné did not long live a recluse. She saved her property, returned to society, and passed much of her time in Paris, where she was the idol of her circle, people of the first rank in letters and worth of character, as well as stars in the fashionable world. She was also a frequent visitor at court, where the king, Louis XIV, always received her with respect.

Madame de Sévigné had many adorers, among whom were the Seigneur Turenne and the Prince de Conti, and her friends were most devoted—Fouquet was one of them, and she was true to him in his great misfortune, as her letters show. But she appears never to have had the least intention of a second marriage; to promote the happiness of her children and the enjoyment of her friends, was the object of her life. Her son, the Marquis de Sévigné, who entered the army, was very frivolous, weak, and dissipated in his youth; his mother's watchful care and patient forbearance saved him from utter degradation. About middle age he married an amiable wife of noble family, left the army, and cultivated a taste for literature. To effect this marriage, and thus secure the reformation of her son, Madame de Sévigné gave up to him so large a portion of her estate that she was afterward in comparatively straitened circumstances.

But the daughter, Margaret Frances, was her mother's glory, the idol that seemed to claim the worship of the mother's soul. Passion rather than affection possessed Madame de Sévigné when writing to or of her "infinitely dear child." That the daughter did not reciprocate this love in its full flow has been urged to prove that Madame de Grignan was cold in temperament or selfish in feeling. We do not find evidences to support this charge. The mother, ambitious for her daughter, and wishing to keep her in Paris had married her to the Count de Grignan, who was rich, and of the high nobility, and had a place at court. But he was also Lieutenant-Governor of Provence, and ordered, soon after his marriage, to his government. His wife had to follow him; she seems to have loved and respected her husband, as was her duty. She had children; she was at the head of a great establishment, and she could not give the whole of her heart, thoughts, and time to her mother, as the latter did to her daughter.

The separation was a terrible privation to Madame de Sévigné, but it was the cause of her moral and literary improvement, as well as of the series of "Letters to Madame de Grignan," which, of their kind, are unequaled in any language. The mother's genius lives in this correspondence; her pen gives importance to the most trifling occurrences, and makes hard facts as interesting as fairy stories.

Among other advantages of life, Madame de Sévigné retained her good looks, as she did her cheerful disposition, to the last; hence the name of *Mère Beauté* (Mother Beauty) given her by M. de Coulanges. Her constitution was good, and she managed it with great judgment. In thirty years the only disorder she had known was rheumatism. Happy all her life by the exercise of natural affections, Madame de Sévigné thought less of the ravages of time; and when death terminated her existence in 1696, her illness, the result of the fatigue and uneasiness she had endured for some months on her daughter's account, took her by surprise, and was announced by no symptom. It was short. In her last moments she was resigned, and perfectly calm. Thus died Madame de Sévigné, aged about seventy years, and was interred in the Collegiate Church of Grignan, leaving to posterity in the record of her blameless life, as in her exquisite writings, the brightest and purest model which her age affords.

S. J. H.

LETTERS OF MADAME DE SÉVIGNÉ,

FROM 1655 TO 1669.

ADDRESSED TO THE COUNT DE BUSSY.*

LETTER I.

IN THE COUNTRY, June 26, 1655.

I HAD no doubt that you would take some opportunity of bidding me adieu, either at my own house or from the camp at Landrecy. As I am not a woman of ceremony, I am content with the latter; and have not even thought of being angry, that you failed in coming to me before you set out.

I have not stirred from this desert, since your departure; and, to speak frankly, I am not much afflicted to find that you are with the army. I should be an unworthy cousin of so

---

* The Count Bussy de Rabutin, first cousin to the father of Madame de Sévigné, was, on account of his relationship, always on terms of intimacy with her. He was a famous wit and satirist, as his Letters and Memoirs show, but not of principles or character to excite love or esteem in the soul of such a woman as Madame de Sévigné. However, they were cousins, and though she refused his suit, she seems to have felt a deep interest in his welfare. She corresponded with him occasionally till her death, but her letters to him have less interest than those she wrote to others, especially to her daughter. We give a few of her first and best letters to Count de Bussy, as preliminary to the real work of her heart and mind, her correspondence with Madame de Grignan.

brave a cousin, if I were sorry to see you, during the present campaign, at the head of the finest regiment in France, and in so glorious a post as the one you hold. I dare say you would disown any sentiments less worthy than these; I leave weaker and more tender feelings to the true bagnio gentry. Every one loves in his own way. I profess to be heroic as well as you, and am proud to boast of these sentiments. Some women, perhaps, would think this a little in the old Roman style, and *would thank God they were not Romans*,* that they might still preserve some feelings of humanity. But on this subject I can assure them I am not so inhuman as they suppose; and, with all my heroism, I wish your safe return as passionately as they can do. I trust, my dear cousin, you will not doubt the truth of this, nor that I fervently pray your life may be spared. This is the adieu you would have received from me in person, and which I now beg you to accept from hence, as I have accepted yours from Landrecy.

LETTER II.

Paris, July 14, 1655.

Will you always disgrace your relations? Will you never be weary of making yourself the subject of conversation in every campaign? Do you imagine it can give us pleasure to hear that M. de Turenne has sent word to court that you have done nothing worthy of notice at Landrecy?† This is really very mortifying to us, and you may easily comprehend how deeply I feel the affronts you bring upon your family. But I know not why I thus amuse myself, for I have no leisure to carry on the jest. I must tell you, therefore, that I am delighted with the success which has attended your exploits. I wrote you a long letter from the country, which I

---

* Verse from Corneille's tragedy of the Horatii.

† Mere jesting. Bussy had merited and obtained the praises of Turenne.

fear you have not received. I should be sorry it were lost, for you would laugh heartily at its contents.

I was yesterday at Madame de Montglas's; she had just received a letter from you, as also had Madame de ———. I expected one likewise, but was disappointed. I suppose you were unwilling to effect too many wonders at once. I am not sorry, however, and shall some day claim a whole cargo for myself. Adieu, my cousin. The gazette speaks of you but slightly, which has given offense to many, and to me especially, for no one can be so much interested in your affairs as myself.

LETTER III.

Paris, July 19, 1655.

This is the third time I have written to you since you left Paris, a sufficient proof that I have nothing upon my mind against you. I received your farewell letter from Landrecy while I was in the country, and answered it immediately. I see plainly that my letter has never reached you, and I am extremely vexed at it; for, besides its being written with becoming affection, it was in my opinion a very pretty composition; and as it was designed for you only, I am wroth that another should have the pleasure of reading it. I have since written to you by the servant you dispatched hither with letters to some of your favorites. I did not amuse myself by quarreling with you for not remembering me at the same time, but wrote you a line or two at full speed, which, however incoherent, would inform you of the pleasure I received from the success of your regiment at Landrecy. This intelligence came to us in the most acceptable manner possible, by some of the court, who assured us that Cardinal Mazarin had spoken very handsomely of you to the king, who afterward joined with the whole court in extolling your conduct. You may conceive that my joy was not inconsiderable at hearing all this; but to return to my story. This was the subject of my second letter, and five or six days after I received one from you, full of complaints against me. You see, however, my poor cousin, with how little justice you complain; and hence I draw this fine moral reflection, that we should never condemn a person unheard. This is my justification. Another, perhaps, would have expressed the same thing in fewer words. You must bear with my imperfections, in consideration of my friendship. Every one has his peculiar style; mine, as you see, is by no means laconic.

LETTER IV.

PARIS, November 25, 1655.

You affect great things, M. le Comte: under the pretense that you write like a second Cicero, you think yourself entitled to ridicule people. The passage you remarked, in reality, made me laugh heartily; but I am astonished that you found no other equally ludicrous; for, in the way I wrote to you, it is a miracle that you comprehended my meaning; and I see plainly that either you have a greater share of wit, or that my letter is better, than I imagined. I am glad, however, you have profited by my advice.

I am told that you have asked leave to stay at the frontiers. As you know, my poor count, that mine is a blunt and honest sort of love, I am desirous your request may be granted. This is the road, it is said, to preferment, and you know how interested I am in your welfare; but I shall be pleased either way. If you remain, true friendship shall find its account; if you return, affectionate friendship shall be satisfied.

Madame de Roquelaure is returned so handsome that she yesterday completely challenged the Louvre; this kindled such jealousy in the beauties that were present, that they have resolved, out of spite, she shall not be a party at any of the *after-suppers,* and you know how gay and pleasant they are. Madame de Fiennes would have retained her there yesterday, but it was understood by the queen's answer that her presence would be dispensed with.

Adieu, my dear cousin; believe me to be the most faithful friend you have in the world.

LETTER V.

Paris, May 20, 1667.

I received a letter from you, my dear cousin, when I was in Brittany, in which you talked of our ancestors, the Rabutins, and of the beauty of Bourbilly. But as I had heard from Paris that you were expected there, and as I had hoped myself to arrive much sooner, I deferred writing to you; and now I find you are not coming at all. You know that nothing is now talked of but war. The whole court is at camp, and the whole camp is at court; and every place being a desert, I prefer the desert of Livri forest, where I shall pass the summer,

> En attendant que nos guerriers
> Reviennent couverts de lauriers.*

There are two lines for you, but I do not know whether I have heard them before, or have just made them. As it is a matter of no great importance, I shall resume the thread of my prose. My heart has been very favorably inclined toward you, since I have seen so many people eager to begin, or rather to revive, a business in which you acquired so much honor during the time you were able to engage in it. It is a sad thing for a man of courage to be confined at home when there are such great doings in Flanders.† As you feel, no doubt, all that a man of spirit and valor can feel, it is imprudent in me to revive so painful a subject. I hope you

---

* Waiting the return of our warriors covered with laurels.
† Bussy was exiled to his estates.

will forgive me, in consideration of the great interest I take in your affairs.

It is said you have written to the king. Send me a copy of your letter, and give me a little information respecting your mode of life, what sort of things amuse you, and whether the alterations you are making in your house do not contribute a good deal toward it. I have spent the winter in Brittany, where I have planted a great number of trees, and a labyrinth, that will require Ariadne's clew to find the way out of it. I have also purchased some land, to which I have said, as usual, "I shall convert you into a park." I have extended my walks at a trifling expense. My daughter sends you a thousand remembrances. I beg mine to all your family.

LETTER VI.

PARIS, June 3, 1668.

I wrote to you the last; why have you not answered my letter? I have been expecting to hear from you, and have at length found the Italian proverb true: *chi offende non perdona*—the offender never pardons.

Madame d'Assigny has informed me that part of a cornice has fallen upon your head, and hurt you considerably. If you were well, and I dared exercise a little wicked wit upon the occasion, I should tell you that they are not trifling ornaments like these that injure the heads of husbands in general; and that it would be a fortunate circumstance for them if they met with no worse evil than the fall of a cornice. But I will not talk nonsense; I will first know how you are, and assure you that the same reason which made me languid when you were bled, gives me the headache from your accident. The ties of relationship can not, I think, be carried further than this.

My daughter was on the point of marriage. The affair is broken off, I hardly know why. She kisses your hand; I do the same to your whole family. Have you done any thing yet with regard to the court? Pray let me know how you stand there.

LETTER VII.

Paris, July 26, 1668.

I begin by thanking you, my dear cousin, for your letters to the king. They would afford me pleasure even if they were written by a stranger. They have awakened in me sentiments of pity, and I should think they must produce the same effect on our sovereign. It is true, he does not bear the name of Rabutin, as I do.

The prettiest girl in France sends her compliments to you. This title is due to her; I am, however, weary of doing the honors of it. She is more worthy than ever of your esteem and friendship.

You do not know, I believe, that my son is gone to Candia with M. de Roannes, and the Count de Saint Paul. He consulted M. de Turenne, Cardinal du Retz, and M. de Rochefoucauld upon this: most important personages! and they all approved it so highly that it was fixed upon, and rumored abroad, before I knew any thing of the matter. In short, he is gone. I have wept bitterly, for it is a source of great grief to me. I shall not have a moment's rest during his voyage. I see all its dangers, and terrify myself to death; but alas, I am wholly out of the question; for, in things of this nature, mothers have no voice. Adieu.

LETTER VIII.

Paris, September 4, 1668.

Rise, count; I will not kill you while prostrate at my feet, and take your sword to resume the combat. But it is better that I should give you life, and that we should live in peace.*

---

* Bussy and his cousin had frequent quarrels: the reason has before

I exact but one condition: that you own the thing as it has happened. This is a very generous proceeding on my part; you can no longer call me a little brute.

M. de Montausier has just been appointed governor to the Dauphin.

Je t'ai comblé de biens, je t'en veux accabler.*

Adieu, count. Now I have conquered you, I shall every where proclaim that you are the bravest man in France; and whenever extraordinary duels are mentioned, I shall relate ours. My daughter sends her compliments. The idea you express of her good fortune in the late affair is some consolation to us.

LETTER IX.

PARIS, December 4, 1668.

Have you not received the letter, sir, in which I gave you life, disdaining to kill you at my feet? I expected an answer to this noble action; but you have thought it unworthy your notice: you have contented yourself with rising from the ground, and taking your sword as I commanded you. I hope you will never again employ it against me.

I must tell you a piece of news that will, I am sure, give you pleasure. It is, that the prettiest girl in France is going to be married, not to the handsomest youth, but to one of the worthiest men in the kingdom—to M. de Grignan, whom you have long known. All his wives died to give place to your cousin; and, through extraordinary kindness, even his father and mother died too; so that knowing him to be richer than ever, and finding him besides, by birth, situation, and good qualities, every thing we could wish, we have not trafficked with him, as is customary, on the occasion, but confided in the two families that have gone before us. He seems very well pleased with the alliance, and, as soon as we have heard

been given. The new difference to which she alludes seems to have been a slight one.

* I have loaded thee with favors, I will add to the burden.

from his uncle, the Archbishop of Arles, his other uncle, the Archbishop of Usèz, being on the spot, the business will be finished—probably before the end of the year. As I am a lover of decorum, I could not fail asking your advice and approbation. The public seem pleased. This is a great deal, for we are such fools as to be almost always governed by its opinion.

LETTER X.

Paris, January 7, 1669.

It is as true that I did not receive an answer to the letter in which I gave you life, as that I was in pain, lest, with the best intention possible to pardon you, I had unintentionally killed you, being little accustomed to wield a sword. This was the only good reason I could assign to myself for your silence. In the mean time you had written, though your letter had never reached me. Allow me still to regret the circumstance. You always write pleasantly; and if I had wished to lose any portion of your correspondence, it would not have been that letter. I am glad you approve of the marriage with M. de Grignan; he is a very good man, and very gentlemanly—has wealth, rank, holds a high office, and is much esteemed and respected by the world. What more is necessary? I think we are fortunate, and as you are of the same opinion, sign the deed I sent you; and be assured, my dear cousin, that if it depended on me, you should be first at the entertainment. How admirably well you would act your part! Since you left us, I have heard no wit equal to yours, and I have said to myself a thousand times, "Good heavens, what a difference!" War* is talked of, and it is said the king will take the field in person.

* It was a vague report. No idea was yet entertained of breaking the peace of Aix-la-Chapelle, concluded only seven months before. But it was in contemplation to interfere in the quarrel between the Count Palatin and the Duke of Lorraine, and force the latter to lay down his arms.

LETTERS TO MADAME DE GRIGNAN *

FROM 1671 TO 1690.

LETTER I.

PARIS, Monday, February 9, 1671.

I receive your letters in the same way in which you received my ring. I am in tears while I read them. My heart seems ready to burst. Bystanders would think that you had treated me ill in your letters, or were sick, or that some accident had happened to you; whereas every thing is the reverse. You love me, my dear child; you love me, and you tell me so in a manner that makes my tears flow in torrents. You continue your journey without any disagreeable accident.†

---

* Margaret de Sévigné, only daughter of Madame de Sévigné, was born in 1649, a short time before her father was killed. The education and happiness of this "lovely and infinitely dear child," was the occupation, delight, and anxiety of the mother's long life. For her, Madame de Sévigné thought, read, observed, and wrote. The following letters are not only charming as specimens of epistolary style, but also full of interest and instruction to those who would study the human mind in its most sacred development of maternal love.

† In January, 1670, this idolized daughter of Madame de Sévigné was married to the Count de Grignan, who was Lieutenant-General of the Government of Provence, where he found it necessary to reside. The separation of mother and daughter, which took place early the following year, was the occasion for the world-renowned correspondence, which has immortalized the genius of one, and the names of both.

To know this, is the thing I could the most desire; and yet am I in this deplorable condition! And do you then take a pleasure in thinking of me? in talking of me? and have more satisfaction in writing your sentiments to me than in telling them? In whatever way they come, they meet with a reception, the warmth of which can only be known to those who love as I do. In expressing yourself thus, you make me feel the greatest tenderness for you that is possible to be felt; and if you think of me, be assured that I, on my side, am continually thinking of you. Mine is what the devotees call an habitual thought; it is what we ought to have for the Divine Being, were we to do our duty. Nothing is capable of diverting me from it. I see your carriage continually driving on, never, never to come nearer to me; I fancy myself on the road, and am always in apprehensions of the carriage overturning. I am almost distracted at the violent rains we have had the last three days, and am frightened to death at the thoughts of the Rhône. I have at this instant a map before me; I know every place you sleep at. To-night you are at Nevers, Sunday you will be at Lyons, where you will receive this letter. I could only write to you at Moulins by Madame de Gueneguad. I have had but two letters from you; perhaps a third is on the road; they are my only comfort. I ask for no other. I am utterly incapable of seeing much company at a time; I may recover the feeling hereafter, but it is out of the question now. The Duchesses of Verneciel and Arpajon have used all their endeavors to divert me, for which I am much obliged to them. Never, surely, were there better people than in this country. I was all the day on Saturday at Madame de Villars,* talking of you, and weeping; she takes a great share in my sorrow. Yesterday I heard Monsieur d'Agen† preach, and was at Madame de Puisieux and Madame du Pui-du-Fou's, who both send you a thousand

---

* Marie de Bellefond, Marchioness of Villars, mother to the late marshal of that name.

† Claude Joli, a celebrated preacher, afterward Bishop of Agen.

remembrances. This evening I shall sup *tête-à-tête** in the Fauxbourgs. These are my carnivals. I have a mass said for you every day. This is no superstitious devotion. I have seen Adhémar† but for a moment; I am going to write to him and thank him for his bed, for which I am more obliged to him even than you are. If you would give me real pleasure, take care of your health, sleep in that little snug bed, eat broth, and exert that courage which I want. Continue to write to me. The friendships you left behind you here are all increased, and I should never have done with compliments if I were to tell you how much every one is concerned about your health.

LETTER II.

Paris, Wednesday, February 11, 1671.

I have received but three of those delightful letters that so affect my heart. One is still on the road. If I were not so fond of them, and loth to lose any thing that you write me, I should not think I had lost much; for nothing can be wished for beyond what I find in those I have already received. In the first place, they are well written, and are besides so tender, so natural, that it is impossible not to believe every thing

---

* With Madame de la Fayette.

† Joseph Adhémar de Monteil, brother to M. de Grignan, known at first by the name of Adhémar, was, after the death of Charles Philip d'Adbémar, his brother, which happened the 6th of February, 1672, called the Chevalier de Grignan; but being afterward married to N*** d'Oraison, he resumed the name of Count Adhémar. In 1675 he was colonel to a regiment of horse, at the head of which he signalized himself on several occasions, particularly at the battle of Altemheim. He was made field-marshal in 1688, and, had not repeated attacks of the gout prevented him from continuing in the service, he would, doubtless, from his reputation, merit, and illustrious birth, have obtained the most considerable military honors. He died without issue the 19th of November, 1713, at the age of sixty-nine.

contained in them. Distrust itself would here stand convinced. They wear that air of truth which, as I have always maintained, carries authority with it; while falsehood and lies skulk under a load of words, without having the power of persuasion; the more they attempt to show themselves, the more they are entangled. Your expressions are sincere, and they appear so; they are used only to explain your meaning, and receive an irresistible force from their noble simplicity. Such, my dear child, do your letters appear to me. As for me, I appear to myself quite divested of every thing that made me agreeable; I am ashamed to appear in society; and notwithstanding the endeavors that have been used to bring me back to it, I have latterly been like one just come out of the woods; nor could I be otherwise. Few are worthy of understanding what I feel; I have sought those chosen few, and avoided all others. I fancy you are at Moulins to-day; if so, you will receive one of my letters. I did not write to you at Briafre; if I had, it must have been on that cruel Wednesday, the very day you set off; and I was so overwhelmed with grief that I was incapable even of tasting the consolation of writing to you. This is the third letter; my second is at Lyons. Be sure you let me know if you receive them. When at a distance, we no longer laugh at a letter beginning with, "I received yours," etc. The thought of your going still further and further from me, and of seeing the carriage continually driving on, is what harrows me most. You are always going on, and at last, as you say, you will find yourself at two hundred leagues' distance from me; resolved, therefore, not to suffer such injustice without repaying it in my turn, I shall set myself about removing further off, too, and shall do it so effectually as to make it three hundred. A very pretty distance you will say. And would it not be a step highly worthy the love I have for you, to undertake to traverse all France to find you out? I am delighted at the reconciliation between you and the coadjutor; you know how necessary I always thought it to the happiness of your life.

Preserve this treasure with care. You own yourself charmed with his goodness: let him see you are not ungrateful. I shall soon finish my letter; perhaps when you get to Lyons you will be so giddy with the honors you will receive there, that you will not find time to read it; find enough, however, I beseech you, to let me hear of you, and whether you embark upon that horrible Rhône.

Wednesday night.

I have this moment received yours from Nogent; it was given me by a very honest fellow, whom I questioned as much as I could; but your letter is worth more than any thing that could have been told me. It was but justice, my dear, that you should be the first to make me smile, after having caused me so many tears. What you tell me of Monsieur Busche is quite original; it is what may be called a genuine stroke of eloquence. I did laugh then, I own, and I should have been ashamed of it had I done any thing else than cry for this week past. I met this Monsieur Busche in the street, when he was bringing your horses for you to set out; I stopped him, and all in tears asked him his name, which he told me. "Monsieur Busche," said I, sobbing all the while, "I recommend my daughter to your care; do not, dear Monsieur Busche, do not overturn her; and when you have taken her safely to Lyons, if you will call upon me with the agreeable news, I will give you something to drink." I shall, therefore, certainly do so. What you say of him has greatly added to the respect I had for him before.

LETTER III.

Paris, Thursday, February 12, 1671.

This is only a line precursory, for I shall not write to you till to-morrow; but I wish you to know what I have just heard.

Yesterday the president, Amelot, after having made a great number of visits, toward night found himself a good deal out of order, and was soon afterward seized with a violent apoplectic fit, of which he died about eight o'clock this morning. I would have you write to his wife; the whole family are in the greatest affliction.

The Duchess de la Vallière sent a letter to the king, the contents of which have not transpired, and then a message by the Marshal de Bellefond, to say, " that she would have quitted the court, after having lost the honor of his good opinion, had she been able to prevail with herself to see him no more; but that her weakness on that head had been so great that she was scarcely capable, even now, of making a sacrifice of it to her God; she was resolved, however, that the remains of the passion she had felt for him should constitute part of her penance, and, as she had devoted her youth to him, it could not be thought much if the rest of her life were spent in cares for her own salvation." The king wept bitterly, and sent Monsieur Colbert to Chaillot, to beg her to come directly to Versailles, that he might speak to her once more. Monsieur Colbert accordingly conducted her thither. The king had a whole hour's conversation with her, and wept a great deal. Madame de Montespan ran with open arms, and tears in her eyes, to receive her. We do not rightly understand all this. Some say she will remain at Versailles, and continue about the court; others that she will return to Chaillot. We shall see.

LETTER IV.

Paris, Tuesday, March 3, 1671.

If you were here, my dear child, you would certainly laugh at me. I am set down to write beforehand, but from a very different reason to that which I once gave you for writing to a person two days before I could send my letter: it was a matter of indifference to me, when I wrote, as I knew I should have no more to say to him at the two days' end than I had then. But here the case is otherwise. I do it now from the regard I have for you, and to satisfy the pleasure I take in writing to you every moment, which is the sole comfort I have now left. To-day I am shut up by myself in my room, through excess of ill-humor. I am weary of every thing. I took a pleasure in dining here, and still a greater one in writing to you out of season. Alas! you have none of these leisure moments! I write quite at my ease, but can hardly suppose you will be able to read what I write in the same manner. I do not see how it is possible for you to be a minute by yourself. On one side I behold a husband who adores you, who is never tired of being with you, and who scarcely knows the end of his happiness; on the other side, harangues, compliments, visits, and honors paid you without end; all this must be answered. Indeed, you have enough upon your hands. I could not bear it myself in my little circle. But what became of your favorite Indolence amid all this noise and bustle? It suffers now; it retires into a corner, just dead with apprehension of losing its place in your heart forever; it seeks some vacant moment to put you in remembrance, and just drop a word to you by the by. "Alas!" it says, "and have you then forgotten me? Remember, I am your oldest acquaintance; the friend that has never abandoned you; the faithful companion of your happy hours, who made you amends for the want of every pleasure, and for whose sake you have sometimes hated them. It was I that prevented your dying of the vapors while you were in Brittany. Sometimes, indeed, your mother would break in upon our joys, but then I knew where to have you again. Now I know not what will become of me. These shows, all this pageantry, will be my death, unless you take some care of me." Methinks I hear you speak a kind word to it as you go by; you give it some hopes of possessing you when at Grignan; but you are gone in an instant, and can not find time to say more. Duty and reason are with you, and allow you not a moment's repose; I, who have always so highly honored these personages, am now quite out with them, and they with me. How then will they permit you to waste your time in reading such trifles as these? I assure you, my dear child, I am continually thinking of you; and I experience every day the truth of what you once told me, that there are certain thoughts which are not to be dwelt upon, but passed over as lightly as possible, unless we would be forever in tears. This is my case: for there is not a place in the house which does not give a stab to my heart when I see it; but your room especially deals a deadly blow from every part of it. I have placed a screen in the middle of it, that I may at least take something from the prospect. As for the window from which I saw you get into D'Hacqueville's coach, and then called you back again, I shudder every time I think how near I was throwing myself out of it after you. I was likely enough to have done it, for at times I am not in my senses. The closet where I held you last in my arms, without knowing what I did; the Capuchins, where I used to go to mass; the tears that fell so fast from my eyes that they wetted the ground, as if water had been thrown on it; Saint Mary's, Madame de la Fayette, my return to the house, your room, that night, the next morning, your first letter, and every one since, and still every day, and every conversation of those who feel with me, are so many remembrancers of my loss. Poor D'Hacqueville holds the first rank; I shall never forget the compassion he showed me. These are the thoughts incessantly uppermost; yet these are to be passed over, it seems; we are not to abandon ourselves to our thoughts, and the emotions of our heart. I had rather, however, continue my reveries on the kind of life you are leading. It occasions a sort of diversion, without making me abandon my principal, my beloved object. I do then think of you. I am always wishing for letters from you. One wish of this nature, when gratified, is followed by another continually. I am in this state of expectation now, and shall go on with my letter when I have received one from you

LETTER V.

Paris, Wednesday, March 18, 1671.

I have received two packets at once, which have been delayed for a considerable time. By these I am at length informed from yourself, of your entry into Aix, but you do not mention whether your husband was with you, or in what manner Vardes honored your triumph; but you describe the triumph itself very humorously, as well as the embarrassment you were under, and your many misplaced civilities. I wish that I had been with you; not that I should have done better than yourself, for I have not so good a gift of fixing names upon faces—on the contrary, I daily commit a thousand blunders in that way—but I think I could have been of some assistance to you, at least I should have made courtesies enough. It is true, that such a multiplicity of ceremonies and attentions is very tiresome. You should, nevertheless, endeavor not to be deficient in any of these points, but accommodate yourself, as much as possible, to the customs and the manners of those among whom you are to live.

An event has just taken place, which engrosses the whole conversation of Paris. The king has ordered Monsieur de S—— to resign his post, and to quit Paris immediately. Can you guess the reason? For having cheated at play, and won upward of five hundred thousand crowns with false cards! The man who made these cards was examined by the king himself; he denied the fact at first; but, upon his majesty's promising him a pardon, he confessed that he had followed the trade for a long time. It is said that the affair will not stop here, for that there are several houses which he used to furnish with these cards. It was some time before the king could prevail upon himself to disgrace a man of Monsieur de S——'s quality; but as, for several months past, every body that had played with him had been in a manner ruined, he thought he could not in conscience do less than bring such a scene of villainy to light. S—— was so perfectly master of his adversaries' game, that he always made *sept et le va* upon the queen of spades, because he knew the spades lay all in the other packs. The king as constantly lost one-and-thirty upon clubs, and used to say, clubs never win against spades in this country. This man had given thirty pistoles to Madame de la Vallière's *valets de chambre* to throw all the cards they had in the house into the river, in the pretense that they were not good, and had introduced his own card-maker. He was first led into this fine way of life by one Pradier, who has since disappeared. Had S—— known himself innocent, he would immediately have delivered himself up, and insisted upon taking his trial; but, instead of this, he took the road to Languedoc, as the surest way of the two; many, however, advised him to take a journey to La Trappe,* after such a misfortune.

Madame d'Humieres has charged me with a thousand good wishes for you. She is going to Lille, where she will receive as many honors as you did at Aix. Marshal Bellefond, through a pure motive of piety, has settled with his creditors. He has given up to them the principal part of his property, besides half the profits of his post,† to complete the payment of the arrears. This is a noble action, and shows that his visits to La Trappe have not been without effect. I went the other day to see the Duchess of Ventadour; she was as handsome as an angel. The Duchess of Nevers came in, with her head dressed very ridiculously. You may believe me, for you know I am an admirer of fashion. Martin had cropped her to the very extremity of the mode.

Your brother is at St. Germain; he divides his time with Ninon, a young actress,‡ and, to crown the whole, Despréaux. We lead him a sad life.

---

* *La Trappe* is a society of religious monks, remarkable for the austerity of their lives, and the severe discipline practiced among them.

† That of chief maître d'hôtel, or master of the household, to the king.

‡ Called la Champêlée.

LETTER VI.

PARIS, Friday, April 1, 1671.

I returned yesterday from St. Germain with Madame d'Arpajon. Every one at court inquired after you; among the rest, it will not be amiss, I think, to distinguish the queen, who accosted me, and asked how my daughter was after her affair upon the Rhône. I returned her majesty thanks for the honor she did you in remembering you. She then desired me to tell her in what manner you had like to have been lost; I accordingly gave her an account of your crossing the river in a storm of wind, and that a sudden gust had thrown you under an arch, within an inch of one of the piles, which if you had once touched, all the world could not have saved you. But, says the queen, "Was her husband with her?" "Yes, madam, and the coadjutor too." "Really," said she, "they were greatly to blame." She gave two or three alasses! while I was talking to her, and said many obliging things of you. Afterward a number of ladies came in, and among the rest the young Duchess of Ventadour, very fine and very handsome; it was some time before they brought her the divine tabouret;* "Ah," said I, turning to the grand master,† "why do they not give it to her, she has purchased it dearly enough?"‡ He was of my opinion. In the midst of a silence in the circle, the queen turned to me, and asked me who my granddaughter was like? "M. de Grignan, madam," replied I. Upon which her majesty exclaimed, "Indeed! I am sorry for it;" and added, in a low tone of voice, "She had better have resembled her mother or grandmother." So you see how much I am indebted to you in making my court. Marshal Bellefond made me promise to distinguish him from

---

* The tabouret is a stool to sit on in the presence of the queen, a privilege never enjoyed but by ladies of the first quality.

† The Count de Lude, grand master of the artillery.

‡ Monsieur de Ventadour was not only very ugly and deformed, but, at the same time, a great debauchee.

the crowd. I made your compliments to Monsieur and Madame Duras, and to Messieurs de Charôt and Montausier, and *tutti quanti*, not to forget the dauphin and mademoiselle, who both talked a great deal to me about you. I likewise saw Madame de Ludre; she accosted me with an excess of civility and kindness that surprised me, and talked in the most affectionate manner of you, when all on a sudden, as I was going to make her a suitable answer, I found she was not attending to me, and saw her fine eyes wandering round the room. I presently perceived it, and those who saw I took notice of it were pleased with me, and could not help laughing.

I have been extremely diverted with our hurly-burly headdresses; some of them looked as if you could have blown them off their shoulders. Ninon* said that La Choiseul was as like the flaunting hostess of an inn, as one drop of water to another; a most excellent simile! But that Ninon is a dangerous creature; if you only knew how she argues upon religion it would make you shudder. Her zeal to pervert the minds of young people is much the same as that of a certain gentleman of St. Germain, that we saw once at Livri. She says your brother has all the simplicity of the dove, that he is just like his mother; but that Madame de Grignan has all the fire of the family, and has more sense than to be so docile. A certain person would have taken your part, and put her out of conceit with you on that head, but she bid him hold his tongue, and told him that she knew more of the matter than he did. What a depravity of taste! Because she knows you to be handsome and witty, she must needs saddle you with the other qualification, without which, according to her rule, there is no being perfect. I am greatly concerned for the harm she does my son in this point; but do not take any notice of it to him. Madame de la Fayette and I use all our endeavors to disengage him from so dangerous an attachment. Besides her, he has a little actress,† and all the players of the

---

* Ninon de l'Enclos, famous for her wit and free-thinking.
† La Champêlée.

town upon his hands, to whom he gives suppers; in short, he is perfectly infatuated. You know what a joke he makes of Mascaron. I fancy your Minim* would suit him. I never read any thing more diverting than what you wrote to me about that man; I read it to Monsieur de la Rochefoucault, who laughed heartily at it. He desires me to tell you, that there is a certain apostle who is running up and down after his rib, which he would fain appropriate to himself, as a part of his goods and chattels; but, unluckily for him, he is not clever at enterprise. I fancy Mellusina is fallen into some pit, we do not hear a single word about her. M. de la Rochefoucault says besides, that if he was only thirty years younger, he should certainly have a great inclination for M. de Grignan's third rib.† That part of your letter, where you say he has already had two of his ribs broken, made him laugh heartily; we always wish for some oddity or other to divert you, but we very much doubt whether this has not turned out rather more to your satisfaction than ours. After all, we pity you extremely, in not having the word of God preached in a suitable manner. Ah, that Bourdaloüe! his sermon on the Passion was, they say, the most perfect thing of the kind that can be imagined; it was the same he preached last year, but revised and altered with the assistance of some of his friends, that it might be wholly inimitable; how can one love God, if one never hears him properly spoken of? you must really possess a greater portion of grace than others. We went the other day to hear the Abbé Montmort;‡ I never heard a prettier sermon for so young a beginner. I wish you had such a one in the room of your Minim. He made the sign of the cross, and gave out his text; he did not anathematize his audience, he did not load us with abuse; he told us not to be under any apprehensions concerning death, since it was the only passage we had to a glorious resurrection with Jesus

---

* The priest who preached at Grignan.
† That is, to Mme. de Grignan, who was M. de Grignan's third wife.
‡ Afterward Bishop of Bayonne.

Christ. We agreed with him in this, and every one went away contented. He has nothing offensive in his manner; he imitates Monsieur d'Agen without copying him; he has a modest confidence, is learned, and pious. In short, I was highly pleased with him.

LETTER VII.

PARIS, Friday, April 10, 1671.

I wrote to you on Wednesday by the post, yesterday by Magalotti, and to-day again by the post; but last night I lost a charming opportunity. I went to walk at Vincennes, *en Troche*,* and by the way met with a string of galley-slaves; they were going to Marseilles, and will be there in about a month. Nothing could have been surer than this mode of conveyance, but another thought came into my head, which was to go with them myself. There was one Duval among them, who appeared to be a conversible man. You will see them when they come in, and I suppose you would have been agreeably surprised to have seen me in the midst of the crowd of women that accompany them. I wish you knew of what importance the words Provence, Marseilles, Aix, are become to me; even the Rhône, that devilish Rhône, and Lyons, are something to me. Brittany and Burgundy appear like places under the pole, in which I take no sort of interest. I may say with Coulanges, "O, the surprising power of my orvietan!" Really, my child, it was admirable in you to desire the abbé† to prevent my sending you any more presents! What nonsense! Do I in reality make you any? You call the newspapers I send you by that name. You never can divest me of the desire of thus giving; it is the most sensible pleasure I can enjoy. You should rather re-

---

* With her friend, Madame de la Troche.

† The Abbé de Coulanges, who lived with his niece, Madame de Sévigné.

joice with me, if I indulged myself more frequently in it. The method you took of thanking me was highly pleasing to me.

Your letters are excellent; one might venture to say they were not dictated by the good ladies of the country where you reside. I find that M. de Grignan, to his other connections with you, adds that of being your companion; he seems to me the only one who understands you. Be careful to preserve the happiness of his heart by the tenderness of yours, and consider that if you do not both love me, each according to your proper degree of estimation, you will be the most ungrateful of beings. The new opinion, that there is no such thing as ingratitude in the world, appears to me, for the reasons which we have so frequently discussed, like the philosophy of Descartes, and the contrary one like that of Aristotle. You know the deference I always paid to the authority of the latter; it is the same with respect to my opinion of ingratitude. I should pronounce you then, my child, to be a little ungrateful wretch; but, happily, and the idea constitutes all my comfort, I know you to be incapable of such conduct, and I therefore yield without reserve to the feelings of my heart. Adieu, my dearest love, I am going to close this letter. I shall write you another to-night, in which I shall give you an account of the occurrences of the day. We are every day in hopes of letting your house; you may suppose I can forget nothing that relates to you; I am as interested in your affairs as the most selfish being ever was in his own.

LETTER VIII.

Friday night, April 10, 1671.

I make up my packet at Monsieur de la Rochefoucault's, who embraces you very heartily; he is delighted with your answer about the canons and Father Desmares. There is some pleasure in sending you these trifles, you answer them so prettily. He begs you to be assured that you still live strongly in his remembrance, and that if he hears any thing worth your notice he will certainly communicate it to you. He is at his Hôtel de Rochefoucault, having no longer any hopes of recovering the use of his feet; he talks of going to the waters; I am for sending him to Digne, others to Bourbon. I dined *en Bavardin*,* and in so complete a style that I thought we should have died. We did not talk, merely, as we used to do; we did nothing but chatter.

Brancas was overturned the other day into a ditch, where he found himself so much at his ease, that he asked those who came to help him out if they had any occasion for his services. His glasses were all broken, and his head would have been so, too, if he had not been more lucky than wise; but all this did not seem to have destroyed his reverie in the least. I wrote this morning to let him know he had been overturned, and was very near breaking his neck, as I supposed he was the only person in Paris who was ignorant of it; and that I took the opportunity of expressing the concern it gave me. I expect his answer.

LETTER IX.

From Monsieur De la Rochefoucault's,
Friday evening, April 24, 1671.

Here, then, I make up my packet. I had intended to tell you that the king arrived yesterday evening at Chantilly: he hunted a stag by moonlight; the lamps did wonders; the fire-works were a little eclipsed by the brightness of our serene friend, the moon; but the evening, the supper, and the entertainment, went off admirably well. The weather we had yesterday gave us hopes of an end worthy of so fine a begin-

* That is, at Madame de Lavardin's, who was extremely fond of news.

ning. But what do you think I learned when I came here? I am not yet recovered, and hardly know what I write. Vatel, the great Vatel, late maître-d'hôtel to M. Fouquet, and in that capacity with the prince, a man so eminently distinguished for taste, and whose abilities were equal to the government of a state—this man, whom I knew so well, finding, at eight o'clock this morning, that the fish he had sent for did not come at the time he expected it, and unable to bear the disgrace that he thought would inevitably attach to him, ran himself through with his own sword. Guess what confusion so shocking an accident must have occasioned. Think, too, that perhaps the fish might come in just as he was expiring. I know no more of the affair at present, and I suppose you think this enough. I make no doubt the consternation was general; it must be very disagreeable to have so fatal an event break in upon an entertainment that cost fifty thousand crowns.

Monsieur De Menars is to be married to Mademoiselle De la Grange-Neuville; but I do not know how I can have the heart to speak to you about any thing but Vatel.

LETTER X.

PARIS, Sunday, April 26, 1671.

This is Sunday, April 26th, and this letter will not go out till Wednesday; but it is not so much a letter as a narrative that I have just learned from Moreuil, of what passed at Chantilly with regard to poor Vatel. I wrote to you last Friday that he had stabbed himself—these are the particulars of the affair: The king arrived there on Thursday night; the walk, and the collation, which was served in a place set apart for the purpose, and strewed with jonquils, were just as they should be. Supper was served, but there was no roast meat at one or two of the tables, on account of Vatel's having been obliged to provide several dinners more than were expected. This affected his spirits, and he was heard to say, several times: "I have lost my honor! I can not bear this disgrace!" "My head is quite bewildered," said he to Gourville. "I have not had a wink of sleep these twelve nights; I wish you would assist me in giving orders." Gourville did all he could to comfort and assist him; but the failure of the roast meat (which, however, did not happen at the king's table, but at some of the other twenty-five), was always uppermost with him. Gourville mentioned it to the prince, who went directly to Vatel's apartment, and said to him: "Every thing is extremely well conducted, Vatel; nothing could be more admirable than his majesty's supper." "Your highness's goodness," replied he, "overwhelms me; I am sensible that there was a deficiency of roast meat at two tables." "Not at all," said the prince; "do not perplex yourself, and all will go well." Midnight came: the fireworks did not succeed, they were covered with a thick cloud; they cost sixteen thousand francs. At four o'clock in the morning Vatel went round and found every body asleep; he met one of the under-purveyors, who was just come in with only two loads of fish. "What!" said he, "is this all?" "Yes, sir," said the man, not knowing that Vatel had dispatched other people to all the sea-ports around. Vatel waited for some time; the other purveyors did not arrive; his head grew distracted; he thought there was no more fish to be had. He flew to Gourville: "Sir," said he, "I can not outlive this disgrace." Gourville laughed at him. Vatel, however, went to his apartment, and setting the hilt of his sword against the door, after two ineffectual attempts, succeeded in the third, in forcing his sword through his heart. At that instant the carriers arrived with the fish; Vatel was inquired after to distribute it. They ran to his apartment, knocked at the door, but received no answer, upon which they broke it open, and found him weltering in his blood. A messenger was immediately dispatched to acquaint the prince with what had happened, who was like a man in despair. The duke wept, for his Burgundy journey depended upon Vatel. The prince related the whole affair to his majesty with an expression of great concern; it was considered as the consequence of too nice a sense of honor; some blamed, others praised him for his courage. The king said he had put off this excursion for more than five years, because he was aware that it would be attended with infinite trouble, and told the prince that he ought to have had but two tables, and not have been at the expense of so many, and declared he would never suffer him to do so again; but all this was too late for poor Vatel. However, Gourville attempted to supply the loss of Vatel, which he did in great measure. The dinner was elegant, the collation was the same. They supped, they walked, they hunted; all was perfumed with jonquils, all was enchantment. Yesterday, which was Saturday, the same entertainments were renewed, and in the evening the king set out for Liancourt, where he had ordered a *media-noche* ;* he is to stay there three days. This is what Moreuil has told me, hoping I should acquaint you with it. I wash my hands of the rest, for I know nothing about it. M. D'Hacqueville, who was present at the scene, will, no doubt, give you a faithful account of all that passed; but, because his hand-writing is not quite so legible as mine, I write too; if I am circumstantial, it is because, on such an occasion, I should like circumstantiality myself.

LETTER XI.

Monday, May 18, 1671.
Just going to set out.

At last, my dear child, I am just ready to step into my carriage: there!—I am in—adieu! I never shall use that word to you without real grief. I am now on my way for

* *Media-noche* is a flesh-meal just after midnight, among the Roman Catholics.

Brittany. Is it possible that any thing can increase the distance between us, when we are already separated from each other more than two hundred leagues? But so it is; I have found a way to complete it; and as you thought your town of Aix not quite far enough from me, I also, look upon Paris as too much in your neighborhood. You went to Marseilles to fly me, and I, to pay you in your own coin, am going to Vitré. But to be serious, my dear, our correspondence will suffer by this; it used to be a great source of consolation and amusement to me. Alas! what shall I have to say to you from the midst of my woods? I shall have nothing to entertain you with but accounts of Mademoiselle du Plessis and Jaquine;* charming subjects these! I am very happy in what you tell me of your health, but, in the name of God, if you have any love for me, take care of yourself; do not dance, do not fall, take a good deal of rest, and, above all things, arrange your plans so as to lie-in at Aix, where you may have the best and the most timely assistance. You know how expeditious you are on those occasions; be sure to have every thing ready rather too soon than too late. Good Heavens! what shall I not suffer at that period!

You relate the dispute you had with our friend Vivonne very agreeably. I think the fault lies entirely on his side. You laid a famous trap in which you caught him completely. His confusion made me sweat for him, and he did so himself, I dare say; but in the end you made it up and embraced him! a great† undertaking that, for one in your situation. If your quarrels must end thus, you ought to have no quarrels nor enemies upon your hands.

* A pretty servant girl of Madame de Sévigné's at her house in Brittany.
† Monsieur de Vivonne was remarkable for his great bulk.

LETTER XII.

FROM THE ROCKS,* Sunday, May 31, 1671.

At last, my child, I am at the Rocks. Can I behold these walks, can I view these ornaments, this little closet, these books, these rooms, and not die with grief? Some recollections are agreeable, but there are others again so lively and so tender that they are hardly supportable; such are mine with respect to you. And you may easily guess the effect this is likely to produce in a heart like mine.

If you continue pretty well, my dear child, I believe I shall not come to you till next year. Brittany and Provence are not very compatible; long journeys are strange things. If we were always to continue in the same mind we are in at the end of a journey, we should never stir from the place we were then in; but Providence, in kindness to us, causes us to forget it. It is much the same with lying-in women. Heaven permits this forgetfulness that the world may be peopled, and that folks may take journeys to Provence. Mine, therefore, will afford me the greatest joy I ever received in my life, but how cruel a thought is it to see no end to your stay there! I more and more admire and applaud your prudence, though, to tell you the truth, I am greatly affected with this impossibility; but I hope time will make us see things in a different light. We must always live in hope; without that consolation there would be no living. I sometimes pass such melancholy moments in the woods, that I return as changed as one just out of a fever. I fancy you pass your time pretty well at Marseilles. Do not fail to tell me how you were received at Grignan. The people here had designed to make a kind of triumphal entry for my son; Vaillant had drawn out near fifteen hundred men under arms, very well dressed, with new ribbons round their necks, and had marched them within a league of the Rocks. But guess what happened! Our

* The name of Madame de Sévigné's estate in Brittany.

abbé had written word that we should be there on Tuesday, and afterward forgot to mention it to us. Accordingly these poor people were waiting under arms the whole day till ten o'clock at night, when they returned home very much chagrined at their disappointment; and behold the next day, which was Wednesday, we came in as quiet and peaceable as lambs, without dreaming that a little army had been drawn out to receive us! We were a good deal vexed at this mistake, but there was no remedy; so much for our first setting out. Mademoiselle du Plessis is just as you left her. She has formed a new acquaintance at Vitré that she plumes herself mightily upon, because she is a great genius, has read all the romances, and, more than that, has had two letters from the Princess de Tarante. I was wicked enough to set Vaillant upon telling her that I was jealous of this new friend of hers, and that, when I heard of their intimacy, it had given me the greatest uneasiness, though I had taken no notice of it to her. It requires the pen of a Molière to describe all she says upon the occasion; and it is highly amusing to see how artfully she manages me, and with what care she avoids speaking of my supposed rival before my face; I too play my part very well. My little trees are grown surprisingly; Pilois* is raising their stately heads to the clouds. In short, nothing can be more beautiful than these walks, which you first saw planted. You may remember I once gave you a little device which was thought very suitable. Here is a motto I wrote the other day upon a tree, which I intend for my son, who is just returned from Candia. *Vago di fama.*† Is it not pretty, notwithstanding its conciseness? Yesterday I had another inscribed in honor of the idlers, *Bella cosa far niente!*‡ Ah! my dear child, what a wild romantic air my letters have! What is become of the time when I used to talk of Paris like other people? Now you will hear of nothing but myself; and, to show you what confidence I have in your affection, I am

---

* The gardener at the Rocks. † Anxious for fame.
‡ What a fine thing it is to do nothing.

persuaded this will be the most agreeable intelligence I can give you. I am highly pleased with my company here. Our abbé is at all times an excellent companion. La Mousse and my son are satisfied with me, and I with them. We always seek one another; and if business at any time takes me from them, they are at their wit's end, and think it very odd in me to prefer a farmer's account to a tale of La Fontaine's. They are all passionately in love with you. I fancy you will hear from them soon. I choose however to be beforehand with them, for I do not love talking to you in a crowd. My dearest child, will you always love me? my life depends upon your affection! That, as I told you the other day, constitutes all my joy and all my sorrow.

LETTER XIII.

The Rocks, Wednesday, June 10, 1671.

I am going to entertain you to-day, my dear child, with what is called rain and fine weather. I had not your letters till Friday, and I answered them the Sunday following. I begin then with the rain, for fair weather is out of the question. For this week past it has rained incessantly; I say incessantly—for the rain has only been interrupted by storms. I can not stir abroad, my workmen are all dispersed, and I am devoured with melancholy; La Mousse, too, is very low-spirited. We read, indeed, and that just keeps us alive. My son is gone to Rennes, whither we thought it necessary to send him, to pay a visit to the first president, and several other friends that I have there; if he has time, I shall prevail on him to go and see Monsieur de Coësquen; he is old enough now for these things. There was a ball at Vitré again on Sunday. I very much fear that my son will become too fond of the company of ten or a dozen men that supped with him the other night at the castle of Sévigné; they may be borne with, but he should be very cautious of forming too great an intimacy with them. A dispute arose between two of the party about some trifle or other; the lie was given; to it they went; the company endeavored to part them; there was a great deal of talk and very little sense; however, monsieur le marquis* had the honor of making up the difference, and afterward set out for Rennes. There have been great cabals at Vitré: Mademoiselle de Croqueoison complains that, at a ball the other day, Mademoiselle du Cerni did not offer her part of some oranges she had. We must hear what Mademoiselle du Plessis and the Launayes have to say on this subject, as they know all the circumstances relating to it. As to Mademoiselle du Plessis, she lets all her affairs at Vitré run to ruin, because she will not stir in them, from the fear of making me jealous on account of her new friend; and it was but the other day that, to make me quite easy, she said as many ill-natured things of her as she could. When it is fine weather, this nonsense makes me laugh, but when it is bad and gloomy, I could give her a box on the ear, as you once did. Madame de Coulanges writes me word that she has heard nothing of Brancas, except that out of his six coach-horses he has only one left, and that he was the last person to discover it. I hear no news. Our little Alégre is at her mother's, and it is thought that M. de Seignelai is to be married to her. I suppose you are in want of persons to furnish you with intelligence; for my part, I despise trivial occurrences; I am only for those that surprise and astonish; such a one I met with this very morning while the abbé and I were in his study together. We found, in reckoning with those counters of his which are so good, that with all that has fallen to me, I ought to be worth 530,000 livres.† Do you know that what our dear abbé has left me will not amount to less than 80,000 francs? And do you think I am not impatient to be in possession? And 100,000 francs from Burgundy; this has come since you were married, the rest, viz.: 100,000 crowns by my marriage; 100,000

---

* Meaning her son, the Marquis of Sévigné.
† Upward of 20,000*l.* sterling, reckoning a livre at 10d. halfpenny.

crowns since by M. de Chalons, and 20,000 francs, in little legacies, from one or two of my uncles; but do you not wonder whither my pen is running with me? I should do much better to tell you what I suffer every day, when I reflect in what places Providence has destined us to pass our lives. This is a continual source of uneasiness to me, but let it not be so to you; you have not the same reason; you are with a husband that adores you, and in the midst of honors and splendor; but endeavor, if possible, to work some miracle in your affairs, so that your return to Paris may be retarded only by the duties of your post, and not from necessity. It is very easy to talk thus; I wish it was as easily carried into execution, and wishes are not forbidden us. They write me word that Madame de Valavoire is at Paris, and that she is forever talking of your beauty, politeness, wit, talents, and, in short, of the new head-dress you have invented, which it seems you have executed in as good a style as if you had been in the midst of the court. Madame de la Troche and I have at least the honor of having described it so well as to put you in the way of performing these wonders. She is at Paris still, that La Troche. She is going to her own house about the latter end of this month. As for me, I do not know what the States intend doing; but I fancy I shall run away for fear of being ruined. It is a mighty pretty thing to put myself to the expense of near a thousand crowns in dinners and suppers, and all for the honor of keeping a summer-house for M. and Madame de Chaulnes, Madame de Rohan, M. de Lavardin, and half Brittany, who, without knowing any thing of me, will, to be in the fashion, honor me with their company. Well, we shall see how it will turn out. I shall only regret leaving M. d'Harroüis and this house, before I have half finished my business. But, my dear child, the greatest inclination I have at present is to be a little religious. I plague La Mousse about it every day. I belong neither to God nor to the devil. I am quite weary of such a situation, though, between you and me, I look upon it as the most natural one in the world. I am not the devil's, because I fear God, and have at the bottom a principle of religion; then, on the other hand, I am not properly God's, because his law appears hard and irksome to me, and I can not bring myself to acts of self-denial; so that altogether I am one of those called lukewarm Christians, the great number of which does not in the least surprise me, for I perfectly understand their sentiments and the reasons that influence them. However, we are told that this is a state highly displeasing to God; if so, we must get out of it. Alas! this is the difficulty. Was ever any thing so mad as I am, to be thus eternally pestering you with my rhapsodies? My dear child, *I ask excuse*, as they say here; but I must chat with you, it is so truly delightful to me. Be sure, however, not to return me an answer, only let me hear of your health, with a little spice of your sentiments, that I may see that you are happy, and that you like Grignan; that is all. Love me; though we have turned the world into ridicule, it is natural, it is good.

LETTER XIV.

The Rocks, Sunday, June 28, 1671.

You have amply made up to me my late losses; I have received two letters from you which have filled me with transports of joy. The pleasure I take in reading them is beyond all imagination If I have in any way contributed to the improvement of your style, I did it in the thought I was laboring for the pleasure of others, not for my own. But Providence, who has seen fit to separate us so often, and to place us at such immense distances from each other, has repaid me a little for the privations in the charms of your correspondence, and still more in the satisfaction you express in your situation, and the beauty of your castle; you represent it to me with an air of grandeur and magnificence that enchants me. I once saw a similar account of it by the first Madame de Grignan;

but I little thought, at that time, that all these beauties were one day to be at your command. I am very much obliged to you for having given me so particular an account of it. If I could be tired in reading your letters, it would not only betray a very bad taste in me, but would likewise show that I could have very little love or friendship for you. Divest yourself of the dislike you have taken to circumstantial details. I have often told you, and you ought yourself to feel the truth of this remark, that they are as dear to us from those we love, as they are tedious and disagreeable from others. If they are displeasing to us, it is only from the indifference we feel for those who write them. Admitting this observation to be true, I leave you to judge what pleasure yours afford me. It is a fine thing, truly, to play the great lady, as you do at present. I perfectly comprehend Monsieur de Grignan's feelings in seeing you so much admire his castle; had you appeared insensible, or even indifferent, on the occasion, it would have given him a chagrin that I can conceive better perhaps than any other; and I share in the pleasure he has in seeing you pleased. There are some hearts which sympathize for each other so truly, that they judge by themselves what others feel. You do not mention Vardes* often enough to me, nor poor Corbinelli. Was it not very agreeable to you to be able to speak their language? How goes on Vardes' love for the fair T——? Tell me whether he is much hurt by the infinite length of his banishment, or whether his philosophy, and a little dash of misanthropy, can support his heart against these vicissitudes of love and fortune. The books you read are well chosen. Petrarch must certainly give you a good deal of pleasure, especially with the notes you have. Those of Mademoiselle de Scuderi on some of his sonnets, rendered them very agreeable. As for Tacitus, you know how much I was charmed with it, when we read it together here; and how often I used to interrupt

* The Marquis de Vardes was banished to Provence in 1665, for having been concerned in some court intrigues, and remained in exile till the year 1682. He was a man of amiable manners.

you, to make you observe the periods, where I thought the harmony particularly striking. But if you stop half way I shall scold you; it will be doing great injustice to the dignity of the subject, and I shall say to you, as a certain prelate did to the queen mother, "This is history; you know what stories are already." A reluctance, in this respect, is only pardonable in romances, which I know you do not like. We read Tasso with pleasure, and I am a pretty good proficient in the language, from the excellent masters I have had. My son makes La Mousse read Cleopatra,* and I listen to him, whether I will or not, and am amused. My son is going to Lorraine; we shall be very dull in his absence. You know how it vexes me to see the breaking up of an agreeable party, and how transported I am when I see a train of carriages driving off that have wearied me to death for a whole day; upon which we made this just observation, that bad company is more desirable than good. I recollect all the odd things we used to say when you were here, and all you said yourself, and all you did; your idea never leaves me; and then again, on a sudden, I think where you are; my imagination represents to me an immense space, and a great distance; on a sudden your castle bounds the prospect, and I am displeased at the walls that inclose your mall. Ours is surprisingly beautiful, and the young nursery is delightful. I take pleasure in rearing their little heads to the clouds, and frequently, without considering consequences or my own interest, cut down large trees, because their shade incommodes my young ones. My son views all these proceedings, but I do not allow him to interfere. Pilois† continues to be a very great favorite with me, and I prefer his conversation to that of many who have the title of chevalier in the parliament of Rennes. I am grown rather more negligent than you; for the other day I let a coachful of the Fouesnelle family go home through a tremendous rain, for want of pressing them with a good grace to

---

* A famous romance of La Calprenede's. † The gardener.

stay; but I could not get the compliment to pass my lips. It was not the two young women, but the mother, and an old woman from Rennes, and the two sons. Mademoiselle du Plessis is exactly as you represent her, only if possible, more impertinent. What she says and does every day to keep me from being jealous, is perfectly original, and I am quite provoked, sometimes, that I have nobody to laugh at it with me. Her sister-in-law is very pretty, without being ridiculous, and speaks Gascon in the midst of Brittany. I think you are very happy in having Madame de Simiane* with you; she has a fund of knowledge that will relieve you from all kinds of restraint; this is a great deal. You will have, too, a very agreeable companion in her.

I now return to you, that is, to the divine fountain of Vaucluse! How beautiful! Well might Petrarch make such frequent mention of it! But, remember, I shall some day see all these wonders with my own eyes; I, who have such a veneration for antiquities. I shall certainly be transported with them, and the magnificence of Grignan. The abbé will find employment enough there. After the Doric orders and splendid titles of your house, nothing is wanting but the order you are going to establish there; for, let me tell you, without something substantial at the bottom, all is bitterness and anxiety. I have great pity for those who ruin themselves; it is the only affliction in life that is felt alike by all, and which is increased, instead of being diminished, by time. I have frequent conversations on this subject with a certain friend of ours. If he has a mind to benefit by them, he has had opportunity enough to lay in a good stock, and of such a nature he need not forget them. I am glad that you are to have two of your brothers-in-law with you this autumn. I think you have planned your journey well. We can travel a great way without being fatigued, provided we have something to amuse us by the way, and do not lose

---

* Magdelen Hai-du-Châtelet, wife to Charles Louis, Marquis of S'miane; she was afterward mother-in-law to Paulina de Grignan.

our courage. The return of fine weather has brought all my workmen back again, which is a great amusement to me. When I have company, I work at that fine altar-piece you saw me drawing when you were at Paris; when I am alone, I read, I write, or am with the abbé in his closet upon business. I wish him with you sometimes, but it is for two or three days only.

I consent to the commerce of wit which you propose. The other day I made a maxim off-hand, without once thinking of it, and I liked it so well that I fancied I had taken it out of M. de la Rochefoucault's. Pray tell me whether it is so or not, for in that case my memory is more to be praised than my judgment. I said, with all the ease in the world, that "ingratitude begets reproach, as acknowledgment begets new favors." Pray where did this come from? Have I read it? did I dream it? is it my own idea? Nothing can be truer than the thing itself, nor than that I am totally ignorant how I came by it. I found it properly arranged in my brain, and at the end of my tongue. As for that sentence, "*bella cosa far niente*," you will not think it so dull when I tell you it is intended for your brother: remember last winter's disaster. Adieu, my dearest child; take care of yourself, continue handsome, dress well, amuse yourself, and take proper exercise. I have just been writing to Vivonne,* about a captain of a troop of Bohemians, whose confinement I have begged him to render as easy as possible, without detriment to the king's service. You must know that there was among the troop of Bohemians† that I was mentioning to you the other day, a young girl who danced extremely well, and put me very much in mind of your manner. I was pleased with her. She begged me to write to Provence in favor of her grandfather. "Where is he?" said I. "He is at Marseilles," said she, with as much composure and unconcern as if she had said, "He is at Vincennes." He was a man of singular

---

* General of the galleys.   † Gipseys.

merit, it seems, in his way;* in short, I promised her to write about him; I immediately thought of Vivonne. I send you my letter; if you are not sufficiently upon terms with him to allow of my jesting with him, you may burn it; if it is an ill-written letter you may burn it; but if you are friendly with his corpulency, and my letter will save you the trouble of writing one, seal it and send it to him. I could not refuse this request to the poor girl, and to the best-danced minuet that I have seen since the days of Mademoiselle de Sévigné. She had just your air, was about your height, has good teeth, and fine eyes. Here is a letter of so enormous a length that I can easily forgive your not reading it through. Monsieur de Grignan can not conceive how one can possibly read such long letters; but, in good earnest, can you read them in a day?

LETTER XV.

THE ROCKS, Sunday, July 5, 1671.

It is a great proof of your love, my dear child, that you can bear with all the nonsense I send you from hence. You defend Mademoiselle de Croqueoison extremely well. In return, I assure you there is not a single word in your letters that is not dear to me. I am afraid to read them for fear of ending them, and if it were not for the consolation that I can read them over as often as I please, I should make them last much longer; but then, on the other hand, my impatience makes me ready to devour them. What should I do if your writing was as illegible as D'Hacqueville's? Would the greatness of my affection help me to decipher it? Really, I am afraid not; but I have heard of such instances. In short, I greatly esteem D'Hacqueville, and yet I can not accustom myself to his handwriting; I never can read his letters; I

---

* And had been condemned to the galleys for having distinguished himself rather too much in his Bohemian faculty.

hunt out word by word; I puzzle myself with guessing at them; I say one word for another, and at last, when I can make neither head nor tail of it, away I fling the letter in a rage. But I tell you this as a secret, for I would not have him know that his letters give me all this trouble. He thinks, poor man, his hand is like print; but you, who know the contrary, tell me how you manage. My son set out yesterday, greatly concerned at parting with us. I endeavored to inspire him with every good, just, and noble sentiment that I was mistress of, and to confirm all the good qualities I had remarked in him. He received my advice with all imaginable sweetness and marks of approbation; but you know the weakness of human nature; I leave him, therefore, in the hands of Providence, reserving to myself the comfort of having nothing to reproach myself with in regard to him. As he has a fund of wit and humor, we shall necessarily miss him extremely. We are going to begin a moral treatise of Nicole's. If I were at Paris I would send it to you; I am sure you would admire it. We continue to read Tasso with pleasure. I am almost afraid to tell you that I am returned to Cleopatra; and, by good fortune, the short memory I have makes it still pleasing to me. I have a bad taste, you will say; but you know I can not affect a prudery which is not natural to me, and as I am not yet arrived at a time of life that forbids the reading such works, I suffer myself to be amused with them, under the pretense that my son brought me into it. He used to read us some chapters, too, out of Rabelais, which were enough to make us die with laughing; in return, he seemed to take a good deal of pleasure in talking with me; and, if he is to be believed, he will remember what I have said to him. I know him well, and can often discern good sentiments through all the levity of his conversation. If he is dismissed this autumn, we shall have him again.

I have mentioned Launaye to you; she was bedaubed the other day like a twelfth-day taper; we thought she resembled the second volume of a sorry romance, or the Romance of the Rose, exactly. Mademoiselle du Plessis is always at my elbow; when I read the kind things you say of her, I am as red as fire. The other day La Biglesse played Tartuffe to the life. Being at table, she happened to tell a fib about some trifle or other, which I noticed, and told her of it; she cast her eyes to the ground, and with a very demure air, "Yes, indeed, madam," said she, "I am the greatest liar in the world; I am very much obliged to you for telling me of it." We all burst out a-laughing, for it was exactly the tone of Tartuffe: "Yes, brother, I am a wretch, a vessel of iniquity." She attempts sometimes to be sententious, and gives herself airs of understanding which sit still worse upon her than her own natural way. There! I think you know every thing about the Rocks.

LETTER XVI.

The Rocks, Sunday, July 12, 1671.

I have received but one letter from you, my dear child, which vexes me; I used generally to have two. It is a bad thing to use one's self to such dear and tender cares as yours; there is no being happy without them. If M. de Grignan's brothers come to you this summer, they will be good company for you. The coadjutor has been a little indisposed, but is now perfectly recovered; he is incredibly lazy, and is the more to blame, as he can write extremely well when he sets about it. He has a great regard for you, and intends visiting you about the middle of August—he can not before. He protests, but I believe it is false, that he has no branch to rest upon, which hinders him from writing, and makes his eyes ache. This is all I know about Seigneur Corbeau. How odd it is of me to tell you all this, when I do not know myself how I stand with him! If you should know any thing of the matter, pray inform me. I reflect every hour of the day upon the times when I used to see you always about me, and am perpetually regretting the loss of those happy moments. Not that I can reproach my heart with having been insensible of the pleasure of your company; for I solemnly protest to you, I never looked on you with the indifference or coolness that grows upon long acquaintance; no, I can not reproach myself with that. What I regret is, that I did not see you so constantly as I could now wish I had, but suffered cruel business sometimes to tear me from you. It would be a fine thing to fill my letters with what fills my heart; alas! as you say, we should glide over many thoughts, without seeming to regard them. Here then I rest, and conjure you, if I am at all dear to you, to be particularly careful of your health. Amuse yourself, do not study too much, carry yourself safely through your pregnancy; after that, if M. de Grignan really loves you, and is resolved not to kill you outright, I know what he will do, or rather what he will not do.

Have you cruelty enough not to finish Tacitus? Can you leave Germanicus in the midst of his conquests? If you really intend to serve him so paltry a trick, let me know where you leave off, and I will finish for you, which is all I can do to serve you at present. We have gone through Tasso, and with a great deal of pleasure; we found beauties in him, that are unknown to those who are only half read in the language. We have begun our *morality*,* it is of much the same nature as Pascal's. Talking of Pascal, I have taken into my head to almost adore those gentlemen, the postillions who are incessantly carrying our letters backward and forward. There is not a day in the week, but they bring one either to you or to me; there is one every day, and every hour of the day, upon the road. Kind-hearted people, how obliging it is of them! What a charming invention is the post, and what a happy effect of Providence is the desire of gain! I sometimes think of writing to them to show my gratitude; and I believe I should have done it before, had I not remembered that chap-

---

* M. Nicole's Moral Essays.

ter in Pascal, and been afraid that they might have perhaps thought proper to thank me for writing to them, as I thanked them for carrying my letters. Here is a fine digression for you. But to return to our reading. It was without prejudice to Cleopatra that I laid a wager I would read it through; you know how I support my wagers. I often wonder how I could like such ridiculous stuff; I can hardly comprehend it. You may perhaps remember enough of me to know how much a bad style displeases me; that I have some taste for a good one, and that no person is more sensible to the charms of eloquence. I well know how wretched La Calprenedre's style is in many places, on account of its long-winded periods, and bad choice of words. I wrote a letter to your brother in that style the other day, which was pleasant enough. However, though I find such glaring faults in Calprenedre, though I know how detestable that way of writing is, yet I can not leave it. The beauty of the sentiments, the violence of the passions, and the miraculous success of their redoubtable swords, entices me away like a child; I become a party in all their designs, and if I had not the example of M. de la Rochefoucault and D'Hacqueville to comfort me, I should be ready to hang myself for being guilty of such a weakness. You appear before me, and cry "Shame!" yet still I go on. I shall have great honor in being intrusted by you with the care of preserving you in the abbé's friendship. He loves you tenderly; you are often the subject of our conversation, with your state, your grandeur, and so forth. He would not willingly die without having first taken a trip to Provence, and rendered you some service. I am told, that poor Madame de Montluet is on the point of losing her senses; she has been raving hitherto without once shedding a tear, but now she has a violent fever, and begins to cry. She says she will be damned, since her dear husband is inevitably so. We go on with our chapel. The weather is very hot; but the mornings and evenings are delightful in the woods, and under the shade of the trees before the house. My apartment is extremely cool. I am afraid you suffer from the heat in Provence.

LETTER XVII.

THE ROCKS, Wednesday, August 19, 1671.

You describe very humorously the disorder my perfumed paper occasioned you. Those who saw you read my letters must have thought I was dead, and could never imagine that they contained nothing but chit-chat. I am very far from correcting myself in the way you imagined. I shall always run into extremes in what is for your good, if it depends on me. I already began to think that my paper might do you harm, but I did not intend to change it till about November. However, I begin from this day, and for the future you will have nothing to guard against but the smell.

You have a tolerable number of the Grignans with you; the Lord deliver you from the aunt,* I feel her troublesome even here. The chevalier's sleeves must have had a curious effect at table; but though they draw every thing along with them, I much question whether they would draw me; fond as I am of fashion, I have a great aversion to slovenliness. Vitré would be a famous place for him. I think I never saw such profusion before. There is not a table at court that can come up to the meanest of the twelve or fifteen that are constantly kept up here; and, indeed, there is occasion for all this, for there are no less than three hundred people to be provided for, who have nowhere else to eat. I left this good town last Monday, after having made your compliments to Mme. de Chaulnes and Mme. de Murinais. Nothing could be more cordially received, or more warmly returned. All Brittany was drunk on that day. We dined apart. Forty gentlemen dined in a lower room, each of whom drank forty toasts; the king's was the first, and then the glasses were broken. All this was done under pretense of extreme joy and gratitude for a hundred thousand crowns which his majesty had remitted out of the free gift the province had made him, as a recompense for their having so

---

* Ann d'Ornano, Countess of Harcourt, aunt to M. de Grignan.

cheerfully complied with his request. So now there is only two millions two hundred thousand livres, instead of five hundred thousand. The king, too, has written a letter with his own hand, full of the kindest expressions to his good province of Britany. This letter the governor read to the States assembled, and a copy of it was registered. Upon this they shouted *Vive le roi!* and immediately fell to drinking; and drink they did, God knows! M. de Chaulnes did not forget the gouvernante of Provence; and a Breton gentleman going to toast you by your name, and not well remembering it, got up, and, in a loud voice, exclaimed, "Here is to Madame de *Carignan.*" This ridiculous mistake made M. de Chaulnes laugh till the tears came into his eyes. The Bretons drank it, thinking it was right; and, for a week to come, you will be nothing but Madame de Carignan; some called you the Countess of Carignan. This was the state of things when I left them.

I have shown Pomenars what you say of him. He is highly delighted with it; but I assure you he is so hardened and impudent, that once or twice in a day he makes the first president leave the room, to whom he is a mortal enemy, as well as to the procurator-general. Madame de Coëtquen had just received the news of the death of her little girl, and fainted away. She is in great affliction, and says she shall never have so pretty a one. Her husband is quite inconsolable; he is just returned from Paris, after having made matters up with Le Bordage. This was a most extraordinary affair; he has transferred all his resentments to M. de Turenne.* I suppose you know nothing of this, but it fell unintentionally from my pen. There was a pretty ball on Sunday. We saw a *girl of Lower Brittany* who, they said, bore away the palm. She was the most ridiculous creature I ever saw, and threw herself into such attitudes as made us die with laughing. But there were

---

* Glory, which is the last passion of the sage, was not the only passion of Turenne; for, at the age of sixty, he was in love with Madame de Coetquen.

other dancers, both men and women, that were really admirable.

If you ask me how I like my Rocks after all this hurry, I shall tell you that I am delighted to be here again. I shall stay for a week or ten days at least, in spite of their endeavors to get me back. I want rest more than I can describe to you. I want to sleep; I want to eat, for I am starved at these fêtes. I want the fresh air; I want silence, for I was attacked on all sides, and my lungs were almost worn out with talking. In short, my dear, I found our abbé, La Mousse, my dog, my mall, Philois, and my masons, all as I left them, and they are the only things that can do me any good in my present condition.

LETTER XVIII.

THE ROCKS, Sunday, August 23, 1671.

You were with the president of Charme's lady, then, when you wrote to me. Her husband was the intimate friend of Monsieur Fouquet. Am I right in this? In short, my dear, you were not alone; and M. de Grignan acted wisely in making you leave your closet to entertain your company. He might, however, have spared his capuchin's beard, though he did not appear much the worse for it in your eyes, for when he was at Livri, with *his bushy tuft*,* you thought him handsomer than Adonis. I often repeat these four verses with admiration. It is surprising what an impression the remembrance of any particular time makes upon the mind, whether good or bad. Sometimes I 'hink of that delicious autumn; and then again, when I reflect on the latter part of it, I sweat with horror;† yet we ought to be thankful to Providence, who delivered you out of the danger you were in.

* *Sa touffe ébouriffée.* Part of a *bout rimé*, filled up by Madame de Grignan.
† On account of a miscarriage that Madame de Grignan had at Livri, the 4th November, 1669.

Your reflections upon the death of M. de Guise are admirable; they have made me plow up my mall with my eyes; for it is there I meditate with most pleasure. Poor La Mousse has been afflicted with the tooth-ache, so that for a long time I have walked alone till night, and thought of—God knows what I have not thought of. Do not be under apprehensions of my growing weary of solitude: set aside the ills that arise from my own heart, and against which I have not strength to struggle, and I am not to be pitied in any respect. I am of a happy temper; I can accommodate myself to, and be pleased with any thing; and I prefer my retirement here to all the noise and pageantry of Vitré. I have been here a week, and the tranquillity I have enjoyed has cured me of a dreadful cold. I have drank nothing but water; have talked very little; have left off suppers; and by this method, without having shortened my walks, I am quite well again. Madame de Chaulnes, Madame de Murinais, Madame Fourché, and a very fine girl from Nantes, came here last Thursday. Madame de Chaulnes told me, as she came into my room, that she could exist no longer without seeing me; that she had the weight of all Brittany upon her shoulders, and should die with fatigue. She then flung herself upon my bed; we sat round her, and she was fast asleep in a minute, from mere fatigue, though we continued talking. At last she awoke, highly charmed with the ease and freedom we enjoy at the Rocks. We then took a walk. Afterward she and I sat down to rest ourselves in the center of the wood, and while the rest were diverting themselves at mall, I made her tell me how she came to marry M. de Chaulnes; for I always love to fish out something by way of amusement; but in the midst of our entertainment there came on just so treacherous a shower like the one you may remember at Livri, that we were nearly drowned. The water ran from our clothes in streams; it came through the trees in a moment, and we were instantly wet to the skin. We ran as fast as we could, some screaming, others sliding, others falling. At last we got in, a roaring fire was made, we changed our dress from head to foot, I furnishing the whole wardrobe. We dried our shoes, and were ready to die with laughing all the while. In this manner was the gouvernante of Brittany treated in her own government. After this we had a slight repast, and then the poor woman left us, more vexed, I dare say, at the part she had to play when she got home, than at the affront she had received here. She made me promise to relate this adventure to you, and to come and assist her to-morrow in entertaining the States, which will break up in about a week. I engaged to do both; of the one I now acquit myself, and of the other I shall acquit myself to-morrow, as I can not help showing her this civility.

LETTER XIX.

The Rocks, Wednesday, September 16, 1671.

I am wicked to-day, my child. I am just in the same humor as when you used to say, "*You are wicked*." I am very dull and spiritless: I have not heard from you. "Warm affections are never tranquil;" *a maxim*. It rains; we are quite alone; in short, I wish you a pleasanter day than I am likely to have. What greatly perplexes the abbé, La Mousse, and the rest of my party, is, that there is no remedy for the evil. I want it to be Friday, that I may have a letter from you, and it is but Wednesday. This puzzles them. They do not know what to do for me in this case, for if, in the excess of their friendship, they were to assure me it was Friday, that would be still worse; for if I had not a letter from you then, I should be lost to all reason. I am obliged to have patience; though patience, you know, is a virtue that I am not much in the habit of practising; but I shall be easy before three days have passed. I am very anxious to know how you are after your alarm. These alarms are my aversion; for though I am not with child myself, they make me become so, that is, they put me in a condition that entirely destroys my health. However, my uneasiness does not at present reach so far; for I am persuaded you have been prudent enough to keep your bed, and that will have set all matters right again. Do not tell me, that you will not let me know any thing about your health; that would make me desperate, and having no longer any confidence in what you say, I should be always in the way I am in at present. We are, it must be owned, at a fine distance from each other, and if either of us had any thing upon the mind that required immediate relief, we should have plenty of time to hang ourselves in.

I thought it necessary yesterday to take a small dose of morality, and I found myself a great deal the better for it; and still more so for a little criticism on the Bérénice of Racine, which I thought very diverting and ingenious. It is by the author* of the sylphs, gnomes, and salamanders. There are a few words which are not quite so good as they should be, and even unbecoming a man who knows the world; these grate the ear; but, as they occur only here and there, they ought not to prejudice us against the whole, which, I assure you, upon examination, I found a very well-written critique. As I fancied this trifle would have diverted you, I heartily wished for you by my side in the closet, provided you could return again to your magnificent castle as soon as you had read it. And yet I own I should have felt some pain in letting you go so soon. I know too well what the last parting cost me. It would partake of the humor I have just been complaining of. I can not think of it even now without shuddering; but you are safe from this inconvenience. I hope this letter will find you cheerful; if so, I beg you will burn it directly, for it would be very extraordinary if it should be agreeable to you, considering the horrid humor I write it in. It is very happy for the coadjutor that I do not answer his letter to-day.

I have a great inclination to ask you a thousand questions

* The Abbé Villars, author of the Count de Gabalis.

by way of finishing this performance worthily. Have you many grapes? you tell me only of figs. Is the weather very hot? you do not say a word about it. Have you such charming cattle as we have at Paris? Has your aunt D'Harcourt been with you long? You see that, having lost so many of your letters, I am quite ignorant how matters stand, and have entirely lost the thread of your discourse. Ah! how I long to beat somebody! and how much I should be obliged to any Breton that would come and say something very silly, to put me in a passion! You told me the other day that you were glad I was returned to my solitude that I might think of you. Very pretty that! as if I did not think sufficiently of you in every other place. Farewell, my dear—this is the best part of my letter. I finish, because I think I talk foolishly, and I must preserve my credit.

LETTER XX.

THE ROCKS, Wednesday, Sept. 30, 1671.

I believe the *Leonic* opinion is now the most ascertained. He understands the subject completely, can tell whether matter reasons or not, what kind of intelligence God has given to the brute creation, with other subjects that occupied his thoughts. You may perceive by this that I suppose him in heaven, *O che spero!** He died on Monday morning; I was then at Vitré and saw him, but I wish I had not seen him. His brother seems inconsolable; I invited him to my woods that he might weep at liberty, but he told me he was too deeply afflicted to seek consolation. The poor bishop was only five and thirty years of age; he was well provided for, and had an admirable taste for science; this was, in fact, the cause of his death, as it was of Pascal's—he wore himself out with study. You are not much interested in this detail; but it is the news of the place, and you must, therefore, bear with

* O, how I wish it!

it. Death, in my opinion, is the concern of every one, and its consequences strike home to our bosoms.

I read M. Nicole with a degree of pleasure that lifts me above the earth. I am particularly charmed with his third treatise on the means of preserving peace and harmony among mankind. Read it, I beseech you, and with attention; you will see how clearly he develops the intricacies of the human heart, in which every sect is alike included—philosophers, Jansenists, Molinists, in short, all mankind: this may truly be called searching to the bottom of the heart with a lantern. He discovers to us sensations that we feel daily, but which we have neither the wit to comprehend nor the sincerity to acknowledge. In a word, I never read any thing like it, except Pascal. Were it not for the amusement of our books we should be moped to death for want of employment. It rains incessantly. I need say no more to make you conceive how dull our situation is. But you who enjoy a sunshine which is so much the object of my envy, how do I pity you to be torn from Grignan, while the weather is delightful, in the middle of autumn, and from an agreeable society, and all this to be shut up in a little dirty town! I can not bear the idea. Could not M. de Grignan have put off the assembly a little longer? Is he not master in this respect? And poor Coulanges, what will become of him? Our recluse mode of life has so turned our brains that we make matters of consequence of every thing. Receiving and answering letters takes up some of our time, indeed, but we have always enough left upon our hands. You make our abbé proud by the kind things you say of him in your letters. I am satisfied with him on your account. As for La Mousse, he catechises Sundays and holidays; he is resolved to go to heaven. I tell him it is only out of curiosity, to see whether the sun is a heap of dust, continually in motion, or a globe of fire. The other day he assembled all the children of the village about him, and was catechising them, but after several questions they had so confounded things, that when he asked them who the Blessed

Virgin was, they all with one accord answered, "The Creator of heaven and earth." His faith was not shaken by the children, but finding the men and women, and even the old people, all in the same story, he began to doubt, and at length joined in the opinion; in short, he did not know what he was about, and if I had not luckily come to his aid he would never have got out of the scrape. This new opinion would certainly have been productive of more mischief than that of the motion of atoms. Farewell, my dear child, you see we tickle ourselves in order to laugh, to so low an ebb are we reduced.

LETTER XXI.

The Rocks, Wednesday, October, 7, 1671.

You know I am always carried away by what I read, so that it is for the interest of those I converse with, that I should read none but the best books. I can think of nothing at present but M. Nicole's Moral Reflections. His treatise on the means of preserving peace among men, delights me. I never met with any thing so truly practical, yet so full of fire and imagination. If you have not yet read it, I beg you will. If you have read it, read it again with additional attention. For my part, I think all mankind are included in it. I am persuaded it was made for me, and hope to profit by it; at least I shall endeavor to do so. You know I could never bear the old saying, "I am too old to mend;" I could much sooner pardon the young for saying, I am too young. Youth is in itself so amiable, that were the soul as perfect as the body, we could not forbear adoring it; but when youth is past, it is then we ought to think of improvements, and endeavor to supply the loss of personal charms by the graces and perfections of the mind. I have long made this the subject of meditation, and am determined to work every day at my mind, my soul, my heart, and my sentiments. I am full of this at present, and therefore fill my letter with it, having besides nothing of greater consequence to tell you.

I suppose you are at Lambesc, but I can not see you clearly from hence; there is a mist about my imagination that conceals you from my sight. I had formed an idea of Grignan, I saw your apartment, used to walk upon your terrace, and went to mass at your beautiful church. But now I am quite at a loss; I wait with great impatience for intelligence from your new quarters. I will write no more to-day, though I have a great deal of time upon my hands; for I have nothing but trifles to tell you, which would be an affront to the lady-lieutenant of a province, who is holding the States, and, consequently, has weighty affairs upon her hands. It may do well enough when you are in your little palace of Apollo. Our abbé and La Mousse are very much yours; and I, my dear child, need I tell you what I am, or what you are to me?

LETTER XXII.

The Rocks, Wednesday, November 4, 1671.

Let us talk of M. Nicole, it is a long time since we have said a word about him. There is a great deal of justice in your observation respecting the indifference he requires us to show to the opinion of the world; I think with you, that philosophy will hardly be found sufficient of itself, without the assistance of grace. He lays so great a stress on preserving peace and good fellowship with our neighbor, and recommends so many things to us in order to attain these, that it is next to an impossibility, after this, to be indifferent to what the world thinks of us. Guess what I am doing; I am beginning this treatise again—methinks I could wish to swallow it, like Ezekiel's roll. I am delighted with what he says on the subject of pride and self-love, which enter into all disputes, under the feigned name of the love of truth. In short, this treatise will apply to more than one in the world; but I can not help thinking that he had me principally in view when he wrote it. He says, eloquence, and a flow of words, give a *luster* to the thoughts. I greatly admire that expression; I thought it beautiful and new. The word *luster* is extremely apposite there, do you not think so? We must read this book together at Grignan. I pass my time in having masses said for you every day, and in a multitude of disagreeable thoughts, which can be of no service to you, but which, however, it is impossible to avoid. I have at present ten or twelve workmen in the air, raising the timbers of our chapel. They run backward and forward upon the outside of it like so many rats; they hold by nothing, and are every instant in danger of breaking their necks, and make my back ache with endeavoring to help them below. One can not but admire the wonderful effects of Providence in the desire of gain, and be thankful such people are created, who are willing to do for a shilling what others would not do for a hundred thousand pounds. "O, thrice happy they who plant cabbages! when they have one foot on the ground, the other is not far off." I have this from a very good author.* We have planters too with us, who are forming new avenues. I hold the young trees myself while they set them in the ground, unless it rains so that there is no being abroad; but the weather almost drives me to despair, and makes me wish for a sylph to transport me to Paris. Madame de la Fayette says, that since you tell the story of Auger in so serious a manner, she is persuaded nothing can be more true, and that you are by no means jesting with me. She thought at first that it had been a joke of Coulanges', and it looks very like it. If you write to him upon the subject, pray let it be in that style.

---

* Panurge, in Rabelais.

LETTER XXIII.

PARIS, Wednesday, Jan. 13, 1672.

For Heaven's sake, my dear child, what do you mean? What pleasure can you take in thus abusing your person and understanding, vilifying your conduct, and saying, that one must have great good-nature to think of you sometimes? Though I am certain you can not believe all you say, yet it hurts me to hear it; you really make me angry with you; and though, perhaps, I ought not to answer seriously things that are only said in jest, yet I can not help scolding you before I go any further. You are excellent again, when you say you are afraid of wits. Alas! if you knew how insignificant they are when you are by, and how encumbered they are with their own dear persons, you would not value them at all. Do you remember how you used to be deceived in them sometimes? Do not let distance magnify objects too much; but it is one of its common effects.

We sup every evening at Madame Scarron's; she has a most engaging wit, and an understanding surprisingly just and clear. It is a pleasure to hear her sometimes reason upon the horrid confusion and distractions of a country with which she is very well acquainted. The vexations that Heudicourt undergoes in a place that appears so dazzling and glorious; the continual rage of Lauzun; the gloomy chagrin and cares of the court ladies, from which the most envied are not always exempt; are things which she describes in the most agreeable and entertaining manner. Such conversations as these lead us insensibly from one moral reflection to another, sometimes of a religious, sometimes of a political kind. You are frequently one of our subjects; she admires your wit and manners; and, whenever you return hither, you are sure of being highly in favor.

But let me give you an instance of the king's goodness and generosity, to show you what a pleasure it is to serve so amiable a master: He sent for Marshal Bellefond into his closet the other day, and thus accosted him: "Monsieur le maréchal, I insist upon knowing your reasons for quitting my service. Is it through a principle of devotion? Is it from an inclination to retire? Or is it on account of your debts? If it be the latter, I myself will take charge of them, and inform myself of the state of your affairs." The marshal was sensibly affected with this goodness: "Sire," said he, "it is my debts; I am overwhelmed with them, and can not bear to see some of my friends, who assisted me with their fortunes, likely to suffer on my account, without having it in my power to satisfy them." "Well, then," said the king, "they shall have security for what is owing to them: I now give you a hundred thousand francs on your house at Versailles, and a grant of four hundred thousand more, as a security in case of your death. The hundred thousand francs will enable you to pay off the arrears, and so now you remain in my service." That heart must be insensible indeed, that could refuse the most implicit obedience to such a master, who enters with so much goodness and condescension into the interest of his servants. Accordingly the marshal made no further resistance; he is now reinstated in his place, and loaded with favors. This is all strictly true.

Not a night passes at St. Germains without balls, plays, or masquerades. The king shows an assiduity to divert this madame that he never did for the other. Racine has brought out a new piece called Bajazet, which they say carries every thing before it: indeed it does not go *in emperando*, as the others did. Monsieur de Tallard says, that it as much exceeds the best piece of Corneille's, as Corneille's does one of Boyer's; this now is what you may call praising by the lump; there is nothing like telling truth; however, our eyes and ears will inform us more fully; for

   Du bruit de Bajazet mon ame importunée *

---

    * A line in Despreaux.

obliges me to go immediately to the play; we shall see what it is.

I have been at Livri. Ah, my dear child, how well did I keep my word with you, and how many tender thoughts of you filled my breast! It was delightful weather, though very cold; but the sun shone finely, and every tree was hung with pearls and crystals, that formed a pleasing diversity of colors. I walked a great deal. The next day I dined at Pomponne. It would not be an easy matter to recount all that passed during a stay of five hours; however, I was not at all tired with my visit. Monsieur de Pomponne will be here in three or four days. I should be very much vexed if I was obliged to apply to him about your Provence affairs; I am persuaded he will not hear me. You see I give myself airs of knowledge. But really nothing comes up to M. d'Usèz; I never saw a man of better understanding, nor one more capable of giving sound advice. I wait to see him, that I may inform you of what he has done at St. Germain.

You desire me to write you long letters; I think you have now sufficient reason to be contented; I am sometimes frightened at the length of them myself; and were it not for your agreeable flattery, I should never think of venturing them out of my hands. Madame de Brissac is excellently provided for the winter, in M. de Longueville and the Count de Guiche; but nothing is meant but what is fair and honorable, only she takes a pleasure in being adored. La Marans is never seen now, either at Madame de la Fayette's or at M. de la Rochefoucault's; we can not find out what she is doing; we are apt to judge a little rashly now and then; she took it into her head this summer, that she should be ravished, as if she wished it; but I am of opinion that she is in no great danger. Good Heavens, what a mad creature she is, and how long have I looked on her in the same light as you do now! But now let me tell you, my dear, it is not my fault that I do not see Madame de la Valavoire.* I am sure there is no occasion to

---

* A lady of quality in Provence, who was just then come to Paris.

bid me go and see her, it is enough that she has seen you, for me to run after her; but then she is running after somebody else; for I might forever desire her to wait at home for me; I can not get her to do me that favor. Your jest applies admirably to M. le Grand, and a very good one it is. Poor Châtillon is every day teasing us with the most wretched ones imaginable.

LETTER XXIV.

PARIS, Wednesday, June 20, 1672.

I send you M. de Rochefoucault's Maxims, revised and corrected, with additions; it is a present to you from himself. Some of them I can make shift to guess the meaning of; but there are others that, to my shame be it spoken, I can not understand at all. God knows how it will be with you. There is a dispute between the archbishop of Paris and the archbishop of Rheims about a point of ceremony: Paris will have Rheims ask leave of him, as his superior, to officiate, which Rheims will not consent to. It is said that these two right reverends will never agree till they are thirty or forty leagues asunder; if that is the case, they are both of them likely to continue as they are. The ceremony it relates to is the canonization of one Borgia, a Jesuit. The whole opera band is to exert itself on the occasion; the streets will be illuminated, even to the Rüe St. Antoine; the people are all mad about it: old Mérinville, however, has died without having seen it.

Do not deceive yourself, my child, by entertaining too good an opinion of my letters. The other day an impertinent fellow, seeing the monstrous length of a letter I was writing to you, asked me very seriously, if I thought any body could possibly read it all: I trembled at the thought of it, but without any intention of amendment; for the correspondence I have with you is my existence, the sole pleasure of my life; and every other consideration is but mean, when put in competition with it. I am uneasy about your brother; poor fellow! The weather is very cold: he lies in camp, and is still on the march to Cologne, for the Lord knows how long! I was in hopes of seeing him this winter, and see where he is now! After all, I find little Mademoiselle Adhémar must be the comfort of my old age: I wish you could but see how fond she is of me; how she cries after me, and hangs about me. She is not a beauty, but she is very pleasing—has a delightful voice, and a skin as clear and white . . . In short, I doat on her. You, it seems, doat on your boy; I am very glad of it; we can not have too many things to amuse us; real or imaginary, it does not signify.

To-morrow there is to be a ball at Madame's. I saw a heap of jewels tossing about at mademoiselle's, which put me in mind of past troubles: and yet, would to Heaven we were at the same work again! For how can I be unhappy while you are with me? Alas! my whole life is one continued scene of sorrow and disappointment. Dear Monsieur Nicole! have pity on me; and teach me to bear, with patience, the dispensations of Providence. Farewell, my dearest child, I dare not say I adore you; but I can not conceive any degree of love superior to mine: the kind and pleasing assurances you give me of yours, at once lighten and increase my sorrows.

LETTER XXV.

PARIS, Wednesday, March 16, 1672.

You talk to me of my departure: alas! my dear, I languish in the pleasing hope of it; nothing now stops me, but my poor aunt,* who is dying with violent pain and dropsy: it breaks my heart to see her sufferings, and to hear the tender and affecting manner in which she talks to me: her courage, patience, and resignation, are all together admirable. M. d'Hacqueville and I observe her distemper from day to day;

* Henrietta de Coulanges, Marchioness de la Trousse.

he sees my inmost heart, and knows what grief it is to me not to be at liberty at present: I am entirely guided by him, and we shall see, between this and Easter, whether her disorder increases as much as it has done since I came hither; if it does, she will die in our arms; but if she receives any relief, and is likely to languish for any length of time, I shall then set out as soon as M. de Coulanges comes back. Our poor abbé is as vexed at this as myself; but we shall be able to judge how it will turn out by next month. I can think of nothing else: you can not wish to see me so much as I do to embrace you; so put some bounds to your ambition, and do not hope ever to equal me in that respect.

My son tells me, they lead a wretched life in Germany, and are working all in the dark. He was greatly concerned at the death of the poor chevalier. You ask me if I am as fond of life as ever: I must own to you that I experience mortifications, and severe ones too; but I am still unhappy at the thoughts of death: I consider it so great a misfortune to see the termination of all my pursuits, that I should desire nothing better, if it were practicable, than to begin life again. I find myself engaged in a scene of confusion and trouble: I was embarked in life without my own consent, and know I must leave it again: that distracts me; for how shall I leave it? in what manner? by what door? at what time? in what disposition? Am I to suffer a thousand pains and torments that will make me die in a state of despair? Shall I lose my senses? Am I to die by some sudden accident? How shall I stand with God? What shall I have to offer to him? Will fear and necessity make my peace with him? Shall I have no other sentiment, but that of fear? What to hope? Am I worthy of heaven? or have I despaired the torments of hell? Dreadful alternative! Alarming uncertainty! Can there be greater madness than to place our eternal salvation in uncertainty? Yet what is more natural, or can be more easily accounted for, than the foolish manner in which I have spent my life? I am frequently buried in thoughts of this nature, and then death appears so dreadful to me that I hate life more for leading me to it, than I do for all the thorns that are strewed in its way. You will ask me then, if I would wish to live forever? Far from it; but if I had been consulted, I would very gladly have died in my nurse's arms; it would have spared me many vexations, and would have insured heaven to me at a very easy rate: but let us talk of something else.

I am quite provoked that you have received Bajazet from any hand but mine; that fellow Barbin* has served me this trick, out of spite, because I do not write Princesses of Cleves and Montpensier.† You form a very just and true judgment of Bajazet, and you will find that I am of your opinion: I wish I could send you Champmêlée to enliven it a little. The character of Bajazet wants life, and the manners of the Turks are ill preserved: their marriages have less ceremony; the plot is badly managed; and we are at a loss to account for so much slaughter: the piece has doubtless its beauties; but there is nothing superlative; nothing perfect; none of those fine strokes, that, like Corneille's, make one tremble. Let us be cautious how we compare Racine with him; the difference between them is great: the pieces of the latter are in many places cold and feeble; nor will he ever be able to surpass his Alexander and Andromache. Many persons consider Bajazet as inferior to both these, and it is my opinion also, if I may be allowed to give it. Racine's plays are written for Champmêlée, and not for posterity;‡ whenever he grows old and ceases to be in love, it will be seen whether I am mistaken or not. Long live then our old friend Corneille; let us forgive the bad lines we occasionally meet with for the sake of those

---

* A famous bookseller of that name.

† Two romances written by Madame de la Fayette, by which Barbin got a great deal of money.

‡ The event has proved, by Mithridates, Phædra, and Athaliah, that Madame de Sévigné's judgment partook of the prejudice of the times in which she wrote.

divine sallies that so often transport us, those masterly strokes that bid defiance to imitation. Despreaux has said as much before me; and it is in general the opinion of every one of good taste; let us therefore maintain it.

I send you a witticism of Madame de Cornuel's, which has highly diverted the crowd. Young M. Tombonneau has quitted the long robe, and taken to the jacket and trowsers: in short, he is resolved to go to sea; I do not know in what way the land has offended him; however, somebody told Madame de Cornuel that he was going to sea. "Lord bless the man!" said she, "has he been bitten by a mad dog?" As this was said off hand, it raised a great laugh.

LETTER XXVI.

PARIS, Wednesday, May 4, 1672.

It is impossible, my dear child, to tell you how much I pity, how much I praise, and how much I admire you: thus I divide my discourse into three heads. First, *I pity you* in being so subject to the vapors and low spirits, as they will certainly do you much harm. Secondly, *I praise you* for subduing them when there is occasion, especially on M. de Grignan's account, whom they must make very uneasy; it is a pleasing proof of the regard and consideration you have for him. Thirdly and lastly, *I admire you* for suppressing your natural inclination, to appear what you are not: this is really heroic, and the fruit of your philosophy: you have ample matter in yourself to call it into exercise. We were saying the other day that there is no real evil in life, except great pain; all the rest is merely imaginary, and depends on the light in which we view things. All other evils are curable either by time, moderation in our wishes, or strength of mind; and may be lightened by reflection, religion, or philosophy. But pain tyrannizes over both soul and body. Confidence in

God may indeed enable us to bear it with patience, and turn it to our advantage, but it will not diminish it.

This seems to savor of the Fauxbourg Saint Germain,* but it comes from my poor aunt's apartment, where I was the leader of the conversation. The subject arose naturally from her extreme sufferings, which, she maintains, are infinitely superior to every evil that life is subject to. M. de la Rochefoucault is of the same opinion: he is still tormented with the gout; he has lost his true mother,† and he lamented her death so tenderly and affectionately that I almost adored him: she was a woman of extraordinary merit, and was the only person in the world, he said, who was unchangeable in her love to him. Fail not to write to him; both you and M. de Grignan. M. de Rochefoucault's affection for his family is unparalleled: he maintains that it is one of the chains that attach us to one another. We have discovered, and related, and reconciled many things relative to his foolish mother (Madame de Marans), which explain to us clearly what you once said, that it was not what we thought, but quite another thing; yes truly it was quite another thing, or perhaps better still, it was this and that too; one was without prejudice to the other; she wedded the lute to the voice, and spiritual things to coarseness and indelicacy. My child, we have found a good vein, and one which explains the mystery of a quarrel you once had in the council-chamber of Madame de la Fayette. I will tell you the rest in Provence.

My aunt is in a state which does not seem likely to terminate. Your journey is exceedingly well-timed, perhaps ours may tally with it. We have a great desire to pass some part of our Whitsuntide on the road, either at Moulins or at Lyons. The abbé wishes it no less than myself. There is not a man of quality (of the sword I mean) in Paris. I went on Sunday to hear mass at the Minims. "We shall find our poor

---

* That is, from Madame de la Fayette, at whose house M. de Rochefoucault, and some of the most select company in Paris, used to meet.
† Gabrielle du Plessis Liancourt.

Minims quite deserted," said I to Mademoiselle de la Trousse, "we shall not find a creature there, except the Marquis d'Alluye." * Well, we went into the church, where the first and only creature we saw was the Marquis d'Alluye: I could not help laughing till I fairly cried at the oddity of the thing; in short he is left behind, and is going to his government on the sea-coast. The coast must be guarded, you know.

The lover of her whom you style *the incomparable*,† did not meet her at the first stage, but on the road, in a house of Sanguin's, a little beyond that which you know; he remained there two hours. It is thought he then saw the children for the first time. The fair one stays there, attended by a guard and a female friend; she is to be there for four or five months. Madame de la Vallière is at St. Germains. Madame de Thianges is here with her father; I saw her daughter the other day, she is beautiful beyond all imagination. Some people pretend that the king went straight to Nanteuil, but it is certain that the fair one is at the house called Genitoi. I tell you nothing but the truth; there is nothing I have a greater aversion and contempt for than idle stories.

You have taken your departure, then, my dear. Well, I will live in the hope of hearing from you at every stage. I shall not be behindhand on my side. I have managed so well as to find a friend at the post-office, who is very careful of our letters. I have for these several days past been occupied in adorning my cottage; Saint Aubin has effected wonders. I shall sleep there to-morrow. I swear to you that the reason I like it so well is because it is intended for you. You will be very well accommodated in my apartment, and I shall not be less so. I will tell you how charmingly every thing is contrived. I am extremely uneasy about your poor brother; this terrible war makes us tremble for those we love; whenever I think of it it fills me with horror; but then, again, I

---

* Paul d'Escloubleau, Marquis d'Alluye and de Sourdis, governor of the city and country of Orleans, and of the Pays Chartrain.

† The king and Madame de Montespan.

comfort myself with the thought that it may not be so bad as I apprehend, for I have remarked that things seldom happen as we expect them to do.

Pray let me know what has happened between the Princess Harcourt and you.* Brancas is dreadfully chagrined that you do not love his daughter. M. d'Usèz has promised to reestablish peace between all parties: I should be glad to know what has occasioned the coolness between you.

You tell me of your son, that his beauty grows less, and his merit increases: I am sorry for the loss of his beauty, and I am rejoiced to find that he loves wine; this is a little spice of Brittany and Burgundy together, which will produce a charming effect with the prudence of the Grignans. As for your daughter, she is quite the reverse; her beauty increases, and her merit lessens. I assure you, she is very pretty, but as obstinate as a demon; she has her little wills and little designs of her own; she diverts us extremely; she has a beautiful complexion, blue eyes, black hair, a nose neither handsome nor ugly; her chin, her cheeks, and the turn of her face are faultless. I shall say nothing of her mouth, it will do very well. She has a very sweet voice: Madame de Coulanges thinks it suits her mouth admirably.

I fancy, my dear child, that I shall at last be a convert to your opinion. I meet with vexations in life that are insupportable, and find, notwithstanding my fine reasoning at the beginning of this letter, there are many evils which, though less severe than bodily pain, are nevertheless equally to be dreaded.

LETTER XXVII.

PARIS, Friday, May 30, 1672.

I had no letter from you yesterday, my poor child. Your journey to Manaco had put you quite out of sorts. I was

---

* Frances de Brancas, wife of Alphonso Henry Chartres, of Lorrain, afraid some little disaster of this kind would befall me. I now send you news from M. de Pomponne; the fashion of being wounded is already begun; my heart is very heavy with the fears of this campaign. My son writes by every opportunity; he is at present in good health.

My aunt is still in a deplorable state, and yet we have the courage to think of appointing a day for our departure, assuming a hope which in reality we can not entertain. I can not help thinking that many of the events of life are ill-arranged; they are, as it were, rugged stones lying across our way, too unwieldy to be removed, and which we must get over as well as we can, though not without pain and difficulty. Is not the comparison just? I shall not bring my little girl with me; she goes on very well at Livri, and is to stay there during the summer. You never saw Livri in such perfection as it is at present; the trees are beautifully green, and the honeysuckles are every where in profusion. I am not yet tired of their perfume. But you despise our shrubberies since you have been accustomed to your groves of orange-trees.

I have a very tragical history to communicate to you from Livri. Do you remember that pretended devotee, who walked so steadily without turning his head that you would have thought he was carrying a glass of water upon it? His devotion has turned his brain. One night he gave himself five or six stabs with a knife, and fell on his knees in his cell, naked, and weltering in his blood. On entering, he was found in this posture. "Good God! brother, what have you done? Who has treated you thus?" He replied, very calmly, "Father, I am doing penance." He fainted away; he was put to bed; his wounds, which were found very dangerous, were dressed; with uncommon care and attention he recovered at the end of three months, and was sent back to his friends.

If you do not think such a head sufficiently disordered, tell

---

Prince of Harcourt, and daughter of Charles de Brancas, gentleman of honor to Queen Anne of Austria.

me so, and you shall have the story of Madame Paul,* who is fallen desperately in love with a great booby of five or six and twenty, whom she had taken to be her gardener. The lady has managed her affairs admirably; she has married him. The fellow is a mere brute, and has not common sense; he will beat her soon, he has already threatened to do it; no matter, she was resolved to have him. I have never seen such violent love; there is all the extravagance of sentiments imaginable, were they but rightly applied; but they are like a rough sketch of an ill painting; all the colors are there, they want only to be properly disposed. It is extremely amusing to me to meditate on the caprices of love. I feel frightened for myself when I see such things! What insolence, to attack Mme. Paul—that is to say, austere, old, straight-laced virtue herself!

LETTER XXVIII.

PARIS, Monday, June 20, 1672.

I can not reflect upon the situation you have been in, without great emotion; and though I know you are out of danger, yet I can not turn my eyes on what has passed without a horror that distracts me. Alas, how much was I in the dark about a health that was so dear to me! If any one had told me that my daughter was in greater danger than if she had been in the army, how little should I have believed it! Must I suffer this useless grief in addition to so many other sorrows that afflict my heart? The extreme danger my son is in; the war, which rages every day with greater violence; the couriers, who bring no other news but the death of some friend or acquaintance, and may bring accounts more fatal; the fear of hearing ill news, and yet the curiosity of knowing it; the desolation of those who are in excess of grief, and with whom I pass a great part of my time; the strange state of health my aunt is in, and my extreme desire of seeing you;

* Widow to the gardener at Livri.

all this afflicts and consumes me, and forces me to lead a life so contrary to my inclination, that I have need of more than a common share of health to support it.

You have never seen Paris as it is at present; all the world is in tears, or fears to be so. Poor Madame de Nogent is almost beside herself. Madame de Longueville pierces every heart with her complaints. I have not seen her indeed, but this is what I am told. Mademoiselle de Vertus returned two days since from Port-Royal, where she resides. They sent for her and M. Arnauld, to impart to Madame de Longueville the terrible news. The very sight of Mademoiselle de Vertus was sufficient; her sudden return was too sure a sign that some fatal accident had happened. As soon therefore as she appeared—"Ah! mademoiselle, how is it with my brother?"* She did not dare, even in thought, to inquire further. "Madam, he is recovered of his wound—there has been a battle—" "And my son?" No answer was made. "Ah! mademoiselle, my son, my dear child! answer me; is he dead?" "I have no words to answer you, madam." "Oh, my dear son! Was he killed on the spot? Had he not a single moment? Oh, God! what a sacrifice is this!" And she threw herself upon the bed, and by expressions of the most lively sorrow, by fainting-fits, by convulsions, by the silence of despair, by stifled cries, by sudden bursts of passion, by floods of bitter tears, by eyes uplifted to heaven, and by heart-rending complaints, she exhibited all the various emotions of grief. She sees a few friends; and, in pure submission to Providence, consents to receive such nourishment as is just sufficient to keep life and soul together. She takes no rest; her health, before in a declining state, is visibly altered for the worse. For my part, I wish her death earnestly, as I can not think she can survive such a loss. There is a certain gentleman† who is scarcely less affected. I can not help thinking, that if they had met, in the first moments of their grief, and had been alone together, all other sentiments would have given place

---

* The Prince of Condé.   † M. de la Rochefoucault.

to sighs and tears, redoubled without intermission; there would have been a dumb scene of sorrow, a dialogue of inarticulate sighs and groans. This is a mere thought of my own. But, my dear, how great affliction is this! The very mistresses of poor De Longueville do not constrain themselves; his domestics are disconsolate; and his gentleman, who came yesterday with the ill news, scarcely appears a reasonable creature. This death effaces the thoughts of all others.

A courier, who arrived yesterday evening, brings an account of the death of the Count du Plessis,* who was killed by a cannon-shot, as he was giving directions for making a bridge. Arnheim is besieged by M. Turenne. They did not attack the fort of Skeing, as it was defended by eight thousand men. Alas! these successful beginnings will be followed with a tragical end for a great number of families. May Heaven preserve my poor son! He was not upon this expedition; but the campaign is not yet finished.

In the midst of our afflictions, the description you have given me of Madame Colonna and her sister,† is really divine; it rouses one under the most melancholy circumstances. It is an admirable picture. The Countess de Soissons, and Madame de Bouillon,‡ are quite in a rage with these fools, and say they ought to be confined. It is thought that the king will not disoblige the constable§ (Colonna), who is certainly one of the greatest men in Rome. In the mean time we are in expectation of seeing them arrive here like Mademoiselle de l'Etoile;‖ this comparison is good.

The accounts I send you are from the best authority; you will find by all you receive, that M. de Longueville has been the cause of his own death, as well as of the death of many

---

* Alexander de Choiseul, Count du Plessis, son of Cæsar de Choiseul, Marshal of France.

† Hortensia Mancini, Duchess of Mazarin.

‡ Sisters to Mesdames de Colonna and Mazarin.

§ The father of these ladies, and of one of the most powerful families in Rome. ‖ In Scarron's comic romance.

others; and that the prince has showed himself, through the whole of this expedition, more like a father than the general of an army. I said yesterday, and others agreed with me, that if the war continues, the duke* will certainly occasion the death of the prince. His love for him surpasses every other consideration.

La Marans affects to appear overwhelmed with grief. She says that she sees very plainly there is something in the news from the army which is concealed from her; and that the prince and the duke are dead, as well as M. de Longueville. She conjures people, by all that is sacred, to speak out, and not to spare her; and tells them, that in her deplorable situation, it is in vain to hide any thing from her. If it were possible to laugh under these circumstances, we should laugh at her. Alas! if she knew how little any of us think of concealing any thing from her, and how much every one is taken up with his own griefs and his own fears, she would not have the vanity to believe we paid so much attention to her as to deceive her.

The news I send you comes, as I before said, from good authority; I had it from Gourville, who was with Madame de Longueville when she heard of her son's death. All the couriers come straight to him. M. de Longueville had made his will before he set out. He leaves a great part of his property to a son he has, who, as I believe, will take the title of Chevalier d'Orleans,† without expense to his relations. Have you heard how the body of M. de Longueville was disposed of? It was laid in the same boat in which he passed the river two hours before. The prince, who was wounded, ordered him to be placed near him, covered with a cloak, and, with several others who were wounded, repassed the Rhine to a town on this side of the river, where they came to have their

---

* Henry Juliers de Bourbon, son of the prince.

† He appeared under the name of the Chevalier de Longueville, and was accidentally killed at Philipsbourg in 1688, by a soldier, who was shooting at a snipe. See the letter of the 8th of July following

wounds dressed. It was the most melancholy sight in the world. They say the Chevalier de Monchevreuil, who was attached to M. de Longueville, will not have a wound dressed which he received as he stood next to him.

I have received a letter from my son: he is very much grieved at the death of M. de Longueville. He was not in this expedition, but he is to be in another. What safety can be hoped for in such a profession? I advise you to write to M. de la Rochefoucault, on the death of the chevalier, and the wound of M. de Marsillac. This fatal event has given me an opportunity of seeing his heart without disguise: for constancy, worth, tenderness, and good sense, he infinitely surpasses any one I have ever met with; his wit and humor are nothing in comparison. I will not amuse myself at present with telling you how much I love you. I embrace M. *. Grignan, and the coadjutor.

The same evening, at 10 o'clock.

I made up my packet two hours ago, and on my return to town I found a letter for me, with the news that a peace was concluded with Holland. It may easily be imagined that the Dutch are in the greatest consternation, and glad to submit to any terms; the king's success is beyond all that has ever been known. We shall once more breathe again; but what a cruel addition must this be to the grief of Madame de Longueville, and all those who have lost children and near relations! I have seen Marshal du Plessis; he is greatly afflicted, but demeans himself like a brave soldier. His lady* weeps bitterly; the countess† is only disconcerted at not being a duchess. I think, my dear child, that if it had not been for the rashness of M. de Longueville, we should have gained Holland without losing a man.

* Columba de Charron.
† Maria Louisa le Loup de Bellenave.

LETTER XXIX.

PARIS, Friday, Dec. 8, 1673.

I must begin, my dear child, by telling you of the death of the Count de Guiche: this is the chief subject of conversation at present. The poor youth died of sickness and fatigue in M. de Turenne's army; the news came on Tuesday morning. Father Bourdaloüe went to acquaint the Marshal de Grammont with it; who feared it the moment he saw him, knowing the declining state of his son. He made every one go out of his chamber, which was a little apartment near the convent of the Capuchins, and as soon as he found himself alone with Bourdaloüe, he threw himself upon his neck, saying, that he guessed but too well what he had to tell him; that it was his death-stroke, and that he received it as such from the hand of God; that he lost the true, the only object of his tenderness and natural affection; that he had never experienced any real joy, or violent grief, but through his son, who was not a common character. He threw himself on a bed, unable to support his grief, but without weeping, for this is a situation that denies the relief of tears. Bourdaloüe wept, but had not yet spoken a word. At last he began to comfort him with religious discourse, in which he employed his well-known zeal and eloquence. They were six hours together; after which Bourdaloüe, to induce him to make a complete sacrifice, led him to the church of these good Capuchins, where vigils were said for his son. He entered the church fainting and trembling, supported more by the crowd that pressed round him on every side, than by his feet; his face was so much disfigured with grief, that he could scarcely be known. The duke saw him in this lamentable condition, and related it to us at Madame de la Fayette's, with tears. The poor marshal returned at last to his little apartment, where he remains like a man under sentence of death. The king has written to him. No one is admitted to see him. Madame de Monaco* is in-

---

* Catherine Charlotte de Grammont, sister to the Count de Guiche.

consolable, and refuses to see company. Madame de Louvigny* is likewise incapable of receiving comfort; but it is only because she is not at all grieved. Do not you wonder at her good fortune? She is in a moment become Duchess of Grammont. The chancellor's lady† is transported with joy: the Countess de Guiche‡ behaves admirably well; she weeps when they tell her all the kind things her husband said, and the excuses he made to her when he was dying. "He was a very amiable man," she says; "I should have loved him passionately, if he had loved me in the slightest degree; I suffered his contempt with grief, and his death affects me with pity; I always hoped he would change his sentiments with regard to me." This is certainly true; there is not the least fiction in it. Madame de Verneuil§ feels real concern on this occasion. I believe it will be sufficient, if you only desire me to make your compliments to her; so you need only write to the Countess de Guiche, to Madame de Monaco, and Madame de Louvigny. The good D'Hacqueville has been desired to go to Frasé, thirty leagues from hence, to tell the news to Madame de Grammont, and to carry her a letter written by the poor youth a little before he died. He made a full confession of the faults of his past life, asked pardon publicly, and sent to tell Vardes a great many things which may benefit him. In a word, he ended the comedy well, and has left a rich and a happy widow.‖ The chancellor's lady is so fully sensible, she

---

* Maria Charlotte de Castelnau, sister-in-law to the Count.

† Relict of the late Chancellor Seguier, and grandmother to the Countess de Guiche.

‡ Margaret Louisa Susan de Bethune Sulli.

§ Charlotte de Seguier, mother to the Countess de Guiche: she first married the Duke de Sulli, and afterward Henry de Bourbon, Duke de Verneuil.

‖ She was married afterward to the Duke de Lude, in 1688. The Count de Guiche had been the lover of Henrietta of England. He also entered into the intrigues of M. de Vardes. He had made a brilliant campaign in Poland, and to him was owed the passage of the Rhine. He was as handsome and witty as he was brave.

says, of the little happiness this poor lady must have had in her marriage, that she thinks of nothing but repairing this misfortune. We are at a loss for a proper match for her. You will perhaps name for her M. de Marsillac, as we did; but they do not like each other: the other dukes are too young. M. de Foix is destined for Mademoiselle de Roquelaure. Think a little for us, for the affair is pressing. I have sent you, my dear child, a tedious account, but you sometimes tell me you like minuteness.

LETTER XXX.

PARIS, Monday, Dec. 11, 1673.

I am just returned from St. Germain, where I have been two whole days with Madame de Coulanges at M. de la Rochefoucault's. In the evening we went to pay our court to the queen, who said a thousand obliging things to me of you; but if I were to enumerate all the how-d' ye-do's and compliments that I had, both from men and women, old and young, who crowd about me to inquire after you, I should have to name the whole court. "And how does Madame de Grignan do? and when will she return?" and so on. In short, only figure me to yourself in the midst of a crowd of idle people, who, having nothing else to do, would every one ask me some question, so that I was frequently obliged to answer twenty at once. I dined with Madame de Louvois: it was who should be the first to invite me. I would have returned yesterday, but we were stopped by force to sup with M. Marsillac in his enchanted apartments with Madame de Thianges, Madame Scarron, the duke, M. de la Rochefoucault, M. de Vivonne, and a band of heavenly music. This morning, with much ado, we got away.

A quarrel of a singular nature is the news of the day at St. Germain. The Chevalier de Vendôme, and M. de Vivonne are the humble servants of Madame de Ludre. The chevalier expressed a wish of compelling M. de Vivonne to resign his pretensions. But on what grounds? he was asked. Why, he would fight M. de Vivonne. They laughed at him. It was, however, no joke, he said, he would fight him; and he mounted his horse to take the field. But the best of the story was Vivonne's reply to the person who brought him the challenge. He was confined to his room by a wound in his arm, and, receiving the condolence of the whole court, ignorant of the threat of his rival: "I, gentlemen," said he, "I fight! He may fight if he pleases, but I defy him to make me fight. Let him get his shoulder broken, let the surgeon make twenty incisions in his arm, and then"—it was thought he was going to say, *we will fight*—" and then," said he, " perhaps we may be friends. But the man must be jesting to think of firing at me! A pretty project, truly! He might as well fire at the door of a house.* I repent, however, having saved his life in crossing the Rhine, and will do no more such generous actions till I have the nativity cast of those I intend to assist. Would any one have thought, when I was remounting this fellow on his horse, that a few weeks afterward he would want to shoot me through the head for my kindness?" This speech, from the tone and manner in which it was delivered, had so droll an effect, that nothing else is talked of at St. Germain.

I found your siege of Orange very much magnified at court. The king had spoken of it very agreeably, and it was thought highly honorable to M. de Grignan, that, without the king's order, and merely to follow him, seven hundred gentlemen should have assembled upon the occasion; for the king having said *seven hundred*, every one else said *seven hundred*; it was added, with a laugh, that two hundred litters also followed him. But it is thought, seriously, that few governors could have obtained such a retinue.

I have had two hours' conversation at two different times with M. de Pomponne. He exceeds my most sanguine hopes. Mademoiselle de Lavocat is in our confidence: she is a **very**

---

* M. de Vivonne was remarkably corpulent.

amiable girl. She knows all our affairs—the business of the syndic, of the procurator, our gratuity, opposition, deliberation, etc., as well as she does the map of the empire and the interest of princes; that is, she has them at her finger's end. We call her the *little minister*. We have interludes in our conversation, which M. de Pomponne calls flashes of rhetoric to secure the good humor of the audience. There are some points in your letters I can not reply to; we often answer ridiculously when we write from such a distance. You know how grieved we once were at the loss of some town, when they had been rejoicing for ten days at Paris because the Prince of Orange had raised the siege; but this is one of the evils of distance. Adieu, my beloved child; I embrace you very affectionately.

LETTER XXXI.

PARIS, Friday, Dec. 22, 1673.

A piece of political news is just come into my head, and, contrary to my custom, I shall give it you. You know the King of Poland* is dead. The grand marshal,† the husband of Mademoiselle d'Arquien, is at the head of an army against the Turks; he has lately gained so complete a victory over them, that fifteen thousand were left dead on the field of battle, two bashaws are taken prisoners, and he himself occupies their general's tent. After so distinguished a victory, it is not in the least doubted that he will be declared king, especially as he is at the head of such an army, and that fortune generally declares in favor of numerous battalions. This piece of news has given me pleasure.

I never now see the Chevalier de Buous. He is enraged at

---

* Michael Koribert Wiesnowieski, who died November 1673.

† John Sobieski, elected King of Poland, May 20, 1674. He married the grand-daughter of Marshal d'Arquien, who, after his death, returned to France. The victory Sobieski gained in 1685, under the walls of Vienna, and which saved the emperor and the empire, is still more celebrated than that which is here spoken of.

not being made a *chef d'escadre*.* He is at St. Germain, and I am in hopes he will manage his affairs so well as to obtain his desire at last: I sincerely wish it. The Archbishop (of Arles) has written to assure me of the joy the affair of Orange has given him, and that he hopes that of the Syndicate will end no less happily. He finds himself obliged to own, by the event, that your vigor was of more service than his prudence, and that from your example he is become a perfect bravo. This has rejoiced me exceedingly.

And now, my dear child, when I picture you to myself, pale and thin, when I think of the agitations you endure, and that the slightest degree of fever endangers your life, I suffer night and day from apprehensions for you. What happiness would it be to have you with me, in a less destructive climate, in your native air, which would again restore you to health and vigor! I am surprised that loving you as the Provençals do, they do not urge this remedy to you. I consider you as having been so useful till now, and as having relieved M. de Grignan so much in all his affairs, that I dare not regret I did not bring you with me; but when every thing is finished, why not give me this satisfaction? Adieu, my dearest child, I am very impatient to hear from you. You would throw yourself into the fire, you say, to convince me of your love: my child, I have no doubt of your affection, and without this extraordinary proof of it, you may give me a much more pleasing and a much more convincing one.

LETTER XXXII.

Paris, Friday, December 29, 1673.

M. de Luxembourg is a little pressed near Maestricht, by the army of M. de Montereï† and the Prince of Orange; he dares not venture to remove his camp, and he must perish

---

* A rank somewhat inferior to that of rear-admiral.
† Governor of the Spanish Low Countries.

where he is, unless they send him speedy and effectual succor. The prince is to set out four days hence with the duke and M. de Turenne; the latter is to serve under the two princes, and there is a perfectly good understanding between the three. They have twenty thousand foot, and ten thousand horse; the volunteers and those companies which are not to march, do not go, but all the rest do. La Trousse and my son, who arrived here yesterday, are to be of the number; they have scarcely had time to pull off their boots before they are in the mud again. The rendezvous is appointed at Charleroi, on the 16th of January. D'Hacqueville has written you word of this, but you will read it more distinctly in my letter.* It is certainly very important news, and has occasioned a great bustle every where. We know not what to do for money. It is certain M. de Turenne is not on terms with M. de Louvois, but it is not generally known; and while he continues to keep in with M. Colbert, there will be nothing said about it. This afternoon I had some great folks with me, who desired their compliments to M. de Grignan, and to *Grignan's wife*. They were the grand-master, and the *charmer*.† I had besides, Brancas, the Archbishop of Rheims, Charôt, La Trousse, etc., who all in like manner desired to be remembered to you. They talk of nothing but war. The *charmer* knows all our affairs, and enters admirably into our little perplexities. He is governor of a province, which is sufficient to give him an idea of our feelings on those subjects. Adieu, my dearest child. I participate in all the joys of your conquests.

LETTER XXXIII.

PARIS, Monday, New Year's Day, 1674.

I wish you a happy year, my child; and in this wish I comprehend so many things, that I should never have done if I

---

* M. d'Hacqueville wrote a hand very difficult to be read.
† The Count de Lude and the Duke de Villeroi.

were to enumerate them. I have not yet asked leave for you to return to Paris, as you feared; but I wish you had heard what La Garde said of the necessity of your coming hither, that you may not lose your five thousand francs, and of what he thinks proper for M. de Grignan to say to the king. If it were a suit which you were obliged to solicit against any one who designed to injure you, you would doubtless come to solicit it; but as it is to come to a place where you have a thousand other affairs, you are both guilty of the greatest indolence. Ah, what an enchanting thing is indolence! you feel its power too much; read La Garde upon this subject, chapter the first. Consider, in the mean time, that you would have the pleasure of seeing the king, and receiving his approbation.

The edicts are revoked which gave us so much uneasiness in our province. The day that M. de Chaulnes declared it to the States, there was a cry of "Long live the king!" which made every one present weep for joy. They embraced each other, broke out into the highest expressions of rapture, ordered Te Deum to be sung, made bonfires; and the thanks of the public were given to M. de Chaulnes. But do you know what we are to give the king as a mark of our gratitude? six hundred thousand livres, and as much more by way of a voluntary gratuity. What think you of this little sum? You may judge by this of the favor that has been done us, in taking off the burden of these edicts.

My poor son has arrived here, as you know; he is to return on Thursday, with many others. M. de Monterei is a very clever fellow; he disturbs the whole world, he fatigues the army, and puts it out of condition to take the field, and begin the campaign, till the end of the spring. The troops were all at ease in winter-quarters; and when, after a tedious march, they are arrived at Charleroi, he has only a single step to take to make good his retreat—till when, M. de Luxembourg can not be extricated. By appearances, the king will not set out so soon as he did last year. If, when in the field, we had to make an attack on some great town, or the enemy would come out and oppose our two heroes, as we should probably beat him, peace might almost be depended upon. This is what is said by persons of the profession. It is certain that M. de Turenne is out of favor with M. de Louvois; but as he is in favor with the king and M. Colbert, it has not made much noise.

Five ladies of the palace are appointed : Madame de Soubise, Madame de Chevreuse, the Princess d'Harcourt, Madame d'Albret, and Madame de Rochefort. The maids of honor are to serve no more, and Madame de Richelieu as a lady of honor, is also discharged. There are to be only the gentlemen in waiting, and the maîtres-d'hôtel, as formerly. But that the queen may not be without women, Madame de Richelieu and four other ladies are to wait constantly behind her chair. Brancas is in raptures that his daughter* is so well provided for.

The Grand Marshal of Poland has sent a letter to the king, in which he tells his majesty, that if he has any person in view to raise to the crown of Poland, he will assist him with all the forces under his command; and if not, requests his protection and assistance for himself. The king has promised it to him. However, it is imagined he will not get himself elected, because he is not of the established religion of the nation.

LETTER XXXIV.

PARIS, Friday, Jan. 5, 1674.

It is a year ago this very day since we supped with the archbishop: at this moment perhaps you are supping with the intendant: I am afraid, my dear child, your mirth is feigned. All you say on this subject to me, and to Corbinelli, is admirable. My heart thanks you for the good opinion you have

* The Princess d'Harcourt.

of me, in believing I hold in abhorrence all villainous proceedings. You are not deceived.

M. de Grignan tells you true; Madame de Thiange has left off paint, and covers her neck; you would hardly know her in this disguise. She is frequently with Madame de Longueville, and is the very pink of modish devotion. But she is still good company, and has not at all the air of a recluse. I dined with her the other day; a servant brought her a glass of liquor; she turned to me and said, "The fellow does not know that I am become a devotee;" this made us all laugh. She spoke very naturally of her intentions, and of her change. She is very cautious of saying any thing that may injure the reputation of her neighbor, and stops short when any thing of that nature escapes her; for my part, I think her more agreeable than ever. Wagers are laid that the Princess d'Harcourt will not turn nun these twelve months, now she is become a lady of the palace, and paints again: this rouge is the law and the prophets; it is the great point that our new devotion turns upon. As for the Duchess d'Aumont, her taste is burying the dead.* They say the Duchess de Charost kills people for her, with ill-compounded medicines, and then buries them in a religious retreat. The Marchioness d'Huxelles is very good; but La Marans is more than good. Madame de Schomberg tells me very seriously that she is of the first order for seclusion and penitence, not admitting any society, and refusing even the amusements of devotion; in a word, she is a penitent in the true sense of the word, and in all the simplicity of the primitive church.

The ladies of the palace are kept in great subjection. The king has explained himself upon this subject, and will have the queen always attended by them. Madame de Richelieu,

---

* If we may believe Bussy, she rendered a service of a different kind to the living. The Duchess of Charost was the daughter of the Superintendent Fouquet. She apparently had her recipe from her grandmother, by whom we have a printed collection in two volumes, under the title of *Family Recipes by Madame Fouquet.*

though she does not serve any longer at table, is always present when the queen dines, with four ladies, who wait by turns. The Countess d'Ayen* is the sixth: she does not like the confinement of this attendance, and of being constantly at vespers, sermons, and other religious ceremonies; but there is no perfect happiness in this world. The Marchioness de Castelnau is fair, blooming, and perfectly recovered from her grief. *L'Eclair*, they say, has only changed her apartment at court, not very much to her satisfaction. Madame de Louvigny does not seem sufficiently delighted at her good fortune. She is thought unpardonable for not adoring her husband in the same manner as when she was first married; this is the first time the public was ever offended at a thing of this nature. Madame de Brissac is beautiful, and follows the Princess of Conti like her shadow. La Coëtquen is still the same as ever. She has a petticoat of black velvet, embroidered with gold and silver, and a brocade cloak. This dress cost her an immense sum; and when she thought she made the most splendid figure imaginable, every one said she was dressed like an actress; and she has been so much rallied in consequence, that she has thrown it aside. La Manierosa† is a little vexed at not being a lady of the palace. Madame de Duras, who would not accept this honor, laughs at her. La Troche is, as usual, very much interested in your affairs; but I can not express how strongly Madame de la Fayette and M. de la Rochefoucault have your interest at heart.

Madame de la Fayette and I went to see M. de Turenne a few days ago; he has a slight fit of the gout. He received us with great civility, and talked much of you. The Chevalier de Grignan has given him an account of your victories; he would have offered you his sword if there had been any occasion for it. He intends to set out in three days. My son went yesterday very much out of humor: I was not less so, at this ill-judged and in every respect disagreeable journey.

* A feigned name.
† Mary Frances de Bournouville, afterward Marchioness de Noailles

The dauphin saw Madame Schomberg the other day; they told him his grandfather had been in love with her: he asked in a whisper, "How many children has she had by him?" They informed him of the manners* of that time.

The Duke du Maine† has been seen at court, but he has not yet visited the queen: he was in a coach, and saw only his father and mother.

The Chevalier de Chatillon has no longer any thing to seek for; his fortune is made. Monsieur chose rather to give him the office of captain of his guards, than Mademoiselle de Grancey that of lady of the wardrobe. This young man therefore has the post of Vaillac, and is well provided for: they say Vaillac is to have D'Albon's, and that D'Albon is discarded. I told you how our States ended, and that they repurchased the edicts at two millions six hundred thousand livres, and gave the same sum as a gratuitous gift, making together five million two hundred thousand livres; that the air was rent with cries of "Long live the king!" that we had bonfires, and sung *Te Deum*, because his majesty was kind enough to accept it. Poor Sanzei is ill with the measles; it is a disorder that soon passes, but is alarming from its violence.

I see no reason to ask the king's pardon for the humane gentleman who was guilty of assassination; the crime is of too black a nature. The criminals who were pardoned at Rouen were not of this stamp; it is the only crime the king refuses to pardon. So Beavron has mentioned it to the Abbé de Grignan.

* Madame de Schomberg who is here spoken of, mother of the marshal then living, captivated Louis XIII. when she was only a maid of honor, by the name of Mademoiselle d'Hautefort. The king's gallantry exacted so little, that she even jested upon the subject, and said he talked to her of nothing but dogs, horses, and hunting. She was handsome and discreet. She attached herself to Queen Anne of Austria, and shared her disgrace during the life of Louis XIII. She afterward quarreled with her during the regency, for having spoken too freely against Cardinal Mazarin.

† The king's eldest son by Madame de Montespan.

I have heard the ladies at the palace spoken of in a way that made me laugh. I said with Montaigne, "Let us avenge ourselves, by slandering them." It is, however, true that they are under extreme subjection.

The report still prevails, that the prince sets out on Monday. The same day M. de Saint Luc is to espouse Mademoiselle de Pompadour; about this I am quite indifferent.

Adieu, my dear; this letter is growing too long; I conclude it for no other reason but because every thing must have an end. I embrace Grignan, and beg him to forgive me for opening Madame de Guise's letter; I was very desirous to see her style; my curiosity is satisfied forever.

Guilleragues said yesterday, that Pelisson abused the permission men have to be ugly.*

LETTER XXXV.

PARIS, Friday, Jan. 12, 1674.

Well, your peace is then concluded at last. The Archbishop of Rheims and Brancas received their letters before I did mine; M. de Pomponne sent to inform me of this important event from St. Germain; I was ignorant, however, of the particulars, but now I know all. I advise you, my child, to regulate your conduct by circumstances; and since it is the king's will that you should be friendly with the bishop,† endeavor to obey him. But to return to St. Germain: I was there three days ago; I went first to M. de Pomponne's, who had not yet applied for your leave of absence, but is to send for it to-day From thence we went to the queen's; I was with Madame de Chaulnes; there was nobody to talk but me, and you may be sure I was not deficient. The queen said without hesitation that you had been absent for more than three years, and that

---

* An expression that is become common, but which was new at that time, or it would not have been worth noticing.

† Of Marseilles.

it was time for your return. From court we went to Madame de Colbert's, who is extremely civil and well bred. Mademoiselle de Blois* danced; she is very pleasing and graceful. Desairs says she is the only one who reminds him of you: he asked me what I thought of her dancing, for my applause was required, and I gave it with the greatest readiness. The Duchess de la Vallière was there; she calls her little daughter *mademoiselle*, and the young princess in return calls her *pretty mamma*. M. de Vermandois was there too. No other children have yet made their appearance. We afterward went to pay our respects to monsieur and madame; the former has not forgotten you, and I never fail to present your dutiful acknowledgments to him. I met Vivonne there, who accosted me with, " *Little mamma*, I beg you will embrace the Governor of Champagne."†—" And pray who is he ?" said I.—" Myself," replied he.—" You !" said I; " pray who told you so ?"—" The king has just informed me of it." I instantly congratulated him. The Countess de Soissons was in hopes of getting this post for her son.

There is no talk of taking the seals from the chancellor ;‡ the good man was so surprised at this additional honor, that he began to fear a snake in the grass, and could not comprehend the reason of being thus loaded with dignities: " Sire," said he to the king, " does your majesty intend to take the seals from me ?"—" No, no, chancellor," replied the king, " go, sleep in peace." And, indeed, they say he is almost always asleep; there are many wise conjectures on the subject, and people can not understand the reason of this augmentation of favors.

The prince set out the day before yesterday, and M. de Turenne is to follow to-day. Write to Brancas to congratulate

---

* She had been educated by Madame Colbert.

† This government was vacated by the death of Eugene Maurice, of Saxony, Count de Soissons, which happened June 7, 1673.

‡ Stephen d'Aligre was keeper of the seals in 1672, upon the death of Chancellor Seguier, who was made Chancellor of France in 1674.

him on his daughter's being in the queen's household, for he is very proud of it. La Troche returns you many thanks for your kind remembrance of her. Her son has still nose enough to lose half of it at the next siege, without the loss being very apparent. It is said that the *Dew** begins to be less friendly with the *Torrent*, and that after the siege of Maëstricht, they entered into a league of mutual confidence, and saw the *Fire* and the *Snow* every day of their lives. You know all this could not last long without occasioning great tumult, nor without being discovered. The *Hail*† seems to me, with respect to the reconciliation between you and him, like a man who goes to confession, and keeps one great sin upon his conscience—by what other name can you call the trick he has played you? Still the wise heads say you must speak, you must ask, you have time, and that is sufficient; but do not wonder at the faggoting of my letters. I leave one subject, you think I have done with it, and suddenly I resume it again, *versi sciolti*. Do you know that the Marquis de Sessac is here, that he will have a situation in the army, and will probably soon be presented to the king? This is manifestly predestination.

Corbinelli and I talk of Providence every day, and we say, as you know, from day to day and hour to hour, that your journey is determined. You are very glad that you have not to answer for this affair, for a resolution is a wonderful thing for you, quite a wild beast. I have seen you a long time deciding on a color: it is a proof of a too enlightened mind, which, seeing at one glance all the difficulties, remains suspended, as it were, like Mohammed's tomb: such was M. Bignon, the greatest wit of the age; I, who am the least of the present age, hate uncertainty, and love decision. M. de Pomponne

---

* The *Dew*, the *Torrent*, the *Fire*, and the *Snow*, etc., are ciphers between the mother and daughter. These ciphers do not always mean the same persons. In this place, it seems that Madame de Montespan is the *Torrent*, Madame de Vallière the *Dew*, the king is the *Fire*, and the *Snow* represents the queen.

† Apparently the Bishop of Marseilles.

informs me you received your leave of absence to-day; I am consequently ready to do every thing you wish, and to follow, or not to follow, the advice of your friends.

It is said here that M. de Turenne has not yet begun his march, and that there is no further occasion for it, because M. de Monterei has at last retreated, and M. de Luxembourg is freed, with the assistance of five or six thousand men, whom M. de Schomberg assembled, and with whom he so extremely harassed M. de Monterei, that he was obliged to retire with his troops. The prince is to be recalled and all our poor friends with him. This is the news of the day.

The ball was dull, and ended at half past eleven. The king led out the queen; the dauphin, madame; monsieur, mademoiselle; the Prince de Condé, the great mademoiselle; the Count de Roche-sur-Yon, Mademoiselle de Bois, handsome as an angel, dressed in black velvet, with a profusion of diamonds, and an apron and stomacher of point lace. The Princess d'Harcourt was as pale as the Commandeur in the play Du Festin de Pierre. M. de Pomponne has desired me to dine with him to-morrow, to meet Despréaux, who is to read his Art of Poetry.

LETTER XXXVI.

Paris, Monday, January 15, 1674.

Saturday last I dined with M. de Pomponne, as I told you, and was there till five o'clock, enchanted, transported, enraptured with the beauties of Despréaux's Art of Poetry. D'Hacqueville was there, we often talked of the pleasure you would have received from it. M. de Pomponne recollected that one day when you were a very little girl at your Uncle de Sévigné's, you got behind a large window with your brother, and said you were a prisoner, a poor unfortunate princess driven from your father's house; your brother, who was as hansome as yourself, and you were as handsome as an angel, played his part extremely well. You were nine years of age.

He made me remember the day perfectly. He never forgets one moment that he has seen you, and promises himself great pleasure in seeing you again, which is very gratifying to me. I own to you, my dear, that my heart is bursting with joy, but I shall conceal it till I know your resolution.

M. de Villars is returned home from Spain, and has given us a thousand amusing anecdotes respecting the Spaniards. I have at length seen La Marans in her cell, for it is nothing else. I found her quite in dishabille, not a single hair to be seen, with a coarse coif of old Venice point, a black handkerchief on her neck, a faded gray gown, and an old petticoat. She seemed very glad to see me; we embraced each other tenderly. She does not seem at all changed. We began the conversation by talking of you; she appears to love you as well as she ever did, and seemed so humble that it is impossible to help loving her. We then talked of the religious life she had lately embraced. She assured me it was true that God had vouchsafed her a great portion of grace, of which she had the most grateful sense; that this grace consists in great faith, profound love of God, horror of the world and its vanities, and a thorough distrust of herself, adding, that if she were to go abroad for only an hour, this divine spirit would evaporate. In short, she seems to preserve it carefully in her solitude like a bottle of fine perfume; she believes the world would make her lose this precious liquor, and she even fears the parade of devotion might spill it. Madame de Schomberg says she is not to be compared to Madame de Marans. Her savage disposition is softened into a passion for retirement; the disposition does not change; she is even exempt from the folly common to most women, to love their confessor; she does not approve this tie, and never speaks to him but at confession. She goes on foot to her parish church, reads all our books of religion, works, prays, has a fixed time for every thing, takes all her meals in her own room, sees Madame de Schomberg at a certain hour, hates news as much as she used to like it, is as charitable to others as she used to slander them, and loves the Creator as much as she loved the creature. We laughed a good deal at her former manners, and turned them into ridicule. She has not the least air of the Collette sisters. She speaks very sincerely and very agreeably of her situation. I was two hours with her without being at all dull. She reproached herself even for this pleasure, but without the least affectation; in short, she is much more amiable than she ever was. I do not think, my dear child, you can complain that I have not been particular enough.

I have just received your letter of the 7th. I own to you, my dearest, that the joy it has given me is so lively that my heart can scarcely contain it. You know how strongly it feels, and I should hate myself, if I were so warmly interested in my own affairs as in yours. At last, my child, you are coming; this is the most delightful to me of all. But I am going to tell you something you do not expect, which is, that I solemnly swear to you that if M. de la Garde had not deemed your journey expedient, and that if it really were not so for your own affairs, I would not have taken into consideration, at least for this year, the ardent desire I have to see you, nor what you owe to my infinite affection. I know how to keep within the bounds of reason, whatever it cost me, and I have sometimes as much strength in my weakness as those who are wiser. After this sincere confession I can not conceal from you that I am penetrated with joy, and that, reason concurring with my wishes, I am, at the moment I write to you, perfectly satisfied, so that I think of nothing now but of receiving you. Do you know, the best thing after yourself and M. de Grignan, would be to bring the coadjutor? You will not perhaps always have La Garde; and if he fails you, you well know M. de Grignan is not so zealous in his own affairs as in those of the king, his master. He has a religious care of those, which can only be compared to his negligence with regard to his own. When he will take the trouble to speak, no one does it better, and we can not therefore but wish it. You are not like Madame de Cauvisson, to act alone; you must wait eight or ten years. But M. de Grignan, you, and the coadjutor, would do admirably together. Cardinal de Retz is just arrived, and will be delighted to see you. What joy, my dear child, will your return occasion! but, above all things, come prudently. It is to M. de Grignan I give this charge, and I expect him to be accountable to me. I have written to the coadjutor, to entreat him to accompany you. He will facilitate our audience with the two ministers, and will support his brother's interest. The coadjutor is bold and fortunate, and you will mutually heighten each other's consequence. I could talk till this time to-morrow upon the subject. I have written to the archbishop. Gain my point with the coadjutor, and give him my letter.

The prince has come back, after having been thirty leagues on his journey. M. de Turenne did not go. M. de Monterei has withdrawn his forces, and M. de Luxembourg is now at liberty. Within these twenty-four hours the chapel at St. Germain has been robbed of a silver lamp, worth seventy thousand francs, and six candlesticks of the same metal, each of them taller than I am. This is a daring insolence.* The ropes they made use of to get in were found by the Richelieu gallery. No one can conceive how the robbery could have been committed, for there are guards continually going that way, and patrolling about all night.

Do you know that peace is talked of? M. de Chaulnes is since come from Brittany, and is to set out again immediately for Cologne.

---

* The Duke of Saint-Simon relates a still more extraordinary robbery that took place at Versailles. In one night all the gold ornaments and fringes were stolen from the state apartment, from the gallery to the chapel. Whatever inquiries were made, no trace could be found of the robber. But five or six days after, the king being at supper, an enormous packet fell suddenly upon the table at some distance from him; it contained the stolen fringes, with a note fastened to it with these words, "Bontems, take thy fringes again, the pleasure pays not half the pain." Saint-Simon was a witness of this.

LETTER XXXVII.

PARIS, Monday, February 5, 1674.

It is many years ago, to-day, that there came into the world a creature destined to love you beyond every other thing in existence.* I beg you not to suffer your imagination to wander either to the right hand or to the left:—*Cet homme là, sire, c'était moi-même.*†

It was yesterday three years that I felt the most poignant grief of my whole life. You set out at that time for Provence, and you remain there still. My letter would be very long, if I attempted to express all the sorrow I then felt, and what I have since felt, in consequence of this separation. But to leave this melancholy digression. I have received no letters from you to-day. I know not whether I am to expect any, and I fear not, as it is so late; I have, however, expected them with impatience; I wanted to hear of your departure from Aix, and to be able to compute, with some exactness, the time of your return. Every one teases me, and I know not what to answer. I think but of you and your journey. If I receive any letters from you after this is sent away, you may make yourself perfectly easy; for 1 will certainly take care to do whatever you desire me.

I write to-day a little earlier than usual. M. Corbinelli, and Mademoiselle de Méri, are here, and have dined with me. I am going to a little opera of Molière's, that is to be sung at Jellison's. It is an excellent composition; the prince, the duke, and the duchess, will be there. I shall, perhaps, sup at Gourville's, with Madame de la Fayette, the duke, Madame de Thianges, and M. de Vivonne, of whom we are to take our leave, as he sets out from hence to-morrow. If this party is broken up, I shall, perhaps, go to Madame de Chaulnes, where

---

* She refers to her birth-day, 5th February, 1626.

† A line of Marot, in an epistle to Francis I. *This man, sire, was myself.*

I am earnestly invited, as well by the mistress of the house as by Cardinals de Retz and Bouillon, who made me promise them. The first of these is very impatient to see you; he loves you dearly.

It was apprehended that Mademoiselle de Blois had the small-pox, but it does not prove so. There is not a word said of the news from England; this makes me conclude there is nothing good from thence. There has been only a ball or two at Paris during the whole carnival; there were masques at noon, but not many. It is a very dull season. The assemblies at St. Germain are mortifications for the king, and only show the falling off of the carnival.

Father Bourdaloue preached a sermon on the purification of our Lady, which transported every body. There was such energy in his discourse as made the courtiers tremble. Never did preacher enforce with so much authority, and in so noble a manner, the great truths of the Gospel. His design was to show that every power ought to be subject to the law, from the example of our Lord, who was presented at the temple. This was insisted on with all the strength and clearness imaginable; and certain points were urged with a force worthy of St. Paul himself.

The Archbishop of Rheims, as he returned yesterday from St. Germain, met with a curious adventure. He drove at his usual rate, like a whirlwind. If he thinks himself a great man, his servants think him still greater. They passed through Nanterre, when they met a man on horseback, and in an insolent tone bid him clear the way. The poor man used his utmost endeavors to avoid the danger that threatened him, but his horse proved unmanageable. To make short of it, the coach and six turned them both topsy-turvy; but at the same time the coach too was completely overturned. In an instant the horse and the man, instead of amusing themselves with having their limbs broken, rose almost miraculously; the man remounted, and galloped away, and is galloping still for aught I know; while the servants, the archbishop's coachman, and the archbishop himself at the head of them, cried out, "Stop that villain, stop him; thrash him soundly." The rage of the archbishop was so great, that afterward, in relating the adventure, he said, "if he could have caught the rascal, he would have broke all his bones, and cut off both his ears."

Adieu, my dear, delightful child, I can not express my eagerness to see you. I shall direct this letter to Lyons; it is the third; the two first were to be left with the *chamarier*. You must be got thither by this time or never.

LETTER XXXVIII.

PARIS, Friday, May 31, 1675.

I have received only your first letter yet, my dear child; but that is invaluable. I have seen nothing since your absence, and every fresh person reminds me of it; they talk to me of you; they pity me; they —— but stop; is it not such thoughts as these we should pass lightly over? Let us then do so.

I was yesterday at Madame de Verneuil's in my way from St. Maur, where I had been with Cardinal de Retz. At the Hotel de Sully, I met Mademoiselle de Launoi,* who is just married to the old Count de Montrevel; the wedding was kept there; you never saw a bride so pert; she bustles about the house, and calls *husband*, as if she had been married for twenty years. This same husband of hers, you must know, is very much troubled with the ague; he expected his fit the day after he was married, but missed it; upon which Fieubet said, "We have found a remedy for the ague, but who can tell us the dose?" Mesdames des Castelnau, Louvigny, Sulli, and Fiesque, were there. I leave you to guess what these

---

* Adriana-Philippa-Theresa de Launoi, who had been maid of honor to the queen, was married to James-Mary de la Baume Montrevel in 1675, and not in 1672, as it is said by mistake in the history of the great officers of the crown.

charming women said to me. My friends are too solicitous about me; they harass me; but I do not lose a single moment that I can spend with our dear cardinal. These letters will inform you of the arrival of the coadjutor; I saw and embraced him this morning. He is to have a conference this evening with his eminence and M. d'Hacqueville on the steps he is to take. He has hitherto remained incog.

The Duchess has lost Mademoiselle d'Enghein; one of her sons is going to die besides; her mother is ill; Madame de Langeron is already under ground; the prince and the duke in the army; ample subjects for tears, and, as I am told, she is not sparing of them. I leave D'Hacqueville to tell you the news of the war; and the Grignans to write to you about the chevalier; if he should return hither, I will take as much care of him as of my own son. I imagine you are now upon the tranquil Saône; our minds ought to resemble this calm view, but our hearts perpetually seduce them; mine is wholly with my daughter. I have already told you, that my greatest difficulty is to divert my thoughts from you, for they all tend to the same point.

LETTER XXXIX.

Paris, Wednesday, June 5, 1675.

I have not received any of your letters since that from Sens; you will therefore easily conceive how anxious I am to be informed of your health and safety. I am fully persuaded you have written to me, and complain of nothing but the management, or rather mismanagement of the post. According to the calculations of your friends here, you should be by this time at Grignan, unless you were detained at Lyons during the holidays. In short, my dear child, I have accompanied you step by step all the way, and am in hopes the Rhône behaved with proper respect to you. I have been at Livri with Corbinelli; but returned here with all the haste I could, that,

I might not lose a moment in seeing our dear cardinal. The great affection he has for you, and the long friendship which has subsisted between him and me, have attached me to him very sincerely; I see him every evening from eight till ten, and I think he is very glad to have me with him till his bedtime. Our conversation is constantly about you; this is a subject we are fond of expatiating upon, and indeed it seems the master-sentiment of both hearts. He is for coming hither, but I can not bear this house when you are not in it.

The nuncio informed him yesterday that he had just learned by a courier from Rome that he was appointed to a cardinalship. The pope* has lately made a promotion of his creatures, as it is called. The crowns are put off for the ⟩ five or six years, and consequently M. de Marseilles.† The ⟩ ıncio told Bonvoulour, who went to congratulate him on his promotion, that he hoped his holiness would not now accept Cardinal de Retz's resignation of his hat; that he should use all his endeavors to dissuade his holiness from doing so, as he had the honor of being his colleague: so now we have another cardinal, Cardinal de Spada. Cardinal de Retz sets out on Tuesday; I dread the day; for I shall suffer extremely in lo⟨s⟩ing so valuable a friend: his courage seems to increase in pr⟨o⟩portion as that of his friend diminishes.

The Duchess de la Vallière pronounced her vows yester day.‡ Madame de Villars promised to take me to see it; but by some misunderstanding we thought we should not get places. Nothing more, however, was necessary than to present our-

---

* Clement X.

† Toussaint de Forbin-Janson, Bishop of Marseilles, and afterward Bishop of Beauvois, was not made cardinal till 1690, at the promotion by Alexander VIII.

‡ For more than three years she had only received at court insults from her rival and unkindness from the king. She remained there, she said, merely from a spirit of penitence, and added. "When the life of a Carmelite appears to me too severe, I have only to call to mind what those persons made me suffer," pointing to the king and to Madame de Montespan.

selves at the door, though the queen had given out that the admission should not be general; and, after all, we did not go. Madame de Villars was very much vexed at it. The beautiful duchess performed this action like every other of her life, in the most charming manner possible: she is surprisingly handsome: but you will be astonished to hear that M. de Condom's (Bossuet's) sermon was not so good as was expected. The coadjutor was there; he will tell you how well the affair goes on with respect to M. de Paris and M. de St. Paul; but he finds the shade of M. de Toulon and the spirit of M. de Marseilles every where.

Madame de Coulanges goes from hence on Monday with Corbinelli: this deprives me of my companions. You know how good Corbinelli is to me, and how kindly he enters into all my sentiments. I am convinced of his friendship, and feel his absence; but, my child, after having lost you, of what else can I complain? It is true that you are interested in my complaints, because he is one of those with whom I most enjoyed the consolation of speaking of you; for you must not imagine, that those to whom I can not speak freely are as agreeable to me as those who enter into my feelings. You seem to me to be apprehensive that I make myself ridiculous, and that I am too apt to divulge my sentiments on this pleasing subject. No, no, my dear, fear nothing; I am able to govern the torrent. Trust to me, and let me love you, till it shall please God to take you out of my heart, in order to place himself there; for you can yield to none but him. In short, my heart is so entirely occupied with, and so full of you, that finding myself incapable of any other thought, I have been restrained from performing the devotions of the season. Adieu, my dear child, for the present. I shall finish my letter this evening.

I have just received a letter from Macon; I can not yet read it without the fountain playing its old tricks: my heart is so extremely sensible that the least thing that affects it quite overcomes me. You may imagine that, with this fine disposition, I frequently meet with opportunities to try it; but, pray, have no fears for my health. I can never forget the philosophy you inspired me with the evening before we parted; I improve by it as much as I can; but I have such an habitual weakness, that in spite of your good lessons, I often yield to my emotion.

Our cardinal will have left me before you receive this; it will be a melancholy day to me, for I am extremely attached to his person, his merit, his conversation, which I enjoy as much as I can, and the friendship he expresses for me. His soul is of so superior an order that it is not to be expected that his life should be attended with only common events. He that makes it a law to himself, to do always what is most great and heroic, must place his retreat in some proper part of his life, like a shade beautifully disposed in a piece of painting, and leave his friends to lament it.

How facetious you are, my child, with the newspaper in your hand! What! can you derive amusement from it already? I did expect that you would at least have waited till you had crossed the vile Durance. The conversation between the king and the prince appears to me very humorous; I think you would have been entertained with it even here. I have just received a letter from the chevalier, who is well; he is with the army, and has only had five attacks of the ague: this is one subject of uneasiness less; but his letter which is full of friendship, is in the true German style; for he will not believe a syllable of the retreat of Cardinal de Retz: he desires me to tell him the truth, which I shall not fail to do. I shall distribute all your compliments, and I am sure, they will be well received; every body thinks it an honor to be remembered by you; M. de Coulanges was quite proud of it. The coadjutor will relate to you the success of his journey; but he will not boast that he was on the point of being stifled at Madame de Louvois' by twenty women, who each supposed they had a right to embrace him: this occasioned a confusion, an oppression, a suffocation, of which the bare idea almost suffocates me, accompanied by the most high-flown, reiterated, and affected compliments that it is possible to conceive : Madame de Coulanges describes the scene very drolly. I wish you may have the company at Grignan you mention. My son is well; he sends you a thousand remembrances. M. de Grignan will be very willing for me to embrace him, now that he is no longer occupied with the bustle of the boat.

LETTER XL.

PARIS, Friday, June 14, 1675.

Instead of visiting you in your apartment, my dear child, I sit down to converse with you by letter; when I am so unfortunate as not to have you with me, the most natural consolation I can find is to write to you, to receive your letters, to speak of you, or to take some step in your affairs. I passed the afternoon yesterday with Cardinal de Retz; you can not possibly guess what we talk of when we are together. I always begin by telling you that you can not love him too well, and that I think you happy in having so firmly fixed the kindness and affection he before felt for you. Let me know how you bear the air at Grignan, and whether it has already begun to prey upon you; how you enjoy your health and how you look. Your picture is very pleasing, but far less so than your person, without reckoning that it wants the power of speech Be not uneasy about my health ; the rule I observe at presen is, to be irregular; I am not sensible of any indisposition; I dine alone ; stay at home till five or six o'clock, and go in the evening, when I have no business of importance to keep me within, to the house of one of my friends. I walk or ride according to the distance, but I make every thing yield to the pleasure of being with our cardinal. I lose not a moment he can spare me, and he is very obliging in this respect. I shall feel more sensibly his departure and his absence; but this does not prevent my indulging myself in the pleasure of his conversation; I never think of sparing myself; after having endured the pangs of parting with you, I have nothing to fear from any less tender attachment. Were it not for him, and for your affairs, I should go a little to Livri; but I make every consideration yield to these, which are above all my little pleasures.

The queen went to see Madame de Montespan at Clagny on the day I told you she took her up in her carriage as she passed; she went into her room, where she staid half an hour; she then went into M. du Vexin's, who was a little indisposed, and afterward took Madame de Montespan to Trianon, as I informed you. Some ladies have been at Clagny; they found the fair lady so occupied with the building and enchantments that are preparing for her, that I fancy her like Dido building Carthage; but the resemblance will not hold good in any other respect. M. de la Rochefoucault and Madame de la Fayette have entreated me to present their compliments to you. We fear you will have too much of the grand-duchess.* A prison is preparing for her at Montmartre, with which she would be frightened, if she did not hope to change it; but she will be caught; they are delighted in Tuscany to have got rid of her. Madame de Sully is gone; Paris is become a desert. I already wish myself out of it. I dined yesterday with the coadjutor at the cardinal's: I have left him in charge to inform you of that part of ecclesiastical history. M. Joli† preached at the opening of the assembly of the clergy, but as he took an ancient text, and preached only ancient doctrine, his sermon seemed a piece of antiquity altogether. It was a fine subject too for reflection.

The queen dined to-day at the Carmelites de Bouloi, with Madame de Montespan, and Madame de Fontevraud; you will see how this friendship will end. They say that M. de Turenne, as it were, conducts the enemy's troops to their quar-

---

* Marguerite-Louise d'Orléans, daughter of Gaston de France Duke of Orléans, and of Marguerite de Lorraine, his second wife.

† Claude Joli, Bishop of Agen.

ters. My heart is much oppressed with the thoughts of losing the cardinal; the repeated intercourse of friendship and conversation which has so lately passed between us, redoubles my grief; he goes to-morrow. I have not yet received your letters. Believe, my dear, that it is not possible to love you more than I love you; nothing animates me but what has some relation to you. Madame de Rochebonne has written to me very affectionately; she told me with what feelings you received and read my letters at Lyons. I see, my dear, you are grown weak as well as I.

D'Hacqueville has sent you such a large packet that it would be ridiculous to pretend to tell you any news now.

LETTER XLI.

Paris, Friday, June 28, 1675.

Madame de Vins expressed herself very affectionately about you yesterday, my dear; that is, in her way, but it is not a bad one; there seemed no *interlineations* in what she said.

We have no news. The king's good star has brought the Duke of Lorraine and the Prince of Orange across the Meuse again. M. de Turenne has now elbow-room, so that we are no longer confined in any part. I am rejoiced that my letters are so pleasing to you; I can hardly think they are so agreeable as you say they are. I know they have no stiffness in them. Our good cardinal is gone to solitude; his departure gave me sorrow, and reminded me of yours. I have long remarked our cruel separations to the four corners of the world. It is very cold; we are obliged to have a fire, and so are you, which is more astonishing still. You judge well respecting *Quantova;** if she can not return to her old ways, she will push her authority and grandeur beyond the clouds; but she must prepare to be loved the whole year without scruple: in the mean time her house is crowded by the whole court, visits are

---

* Quantova is Mme. de Montespan.

paid alternately, and her consequence is unbounded. Be not uneasy respecting my journey to Brittany; you are too good and too attentive to my health. I will have nothing to do with La Mousse; the dullness of others weighs me down more than my own. I have no time to go to Livri. I have made a vow to expedite your affairs. I shall give your compliments to Madame de Villars and Madame de la Fayette. The latter has still a little fever upon her. Adieu, my dearest child, believe me to be most sincerely yours.

LETTER XLII.

Paris, Friday, July 5, 1675.

I sit down, my dear, to talk to you a little of our good cardinal. I send you a letter he has written to you. Pray advise him to write his history, it is what all his friends press him much to do. He tells me he is very well pleased with his desert, that he can look upon it without the least horror, and humbly hopes that God will support him in his weakness. He expresses the most sincere regard for you, and desires me not to think of leaving Paris till I have finished all your affairs. He remembers the time when you had the ague, and that he desired me, for his sake, to be careful of your health. I answer him in the same tone. He assures me that the most frightful solitude would not make him forget the friendship he owes us. He was received at St. Michael's* with transports of joy; the people were all on their knees, and received him as a protector sent by God. The troops, who were quartered there, are taken off, the officers having waited on him for his orders to send away or to leave as many as pleased. Cardinal Bonzi has assured me that the pope, without staying to receive our cardinal's letter, had sent him a brief, to tell him that he supposes, and even desires, he will keep his hat; that the preserving his

* The place of the cardinal's retreat, a remote village in the province of Brittany.

rank and dignity will in no wise impede the work of his salvation; and it is moreover added, that his holiness expressly commanded him not to make choice of any other place of retirement than St. Denis; but I much doubt this latter part of the report, so I only tell you my author for the former part.

I am convinced he thinks no more about the cassolette. If I had desired him not to send it, it would only have served to put him in mind of it, so I thought it was best to take no notice of it. There is no news of importance stirring. Every thing goes on with spirit on M. de Turenne's side.

The other day there was a Madame Noblet, of the Vitri family, playing at basset with monsieur. Mention was made of M. de Vitri, who is very ill, upon which she said to monsieur, "Ah! sir, I saw him this morning, poor man! his face looked just like a *stratagem.*" What could she mean? Madame de Richelieu has received such kind and affectionate letters from the king, that she is more than repaid for what she has done.* Adieu, my dearest and best-beloved.

LETTER XLIII.

PARIS, Friday, July 19, 1675.

Guess from whence I write to you, my dear—from M. de Pomponne's, as you will perceive by the few lines which Madame de Vins sends you with this. I have been with her, the Abbé Arnauld, and D'Hacqueville, to see the procession of St. Genevieve pass; we returned in very good time; we were back by two o'clock; there are many that will not return till night. Do you know that this procession is considered a very fine sight. It is attended by all the religious orders, in their respective habits, the curates of the several parishes, and all the canons of Nôtre-Dame, preceded by the archbishop of Paris in his pontificals, and on foot, giving his

* The singular attachment of the queen and Madame de Montespan.

benediction to the right and left as he goes, till he comes to the cathedral; I should have said to the left only, for the Abbé de St. Genevieve marches on the right, barefoot, and preceded by a hundred and fifty monks, barefoot also; the cross and miter are borne before him, like the archbishop, and he gives his benedictions in the same manner, but with great apparent devotion, humility, and fasting, and an air of penitence, which show that he is to say mass at Nôtre-Dame. The parliament, in their red robes, and the principal companies follow the shrine of the saint, which glitters with precious stones, and is carried by twenty men clad in white, and barefoot. The provost of the merchants, and four counselors, are left as hostages at the Church of St. Genevieve, for the return of this precious treasure. You will ask me, perhaps, why the shrine was exposed. It was to put a stop to the continual rains we have had, and to obtain warm and dry weather, which happened at the very time they were making preparations for the procession, to which, as it was intended to obtain for us all kinds of blessings, I presume we owe his majesty's return, who is expected here on Sunday next. In my letter of Wednesday I will write you all that is worth writing.

M. de La Trousse is conducting a detachment of six thousand men to Marshal de Créqui, who is to join M. de Turenne. La Fare and the others remain with the dauphin's gens-d'armes, in the army commanded by the prince. The other day madame and Madame de Monaco took D'Hacqueville, at the Hôtel de Grammont, to walk about the streets and the Tuileries incog.; as her highness is not much given to a disposition for gallantry, her dignity sits very easy on her. The Tuscan princess is expected every hour. This is another of the blessings obtained by the shrine of St. Genevieve. I saw one of your letters yesterday to the Abbé de Pontcarré; it is the best letter that ever was written; there is no part of it which has not some point and wit. He has sent a copy of it to his eminence, for the original is kept as sacred as the shrine.

Adieu, my dearest and best-beloved; you are so remarkable

for your inviolable love of truth, that I do not abate myself a single expression of your kindness toward me, and you may judge, then, how happy it makes me.

LETTER LXIV.

Paris, Wednesday, July 24, 1675.

The weather is so extremely hot, my dear, that instead of tossing and tumbling in my bed the whim took me to get up (though it is but five o'clock in the morning) and chat a little with you.

The king arrived at Versailles on Sunday morning; the queen, Madame de Montespan, and all the other ladies, went to take possession of their former apartments. In a short time after his arrival, his majesty began to make the usual visits: the only difference is that they play in the state-apartments. I shall have more intelligence before I conclude my letter. The reason of my being so ill-informed of what passed at Versailles is, that I came but last night from M. de Pomponne's; Madame de Pomponne had invited D'Hacqueville and me in so pressing a manner that there was no refusing. Indeed, M. de Pomponne appeared delighted to see us; you were spoken of with all the friendship and esteem imaginable, during the short time we were there, and there was no want of conversation. One of our whims was to wish we could see through a great many things which we think we understand, but which, in fact, we do not; we should then see into what passes in families, where we should find hatred, mistrust, anger, and contempt, in the room of all those fine things that are set to outward show, and pass upon the world for realities. I was wishing for a closet hung with mirrors of this kind instead of pictures. We carried this odd notion very far, and diverted ourselves extremely with it. We were for opening D'Hacqueville's head to furnish ourselves from thence with some of these curious anecdotes, and pleased ourselves with thinking how the world is in general imposed upon by what they see and take for truth. You think that things are so and so in such a house; that such a couple adore each other; but stay a while and turn up the cards, and you will see that they hate each other most completely. You would imagine that such an event proceeded from such a cause—the little demon that drew aside the curtain would undeceive you; and so through life. This afforded us infinite amusement. You see, my dear, I must have plenty of time to entertain you with such trifles. This is the consequence of rising so early in the morning; this is doing as M. de Marseilles does. If it had been winter I should have visited by torch-light.

You have your cool north-east wind at last. Ah! my child, how uncomfortable it is; we are broiling with heat in this country, and in Provence you are starving with cold. I am convinced that our shrine has effected this change; for, before the procession, we discovered, like you, that the sun and the seasons had changed their course. I thought I had discovered, too, like you, that this was the true reason that had occasioned the days we so much regret to fly so rapidly. For my part, my dear child, I experience as much sorrow to see these days passed and gone forever, as I formerly experienced joy in spending winter and summer, and every season, with you; this painful thought must give way to the hope of seeing you again.

I wait for cooler weather before I take physic, and for cooler councils in Brittany* before I venture thither. Madame de Lavardin, De la Troche, M. d'Haroüis, and I, shall consult together about a proper time for our journey, having no design to run ourselves into the midst of the commotions that at present rend our poor province. They seem to increase daily, and those concerned in them have got as far as Fougères,

---

* The exorbitant taxes that had been imposed upon these unhappy people had obliged numbers of them to have recourse to arms, in order to free themselves from the load of exactions that it was impossible for them to bear.

burning and ransacking all the way as they go along. This is rather too near the *Rocks*. They have begun a second time to plunder the *bureau** at Rennes: Madame de Chaulnes is terrified almost to death at the continual menaces she hears. I was told yesterday that some of the mutineers had actually stopped her in her coach, and that even the most moderate of them had sent notice to M. de Chaulnes, who is at Fort Louis, that if the troops he had sent for took a single step toward entering the province, his wife would run the hazard of being torn to pieces by the insurgents. It is necessary, however, that some troops should march against them, for things are come to such a height that lenitives are no longer of service. But it would not be prudent for us to set out before the storm is a little subsided, and we see the issue of this extreme confusion. It is hoped that the approaching harvest will help to disperse the rioters, for after all they must get in their grain; and there are nearly six or seven thousand of them, not one of whom can speak a word of French.

M. de Boucherat told me the other day, that a curate having received a clock that had been sent him from *France*, as they call this part of the country, in the sight of some of his parishioners, they immediately cried out in their language, that it was a new tax, they were sure of it, they saw it plainly. The good curate, with great presence of mind, and without seeming at all confused, said to them, "My children, you are mistaken, you know not what you are talking of; it is an *indulgence*." This brought them all immediately upon their knees. You may, by this specimen, form a judgment of the understandings of these people. Let the consequence be what it may, I must wait till the hurricane is past; but I am sorry to be obliged to defer my journey. It was fixed at the most convenient time for me, and it can not be put off without interfering with my plans. You know my resignation to Providence; we must all return to this at last, and take things as

---

* A kind of exchequer established in all the principal towns in France for the collection of the king's revenues.

they come. I talk wisely, as you see, but I do not always think wisely. You well know there is one point in which I can not practice what I preach.

LETTER XLV.

Paris, Friday, August 16, 1675.

I could wish all you write to me of M. de Turenne inserted in a funeral oration. There is an uncommon beauty and energy in your style; it has all the force of eloquence that can be inspired by grief. Think not, my child, that the remembrance of him can be lost in this country. The torrent that sweeps every thing away can not remove a memory so well established; it is consecrated to immortality. I was the other day at M. de la Rochefoucault's, with Madame de Lavardin, M. de Marsillac, and Madame de la Fayette. The premier joined us. The conversation, which lasted two hours, turned wholly on the divine qualities of this true hero. The eyes of every one were bathed in tears, and you can not imagine how deeply the grief of his loss is engraved on all their hearts. You have exceeded us in nothing, but in the satisfaction of sighing aloud, and of writing his panegyric. We remarked one thing, which was, that it is not at his death only, that the largeness of his heart, the extent of his knowledge, the elevation of his mind are admired; all this the world acknowledged during his life. How much this admiration is increased by his death you may easily suppose. In a word, my dear, do not think that the death of this great man is regarded here like that of others. You may talk of it as much as you please; but do not suppose your grief can exceed ours. That none of the devotees have yet taken it into their heads to doubt whether his soul was in a good state, proceeds from the perfect esteem every person felt for him. It is not possible that sin or guilt could find a place in his heart; his conversion,* so sin-

* He was originally a Protestant.

cere, appeared to us like a baptism. Every one speaks of the innocence of his manners, the purity of his intentions, his unaffected humility, the solid glory that filled his heart, without haughtiness or ostentation, his love of virtue for its own sake, without regarding the approbation of men, and, to crown all, his generous and Christian charity. Did not I tell you of the regiment he clothed? It cost him fourteen thousand francs, and left him almost penniless. The English told M. de Lorges, that they would continue to serve this campaign to avenge his death; but that they would afterward retire, not being able to serve under any other general after M. de Turenne. When some of the new troops grew a little impatient in the morasses, where they were up to their knees in water, the old soldiers animated them thus: "What! do you complain? It is plain you do not yet know M. de Turenne; he is more grieved than we are when we are in any difficulty. He thinks of nothing at this moment but of removing us hence; he wakes, while we sleep; he is a father to us; it is easy to see that you are but young soldiers." It was thus they encouraged them. All I tell you is true; I do not load you with idle stories to amuse you because you are at a distance; this would be cheating you, and you may rely upon what I write to you as firmly, as on what I should tell you if you were here. I return to the state of his soul. It is really remarkable that no zealot has yet thought fit to doubt whether it has pleased God to receive it with open arms, as one of the best and noblest he ever created. Reflect a little upon this general assurance of his salvation, and you will find it is a sort of miracle, scarcely known but in his case.

The king has said of a certain person, whose absence last winter delighted you, that he had neither head nor heart; these were his very words. M. de Rohan, with a handful of men, has dispersed and put to flight the mutineers, who were formed in troops in his Duchy of Rohan. Our troops are at Nantes, commanded by Fourbin; for Vins is still a subaltern. Fourbin's orders are to obey M. de Chaulnes; but as M. de

Chaulnes is at Fort Louis, Fourbin in effect has the command. You understand what these imaginary honors are, which remain without action in those who have the name of commanders. M. de Lavardin wished much to have this command; he has been at the head of an old regiment, and pretends it was an honor due to him; but his claim was not admitted. It is said that our mutineers have sued for pardon; I suppose they will obtain it, after a sufficient number have been hanged. M. de Chamillart, who was odious to the province, is removed; and M. de Marsillac, who is a worthy man, is made intendant. These disorders no longer prevent me from taking my journey; but there is something here I am unwilling to leave. I have not yet been able to go to Livri, however my inclination may tempt me. Time must be taken as it comes; we wish to be in the center of news in these critical times.

Let me add a word more concerning M. de Turenne. He had made an acquaintance with a shepherd, who knew the roads and the country well; he used to take him along with him, and order his troops to be posted according to his direction. He had a great affection for this shepherd, and esteemed him as a man of good plain sense. He said that Colonel Bec owed his rise to a similar quality; and that he believed this shepherd would make his fortune as he had done. He was pleased with having contrived to make his troops pass without danger; and said to M. de Roye, "In good earnest this seems to me no ill performance, and I believe M. de Montecuculi will not find it so." It is indeed esteemed a masterpiece of military skill. Madame de Villars has seen another account since the day of battle, in which it is said that the Chevalier de Grignan performed wonders, both in respect of valor and prudence. God preserve him! for the courage of M. de Turenne seems gone over to the enemy; and they think nothing impossible, since the defeat of Marshal de Créqui.

M. de la Feuillade went post to Versailles the other day, where he surprised the king, and said to him, "Sire, some (meaning Rochefort) send for their wives, and some come to see them : I am come only to see your majesty, and to thank you a thousand and a thousand times. I shall see nobody besides your majesty, for it is to you I owe every thing." He talked a long while with the king, and then taking his leave, said, "Sire, I am going; I beg you to make my compliments to the queen and the dauphin, and to my wife and children." And he mounted his horse; and in reality saw no other person. This little sally pleased the king much; he told the court, laughing, how he had been made the bearer of M. de Feuillade's compliments. It is a great thing to be happy; every thing then succeeds; nothing is taken amiss.

LETTER XLVI.

Paris, Friday Evening, Aug. 16, 1675.

At length, my dear, M. de la Trousse is found. I admire his good fortune in this affair: after having performed wonders at the head of his battalion, he was surrounded by two squadrons of the enemy's horse, so completely, that no one knew how it would end; when on a sudden he finds himself prisoner to —— Whom ? The Marquis de Grana, with whom he was intimate for six months at Cologne, and with whom he had cultivated a close friendship. You may judge how he will be treated ; he has a pretty little wound, which will furnish him with an excellent plea for passing the vintage at La Trousse; for there is no reason to doubt that he will be released on his parole; and, what is still better, will meet with the most favorable reception at court. Nothing can exceed the congratulations and compliments that have been made him by all his friends on this occasion. I really pity him for having so many thanks to return: if he were to have carved his own fortune, could he have done it more completely to his wish ? As for honest Sanzei, we have no news of him, which does not look well. Marshal de Créqui is at Trèves, at least it is so reported, and that his people saw him cross the river, with three others, in a miserable little boat. His wife is distracted with grief, not having heard a syllable from himself: for my part I really think he has been drowned, or else killed by the peasants on his way to Trèves. In short, matters appear to go badly on all sides, La Trousse excepted.

LETTER XLVII.

Paris, Wednesday, Aug. 28, 1675.

If I had the means of sending letters to you every day I could easily contrive to write them. I sometimes do so even now, though my letters do not go; but the pleasure of writing is reserved for you alone: to every one else I write, because I must. I have particulars to relate respecting M. de Turenne. Madame d'Elbeuf,* who is for a few days at the Cardinal be Bouillon's, invited me to dine with them yesterday, and to share in their grief. Madame de la Fayette was likewise there; the purpose of our meeting was fully answered, for there was not a dry eye among us. Madame d'Elbeuf had a picture of the hero, admirably executed. All his people arrived at eleven o'clock; the poor creatures were already in deep mourning, and bathed in tears; three gentlemen came in who were ready to die at the sight of the picture; their cries pierced every heart; they could not utter a word; his footmen, his pages, his trumpeters, were all in tears, and made every body else weep to see them. The first who was able to speak, answered our mournful questions, and we prevailed on him to relate the manner of his death. It seems he was desirous of confessing, and when he retired for that purpose, he gave his orders for the evening, and was to have communicated the next day, which was Sunday, when he expected to give battle. He mounted on horseback at two o'clock the Saturday, after having taken a little refreshment, and as he had many people with him, he left them all at about thirty paces from the hill,

* Sister to Cardinal de Bouillon.

and said to young d'Elbeuf, "Nephew, stay you there: you move round me so much, that I shall be known." M. Hamilton, who happened to be near the place where he was going, said to him, "Sir, come this way if you please, the enemy's fire is directed to the place in which you are." "You are right, sir," replied M. de Turenne; "I would not willingly be killed to-day; this will do extremely well." He had scarcely turned his horse, when he saw St. Hilaire, who, coming up to him with his hat in his hand, desired him to cast his eye on a battery he had just raised, pointing to the place. M. de Turenne turned back, and at that very instant, without having time to stop his horse, he had his arm and part of his body torn to pieces by the same ball that carried off St. Hilaire's arm and hand in which he held his hat. The gentleman, who was watching him attentively, did not see him fall, for his horse ran away with him as far as the spot where he had left young d'Elbeuf; he was leaning with his face over the pommel of the saddle. The moment his horse stopped, this great man fell off into the arms of his people, who were gathered round him, twice opened wide his eyes, moved his lips a little, and sank to eternal rest. Think of his death, and of part of his heart being carried away! His people immediately burst into loud cries of lamentations, but M. Hamilton quieted them as well as he could, and had young d'Elbeuf removed, who had thrown himself upon his uncle's body frantic with grief, and would not be dragged from it without violence. A cloak was immediately thrown over the body, and it was placed by the side of a hedge, where they kept watch over it in silence till a carriage could be sent for to carry it to his tent; there it was met by M. de Lorges, M. de Roye, and several others, who were ready to expire with grief; but they were obliged to restrain themselves, and think of the important business that had devolved on them. A military service was performed in the camp, where tears and sorrow were the mourning; the officers, however, had each a crape scarf, the drums were covered with the same, they beat only a single stroke, the soldiers marched with their pikes trailing and pieces reversed; but the cries and lamentations of a whole army can not be described without emotion. His two nephews assisted at this mournful ceremony, I leave you to judge in what condition. M. de Roye, though much wounded, would be carried thither. I suppose the poor Chevalier de Grignan was overwhelmed with grief. When the body was removed from the camp, to be brought to Paris, the same scene of grief was renewed, and in every place through which it passed, nothing was heard but lamentations: at Langres, however, they exceeded even this; the bier was met by more than two hundred of the principal inhabitants in mourning, followed by the common people, and all the clergy in sacerdotal habits. In the town a solemn service was performed, and they all voluntarily entered into a contribution toward defraying the expenses, which amounted to five thousand francs; for they conducted the body as far as the next town. What say you to these natural marks of affection, founded on the most extraordinary merit? He is to be brought to St. Denis this evening; the people are all gone to meet the body at a place about two leagues distant, from whence they will conduct it to a chapel, where it is to be deposited for the present; there will be a service performed at St. Denis, till that at Nôtre Dame is celebrated, which will be a solemn one. Such was our entertainment at the cardinal's; we dined, as you may suppose, melancholy enough, and afterward did nothing but sigh till four o'clock. Cardinal de Bouillon mentioned you, and took upon him to answer for you, that, had you been in Paris you would have made one in our sad party; I assured him that you took no small share in his grief. He intends to answer both your letter and M. de Grignan's; he desired me to say a thousand kind things to you, and so did the worthy d'Elbeuf, who, as well as her son, has lost every thing. It was a good idea to undertake thus to tell you what you know already as well as myself; but these originals struck me, and I was glad to show you in what way we forget M. de Turenne in this part of the world.

M. de la Garde told me the other day, that in the enthusiasm of the wonders which were related of the Chevalier de Grignan, he had advised his brothers* to bestir themselves on the occasion, to support his interest at least for the present year; and that he found them both very well disposed to do extraordinary things. This good La Garde is at Fontainebleau, from whence he is to return in three days, to set out at last; for he longs to be gone, though courtiers in general seem to be very leaden-heeled. The situation of poor Madame de Sanzei is really deplorable; we know nothing yet respecting her husband; he is neither dead nor alive, wounded nor prisoner. His people do not take the least notice of him in their letters. M. de la Trousse, after having mentioned the report of his being killed (this was the day of the action), has never since mentioned a syllable about him, either to Madame de Sanzei or to Coulanges,† so that we are quite at a loss what to say to this distracted woman; and yet it is cruel to let her remain in this state of uncertainty; for my part, I am persuaded her husband is killed; the dust and blood must probably disfigure him so much as not to be known again, and he has been stripped with the rest of the slain. Or he was perhaps killed at a distance from any of the rest; or by the country-people on the road, and thrown into a hedge. I think it is more probable that he has met with some such melancholy fate, than that he has been taken prisoner without a word having been heard respecting him.

And now, my dear, I must tell you that the abbé thinks my journey so necessary, that I no longer oppose it; I shall not have him always with me, and therefore I ought to take advantage of his good intentions toward me. It will be only a trip of two months, for the good abbé is not the least disposed to pass the winter there. He expresses himself very sincerely on the subject, and you know I am always the dupe

---

* The Coadjutor of Arles, and the Abbé de Grignan.

† Madame de Sévigné was sister to M. de Coulanges, and M. de la Trousse was first cousin to both.

of every thing that has the appearance of sincerity; so much the worse for those who deceive me. I conceive that it would be very dull there in the winter; long evenings may be compared to long marches for tediousness. I was not dull the winter you were with me; you, who are young, might have felt so, but do you remember our readings? It is true, that if every thing had been taken away that surrounded the table, and even the book too, it is impossible to tell what would have become of me. Providence will arrange every thing. I treasure up all your sayings; we get out of our dullness as we do out of bad roads; we see no one stop short in the middle of a month, because he has not the courage to go through it; it is like dying, we see no one who does not know how to keep out of this dilemma; there are parts in your letters which I neither can nor will forget. Are my friends Corbinelli and M. de Vardes with you? I hope they are. In that case, I dare say, there has been no deficiency of conversation among you; you have talked incessantly of the state of affairs, of the death of M. de Turenne, and are at a loss to guess what will be the consequences of it; in fact, you are just like ourselves, though you are in Provence. M. de Barillon supped here last night. The conversation turned upon M. de Turenne, and the universal grief occasioned by his loss; he entered largely into his virtues, his love of truth, his love of virtue for its own sake, and his reward in the practice of it; he finished this eulogium with adding, that no one could love and esteem M. de Turenne without being the better for it. His company and conversation inspired such hatred of deceit and double-dealing, as raised his friends above the generality of mankind. In this number the chevalier was particularly distinguished as one for whom this great man showed more than common esteem and affection, and who, on his side, was one of his greatest admirers. We shall never see his equal in any age: I do not think we are quite blind in the present day, at least those I meet are not so, and this perhaps is boasting that I keep good company. But I must tell you one word more of M. de Turenne, which I heard yesterday. You know Pertuis well, and his adoration and attachment to M. de Turenne; as soon as he heard of his death, he wrote his majesty the following note: "Sire, I have lost M. de Turenne; I feel my heart unable to support this blow; and being incapable of serving your majesty as I ought to do, I humbly request your permission to resign my government of Courtrai." Cardinal de Bouillon prevented the letter from being given to the king; but, fearing he might come in person, he informed his majesty of the effect Pertuis' grief had on him. The king appeared to enter with great goodness and indulgence into his sentiments, and told Cardinal de Bouillon that he esteemed Pertuis the more for this mark of attachment to his friend and benefactor,* and that he thought him too honest a man not to discharge his duty in whatever situation he was in. This is a specimen of grief for this hero. He had a patrimony of 40,000 livres a year; and M. Boucherat says, that after all his debts, and the several legacies he has bequeathed, are paid, there will not remain more than 10,000. These are the vast treasures he had amassed during a service of fifty years! Adieu, my dearest child, I embrace you a thousand times, and with inexpressible tenderness.

LETTER XLVIII.

Tuesday, September 17, 1675.

Here is an odd date for you:

> Je suis dans un bateau,
> Dans le courant de l'eau,
> Fort loin de mon chateau.

I think I might add,

> Ah quelle folie!‡

for the water is so very low, and we are so often aground, that

---

* He had been captain of the guard to M. de Turenne.

†   I am here in a boat,
        On the water afloat,
        From my castle far remote.

‡   Ah, what folly is this!

I heartily wish for my carriage again, but that is out of reach for some time. The water becomes dull when one is alone. A Count des Chapelles and a Mademoiselle de Sévigné are wanting to enliven the scene. In short, it is mere folly to take a boat at Orléans, or even at Paris; but it is the fashion, as it is at Chartres to buy chaplets. I told you I saw the Abbé d'Effiat at his noble mansion. I wrote to you from Tours; from thence we went to Saumur, where we saw Vineuil, and wept again over M. de Turenne. He seems greatly affected with his loss; you will pity him when I tell you he is in a place where no one ever saw this hero. Vineuil is grown very old, very phthisicky, very driveling, and very devout; but he is still witty. He sends you a thousand and a thousand compliments. It is thirty leagues from Saumur to Nantes; we determined to go there in two days, and to get into Nantes this day. With this view we were upon the water some part of the night, but fortunately we ran aground about two hundred yards from the place where we were to go ashore to sleep, and could not get out of the boat, so we put back and landed at another place, and, following the barking of a dog, we got, about midnight, to a little hut, but the most wretched place you can possibly conceive; there we found two or three old women spinning, and some fresh straw, upon which we all lay down without taking off our clothes. I should have laughed heartily at this scene, had it not been for thinking of our poor abbé, whom I was vexed to have exposed to such a fatiguing journey. At daybreak we re-embarked, but were again so completely stranded, that it was above an hour before we could get afloat again; however, we were resolved to get to Nantes, though against both wind and tide. We were forced to row all the way. When we got there, I received your letters, and as I find the post must pass through Ingrande, I shall leave this little note by the way. I am very well, and only want somebody to chat with. I shall write to you from Nantes, as you may suppose. I am very impatient to hear from you, and about M. de Luxembourg and his army, for my head has been in a sack these nine days. The History of the Crusades is very amusing, particularly to those who have read Tasso, and who see their old friends again in prose and in history, but with respect to the author's style, I am his very humble servant. The Life of Origen is divine.*

LETTER XLIX.

The Rocks, Sunday, Oct. 20, 1675.

I can not sufficiently admire the diligence and fidelity of the post. I received on the 18th your letter of the 9th, that is, in nine days only after date, which is all that can be desired. But, my dear, we must soon put an end to our admirations; for, as you say, you are going still further off, that we may both be exactly in the spot which Providence has assigned us. For my part, God knows, I acquit myself very ill in my residence; but you, heavens! M. d'Angers (H. Arnauld) can not do more. When I think, however, of our separation, and how much I deserve to enjoy the pleasure of being with you, and of all your affection for me, and then reflect that we are placed at two different ends of the globe, you must excuse me if I can not view this part of our history with gayety of heart. Common sense opposes it, and my infinite love still more. I have nothing to do but take refuge in submission to the will of Providence. I am very glad you have seen M. de la Garde; he does me great honor in approving my turn of mind: he is a very good judge. I am sorry you are going to lose him so soon, for he is really a worthy man. Your conversations must have been endless. So he is to take the archbishop away to La Garde. It was very well said of him, that he was like a river which fertilized and made every country flourish through which it passed. I find he did wonders at Grignan.

M. de Chaulnes is at Rennes with four thousand men; he

---

* This is the work of Dufosse, of Port Royal. It had just been published, with the Life of Tertullian, by the same author.

has removed the parliament to Vannes, which has occasioned a terrible desolation. The ruin of Rennes brings with it that of the whole province. Madame de Marbeuf is at Vitré; she has brought me a thousand compliments from Madame de Chaulnes, and from M. de Vins, who intends paying me a visit. I am not under the least apprehension about these troops on my own account, but I can not help feeling for the despair and desolation our poor province suffers at present. It is supposed we shall not have any assembly of the states here, or if we have, it will be only to buy off the taxes which we gave two million five hundred thousand livres to have taken off only two years ago, and which have been all laid upon our shoulders again; and, perhaps, they may set a price too upon bringing the parliament back to Rennes. M. de Montmoron* is fled out of the town, to a seat belonging to one of his friends, at about three leagues distance from hence, that he may avoid hearing the cries and lamentations of the people at seeing their dear parliament removed. You see I am quite a Breton, but, you know, it is owing to the air I breathe, and to something else, for every creature, without distinction, is in affliction throughout the province. Be under no concern about my health, my dearest child; I am extremely well. Madame de Tarente has given me an essence that has cured her of vapors that were worse than mine: two drops are to be taken for fifteen days following, in any beverage that is drunk at table, and it cures effectually. She has told me circumstances of its efficacy, which have all the air of those in the comedy of the Medecin Forcé; but I believe them all, and I would take some of the essence now if it were not that I think it a pity to make use of so admirable a remedy when I have no real occasion for it. I will send you, some time or other, the remainder of the prosperities of the boat. You will make La Plessis too vain, for I shall tell her how much you love her. Except what I told you the other day, I do not think a better creature exists. She is here every day. I have some of your excellent

---

* He was a Sévigné, and dean of the parliament of Brittany.

Hungary water in my pocket; I am quite in love with it; it cures all my sorrows; I wish I could send some of it to Rennes.

My woods continue very beautiful still, and the verdure is a hundred times finer than at Livri; I do not know whether this proceeds from the nature of the trees themselves, or from the refreshing rains we have here; but there is certainly no comparison; every thing here looks as green now as in the month of May. The leaves that fall are brown, it is true, but those that remain on the trees are not at all faded; you never observed this beauty in them. As to that blessed tree that saved your life, I am often tempted to build a little chapel there. It seems to carry its head above all the rest, and exceeds them in bulk as well as stature, and with very good reason, for it saved you. I may, at least, repeat to it the stanza of Medor, in Ariosto, in which he wishes happiness and peace to the cave that had given him so much pleasure. Our sentences are not at all disfigured; I visit them frequently. I think they are rather increased, and two trees that are close to each other, often present us with two contrary sentiments, "*La lontananza ogni grand piaga salda,*" * and "*Piaga d'amor non si sana mais.*"† There are five or six thus contradictory. The good princess was charmed with them, as I am with the letter you have written our good abbé, on Jacob's journey to the land of promise, in your closet.

Madame de Lavardin has informed me of what is still to be kept secret for a few days longer, that D'Olonne is going to marry his brother to Mademoiselle de Noirmoutier. He gives him all his lands in Poitou, besides a great quantity of jewels and furniture. They are at La Ferté-Milon, where this curious affair is to be made up. I never thought D'Olonne would have given himself any concern about his name or family.

* Time is a cure for wounds however deep.
† The wounds of love are never to be healed.

LETTER L.

THE ROCKS, Wednesday, November 6, 1675.

What a delightful letter have you written to me, my dear child! What thanks do I not owe you for employing your hand, your eyes, your head, your time, in composing so agreeable a volume! I have read it over and over, and shall read it again with pleasure and attention. I can read nothing that is more interesting; you satisfy my curiosity in every thing I wish. I admire your care in giving me such punctual answers. This makes a conversation perfect, regular, and extremely entertaining. But I must beg you not to destroy yourself; this fear makes me renounce the pleasure of having frequently such entertainments. You can not doubt my generosity in sparing you the fatigue of immoderate writing.

I comprehend with pleasure the high esteem that is paid to M. de Grignan in Provence, after what I have seen of it. This is a pleasure you are scarcely sensible of; you are too much accustomed to be loved and honored in a province where you command. If you saw the horror, the detestation, the hatred, that the people have here for their governor, you would feel more than you do the pleasure of being adored every where. What affronts! what injuries! what menaces! what reproaches! the very stones fly round him. I do not believe M. de Grignan would accept this post upon such conditions.

You mention to me the paper you have signed so heroically in favor of M. de Grignan.* You say you had no doubt which way the honorable sentiments of Cardinal de Retz† inclined. I do not say any thing of mine; it was enough that you could discern what his counsels tended to. In certain delicate affairs, we do not presume directly to advise, but we represent the case; the common friends of both do what is

---

* It appears that Madame de Grignan had entered into a bond for her husband. † Cardinal de Retz advised her not to sign.

proper, that there may be no jarring opposition in the interest of those they love. But with a soul so perfectly generous and good as yours, we consult only ourselves, and act precisely as you have done. Have you not seen how much you have been admired? Are you not pleased that you owe to none but yourself so noble a resolution? You would have done nothing blamable, if you had refused to sign—you would only have acted like the rest of the world; but by consenting to it, you have exceeded all the world. In a word, my child, enjoy the beauty of your own action, and do not think meanly of us for not having prompted you to it. On a similar occasion, we should perhaps have acted as you have done, and you would have advised as we did; it is all well. I am very much pleased that M. de Grignan is so good as to recompense this mark of your friendship and affection by a greater attention to his affairs. The prudence you commend him for, is the truest mark of his gratitude you could have wished.

LETTER LI.

THE ROCKS, Sunday, December 1, 1675.

Well, my dear, it seems now settled that I am to receive two of your packets together, and miss one post; you should see the faces I make, and how I receive it in comparison with those that come regularly. I am of your opinion, my child, and would give a great deal to be as easy about answering letters as the coadjutor is, and keep them in my pocket for a month or two without troubling my head about them. Well, it is a gift from heaven certainly, this happy indifference! Madame de Langeron used to say of visits, and I apply it to every thing: "What I do fatigues me, and what I omit to do vexes me." I think this is very well said, and I feel it sensibly. I am always exact, however, in my answers. It is with pleasure I give you the top of the basket; that is, you have the very flower of my mind, my head, my eyes, my pen, my desk—the rest fare as they can. I have as much amusement in chatting to you, as labor and fatigue in writing to others. I am perfectly stunned with the great news that abounds in Europe.

I suppose the coadjutor has shown Madame de Fontevraud the letter he received from you. You are ignorant of its value. You write like an angel; I read your letters with admiration. You no sooner set out than you reach the goal. Do you remember the minuet which you danced so well, and closed in such excellent time, when the other creatures were not at the end of theirs till the next day? The late madame and yourself were famous for this; we used to call it *gaining ground*. Your letters are just the same.

As for your poor little *frater*, I know not where he has hid himself; it is three weeks now since I had a line from him. He made no mention of the pretty airing upon the Meuse, though every body believes it here; his fortune is really very hard, poor lad. I do not see how he can manage the affair of his promotion, unless Lauzun will take the guidonage in part of payment, with some other little additions we will endeavor to raise; but to buy the ensign's place, and have the guidonage left upon our hands, will never do. Your reasoning upon the matter is very just; we all acquiesce in it, and shall be very well contented to mount after the other two,* provided the guidon serves as the first step.

I shall finish the year here very peaceably. There are times when all places are indifferent, and a solitude like this not unpleasant. Madame de la Fayette returns you all your civilities; she has very bad health, and poor M. de Limoges still worse; he has resigned all his benefices to the king; I fancy his son, the Abbé de la Fayette, will have one of his abbeys. Poor Gascony has been as roughly handled as we have been. We have six thousand troops sent down to pass

---

* The Marquis de la Trousse, and the Marquis de la Fare; the one captain-lieutenant, and the other sub-lieutenant, in the dauphin's gens-d'armes.

the winter among us: if it were not for the misconduct of the provinces, I do not know how they would be able to dispose of their troops. I can not think peace is so near: do you remember all our reasoning upon the subject of war, and how many there must be killed? This is always a certain prophecy, and so is that, that your letters can never tire me, long as they may be: ah! you will find no chimera in this hope, they are my choicest reading. Ripert brings you a third volume of the Moral Essays, which are worth your perusal. I never met with greater energy than there is in the style of these writers: they make use of no words but what are in common use, and yet they appear perfectly new, by the elegant manner in which they dispose them. In the morning I read the history of France; in the afternoon, some serious subjects in my woods; such as the Essays, the Life of Saint Thomas of Canterbury, which I think delightful, or the Iconoclastes; and in the evening, things of a lighter nature: this is my constant rule. I hope you continue to read Josephus; take courage, my dear, and go on boldly to the end. If you read the history of the Crusades, you will meet with two illustrious men who were your ancestors, but not a word about the great family of V***, that holds its head so high at present: but I am persuaded there are some passages which will make you throw aside the book, and curse the Jesuit;* and yet upon the whole it is an admirable history.

LETTER LII.

THE ROCKS, Wednesday, Dec. 11, 1675.

A little patience, my dear child, brings us to the accomplishment of our wishes: I have received the two packets of letters from you that I should have received before; but they are

* Father Maimbourg, author of the History of the Crusades. The physician, in the Lettres Persanes, gives as a recipe for the asthma, to read all the works of this father, stopping only at each period.

come at last, and you will do me no more than justice to believe that I am highly delighted to have them. I thank you that notwithstanding all your philosophy, you enter into all my melancholy reflections on the immense distance that separates us; you sympathize with me; you seem afflicted as well as myself with this disposition of Providence; but you encounter it with more courage than I do, who always feel from it some new increase of sorrow. I am continually meditating on the past, for which the present and the future can never make me amends. It is an ample field in which to exercise a heart so tender and ill-defended as mine. I can not but admire those good ladies who make a duty of their inclination; there is La Troche for instance, who has so well turned and wound her good fortune, that she is at length settled at her ease in the good city of Paris, making it the seat of her empire and the field of all her operations. She has fixed her son at court, in spite of wind and tide, and makes it her business to be always near him. As for Marbeuf, she had begun, even in her husband's time, and now lays no restraint upon herself; she has taken a lease of a house in Paris for a hundred years, and most humbly takes her leave of poor Brittany: while you, my dear child, who were born and bred in this country, you whom I have always so fondly loved, and so ardently wished to have forever with me, are driven to the furthest end of the world by the storms of adverse fortune; but, if I mean to put an end to my letter, I must pass lightly over these reflections, and resume my courage in the flattering hope of a change: d'Hacqueville and I indulge some pleasing dreams of that kind; but this is not a time to communicate them to you. Let us return to the miseries of this poor province.

Every place is full of warriors; there are to be some at Vitré, notwithstanding the princess is there. Monsieur, when he writes to her, styles her his good aunt; his dear aunt; but I do not find that she is better treated than others. There are to be troops at Guerche, the estate of the Marquis de Villeroi; and from thence they are to spread themselves among the country people, to rob and strip them. This is a heavy disaster upon poor Brittany, that never experienced any thing of the kind before. Our governor has received a power to grant a general amnesty, which he disperses with one hand, and with the other lets loose eight thousand soldiers, over whom he has as much command as you have: they have all their orders. M. de Pommereuil is expected here every day; he has the inspection of this little army, and may very soon boast a fine government. He is the best and wisest of the robe; he is my friend; but I doubt whether he will be as tractable as your intendant, whom you manage so excellently; I am afraid he will be changed. I can give you no information to-day respecting Languedoc; in the mean time content yourself with some from Guienne; I find they are well protected, and have procured a considerable mitigation of their burden. Alas! we are not so happy; our protections, if we had any, would do us more harm than good, by the animosity against us of two individuals. I believe we may still find, or at least promise to find, the three millions demanded of us, without ruining our friend;* for he is so beloved by the states, that they would do any thing rather than he should suffer. And this, I think, is enough upon the subject.

I am rejoiced that you are not returned to Grignan; it would have been only an additional fatigue and expense to you. Prudence and economy, for which the good abbé desires me to thank you, have rendered that step unnecessary. Let me know if the dear little ones are to come to you. We have most delightful weather here, and we are making some new walks, which will be very beautiful. My son is very good, and helps to amuse us; he enters into the spirit of the place, and has brought no more of the warrior or of the courtier with him into this retreat, than is sufficient to enliven conversation. When it does not rain we are not so much to be pitied as at a distance it may be supposed · the time we have fixed to spend here will pass like the rest.

* M. de Harroüis.

My letter has not been given to Louvois; the whole affair is negotiating between Lauzun and myself; if he will take the guidonage, we have offered to make a small addition to it; if he resolves to sell his post outright, which would be very unreasonable, he must look for a purchaser on his side, as we shall on ours; that is all. I have written to the chevalier to condole with him on our not having met at Paris; we should have made curious lamentations together on our last year's party, and should have renewed our tears for the loss of M. de Turenne. I know not what idea you have of our princess; I assure you she is no Artemisia;* her heart is like wax, it easily takes impression; she makes a boast of it, and says pleasantly enough that she has a ridiculous heart; this is spoken in general terms, but the world is rather more particular in its applications. I am in hopes I shall be able to keep this folly within bounds, by the frequent speeches I make (as if I intended nothing by them) on the detestable light in which those women are held, who give too great a rein to their passions, and how much they subject themselves thereby to contempt. I talk miraculously sometimes; I am heard and approved as much as can be expected. Indeed, I consider it quite a duty to talk thus; and should think it an honor to be instrumental in working a reformation.

I am tired to death with the barrenness of news; we stand in great need of some event, as you say, let it be at whose expense it will; as long as we have no more Turennes to lose, *vogue la galère*. You tell me extraordinary things; I read them, admire them, believe them, and then you send me word they are not true; I well know the style and braggart of the provinces. You judge superficially of our governor, when you say you should have acted as he did, had you been in his place; I know you would not; neither did the king's service require it. Ah! what is become of the excellent understand-

---

* The affectionate and chaste wife of Mausolus, king of Caria, whose ashes she drank after his death.

ing you had last winter? This is no time to think of deputations; let us see peace restored, and then we shall have time to think of every thing.

As to the religion of the Jews, I said, when reading their history, that "if God had given me grace to have been born a Jew,"* I should have liked it better than any other except the true religion. I admire its magnificence; but you must admire it still more, on account of its year of rest, and of dressing-gowns, which would have given you an opportunity of being a shining example of piety in your elbow-chair; never would sabbath have been better kept. Ripert has received the Moral Essays; they contain several treatises, and among the rest one that is particularly pleasing; you will guess which I mean. I am delighted with your good health and beauty, for I love you truly. I often wish for you in these woods, the air of which, as well as that of Livri, is a great preservative to the complexion. Our good abbé praises you highly for your care in discharging your debts; for that, in his estimation, is the law and the prophets; and as M. de Grignan is so prudent, I will embrace him notwithstanding his beard; but do you know that your little brother's beard has the presumption to rival it? it is to much purpose! Send me word of your success at play. It seems to me as if I saw your little fingers taking out of the pool; but these times are past; good and evil travel on the same road, but they leave different impressions. You have given a great dinner; where was I? for I know all; I see all the magnificence from hence. You express yourself admirably on the marriage of the little prince (De Marsan) and the maréchale; the disproportion is doubtless great, but suppose he should have escaped it! Believe me, you have no need of my letters, you can write delightfully without a theme. But I must reduce myself at last to Solon's

* In allusion to an expression of M. de Rochefoucault, who said, "If God had given me grace to have been born a Turk, I should have died a Turk."

rule, "Nothing is to be praised on this side the grave;" which is a heavy restriction for me, who dearly love to praise what is praise-worthy; besides, who can stay so long? For my part, I shall always go on in my old way: adieu, my ever-lovely and beloved child.

LETTER LIII.

THE ROCKS, Sunday January 12, 1676.

You may fill your letters with whatever you please, and still be assured that I read them with great pleasure and equal approbation; no one can write better than you do, and it is not my friendship only that leads me to form this opinion.

You delight me by saying you like the Moral Essays; did I not tell you they would suit your taste? As soon as I began to read them, I could think of nothing but of sending them to you; you know I am communicative, and do not like to enjoy a pleasure alone. If this book had been written on purpose for you, it could not have been more calculated to please you. What language! what energy in the arrangement of the words! I think I never read French but in this book. The resemblance of charity to self-love, and of the heroic modesty of M. de Turenne and the prince to Christian humility—but I forbear. This work deserves to be praised from beginning to end, but I should write a strange letter if I were to do so. I am very glad, however, you like it, and I have a better opinion of my own judgment in consequence. You do not admire the life of Josephus; but it is sufficient if you approve his actions and his history. Did you not think him very happy in the cave, where they drew lots who should stab himself the last?

We laughed till we cried at the story of the girl who sung the indecent song, for which she confessed aloud in the church. Nothing can be more novel and amusing. I think she was in the right; the confessor certainly wished to hear the song, for he was not satisfied with the girl's accusation of herself. I fancy I see him bursting with laughter the first at this adventure. We often send you ridiculous stories, but we can not surpass this. I always talk of Brittany, and it is to encourage you to talk of Provence; it is a country in which I am more interested than in any other. My journey thither takes away all possibility of being tired with what you tell me, because I am acquainted with every body, and understand every thing perfectly. I have not forgotten the beauty of your winters. Our season is very fine here; I walk every day, and have almost made a new park round the waste land at the end of the mall. I am planting four rows of trees there; it will be a great improvement, for all this part is now uniform and cultivated.

But I shall take my departure, in spite of all these charms, in February. The abbé's affairs are still more urgent than yours, which has prevented me from offering our house to Mademoiselle de Méri; she has complained of this to several persons, I understand, but I know not what reason she has to do so. The *worthy* is in raptures with your letters; I often show him passages that I know will please him. He thanks you for what you say of the Moral Essays; he was delighted with them himself. The little girl is still with us; she has an active little mind which has never been exercised, and we take pleasure in improving it. She is in perfect ignorance; it is an amusement to us to give her some general knowledge: a few words of this great universe, of empires, countries, kings, religions, and wars, of astronomy and geography. It is pleasant to see the unfolding of all these things in a little head which has never beheld a town or a river, and who thought the whole world extended no further than our park; she amuses us highly. I informed her to-day of the capture of Wismar; she knows we are sorry for it, because the king of Sweden is our ally. Such are our amusements. The princess is delighted that her daughter has taken Wismar; she is a true Dane. She has asked monsieur and madame to exempt her entirely from the soldiery, so that we shall all be safe.

Madame de la Fayette is very grateful for your letter; she thinks you very polite and obliging. But does it not appear strange to you that her brother-in-law is not dead, and that such mistakes should arise at the short distance of Toulon and Aix? Upon the questions you put to the *frater* I decide boldly, that he who is angry, and shows his anger, is preferable to the deceiver, who conceals his malignity under fair and specious appearances. There is a stanza in Ariosto descriptive of guile.* I would transcribe it, but I have not time to look for it. The good D'Hacqueville stills talks to me of the journey of St. Geran, and to prove how short her stay will be, he says she can only receive one of my letters at Palisse. This is how he treats an acquaintance of a week; he is just the same with respect to others, but this is excellent. I forgot to say that I had thought like you of the different ways of

---

* We shall probably gratify the reader by inserting this stanza:

> Havea piaceval viso, abito onesto,
> Un umil valger d'occhi, un andar grave,
> Un parlar si benigno, e si modesto
> Che parea Gabriel, che dicesse: Ave,
> Era brutta e deforme in tutto il resto
> Ma nasconde queste fattezze prave
> Con lungo abito, e largo, e sotto quello
> Attosicato avea sempre il coltello.
> Orlando Furioso. Canto xiv.

> Her garb was decent, lovely was her face,
> Her eyes were bashful, sober was her pace;
> With speech whose charms might every heart assail,
> Like his who gave the blest salute of—Hail!
> But all deformed and brutal was the rest,
> Which close she covered with her ample vest,
> Beneath whose folds, prepared for bloody strife,
> Her hand for ever grasped a poisoned knife.
> Hoole's Translation. Book xiv

painting the human heart, some white and others blacker than black. You know what color mine is of for you.

LETTER LIV.

(MADAME DE SÉVIGNÉ DICTATES—HER SON WRITES.)

THE ROCKS, Monday, Feb. 3, 1676.

Guess, my dear child, what it is that comes the quickest, and goes off the slowest; that brings you nearest to health, and removes you the furthest from it; that throws you into the most agreeable situation imaginable, and, at the same time, hinders you from enjoying it; that flatters you with the most pleasing hopes, and keeps you the longest from the accomplishment of them. Can not you guess? Do you give it up? Why, it is the rheumatism. I have had it these three and twenty days; since the fourteenth day I have been free from fever and pain, and in this delightful situation, thinking myself strong enough to walk, which is the summit of my wishes, I find myself swelled all over—feet, legs, hands, arms; and this swelling, which they call my cure, and in reality is so, is the sole occasion of my present vexation; were I good for any thing, I might gain myself some credit by it. However, I believe the enemy is conquered, and that in two days I shall be able to walk. Larméchin gives me great hope of this. I every day receive letters from our friends at Paris, congratulating me on my recovery. I have taken M. de Lorme's opening powders, which have been of great service to me; I am going to take them again; they are a never-failing remedy in these cases. After this attack I am promised an eternal succession of health. God grant it. My first step will be to return to Paris. I desire you, therefore, my dear, to calm all your fears; you see what a faithful account we have given you of the affair; let that make you easy.

LETTER LV.

PARIS, Wednesday, April 15, 1676.

I am very melancholy, my dear; my poor boy is just gone; he has so many little social virtues that are the charm of society, that were he only an acquaintance I should regret his loss. He desired me, over and over again, to tell you that he forgot to take notice to you of the story of your Proteus, who was at one time a capuchin, at another time a galley-slave; he was highly amused at it. It is supposed we are going to undertake the siege of Cambray; this is so extraordinary a step, that every one thinks we have had intelligence with some one in the place. If we lose Philipsburg, it will be very difficult to repair the breach: *vederemo*, we shall see. But still we reason and make almanacs, all of which end with, *the king's star will prevail*.

At length Marshal Bellefond has cut the thread that tied him here. Sanguin has purchased his place* for 55,000 livres, and a brevet de retenue of 350,000. This is a fine settlement, and an assurance of a cordon bleu.† M. de Pomponne has paid me a very cordial visit; all your friends have exerted themselves wonderfully. I do not go out yet. The cold winds retard the cure of my hands, and yet I write better than I did, as you may see. I turn myself at night on my left side; I eat with my left hand: these are left hand performances. My face is very little altered; you would soon discover that you have seen it somewhere before; it is because I have not been bled, and have endeavored to get cured of my illness without such remedies. I thank you for mentioning the pigeons to me. Where has the little one acquired this timidity? I am afraid you will throw the blame upon me: you cast a sus-

---

* Of premier maître-d'hôtel, or lord chamberlain, to the king.

† M. de Sanguin was not created a knight of the king's order at the promotion in 1688, but the Marquis de Livri his son, who was premier maître-d'hôtel, was comprehended in that of 1724.

picious eye toward me. This humor will, I dare say, pass off, and you will not be obliged to make a monk of him. I am resolved to go to Vichi; they have set me against Bourbon on account of the air. The Maréchale d'Etrées wishes me to go to Vichi; she says it is a delightful country. I have told you what I think of that affair; either resolve to return hither with me, or do not come at all; for a fortnight will only disturb me with constant thoughts of a separation, and will be on the whole a foolish and useless expense. You know how dear the sight of you is to me, so take your own measures.

I wish you had finished the bargain about your estate: M. de Pomponne tells me it is raised to a marquisate. I desired him to make it a dukedom: he assured me it would give him great pleasure to do so, and that he would use all expedition in drawing up the patents. This is a considerable step. I am delighted to hear the pigeons are so well. How does the little tiny, or rather the great fat one do? I love him dearly, for resolving to live against wind and tide. But I can not forget my little girl;* I suppose you will determine on putting her to Saint Marie, according to the resolutions you adopt this summer; all depends upon that. You seem satisfied with the devotions of Passion and Easter weeks: you shut yourself up at Grignan. For my part, my thoughts were not affected with any thing. I had no object to strike the senses. I ate meat till Good Friday, and had only the comfort of being very distant from any opportunity of committing sin. I told La Mousse you remembered him, and he advises you to make the most of your man of wit. Adieu, my dear child.

LETTER LVI.

PARIS, Wednesday, April 29, 1676.

I must begin by telling you that Condé was taken by storm on Saturday night. The news at first made my heart beat;

* Marie-Blanche d'Athémar, born the 15th November, 1670.

I feared the victory had cost us dear, but it does not prove so; we have lost some men, but none of any note; this may be reckoned a complete happiness. Larei, the son of M. Lainé, who was killed in Candia, or his brother, is dangerously wounded. You see how soon our old heroes are forgotten.

Madame de Brinvilliers is not so comfortable as I am; she is in prison, and endeavors to pass her time there as pleasantly as she can; she desired yesterday to play at piquet, because she was dull. Her confession has been found; it informs us that at the age of seven years she ceased to be a virgin; that she had ever since gone on at the same rate; that she had poisoned her father, her brothers, one of her children, and herself; but the last was only to make trial of a counter-poison. Medea was a saint compared with her. She has owned this confession to be her own writing; it was an unaccountable folly; but she says she was in a high fever when she wrote it, and that it was an act of madness or frenzy, which does not deserve a serious thought.

The queen has been twice at the Carmelites with Madame de Montespan. The latter set on foot a lottery; she collected every thing that could be useful to the nuns; this was a great novelty and amusement in the convent. She conversed a long time with sister Louise* de la Miséricorde, and asked her whether it was really true that she was as happy there as it had been generally reported. She replied, "I am not happy, but I am contented." Quanto talked to her a great deal of the brother of monsieur; and asked her if she had no message to send him, and what she should say to him for her. She replied in the sweetest tone and manner possible, though perhaps a little piqued at the question; "Whatever you please, madam, whatever you please." Fancy this to be expressed with all the grace, spirit, and modesty, which you so well understand. Quanto afterward wished for something to eat, and sent to purchase some ingredient that was necessary for a sauce she prepared herself, and which she ate with a wonderful ap-

---

* Madame de la Vallière.

petite. I tell you the simple fact without the least embellishment. When I think of the letter you wrote me last year about M. de Vivonne, I consider all I send you as a burlesque. To what lengths will not folly lead a man who thinks himself deserving of such exaggerated praise!

LETTER LVII.

PARIS, Friday, July 17, 1676.

At length it is all over: La Brinvilliers is in the air; after her execution her poor little body was thrown into a large fire, and her ashes dispersed by the wind, so that whenever we breathe, we shall inhale some particles of her, and by the communication of the minute spirits, we may be all infected with the desire of poisoning, to our no small surprise. She was condemned yesterday; and this morning her sentence was read to her, which was to perform the *amende honorable* in the church of Nôtre-Dame; and, after that, to have her head cut off, her body burned, and her ashes thrown into the air. They were for giving her the question, but she told them there was no occasion for that, and that she would confess every thing; accordingly, she was till five o'clock in the evening relating the history of her life, which has been more shocking than was even imagined. She gave poison to her father ten times successively, but without effect, and also to her brother, and several others, at the same time preserving the appearance of the greatest love and confidence. She has said nothing against Penautier. Notwithstanding this confession, they gave her the question, ordinary and extraordinary, the next morning; but this extorted nothing more from her. She desired to speak with the procurator-general: no one yet knows the subject of their conversation. At six o'clock she was carried in a cart, with no other covering than her shift, and with a cord round her neck, to the church of Nôtre-Dame, to perform the *amende honorable;* after which, she was put again into the same cart, where I saw her extended on a truss of straw, with a confessor on one side, and the hangman on the other; indeed, my child, the sight made me shudder. Those who saw the execution say she mounted the scaffold with great courage. I was on the bridge of Nôtre-Dame, with the good d'Escars; never was Paris in such commotion, nor its attention so fixed upon one event. Yet, ask many people what they saw, and they will tell you they saw no more than I did, who was not present; in short, the whole day has been dedicated to this tragedy.

LETTER LVIII.

Livri, Wednesday, Nov. 4, 1676.

Nothing can be more true than the proverb which says, that liberty is destroyed by uncertainty. Were you under any sort of restraint, you would have determined what to do long ago, and not have been like Mohammed's coffin, suspended between heaven and earth; one of the loadstones would certainly, by this time, have got the better of the other. You would no longer be *dragooned*, which is a very unpleasant state. The voice you heard, in passing the Durance, exclaim, *Ah, mother! mother!* would pierce to Grignan: or at least, that which counseled you to leave it, would not haunt you at Briare; for which reason, I maintain that nothing can be more opposite in its nature to liberty than indifference and indecision. Can it be possible that the sage La Garde, who has, it seems, resumed all his wonted wisdom, has likewise lost his free will? is he incapable of advising you? can he be at a loss to decide in this important point? you have seen that I decide like one of the councils. But how is it that La Garde, who is coming to Paris himself, can not contrive that his journey may take place at the same time with yours? If you do come, it would be no bad thought to take the way of Sully; the little duchess would certainly convey you as far as Nemours; at least, you would find some friend or other, from day to day, so that you would have a relay of friends, till you found yourself in your own apartment. You would have met with a better reception last time, but your letter came so late that you took every body by surprise, and had nearly missed me, which would have been a fine circumstance indeed; but we will contrive to keep clear of this inconvenience in future. I can not help praising the chevalier,* who arrived in Paris on Friday evening, and dined here on Saturday; was is not very good of him? I was delighted to see him, and I assure you we spoke with great freedom of your scruples. I am now going to take a trip to Paris. I must see M. de Louvois on your brother's account, who is still here without leave, which vexes me not a little. I want to talk to M. Colbert likewise, about your pension: these two visits are all I have to make. I have some thoughts of going to Versailles, but will acquaint you whether I do so or not. In the mean time, we have the finest weather imaginable; the country has yet put on none of its horrors, and St. Hubert has favored the hunter extremely.

We are still reading Saint Augustine with pleasure: there is something so great and noble in his ideas, that all the mischief that weak minds can possibly receive from his doctrine, falls infinitely short of the good which others may derive from the perusal. You will imagine I give myself airs of a learned lady; but when you see in what a familiar style this is written, you will cease to wonder at my capacity. You tell me that if you did not love me a great deal more than you say, you should love me very little: I am strangely tempted to scold you for this, even though I should risk the saying an unkind or an uncivil thing: but no; I am fully persuaded you love me; and God knows much better than it is possible for you to do, what a strong affection I entertain for you. I am glad to hear Pauline is like me, she will serve to put you in mind of me. "*Ah! mother, there is no need of that.*"

* De Grignan.

LETTER LIX.

LIVRI, Friday, Nov. 6, 1676.

Surely there never was so brilliant a letter as your last; I had some thoughts of sending it back, that you might have the pleasure of perusing it. I could not help wondering while I read it, how it was possible to wish so ardently to receive no more. This, however, is the affront I put on your letters: you seem to treat mine much more civilly.

This Reimond is certainly *hem! hem!* with the head-dress you know so well; she has dressed in this style, as you properly observe, that she might seem qualified to hear the music of the blessed above; and our sisters have done the same from the wish of obtaining a fund of seven thousand livres, with a pension of a thousand, by which she is enabled* " to go abroad when she likes, and she likes it very often." We have never had such merchandize before; but the beauty of our house causes us to overlook every thing; for my own part, I am quite delighted with it: for in my opinion both her apartments and her voice are divine, *hem, hem.*

The dates you mention in speaking of Madame de Soubise, are, thank, God, among those which have escaped my memory. Some marked incivility must certainly have been shown during the festivities at Versailles. Madame de Coulanges informs me that the tooth has disappeared since the day before yesterday; in that case, you will conclude they can have no tooth against her. You are very amusing upon my friend's† illness, and at the same time it is all true. The quartan ague of our friend of the suburbs,‡ is happily at an end. I have sent your letter to the chevalier, § without apprehension or reproof. I love him sincerely; and as for my *pigeon,* I wish I could give him a kiss; I have some idea in

---

* Madame de Sévigné recants a little. See the Letter of the 21st October.   † Madame de Coulanges.

‡ Madame de la Fayette.   § De Grignan.

my head, I know not how truly, that leads me to think I shall one day or other see all these little folks. I can not understand the eight months' child; pray is she likely to live a century? I fancy the gentlemen that fought it out so bravely in the streets, are in a fair way to live as long. It would really be a very pretty and just punishment for a battle in the midst of summer. Adieu, my dear lovely child, I shall finish this in the good city of Paris.

Friday, at Paris.

So! here I am. I have been dining at the worthy Bagnol's, where I found Madame de Coulanges in this charming apartment, embellished with the golden rays of the sun, where I have often seen you, almost as beautiful and as brilliant as he. The poor convalescent gave me a hearty welcome, and is now going to write two lines to you; it is, for aught I know, something from the other world, which I am sure you will be very glad to hear. She has been giving me an account of a new dress called transparencies. Pray, have you heard of it? It is an entire suit of the finest gold and azure brocade that can be seen, over which is a black robe, either of beautiful English lace, or velvet chenille like the winter laces you have seen; this occasions the name of transparency, which is, you see, a black suit, and a suit of gold and azure, or any other color, according to the fancy of the wearer, as is all the fashion at present. This was the dress worn at the ball on St. Hubert's day, which lasted a whole half-hour, for nobody would dance. The king pushed Madame d'Heudicourt into the middle of the room by main force; she obeyed, but at length the combat ended for want of combatants. The fine embroidered boddices destined for Villers-Côterets serve to walk out on an evening, and were worn on St. Hubert's day. The prince informed the ladies at Chantilly, that their transparencies would be a thousand times more beautiful if they would wear them next their skin, which I very much doubt. The Granceis and Monacos did not share in the amusements, because the mother of the latter is ill, and the mother of the *angels* has been at death's door. It is said, the Marchioness de la Ferté has been in labor there, ever since Sunday, and that Bouchet is at his wit's end.

M. de Langlée has made Madame de Montespan a present of a robe of gold cloth, on a gold ground, with a double gold border embroidered and worked with gold, so that it makes the finest gold stuff ever imagined by the wit of man. It was contrived by fairies in secret, for no living wight could have conceived any thing so beautiful. The manner of presenting it was equally mysterious. Madame de Montespan's mantua-maker carried home the suit she had bespoke, having made it to fit ill on purpose; you need not be told what exclamations and scoldings there were upon the occasion. "Madam," said the mantua-maker, trembling with fear, "as there is so little time to alter it in, will you have the goodness to try whether this other dress may not fit you better?" It was produced. "Ah!" cried the lady, "how beautiful! What an elegant stuff is this? Pray, where did you get? It must have fallen from the clouds, for a mortal could never have executed any thing like it." The dress was tried on; it fitted to a hair. In came the king. "It was made for you, madam," said the mantua-maker. Immediately it was concluded that it must be a present from some one; but from whom? was the question. "It is Langlée," said the king. "It must be Langlée," said Madame de Montespan; "nobody but Langlée could have thought of so magnificent a present—it is Langlée, it is Langlée!" Every body exclaims, "It is Langlée, it is Langlée!" The echoes repeat the sound. And I, my child, to be in the fashion, say, "It is Langlée."

LETTER LX.

Paris, Wednesday, June 30, 1677.

At length you inform me that you are arrived at Grignan. The pains you have taken to keep our correspondence uninterrupted, is a continual mark of your affection. I can assure you that you are not mistaken in the opinion that I stand in need of this support; indeed no one can be more in want of it. It is true, however, and I too often think so, that your presence would have been of much greater service to me; but your situation was so extraordinary, that the same considerations that determined you to go, made me consent to your departure, without doing any thing more than stifle my sentiments. It was considered a crime in me to discover any uneasiness with regard to your health. I saw you perishing before my eyes, and was not permitted to shed a tear. It was killing you, it was assassinating you; I was compelled to suppress my grief. I never knew a more cruel or more unprecedented species of torture. If, instead of that restraint, which only increased my affliction, you had owned that you were ill; and if your love for me had been productive of complaisance, and made you evince a real desire to follow the advice of physicians, to take nourishment, to observe a regimen, and to own that repose and the air of Livri would have done you good, this would indeed have comforted me, but your opposition to our sentiments aggravated my grief and anxiety. In the end, my child, we were so circumstanced, that we could not possibly avoid acting as we did. God explained to us his will by that conduct; but we should endeavor to see whether he will not permit us mutually to reform, and whether, instead of that despair to which you condemned me from a motive of affection, it would not be more natural and more beneficial to give our hearts the liberty they require, and without which it is impossible for us to lead a life of tranquillity. Thus I have declared my mind to you freely once for all. I shall mention the subject no more, but let us each reflect upon the past, that, whenever it pleases God to bring us together again, we may carefully avoid falling into the same errors. The relief which you have found in the fatigues of so long a journey, sufficiently proves the necessity you are under of laying aside restraint. Extraordinary remedies are necessary for persons of an extraordinary character; physicians would never have dreamed of such a one as that I have just mentioned. God grant it may continue to produce the same good effect, and that the air of Grignan may not prove injurious to you! I could not avoid writing to you in this manner, in order to relieve my heart, and intimate to you that we must endeavor, when next we meet, not to give any one an opportunity of paying us the wretched compliment of saying very civilly, that to keep quite well, we should never see one another again. I am astonished at the patience that can bear so cruel a thought.

You brought the tears into my eyes in speaking of your little boy. Alas, poor child; who can bear to see him in such a situation! I do not retract what I always thought of him; but am of opinion that, even from affection, we ought to wish him already in a happier world. Paulina appears to me worthy of being made your play-thing; her resemblance even will not displease you, at least, I hope it will not. That little quadrangular nose is a feature you can not possibly dislike to find at Grignan.* It seems to me somewhat odd that the noses of the Grignan family should admit no shape but this, and should be altogether averse to a nose like yours, which might have been sooner formed; but they dreaded extremes, though they did not care about a trifling modification. The little marquis is a very pretty fellow; you should not be at all uneasy at his not being altered for the better. Talk to me a great deal about the persons you associate with, and the amusements they afford you.

LETTER LXI.

Livri, Saturday, July 3, 1677.

Alas, how grieved I am at the death of your poor child!† it is impossible not be affected at it. Not that I was ever of

* This alludes to Madame de Sévigné's nose, which inclined to the square. † The child that was born in February 1676.

opinion he could live; the description you gave convinced me that his case was desperate. But, it is a great loss to you, who had lost two boys before : God preserve to you the only one that remains! He discovers an admirable disposition; I am much better pleased with sound sense and just reasoning, at his age, than with the vivacity of those who turn out fools at twenty. Be satisfied with him, therefore; lead him like a horse that has a tender mouth, and remember what I told you respecting his bashfulness; this advice comes from persons much wiser than myself; and I am sure it is good. With regard to Paulina, I have one word to say to you; from your description of her she may, perhaps, in time, become as handsome as yourself; when a child, you were exactly like her. God grant she may not resemble me in having a heart so susceptible of tenderness! I see plainly that you love her, that she is amiable, and that she amuses you. I wish I could embrace her, and recognize that face again *which I have seen somewhere.*

LETTER LXII.

Livri, Friday, July 16, 1677.

I wish, my dear child, that you had a tutor for your son; it is a pity his mind should be left uncultivated. I doubt whether he is yet of an age to eat all sorts of food promiscuously; we should examine whether children are strong and robust, before we give them strong meats; otherwise we run the hazard of injuring their stomachs, which is of great consequence. My son stays behind to take leave of his friends; he will then come to me here; he must afterward join the army, and after that he may go and drink the waters. An officer, named M. D****, has lately been cashiered for absenting himself; I know the answer you will make, but this instance sufficiently shows the severity of military discipline. Adieu, my dear child; be comforted for the loss of your son; nobody is to blame concerning him. His death was occasioned by teething, and not by a defluxion upon the lungs; when children have not strength sufficient to force out the teeth at a proper time, they are never able to bear the necessary motion to make them all come at once; I talk learnedly. You know the answer of Sully's green bed to M. de Coulanges, made by Guillerague; it is droll enough; Madame de Thianges repeated it to the king, who sings it; it was said at first, that he had ruined himself by it; but it is not true, it will perhaps make his fortune. If this discourse does not come from a green mind, it comes from a green head, which is the same, and the color of the thing can not be disputed.

LETTER LXIII.

Livri, Wednesday Evening, July 24, 1677.

Love Paulina, love Paulina, my child! indulge yourself in that amusement; do not destroy your peace of mind by depriving yourself of her; what are you afraid of? You may still send her to a convent for a few years, when you think it necessary. Enjoy maternal affection for a while; it is exquisite when it springs from the heart, and the choice falls upon an amiable object. Dear Paulina! methinks I see her here; she will resemble you, notwithstanding she bears the mark of the workman. It is true, this nose is a strange affair; but it will improve, and I will answer for it, she will be handsome.

Madame de Vins is still here; she is now in my closet, engaged in conversation with D'Hacqueville and my son. His heel is still so bad that he may perhaps go to Bourbon when I go to Vichi. Be under no concern about this journey; and since it is not the will of Heaven that I should enjoy the charms of your society, we must yield obedience to his will; it is a bitter evil, but it must be endured; we are the weakest, and to attempt resistance is vain. I should be too happy if your friendship was clothed in all its realities; it is still extremely dear to me, though divested of the charms and pleasures which your presence and company bestow upon it. My son and I will answer all you have said on the subject of epic poetry. The contempt I know he has for Eneas, makes me apprehensive he will be of your opinion. Yet all the great wits have a taste for every thing written by the ancients.

LETTER LXIV.

Epoisses, Wednesday morning, August 25, 1677.

I have here, my beloved child, received your letter of the 11th, which I expected with so much impatience; I am not used to such delays; it renders my whole journey uncomfortable to be thus disappointed. M. Guitaut does all he can to convince me how extremely glad he is to see me here. All our people are at Boubilly, where the farmer treated us yesterday with a most plentiful dinner. M. de Guitaut and M. de Trichâteau were there; this gave an air of comfort to the frightful Boubilly-house. I shall continue here till Sunday, and will write to you once more from this place. There is no sort of constraint in this house, so that I can read, work, or walk out, when I please. My host and I have a great deal of conversation together, and there is hardly a country you can name where we have not been travelers. He tells me a thousand stories of Provence, of the intendant and Vardes, which I was ignorant of till now. He seems very devout; follows good teachers; has a great desire to pay his old debts, and to contract no new ones. This is the first step to be taken when we become acquainted with true religion.

LETTER LXV.

Vichi, Wednesday evening, Sept. 22, 1677.

I have just received a letter of the 15th. I fancy it has taken a trip to Paris. The chevalier has received one from the handsome abbé, of the same date, which shows me you were well, at least on that day. It is true that if Vardes had mentioned your illness to me, in terms ever so little stronger than those he used, no consideration would have kept me from you; but he managed so well, that I have no food for uneasiness but what is passed by. I conjure you, my beloved child, to send me word of the return of your health and beauty. I can not dispense with this intelligence, nor can I endure the thoughts of your being less handsome at your age. Do not fancy, therefore, that you can reconcile me to your extreme thinness, which is too plain a proof of your ill state of health: mine is as perfect as it can be. I put an end to-morrow to all my business, and take my last medicine. I have drunk the waters sixteen days, have twice used the pump and the hot-bath; but the pump was two much for me, and I am sorry for it, but it made me too hot and giddy; in short, I had no occasion for it, and drinking the waters was sufficient. I set out on Friday for Langlar. My messmates, Termes, Flamarens, and Jussac, will follow me thither. The chevalier will come to see me on Saturday, and will return on Monday to begin the pump. He will be only a week without me. He will receive in my absence a thousand presents from my friends, and is very well satisfied with me. My hands are better; the inconvenience is so very slight, that I shall use no remedy but time. I am perfectly in despair, my child, at the frightful ideas you entertain. Heavens! is it possible, that in my present state of health, I can do you any injury? It is certainly very much against my inclination if I do. I know not whether it is your intention to write me such admirable passages as you are accustomed to do. You could not possibly fail to succeed in such attempt, and I can assure you they would not be suffered to be forgotten: you are not sensible of the brilliancy of what you say, and so much the better. You have some little inclination to divert yourself at the expense of your humble servant, as well as at her stays and head-dress; but you would certainly have fallen in love with me had you seen the fine figure I cut at the well. I have a notion the Hôtel de Carnavalet will suit us better than the other house we heard of, which is so small that not one of your people could possibly have been accommodated there. We shall see what the great D'Hacqueville will do. I tremble lest Madame de l'Islebonne should take it into her head to stay. I am still very uneasy about Corbinelli; he has been very severely handled by his ague, his delirium, and every thing that is frightful. He takes the potable gold; we shall see what effect it produces.* I desire you would still talk to me of yourself and your health. Do you use no method to repair the loss of your two bleedings? Good heavens! what a disorder! and what apprehensions must it give to those who love you! Here come the chevalier and the rest of my old companions, with one who certainly plays a better fiddle than Baptiste. We should be delighted to send you and M. de Grignan a chacone and an echo with which he charms us, and with which you would likewise be charmed. You shall hear him this winter.

LETTER LXVI.

PARIS, Friday, October 15, 1677.

We have been at Livri for these two days; Madame de Coulanges, who is quite well, doing the honors of the house,

* The time was at hand when the most pompous names given to the most complicated mixture, served to vail the ignorance of the chemists, physicians, and apothecaries, and to increase their bills. Potable gold was one of those whimsical remedies, of which muriatic acid was the basis. The solution of gold, which was added to it, was only used to swell the expense. Powdered pearls were also sometimes used to make their drugs still dearer. The severe Guy-Patin had no mercy upon these quacks. He calls them *Arabian cooks*, and laughs at their *farrago*. He, and some of his medical friends, prided themselves upon having destroyed this *colossal extortion*. Their triumph was premature. The cheap medicines they pretended to have restored, were not at that time received by people of rank; and it appears that Corbinelli was treated like a nobleman, whether he would or not.

and I the company. We had the Abbé Tetû and Corbinelli with us. Mademoiselle de Meri, who was returning from La Trousse, came there too, thinking to spend some days with Madame de Coulanges; but this lady has ended her campaign, and we all returned yesterday to Paris. Mademoiselle de Meri went directly to Madame de Mereuil's, for her own house was, it seems, in complete disorder; and Madame de Coulanges, the Abbé Tetû and I, paid some visits in the country, like Madame de la Fayette at Saint Maur, and Madame de Schomberg at Rambouillet. I thought of sleeping at Madame de Coulanges', but for that night only. I returned here to visit the good abbé, who has been bled, and is still much indisposed with his cold; I am sorry I could not help leaving him for this little moment. We live quite in the open air; all my people are as busy as bees in packing up for our removal. I encamped in my own bed-chamber; and am now in that of the *worthy*, my whole furniture being a little table, on which I now write to you, and that is sufficient. I fancy we shall all be pleased with our Hôtel de Carnavalet. We think it strange not to have seen Termes, though we have been home these nine days. It is easy to guess that he has returned to his college, and that his regent gives him not a moment's relaxation. I am not at all sorry, as you may very well suppose, and shall not reproach him for it; but ask the chevalier, whether, after the great pleasure he took in talking with me at Vichi, such extreme indifference be not very singular. It would certainly be very indiscreet, if the lady stood in need of being directed, and such conduct would be something to talk of; but it is impossible to do her any injury. I thought he seemed quite delighted at Vichi, on account of the vocation as you say, and to be with a good sort of woman, in full assurance of having no demands made upon him. This repose charmed him; there is sometimes great pleasure in passing from one extreme to another. He was mightily taken with the perpetual gossip of Vichi. You see what the consequence of this has been, at which I am under no sort of concern, but I tell it you as I do a thousand things else. When excess and imprudence are pushed to a certain extreme, I am persuaded they are more injurious to men than women; at least their fortunes are always sure to pay considerably for it. But let us leave Termes under the ferula; there is a good deal to be said of another *old ferula*,* which discovers its severity too much. As for you, my child, you enjoy a real vacation, and make an admirable use of the fine weather; to dine at home in your own house is a very extraordinary affair. You write to me from Rochecourbière—what a pretty place to date from! what a delightful grotto! How amiable you are to remember me at that delightful place, and to be sorry that I am not there to share its pleasures with you! Let us leave Providence to dispose of affairs at his pleasure; we shall see one another again, my love. In the mean time I shall prepare to receive you at Carnavalet, where I shall again have the pleasure of rendering you a thousand little services, which are of no real importance; but I am happy in the opportunity, because you wrote me word the other day, that little attentions were a stronger proof of friendship than any other. It is true, we can not set too high a value upon them; self-love has certainly too large a share in what we do on great occasions. *Tender interest is swallowed up in pride;* this is an idea of yours which I would not for the world deprive you of, as I find my account in it but too well.

I am, in regard to the loss of Bayard, precisely in the same disposition you guessed I was. Madame de la Fayette is utterly inconsolable. I have presented your compliments to

---

* This *old ferula* is apparently the Marchioness de Castelnau, who was long and publicly the mistress of M. de Termes. The *Amours des Gaules*, in which this is found, has very much defamed this marquis. If this part was written by Bussy as well as the rest, he must have been very wicked, for his letters show that the Marquis de Termes was his steady friend. He also possessed all the requisites to excite his jealousy. He was one of those in whom Boileau acknowledged a superior mind. "M. de Termes," said he, "is always of the opinion of others, and this is true politeness." (Vide la Bolcana.)

her. She was then living on a milk diet, which she has discontinued on account of its turning acid on her stomach; so that we have lost this sole ground of hope of the recovery of her desperate state of health. That of M. de Maine is certainly far from being good. He is at Versailles, where no one has seen him; they say he walks worse than he did. In short, I really fancy there is something in it.

LETTER LXVII.

Paris, Wednesday, October 27, 1677.

I shall no longer, my child, ask you why. In three words, my horses are thin, my tooth is loose, and my preceptor has got the king's evil. All this is dreadful. One might well make three grievances of these three answers, and especially of the second. I shall not ask you after this, whether your watch goes right, for you will then tell me it is broken. Paulina answers much better than you do; nothing can be more amusing than the little rogueries she means to be guilty of, when she says she will be *a rogue some day or other herself*. Ah, how sorry I am that I can not see this dear child! I fancy you will soon console me for this, if you pursue the plan I have laid down to you; you will set out at furthest in a week, and will not receive this letter at Grignan. M. de Coulanges is to set out to-day by the stage-coach for Lyons, where you will find him; he will inform you how delightfully we are accommodated. There was no hesitation in choosing the upper part of the house for you and me, and the lower for M. de Grignan and his daughters; so that all will be perfectly well.

I recommend to all your Grignans, who are so careful of your health, to see that you do not fall into the Rhône, by the cruel pleasure you take in exposing yourself to its greatest dangers. I entreat them to turn cowards, and to land with you. I find, besides, that I shall be very happy to administer to you some of my chicken-broth. The place you desire at my table, you may be assured is yours. The regimen which your Grignans prescribe for you is my ordinary fare. I agree with Grisoni to banish all ragouts.

LETTER LXVIII.

LIVRI, Wednesday, October 25, 1679.

I am here alone; I was loath to suffer any irksomeness but my own. No company tempts me to begin my winter so soon. If I chose it, I could assume an air of solitude; but after hearing Madame de Brisac say, the other day, that she was wholly engaged in her meditations, and had rather too much of her own company, I am proud to boast that I have passed this whole afternoon in the meadow, in conference with our sheep and cows. I have store of good books, especially Montaigne; what could I desire more, since I can not have you? I have the favor of your last letter at this place. You fancy I am at Paris, sitting in the chimney-corner, and have, no doubt, sitting by your own, received my lamentations on the fatigue of your journey; what a dreadful thing it is to be at such a distance! It is impossible to be more astonished than I was to find you with M. and Madame de Mêmes; I fancied you had been deceived, and that you were to have received them at Livri. They write to me to express how much they are charmed at the reception you have given them: they are very desirous to see me, which is the strongest inducement for my returning so speedily.

You are in the right to suppress Paulina's modesty; it will be worn out by the time she is fifteen; a premature and ill-timed modesty may have sad consequences. You are in jest, to thank Corbinelli for the compliment he paid your good sense. He merely thinks you superior to others; and when he says so, he says what he thinks, and has no intention to flatter you. He would have said a word or two in my letter, on the compliments you were pleased to make him; but this I intend to wave till my return. M. and Madame de Rohan have not thought of making him a present, out of the two thousand five hundred pistoles they received at the assembly of the States, under the title of the little prince of Leon. Some people have a strange destiny; Corbinelli's seems to be to hold in the most sovereign contempt what other folks prize in the highest degree. It is true, I was very much amused with his conversation, and that of the Abbé de Piles;* they agreed in many things, though there were some of harder digestion, which they seemed to chew upon. M. de Rochefoucault calls this eating hot peas: I am sure they had a good dish of them; for this forest is adapted for such things. The fat abbé has entered on his office of gazetteer, so you need be under no uneasiness about answers; he is better calculated for the office than I am.

Your brother is a strange creature; he could not, for the soul of him, help spoiling all the wonders he performed at the assembly of the States, by an absurd fancy and a pretense of being in love perfectly ridiculous. The object is a Mademoiselle de la Coste, upward of thirty years of age, without fortune or beauty; even her father says he is very sorry for it, and that it is by no means a fit match for M. de Sévigné; he writes me so himself; I commend and thank him for his prudence. What do you suppose your brother has done since? He has never quitted his damsel, but has followed her to Rennes and Lower Brittany, where she has gone under pretense of visiting Tonquedec; he has almost turned her brain, and has put her out of conceit with a very proper match she had in some degree contracted; it is the talk of the whole province. M. de Coulanges, and all my friends in Brittany, write to me about it, and are all persuaded he will certainly

* The same, probably, who has made himself known by his works on painting. He studied in the Sorbonne. He afterward went to Italy with the younger Amelot, whom he educated. He was also employed in several negotiations.

marry her. For my own part, I am convinced of the contrary; but I ask him why he so unnecessarily disgraces his poor head, after such a promising commencement? why he makes the lady reject an offer she now looks upon with the most sovereign contempt? and why this perfidy? If it is not perfidy, it will have some other name, since I am determined, let what will happen, never to sign the marriage-contract. If he be really in love, so much the worse, for this is a source of the most extravagant actions; but as I think him incapable of that passion, I should scruple, were I in his place, thus wantonly to wound the repose and the fortune of one he can so easily dispense with. He is now at the Rocks, from whence he writes to me about this journey to Tonquedec's, but not a syllable of his Dulcinea, or of this noble flame. Only in general terms, a great many fine things, and compliments without number. In short, it is an affair I leave entirely to the disposal of Providence.

LETTER LXIX.

PARIS, Friday, Nov. 10, 1679.

I am no longer a shepherdess, my poor child; I have left with regret my solitary conversation with your letters, and your image, aided by *Louison*, our cows and sheep, and the twilight, which I embraced with eagerness, because I would neither spare nor flatter myself. I am now in the refinements of the Hôtel de Carnavalet, where I find I am not less occupied with you, that your letters are not less dear to me, or that any thing in the world is capable of driving you from my thoughts. I shall have little news to tell you; I know scarcely any at present; but what I hear comes from good authority, and may be depended on. You assure me, my dearest child, you are perfectly well. God grant it be so; this is soon said. I wish you would not write me such long letters; I am certain they do you harm. Were it not for this consideration, you may believe I should be glad they were as long as possible; but this apprehension damps all the pleasure I receive from them. Du Chêne told me the other day nothing could be worse for you than much writing. The time must come, my child, when you will write less; and when you are here, you must think of your health, and your recovery. We will take care to put the Hôtel de Carnavalet in as good order as possible for you. The good abbé wishes this as much as I do. Pray, write me no more bad accounts of yourself, nor imagine that your letters are better than your conversation; I should be unworthy of your love were I capable of entertaining such a thought. I am convinced of your affection, and I have as much relish for your society as those who are most delighted with your conversation. Ah! did you know the power of a word, a look, a kind expression, or a caress from you, and from what distant countries one of these could bring me, you would be convinced, my beauty, that nothing is equal to your presence! The account of your devotion on All-Saints' day has affected me strangely. It was delightful to cram all your little ones into the same litter—dear little party! Had I been of your council, I should have given my vote for doing just as you did, as you will see by my advice to Paulina, in the regular answer I have written her. Lovely child! it is impossible she can ever tire you. Enjoy, my love, all these little comforts, and instead of thinking of depriving yourself of them, think of the numberless evils of this mortal and transitory life.

I finish this letter at Mademoiselle de Meri's, where I also close my packet. She is quite exhausted with the vapors and evacuations, and is incapable of writing a single syllable; she tells you by me all she should write to you if she were able. I have been just visiting that poor chevalier who keeps his bed with pains in his neck and hip. This rheumatic humor never leaves him; I have more compassion than other people for this disorder. I am of opinion his illness will not be of long continuance. He feels the serosities already beginning to dissipate. He wants a good pumping, if the season permitted it. He gave me his letter to inclose in my packet; these poor sick people must be taken care of; all the rest of Paris is ill of a cold:

> Ils ne mouraient pas tous; mais tous étaient frappés.
>
> They died not all; though none escaped a wound:*

as you used to say. Adieu, my dear girl! I embrace you with the warmest affection, with all your great and little party.

LETTER LXX.

PARIS, Wednesday, Nov. 22, 1679.

What I am going to tell you, my dear child, will both surprise and vex you. M. de Pomponne is out of favor; he had orders on Saturday evening, as he was returning from Pomponne, to resign his office. The king has directed that he should receive seven hundred thousand livres, and that his pension of twenty thousand livres a year, which he had as minister, should be continued to him; intending, by this, to show that he was satisfied with his fidelity. It was M. Colbert who gave him his information, assuring him at the same time that he was extremely mortified to be obliged, etc. M. de Pomponne asked him whether he might not be allowed the honor of speaking to the king, to learn from his own mouth what fault he had committed that brought this stroke upon him: he was told, he could not; so he wrote to the king, expressing his extreme sorrow, and his utter ignorance of what could have contributed to his disgrace. He mentioned his numerous family, and besought him to have compassion on his eight children. Immediately after, he caused the horses to be put into his carriage, and returned to Paris, where he arrived

---

* A verse of La Fontaine, in his fable of Les Animaux Malades de la Peste.

at twelve at night. M. de Chaulnes, Caumartin, and I, had been, as I wrote you, on the Friday at Pomponne, where we found him and the ladies, who received us with allt he pleasure imaginable. We chatted all the evening, and played at chess: ah! what a checkmate they were preparing for him at St. Germain! He went thither the next morning, because a courier waited for him; so that M. Colbert, who thought to find him on Saturday evening, as usual, knowing he was set out for St. Germain, returned instantly, and had nearly killed his horses. For ourselves, we did not leave Pomponne till after dinner, where we left the ladies. It was necessary to inform them of what had happened, by letter; this was brought by one of M. de Pomponne's valets, who arrived at nine on the Sunday at Madame de Vins' apartment; the man's precipitation, and his altered looks, made Madame de Vins fancy he had brought the account of M. de Pomponne's death; so that on finding he was only disgraced, she breathed again; but she felt the extent of his misfortune, and when she was sufficiently recovered went to acquaint her sister with it. They set out that instant, leaving all the little boys in tears; and arrived in Paris at two in the afternoon, overwhelmed with grief. You may figure to yourself this interview with M. de Pomponne, and what they felt on meeting each other in so different a situation from what they were in the evening before. I learned this sad intelligence from the Abbé de Grignan, and I confess to you it pierced me to the heart. I went to their house in the evening; they saw no company in public. I went up stairs, and found them all three. M. de Pomponne embraced me without being able to utter a word; the ladies could not restrain their tears, nor I mine. You would have wept too, my child; it was really a melancholy spectacle; the circumstance of our quitting each other at Pomponne so differently, augmented our sorrows. Poor Madame de Vins, whom I left in such spirits, could hardly be recognized; a fever of a fortnight could scarcely have altered her more. She mentioned you to me, and said she was persuaded you would feel for her and M. de Pomponne's affliction, which I assured her you would. We spoke of the blow she felt from this disgrace, both in regard to her affairs, her situation, and her husband's fortune. I do assure you, she feels all this in its greatest horror. M. de Pomponne, it is true, was not a favorite, but his situation gave him an opportunity to obtain certain common things, which often make our fortune. There are many inferior situations sufficient to make the fortunes of individuals. It was besides pleasant to be thus in a manner settled at court. What a change! what retrenching, what economy, must now be made use of in his family! Eight children, and not to have had time to obtain the smallest favor! They are thirty thousand livres in debt; you may suppose how little they will have left: they are going to a miserable retreat at Paris and Pomponne. It is said so many journeys, and sometimes the attendance of couriers, even that of Bavaria, who arrived on the Friday, and whom the king waited for with impatience, have contributed to draw this misfortune upon them.* But you will easily comprehend in this the ways of

* The memoirs and letters of the cotemporary writers all agree that M. de Pomponne's negligence was the cause of his disgrace. The more modern historians, even Hénault, keep to the received opinion. How could they fail to remark, that Louis XIV., in a memorandum written in his own hand, and mentioned by Voltaire, has himself explained very differently the cause of this minister's dismissal? "All that passed through his hands, lost the grandeur and strength it ought to have displayed, as being the orders of a king of France." These are his own words. Every one knows, in reality, that it was from the treaty of Nimeguen, a single year prior to M. de Pomponne's disgrace, the dominion and authority of Louis XIV. affected over all Europe, were dated. From this period his ministers treated the foreign embassadors with insulting arrogance. The famous chambers of reunion were established. Strasbourg was taken possession of by violence. Advances were made into Italy. No conciliatory measures were adopted. All the states were irritated.

But besides M. de Pomponne's having the crime of leaning toward the Jansenists, Louvois and Colbert, though enemies to each other, both labored to ruin him; the first to place his friend M. Courtin in

Providence, when I tell you, the President Colbert has his place; as he is in Bavaria, his brother officiates in his absence, and wrote to congratulate him, and to surprise him, on the back of the letter, as if by mistake; "To M. Colbert, Minister and Secretary of State." I paid my compliments of condolence to the unfortunate family. Reflect a little on the power of this family, as well at home as abroad, and you will easily perceive it far exceeds that of the other house where a wedding is going on.* My poor child, this is a long and circumstantial account; but I think, on such occasions, we can not be too particular; you are pleased we should always be talking to you, and in this instance I have perhaps complied with your desires too much. When your courier arrives, I shall have nowhere to send him; and it is an additional mortification to me to find I shall henceforth be entirely useless to you; though it is true, I was already so, by means of Madame de Vins; but that was meant in mere jest. In short, my child, all is now at an end, and such is the way of the world. M. de Pomponne is better qualified than any man upon earth to support this misfortune with courage and with truly Christian resignation. Those who have acted like him in prosperity, can not fail to be pitied in their misfortunes.

I must, however, add a word or two respecting your letter; it gave me real consolation. You tell me the little boy is quite recovered, and that I should be satisfied with yourself if I were to see you. Ah, my child, it is indeed true; what a delightful sight would it be to me to see you really occupied with the care of your health, by taking the necessary repose to recruit your wasted strength; it is a pleasure you have never yet afforded me. You find this care is by no means useless: you already discover its salutary effects; and if I tor-

his situation, and the second, his brother Colbert de Croissy. The last succeeded, to the great rage of Louvois.

* Madeleine-Charlotte le Tellier, daughter of M. de Louvois, married the next day, 23d November, Francis Duke of Rochefoucault and of Rocheguyon, grandson of M. de la Rochefoucault.

ture myself here by my endeavors to inspire you with the same attention to your welfare, you plainly see I have good reason.

LETTER LXXI.

PARIS, Friday, Nov. 24, 1679.

What a charming letter have I just received from you! what exquisite pleasure is it to hear you reason thus! What you say on the subject of medicine delights me. I am persuaded that, with that understanding and quickness of apprehension with which God has endowed you, you might, with a little application, soon outstrip the physicians themselves. You might, indeed, want a little experience, and perhaps, too, you might not kill with impunity as they do; but I would much sooner trust your judgment of a disease than theirs. The only real concern of life is undoubtedly the care of our health; the world seems to agree in this. The general question is, "How are you? how are you?" and yet we are in general wholly ignorant of every particular relating to this important science. Go on then, go on, my child; finish the course of your studies; the scarlet gown is all the diploma you will stand in need of, as in the play.* Pray, what do you mean by sending us your little physician? I assure you ours have entirely lost their credit here, except three or four of our acquaintance, and who prescribe the Englishman's recipe; all the rest are held in utter abhorrence. This Englishman recovered Marshal de Bellefond the other day from death's door. I do not think the first physician has the right secret.

Is it then true, my child, you have got the better of your complaints? No more pains in the chest, no colic, no pain in the legs? This is as it should be. You see the advantage of repose and taking care to recruit yourself. Can you be angry with me for chiding you when you neglect yourself, and in-

* Molière's Malade Imaginaire.

humanly abandon all care of your health? I could talk for
ten years about this wicked conduct in you, and the benefits
that result from a contrary conduct. Why can not I embrace
you and enjoy your company here in the evenings? I enter
this house with a heavy heart. From nine till twelve at night
I am as desolate as I was at Livri, and yet I prefer this silence
and repose to all the evening parties I am invited to in this
part of the town. I hate going out of an evening. When I
am not tormented with fears for your health, I feel your absence more. The thought of your lungs is like pinching the
ear to prevent the pain of boring it from being felt: this comparison I heard from you, but the former pain soon returns
when I am not checked by the other. I confess I never bear
your absence so well as when I am in fear for your health, and
I thank you a thousand times for removing the pincers from
my ears. Madame de Vins stands in need of some equally
powerful means to remove her affliction at M. de Pomponne's
disgrace, by which she loses her all. I often visit her, and no
misfortune shall ever drive me from the house. M. de Pomponne will easily resolve on what is to be done, and will bear
his ill-fortune with dignity; he will again display the virtues
of a private station, for which we so much admired him at
Frene. They say he was rather remiss in his office, and made
the couriers wait too long for their dispatches. He justifies
himself fully. But, good heavens! do we not plainly see where
the fault lies! Ah! how would poor Madame du Plessis have
adored him now! and how would this similarity of situation
have cemented their union! Nothing in the world would
have been so fortunate for him. I have mentioned this to no
one but Madame de Vins; I suppose you understand me. I
can answer for the justice of my opinion, which is, I dare say,
your own. The whole court pities him, and have been to pay
him their compliments of condolence on the occasion. You will
soon see him recommence the thread of his perfections. We
have talked a great deal about Providence, a doctrine he understands perfectly well. Surely there never was so worthy a

minister. M. Colbert, the embassador,* is to succeed in this office; he is a great friend of the chevalier's. Write all your thoughts to the latter; perhaps Fortune, capricious as she is, intends you should reap more advantage through his means than from our intimate acquaintance. You will easily strike into the right road by what I tell you. How is it possible for us to know what Providence has in store for us?

I continue my attentions to Mademoiselle de Méri; the impression the misfortune of her little domestic makes on her is very extraordinary. She tells me she fancies, when any one speaks to her, they are shooting at her, as if they had an intention to kill her. This really does her as much harm as her illness. It is a circle; her anger increases her disorder, and her disorder increases her anger. The sum total is, that it is a very strange affair, and I employ all my attention to administer to her relief.

Corbinelli gives up the Chevalier de Méri, with his pitiful style,† and the ridiculous critique he makes on a wit so free, so playful, so charming, as Voiture's: those are to be pitied who do not understand him.‡ I would not have you depend on receiving the definition you asked of him, for he has read nothing these three months but the Code and the Cujas. He is delighted with you for resolving to study medicine: you are

---

* Mons. de Colbert de Croissy, brother to the comptroller-general, was then in Bavaria, in order to conclude a marriage between Monseigneur and Maria Anna Victoria of Bavaria.

† M. de Méri had known and loved Madame de Maintenon from her infancy. He had brought her out into the world under the name of the Young Indian. He cultivated her friendship in all circumstances. But what is singular is, that he would have married her, and that he made her the offer of his hand at the very time that Louis thought of making her his wife. The letters of M. de Méri, which were found in Madame de Maintenon's collection, were indeed emphatic, heavy, and pedantic, and well deserved the name " pitiful style" (chien de style).

‡ The French editors observe, justly enough, that as much may be said in regard to those who can not find out the value of these letters of Madame de Sévigné.

a prodigy in his opinion. The calm ingratitude of M. and Madame Richelieu is indeed a prodigy; you describe it very pleasantly. M. le Grand, and some others, said seriously the other day at St. Germain, that M. Richelieu had made an admirable siege: it was supposed he had been reading some book about the great Richelieu's in the civil wars; not so, he meant Richelieu the tapestry-maker, who has made an admirable siege that hangs in his wife's apartment.

Madame de Coulanges has been at court this fortnight; Madame de Maintenon had a cold, and would not part with her. I must tell you of a quarrel she had with the Countess de Grammont.* The latter was scorching her fine complexion over the fire, making chocolate; Madame de Coulanges would have saved her the trouble. The Countess bid her leave her to herself, for it was the only pleasure she had left. Madame de Coulanges answered, "Ah, ingrate!" This expression, which at any other time would have made her laugh, embarrassed and disconcerted her so highly, that she could not get the better of it, and they have not spoken since. The Abbé Tetû said, very rudely, to our neighbor, "But, madame, had she answered you, 'The pot calls the kettle black,' what would you have found to say?" "Sir," said she, "I am no pot, though she is a kettle." So here is another quarrel. *Quanto* and the sick lady are both on the high ropes; the latter is so much in favor with the fountain of all good things, that it occasions a great deal of animosity. I could tell you a thousand trifles if you were here.

Ah, my child, you tell me I have nothing to do but laugh, when I have your absence to support; I could almost find in my heart to say, "Ah! ingrate!" Do not you remember what this absence of yours has made me suffer? Are not you the sensible and true occupation of my heart? You well know, and you ought to feel, what a terrible addition the fear of hearing you are indisposed, and chilled by the piercing air

---

* Elizabeth Hamilton, lady of the bed-chamber to Queen Maria Theresa, of Austria.

of Grignan, makes to this apprehension. You are unjust if you are at a loss to guess my sentiments, which are so very natural, and so full of true affection for you.

LETTER LXXII.

PARIS, Friday, January 26, 1680.

I begin with the state of your health, as the subject nearest my heart. It is without disparagement to this favorite idea, that I see and hear what passes in the world. Events are more or less interesting to me as they are more or less connected with you; even the attention I pay to news springs from the same source. I find you well nursed, my dear child, and kept in cotton. You are not in the whirlwind, so that I am perfectly easy with regard to your quiet; but then I am by no means so with respect to that heaviness, and those heats you are troubled with; and then again that pain you endure, with no north-easterly winds, or extraordinary fatigue to occasion it. I could wish to have a little further information on this particular, which is of so much importance to me. The care that is taken of you can not be wholly owing to precaution, nor without good reason. I wish you may be sincere in your resolution, no longer to destroy yourself with your writing-desk. Confirm me, I beseech you, in my good opinion of you, and never again write me such long letters, since Montgobert acquits herself so well of the office; and, as I have already told you, may also save you the trouble of dictating. I could wish, too, she would now and then add a word or two of her own, relative to the state of your health.

I have at last received a letter from my son, who is at Nantes. He was but twenty days on the road; he traveled only ninety leagues from Brittany in the month of January, to spend the holidays, and without one spark of love in his heart! I have written to him to take care how he tells this story to others, and that, to save his reputation, he ought to allege some flame, real or pretended; otherwise he would appear more a Breton than the Bretons themselves. I have also entreated him not to stay at Nantes, on account of my affairs; they are not a plausible excuse, and I should be sorry to pass for so silly or so covetous a being, as to prefer things which are of no consequence to the necessity of his paying his attendance at court on such an occasion as the present. He seems to me to be under some embarrassment; but he will return soon enough to set out with M. de Chaulnes. Mark my goodness, I have secured him a place in his carriage.

Madame de Soubise is no longer talked of; she even seems forgotten already. In fact, there are a thousand other things to employ our attention at present; and I am foolish enough myself to venture on some other topic. For these two days it has been, as in the affair of mademoiselle and M. de Lauzun, a constant bustle, sending to learn the news, paying visits from house to house, to learn what is passing; curiosity is on the stretch, and this is what has come out, in expectation of the remainder.*

* La Voisin, La Vigoreux, and a priest of the name of Le Sage, known at Paris as conjurers and casters of nativities, added to this jugglery the secret practice of poisons, which they denominated *succession powder*. They did not fail to accuse those who applied to them for one thing, of having had recourse to them for another. It is thus Marshal de Luxembourg was exposed, by his intendant Bonard, for having made some extravagant exorcism with Le Sage, for the purpose of recovering his lost papers. The vindictive Louvois seized the opportunity to ruin, or, at least, to torment him.

Besides the persons here named, Madame de Polignac was decreed to be imprisoned, and Madame de la Ferté, as well as the Countess du Roure, to be personally summoned.

The Countess de Soissons was accused of having poisoned her husband; Madame d'Alluie, her father-in-law; Madame de Tingry, her children; Madame de Polignac, a valet who was in possession of her secret; and this secret was, that she wished to give the king a charm, to make herself beloved by him.

The king gave the Duchess de Foix a note, written by her to La Voisin, expressed in these terms, "The more I rub the less they pro-

M. de Luxembourg was at Saint Germain on Wednesday; the king frowned on him more than usual; he was told there was a warrant issued to apprehend him; he asked to be permitted to speak to the king; you may conjecture what was said. The king told him that if he were innocent, he had nothing to do but to throw himself voluntarily into prison, and that he had appointed such upright judges to make inquiry into affairs of this kind, that he left every thing to them. M. de Luxembourg immediately took coach, and went to Father de la Chaise; Mesdames de Lavardin and De Mouri met him as they were coming here, in a very melancholy mood, in the Rue Saint Honoré; after passing an hour at the convent of the Jesuits, he repaired to the Bastile, and delivered to Barsemeaux* the order he brought from Saint Germain. He was at first shown into a tolerably handsome chamber. Madame de Meckelbourg† came there to visit him, and was almost drowned in tears. About an hour after she left him, an order came to confine him in one of those horrible places in the towers, of which the windows are closed with iron bars, so as scarcely to admit the light of day, and to suffer no one to see him. This, my child, is ample subject for reflection; think of the brilliant fortune of such a man, raised to the honor of commanding in chief the king's armies, and then figure to yourself what his feelings must be on hearing those grating bolts shut upon him, and, if it were possible for him to sleep, what his thoughts must be when he awakes! No one thinks there has been any poison in his affair. This is a misfortune that seems to obliterate every other.

Madame de Tingres is summoned to give evidence on the

ject." He required an explanation. It alluded to a recipe to increase the size of the bosom. She informed La Voisin that her drug was ineffectual.

It may be supposed that La Voisin had many of these secrets for the use of ladies.

* Governor of the Bastile.

† Sister of M. de Luxembourg, formerly Madame de Chatillon.

trial. The Countess de Soissons could not endure the thoughts of a prison; she has been allowed time to make her escape, if she really is guilty. She was playing at basset on the Wednesday when M. de Bouillon came in; he begged her to step with him into the closet, where he told her she must either leave France, or go to the Bastile; she was not long in determining what to do. She immediately called the Marchioness d'Allure from the card-table, and they have never appeared since. When the hour of supper came, they were told the Countess supped in town; the whole company broke up, thinking something very extraordinary had happened. In the mean time, parcels are packed up, with money, jewels, etc., the male servants have gray liveries, and eight horses are put to the carriage. She made the Marchioness d'Allure, who they say was unwilling to go, sit behind, on the same side with her, and two female servants in the front. She told her people not to be uneasy on her account, that she was innocent, but that some vile women* had taken pleasure in implicating her; she wept, called on Madame de Carignan, and left Paris at three in the morning. It is said she is gone to Namur; you may be sure nobody wants to follow her. She will, notwithstanding, be tried in her absence, if it be only to clear her reputation to the world; there is a great deal of detraction in what La Voisin says. It is believed the Duke de Villeroy† is very much concerned at it; he keeps his room, and sees nobody. Perhaps I may be able to tell you more before I seal my letter.

Madame de Vibraye has fallen into the old train of devotion; God, as you well remarked, would not suffer her to pass her whole life in the company of her enemies. Madame de Buri turns her talking-mill with very great address. If the princess is to be seen at Paris, Madame de Vins wishes me to

---

* La Voisin and her associates in their witchcrafts, etc.

† Francis Neuville, afterward Marshal of France. He had been the lover, and was the intimate friend, of the Countess de Soissons.

accompany her when she goes there. Pomenars has been cut for the stone; did I not tell you so? I have seen him; it is pleasant to hear him talk of the poisons; one is almost tempted to say to him, "Is it possible this crime alone should be unknown to you?" Volonne gives his opinion, without any hesitation, and wonders how any one could hold a correspondence with these *vile women*. The Queen of Spain is, in a manner, as much confined as M. de Luxembourg. Madame de Villars wrote to Madame de Coulanges the other day, that were it not for her love to M. de Villars, she would not have consented to pass the winter at Madrid. She gives Madame de Coulanges many pleasant and entertaining narratives, as she thinks they will go further.* I am overjoyed to have the pleasure of perusing her letters, without the trouble of answering them. Madame de Vins thinks as I do. M. de Pomponne is gone to breathe the air of Pomponne, where he means to stay three days; he has received all, and given up all; so that affair is finished. It really pains me to hear him always asking, What news? He is as much a stranger to what is passing as one living on the banks of the Marne; he is in the right to make his mind as happy as he can. Mine, as well as the abbé's, was much affected at what you wrote with your own hand; you did not feel it, my dear child, but it was impossible to read it without tears. Good heavens! you pronounce yourself as good for nothing, as an encumbrance to the earth; to one who sees no object in existence but you! Think of the consequences your talking thus may produce. I beseech you, never henceforth to say any ill of your humor. Your heart and mind are too perfect to suffer such light clouds to be perceived; be a little more tender of truth and justice, as well as of the sole object of my vows and prayers. I shall think myself really dead till I have the gratification of seeing you.

* Madame de Coulanges, passing her life at court, with Madame de Maintenon, and even with Mademoiselle de Fontanges, could easily report these agreeable narratives to the king.

LETTER LXXIII.

Paris, Wednesday, January 31, 1680.

It is impossible for me to see your hand-writing without emotion. I well know the injury writing does you; and though you say the most affectionate and most amiable things to me possible, I regret exceedingly the purchase of that pleasure at the expense of your lungs; I know you are still far from well. You tell me the weather is extremely mild, and that you do not fatigue yourself, and that you write less than usual: whence, then, proceeds this obstinacy in your disorder? You are dumb on that subject, and Montgobert has the cruelty, though she has the pen in her hand, not to say a single word about it. What is the rest of the world to me, and what pleasure can I receive from the account of all the rejoicings at Aix, when I find you are obliged to go to bed at eight in the evening? "But," say you, "do you then wish me to sit up late and fatigue myself?" No, my dearest; God forbid I should be capable of forming so depraved a wish; but when you were here, you were not wholly incapable of relishing the sweets of society. I have at length seen M. de Gordes; he told me, with great sincerity, that you were in a very feeble state in the boat, and that you were much better at Aix: but then, with the same simplicity he assures me, that the air of Provence is too keen, too piercing, and too drying, in your present condition. When we are in health, nothing is amiss; but when the lungs are attacked, and we are thin and delicate, like you, we run the risk of putting it out of our power ever to recover. Tell me no more that the delicacy of your lungs draws our ages nearer together. God forbid that the order established by Providence, so agreeable to nature and reason, and at the same time so dear to me, should be deranged with respect to us.

I must resume the article of news, which I always suffer to rest awhile when I get upon the subject of your health. M. de Luxembourg has been two days without eating; he asked for several Jesuits, but has been refused every one of them: he asked to have the Lives of the Saints, and it has been given him; you will see he is at a loss *to which of the Saints he shall devote himself.* He was interrogated for four hours on Friday or Saturday, I can not recollect which; after that his mind appeared much relieved, and he ate some supper. It is thought he would have done better to have made his innocence take the field, and to have left word he would return, when his proper judges* should think fit to summon him. He has done a real injury to the dukedom, in acknowledging the chamber; but he was willing to yield a blind obedience to the commands of his majesty. M. de Cessac has followed the example of the countess. Mesdames de Bouillon and De Tingry were interrogated on Monday at the chamber of the arsenal. Their noble families attended them to the gate: there is yet no appearance of blackness in the follies which have been laid to their charge, nor even so much as a shade of gray. Should nothing further be discovered, this is a scandal which might very well have been spared, especially to families of their high quality. Marshal de Villeroy † says, these gentlemen and ladies do not believe in God, though they believe in the devil. In reality, a great many ridiculous things are related respecting the private transactions of these abominable women. Madame de la Ferté, who is so properly named, went out of complaisance (to La Voisin's) with the Countess (de Soissons), but did not go up stairs; M. de Langres accompanied Madame de la Ferté; this is very black; the circumstance has given her a pleasure not often enjoyed by her, which is, to hear it said that she is innocent.‡ The Duchess de Bouillon went to ask La Voisin for a small dose of poison, to kill an old tiresome husband she had, and a nostrum to

* The parliament of Paris.

† Nicholas de Neufville, Marshal Duke de Villeroy, father to the last marshal of that name.

‡ The Amours des Gaules have rendered notorious her gallantries, which may be called by a term less mild.

marry a young man she loved. This young man was M. de Vendôme, who led her by one hand, and M. de Bouillon, her husband, by the other. When a *Mancine** is guilty only of a folly like this, information is given of it; and these witches explain it seriously, and shock all Europe with a mere trifle. The Countess de Soissons asked whether she could not recover a lover who had deserted her? this lover was a great prince; and it is asserted that she declared, unless he returned to her, she would make him repent his ingratitude: that is understood to be the king, and every thing is of importance that has relation to him; but let us look to the sequel; if she has committed any greater crime, she has not mentioned it to these baggages. One of our friends says there is an elder branch of the poison, to which they never refer, as it is not a native of France. What we have here, are younger branches only, without shoes to their feet. La T*** † gives us to understand there is something of greater consequence behind, as she was schoolmistress to the novices. She says, "I admire the world; it really believes I have had children by M. de Luxembourg." Alas! God knows whether she has or not; the present prevailing opinion, however, is in favor of the innocence of the persons denounced, and a universal horror for the defamers; to-morrow it may be the reverse. You well know the nature of these general opinions; I shall give you a faithful account of them; it is the only subject of conversation here: indeed there is scarcely an example of such scandal in any court in Christendom. It is said La Voisin put all the infants, whose abortion she had procured, into an oven; and Madame de Coulanges, as you may suppose, when speaking of La T***, says, *it was for her the oven was heating.*

I had a long chat yesterday with M. de la Rochefoucault,

---

* Madame de Bouillon, as well as the Countess de Soissons, was the niece of Cardinal Mazarin. It will be seen that she was innocent.

† Madame de Tingry being named twice in this letter and the preceding one, is it not probable that she is intended by the initial T.? She was related to M. de Luxembourg.

on a subject we have already discussed. There is nothing to oblige you to write; but he entreats you to believe that what could give him the highest gratification in the world would be to have it in his power to contribute to your changing the place of your residence, should an opportunity offer. I never saw so obliging or so amiable a man.

What I am going to tell you, I have heard from good authority. Madame de Bouillon entered the chamber like a queen, sat down on a chair placed there on purpose for her, and, instead of answering to the first question that was asked her, demanded that what she should say might be taken down in writing; it was, "that her sole reason for coming there was from the respect she bore to the king's command, and not in obedience to the chamber, whose authority she in nowise acknowledged, as she would not derogate from the privileges of the dukedom." Every word was written down. When she took off her glove, she discovered a very beautiful hand. Her answers were very sincere; those respecting her age not excepted. "Do you know La Vigoureux?" "No." "Do you know La Voisin?" "Yes." "What reason had you to desire the death of your husband?" "Desire the death of my husband! ask him whether he believes a syllable of it. He gave me his hand to the very gate." "But what was your reason for so often visiting La Voisin?" "Because I wanted to see those Sibyls she promised me I should see; a company which certainly well deserved all this noise and scrutiny." "Did you not show that woman a bag of money?" She answered, "I did not, and for more reasons than one;" and then with a smiling, and at the same time a disdainful air, "Well, gentlemen, have you done with me?" "Yes, madame." She rose, and, as she was going out, said loud enough to be heard, "I really could not have believed that men of sense would have asked so many foolish questions." She was received by all her friends and relations with adoration, she was so pretty, easy, natural, firm, unconcerned, and tranquil.*

* To render this picture complete, it is necessary to cite another

La T*** was by no means so cheerful. M. de Luxembourg is perfectly disconcerted: he is neither a man, nor half a man, nor even a woman, unless it be a foolish woman. "Shut this window; light a fire; give me some chocolate; give me that book; I have abandoned God, and God has abandoned me." This is the conduct he displayed before Baisemeaux and his commissaries, with a countenance pale as death. With nothing better than this to carry to the Bastile, he had better have gained time, as the king, with infinite goodness, had put into his power to do, till the very moment before he committed himself; but we must of necessity have recourse to Providence, in spite of our efforts to the contrary. It was by no means natural to behave as he has done, weak as he appears to be.*
I was misinformed: Madame de Meckelbourg has not seen him; and La T***, who came with him from St. Germain, never intended, any more than himself, to give Madame de Meckelbourg the least notice of it, though he had time enough to have done it if he had been so inclined; but La T*** kept every one from seeing him, and watched him so closely, that not a soul came to him but herself. I have been to see this Meckelbourg at the nunnery of the Holy Sacrament, where she has retired. She is in great affliction, and complains loudly of La T***, whom she blames for all her brother's misfortunes. I made your compliments to her by way of anticipation, and assured her you would be extremely grieved to hear of

stroke related by Voltaire. "La Reynie, one of the presidents of this chamber, was so ill-advised as to ask the Duchess de Bouillon if she had seen the devil. She replied that she saw him at that moment; that he was very ugly, and very dirty, and was disguised as a counselor of state. The questioner proceeded no further.

* Madame de Sévigné seems to have adopted, at this moment, the ridiculous reports spread abroad, in regard to M. de Luxembourg. But is it to be credited that a soul like his was capable of such weakness as was laid to his charge? And does it not rather exhibit the common conduct of envy and malignity, which, in the life-time of men of the first order, are incessantly endeavoring to tarnish the luster of their reputation?

her ill-fortune. She expressed great regard for you. One might, at this time, do almost what one pleased at Paris, it would not be noticed.

LETTER LXXIV.

PARIS, Wednesday, February 7, 1680.

So, my child, you sometimes play at chess. For my own part, I am an enthusiast in this game, and would give the world if I could learn to play it like my son or you. It is the finest and most rational game of any; chance has nothing to do with it; we blame or applaud ourselves, and our success depends upon our skill. Corbinelli would fain make me believe I shall acquire it. He says I have some ideas and schemes of my own; but I can not see three or four moves forward into the game. I assure you I shall be much ashamed and mortified if I do not, at least, attain mediocrity. Every one played it at Pomponne when I was last there—men, women, and children; and while the master of the house was beating M. de Chaulnes, he met with a strange *check* at St. Germain.

There has been a sad melancholy Monday, which you will easily comprehend. M. de Pomponne is at length gone to court. He dreaded this very much. You may guess what his thoughts were on the road, and when he beheld the court at Saint Germain, and received the compliments of the courtiers who surrounded him. He was quite overcome; and when he entered the chamber where the king was waiting for him, what could he say, or how begin? The king assured him he had always been satisfied of his fidelity and services; that he was perfectly at ease as to the state secrets he was acquainted with; and that he would give him and his family proofs of his regard. M. de Pomponne could not help shedding tears when he mentioned the misfortune he had to incur his displeasure. He added, that with respect to his family, he left it entirely to his majesty's goodness; that his only grief was the being removed from the service of a master to whom he was attached, as well by inclination as duty; that it was next to impossible not to feel so heavy a loss in all its severity; that this cut him to the quick, and caused him to betray those marks of weakness, which he hoped his majesty would forgive. The king told him he was himself affected at them, that they proceeded from goodness of heart, and that he ought not to be offended. The whole discourse turned on this, and M. de Pomponne came away with eyes somewhat red, and the looks of a man who had not merited his misfortune. He told me all this yesterday evening: he could have wished to have been more firm, but he could not get the better of his emotion. This is the only occasion in which he has appeared too much affected; though it might be said he had not paid his court badly, if to pay court had been his object. He will soon recover his philosophy, and in the mean time an affair of some importance is concluded; these are renewals which we can not help feeling with him. Madame de Vins has been at Saint Germain: good God, what a difference! She had attentions enough paid her; but to reflect that that had been her home, where she has not now a corner to shelter her head in! I felt what she underwent in that journey. Adieu, my beloved child; I am always impatient to hear from you, but pray write only two words to me; renounce long letters forever, and spare me. It is horrible to think that those who love you, and who are beloved by you, should be the ruin of your health.

LETTER LXXV.

Paris, Friday, Feb. 9, 1680.

I see you are in the midst of the pleasures of the carnival, my beautiful dear; you give little *private* suppers to eighteen or twenty ladies; I am well acquainted with your mode of life, and the heavy expenses you incur at Aix; but yet, amid all this bustle, I fancy you contrive to have plenty of rest.

We say sometimes, I will have pleasure for my money; but I think I hear you say, I will have rest for mine : take your rest then, and enjoy, at least, this advantage. I can not help being surprised that a minuet-tune does not tempt you sometimes; what! not a single step ! no motion of the shoulders! quite insensible! it is not to be believed, it is unnatural; I never yet knew you sit still on these occasions, and, were I to draw such inferences as I commonly do, I should imagine you much worse than you say you are.

There was, yesterday evening, an enchanting entertainment at the Hotel de Condé. The Princess of Conti named one of the duke's daughters, with the Prince de la Roche-sur-Yon. First was the christening, then the dinner; but what a dinner! then a play, but what a play! interspersed with fine pieces of music, and the best opera-dancers. A theater built by the fairies; such perspectives, orange-trees loaded with fruits and flowers, festoons, pilasters, scenes, and other decorations; in short, the whole expense of the evening cost no less than two thousand louis-d'ors, all for the sake of the pretty princess.

The opera (of Proserpine) is superior to every other. The chevalier tells me he has sent you several of the airs, and that he saw a gentleman* who said he had sent you the words; I dare say you will like it. There is a scene in it,† between Mercury and Ceres, which requires no interpreter to be understood; it must have been approved, since it has been performed; but you will judge for yourself.

The poisoning affair is grown quite flat; nothing new is said of it. The report is, that there will be no more blood spilled; you will make your own reflections, as we do. The Abbé Colbert is made Coadjutor of Rouen. They talk of a journey into Flanders. No one knows what this assembling of the forces portends.

Friar Ange has raised Marshal de Bellefond from the dead; he has cured his lungs, that were incurable. Madame de

---

* Quinault.   † See the second scene of the first act.

Coulanges and I have been to visit the grand-master,* who has been almost at death's door for a fortnight past; his gout had returned; add to this an oppression, which made every one suppose he was at his last gasp; cold sweats, light-headedness; in short, he was ill as it was possible to be. The physicians could give him no relief; he sent for Friar Ange, who has cured him, and brought him from the very gates of death, by the gentlest and most agreeable medicines; the oppression went off, the gout fell back into his knees and feet, and he is now out of danger.

Adieu, my dear child! I still lead the same life, either in the suburbs, or with these good widows; sometimes here, sometimes eating chicken with Madame de Coulanges; but always pleased to think I am gliding down the stream with old Time, and hastening the happy moment when I shall see you again.

LETTER LXXVI.

PARIS, Wednesday, Feb. 14, 1680.

I think you extremely fortunate in the society of Madame du Janet, who is come on purpose for you; this is a friendship that pleases me. I am fully persuaded her whole employment will be to take care of your health; pray embrace her for me. You give yourself very little concern about the vanities of this world; I think I see you constantly retiring and going to bed, leaving the rest to sing and dance by themselves; you will have rest for your money, as I told you the other day.

Montgobert has related to me, very pleasantly, the maneuvers of the beautiful Iris, and the jealousy of the count; I dare say he will often see the moon with this beauty; he has revenged himself for this time, by a very pretty song. Montgobert made me laugh at her respect for M. de Grignan. She had written, that he came to the ball *la gueule enfarinée* (full

---

* The Duke de Lude.

of expectation): she recollected herself, erased the *gueule*, and wrote the *bouche*, so that it is now *la bouche enfarinée.* .

The gendarmes are quite bewildered. My son goes to Flanders, instead of meeting the dauphiness. The army is assembling, they say, to take Charlemont.* We know nothing certain, except that the officers are going to the army, and that in a month there will be an army of fifty thousand infantry. The chevalier's regiment is not one of them.

The chamber of the arsenal is again sitting. One of the committee, whose name is not mentioned, said to M. de la Reynie: "But, sir, as far as I see, we are only employed about sorceries and witchcraft, such diabolical proceedings, of which the parliament of Paris never takes cognizance. Our commission is, to try the case of poisoning; how comes it that we inquire into any thing else?" La Reynie was surprised, and said, "Sir, we have secret orders." "Be so good, sir," replied the other, "as to communicate those orders to us, and we will obey them as well as you; but, as we are without your knowledge, I think I say nothing contrary to reason and justice, in thus expressing myself." I am of opinion you will not blame this man's honesty, though he does not wish to be known. There are so many persons of worth belonging to this chamber, that you will find it difficult to guess who he is.

* One of the conditions of the treaty with Spain was, that France, with other places that were given up to her, should have either Dinant or Charlemont. But the emperor, whose consent was necessary, having preferred keeping Dinant, France was put in possession of Charlemont. There was only a military demonstration. It was upon this acquisition of Charlemont, M. de Coulanges wrote some verses ending with,

>Louis est un enfant gâté;
>On lui laisse tout faire.

"Louis is a spoiled child; he is suffered to do what he pleases."

This complaisance throughout Europe cost dear to France. The king, habituated thus to have his own way, adopted three fatal resolutions: he revoked the Edict of Nantes, protected James II., and accepted the testament of the King of Spain.

The little Prince de Léon was baptized yesterday at Saint Gervais, by a bishop of Brittany; M. de Rennes stood godfather, as representing the States of Brittany; the duchess was godmother. The rest were all Brittany folks: the Governor of Brittany, the Lieutenant-General of Brittany, the Treasurer of Brittany, the Deputies of Brittany, several Lords of Brittany, the Presidents of Brittany, father and son. In short, had there been a dance, they would have danced Brittany dances; and have eaten Brittany butter, had it been a meager day. I assure you, my son feels all the secret power which attaches the Bretons to their country; he is returned perfectly enchanted with it. He has begun, for the first time in his life, to admire Tonquedec, and to think him worthy of imitation. It would be like stopping the course of the Rhône, to oppose this torrent, which carries him so far as even to dispose him to sell his place. He said this to Gourville and several others, before he mentioned it to me. He assigns very good reasons. He looks forward. He fears the disgusts which may be occasioned by means of M. de la Trousse. He is sorry for those who are appointed to the gendarmerie, and has no wish to be ruined. The sum of the matter is, that by thus discovering his inmost heart, he would reduce us to the necessity of saying, "Certainly, he is perfectly in the right to sell his place." I can not reproach myself with concealing what my duty obliged me to say on this strange resolution, in which I expressed myself with the freedom I sometimes indulge myself in. I desired him to wait for at least some pretext, some shadow of dissatisfaction; in short, to stay for something that may serve to keep his real thoughts undiscovered. But it was to no purpose; for all M. de la Garde and I have been able to do, is to beg he will not interfere. We are overjoyed at his absence, as it may be a means of preventing his doing injury to his affairs, by decrying his own goods. I told him it was very unfortunate to value commissions merely from whim and caprice, by his liking and disliking; to pay an exorbitant price for the ensigncy, because he was wild for it—to rate the sublieutenancy at nothing, because he is disgusted with it. Is it thus we would buy and sell, unless we were fools, ignorant of business, and wished to ruin ourselves? Adieu, my beloved child; be not uneasy on this account. Let us adore the dispensations of Providence, whose kindness sends us no greater subject of complaint. I shall still possess my mind in liberty, for I shall still be as much yours as ever. This will make no change in me; quite the contrary, quite the contrary.

LETTER LXXVII.

PARIS, Friday, February 23, 1680.

Indeed, my child, this has been a very pretty week for the Grignans; should Providence favor the elder brother in proportion as it has the younger, we might soon expect to see him in a charming situation. In the mean time, I think it no disagreeable thing to have brothers in such favor. The chevalier had scarcely returned thanks for his pension of a thousand crowns, when he was chosen, out of eight or ten persons of quality and merit, to be an attendant upon the dauphin, with a salary of two thousand crowns; so here are appointments to the value of nine thousand livres a year, in the space of three days. He immediately went back to Saint Germain with his second acknowledgments, for it seems he had been appointed in his absence, while he was here in Paris. His personal merit has greatly contributed to this choice. His distinguished reputation, his strict honor and probity, and the regularity of his conduct, have been remarked; and it is the general opinion, that his majesty could not have made a better choice. There are but eight persons named yet, Dangeau, D'Antin, Clermont, Sainte-Maure, Matignon, Chiverni, Florensac, and Grignan.* The last is universally approved.

* These were afterward reduced to six, viz., MM. Dangeau, D'Antin, Saint-Maure, Chiverni, Florensac, and Grignan.

Permit me, then, to pay my compliments of congratulation to M. de Grignan, the coadjutor, and yourself.

My son sets out to-morrow; he has read the reproaches you make him. Possibly the charms of the court he wishes to leave, and where he has so handsome an establishment, will make him change his opinion. We have prevailed on him not to be in a hurry, but to wait quietly till he meets with the temptation of a greater sum than he gave.

You have given me a specimen of M. de Grignan's joy by my own, in hearing that you are better. As your complaints are no longer continual, I am in great hopes that, by taking care of yourself, using a milk diet, and giving up writing, you will in the end restore my daughter to me as lovely as ever.

I am charmed with Montgobert's sincerity. Had she always written me word you were well, I should never have given credit to her. She has managed the whole business to a miracle, and has won my heart by her candor; so natural is it for us to love not to be deceived. May Heaven preserve you, my dear, in this prosperous state! which gives us all such flattering hopes. But to return to the Grignans, for we seem to have forgotten them. Nothing else is talked of here. Nothing but complimenting passes in this house; one has scarcely done when another begins. I have not seen either of them since the chevalier has been made a lady of honor, as M. de Rochefoucault calls it. He will write you all the news much better than I can possibly do. It is supposed that Madame de Soubise will not be one of the traveling party. See how long my letter is growing! Well, I will only mention La Voisin's affair, and conclude.

She was not burned on Wednesday, as I wrote you word; the sentence was not executed till yesterday. She knew her fate on the Monday, a very extraordinary circumstance! In the evening, she said to those who guarded her, "What! no medianoches!" She ate with them at midnight out of whim, for it was no fast-day, drank plentifully of wine, and sang several drinking songs. On Monday she received the question ordinary and extraordinary. She had now dined, and slept nearly eight hours. She was confronted while under the torture with Mesdames de Dreux and Le Feron, and several more. Her answers have not yet transpired, but every one expects to hear strange things. She supped in the evening, and, lacerated and disjointed as she was, gave a loose to her excess, to the disgust of every one present. They endeavored to make her sensible of her ill conduct, and that she would be much better employed in thinking of God, and singing devout hymns, than such songs; upon which she sang a psalm or two in mockery, and then fell asleep. Wednesday was spent in the like confronting, drinking, and singing; she absolutely refused to let a confessor come near her. In short, on the Thursday, that is, yesterday, they denied her all kinds of food, excepting only a little broth, of which she complained greatly, seeming to be apprehensive that she should not have strength to carry her through the business of the day.

She came from Vincennes to Paris in a coach; she seemed embarrassed, and as if she wished to conceal what she felt. They would have had her confess, but she would not hear of it. At five o'clock she was bound and set on the sledge, dressed in white, with a taper in her hand. She was extremely red in the face, and was seen to push away the confessor and the crucifix with great violence. Madame de Chaulnes, Madame de Sully, the Countess (De Fiesque), myself, and several others, saw her pass by the Hôtel de Sully. When she came to the Church of Nôtre-Dame, she refused to pronounce the amende-honorable; and at the Grêve, she struggled with all her might to prevent their taking her out of the sledge; she was, however, dragged out by main force, and made to sit down on the pile, to which she was bound by iron chains, and then covered over with straw. She swore prodigiously, and pushed away the straw five or six times: but at length the fire increased, she sunk out of sight, and her ashes are by this time floating in the air. This is the end of Madame Voisin, celebrated for her crimes and her impiety. One of the judges, to whom my son happened to mention his surprise at persons being burned alive in a slow fire, made answer: "My dear sir, there are some indulgences granted to the women in favor of their sex." "How, pray sir? are they strangled?" "No, sir; they are covered with faggots, and the executioner tears off their heads with iron hooks." So you see, my child, this is not so dreadful as we have been told it was. How do you find yourself after this little story? It made my blood run cold in my veins.

LETTER LXXVIII.

PARIS, Friday, March 15, 1680.

I am much afraid we shall lose M. de la Rochefoucault. His fever still continues. He received the sacrament yesterday. The tranquillity of his mind is really worthy of admiration. He has settled all affairs of conscience, and his disorder and the prospect of approaching dissolution give him no concern; you would think it was his neighbor at the point of death. He hears the physicians dispute without being the least affected by it, and the contentions of the Englishman and Friar Ange, without saying a word. I return to this verse:

Trop au-dessus de lui, pour y prêter l'esprit.*

He would not see Madame de la Fayette yesterday, on account of her tears, and because he was to receive the sacrament; but he sent about noon to know how she was. Believe me, my child, he has not passed his life in making useless reflections: he has rendered death so familiar that the prospect is neither new nor terrific to him. M. de Marsillac arrived the day before yesterday, at midnight, so overwhelmed with grief, that I do not think even you could feel more for me. It was a long time before he could compose himself; at length he came in, when he found M. de Rochefoucault sitting in his chair, with

* Too superior to himself to pay any attention to it.

an air very little different from that he usually wore. As M. de Marsillac is the only one of his children who may be said to enjoy his friendship, it was thought he would be himself affected at seeing him; but of this, however, there was not the smallest appearance, and he even did not name his illness to him. His son, unable to contain himself any longer, withdrew to give vent to his grief; when, after a great deal of altercation, Gourville being against, and Langlade for the Englishman, each of them supported by different parties in the family, and the two Esculapian chiefs keeping up all the warmth of their natural animosity, M. de Marsillac decided in favor of the Englishman; and yesterday, at four in the afternoon, M. de la Rochefoucault took his medicines, and at eight repeated them again. As there is no getting admittance at present, it is difficult to learn the truth; however, I have been told that after having been last night within an instant of giving up the ghost through the struggle between the medicine and the gouty humor, he had so considerable an evacuation that though the fever has not yet abated, there is reason to hope for a favorable issue. I am convinced in my own mind that he will recover, though M. de Marsillac does not yet venture to admit a ray of hope. I can compare him, in his affections and grief, to no one but yourself, my dear child, who can not bear the thoughts of my death. You may well believe that I shall not give him M. de Grignan's letter at present: it shall go, however, with those that may come afterward; for I am convinced, with Langlade, from whom I learned all I tell you, that the remedy given will complete the cure.

I want to know how you are, after your journey to Marseilles; I must chide M. de Grignan for taking you with him; I can not approve of such useless jaunts. Must not you also show Toulon, Hieres, Saint Baume, Saint Maximin, and the Fountain of Vaucluse, to the Mademoiselles de Grignan?

I am almost constantly with Madame de la Fayette, who must be totally insensible to the charms of friendship, and the affections of the heart, were she less afflicted than she is. I close this packet at her house, at nine in the evening; she has read your little note; for, in spite of her fears, she has hope enough to be able to read it. M. de la Rochefoucault is still the same; his legs begin to swell, which the Englishman does not like; he seems certain, however, that his medicines will have the desired effect. If this be true, I shall admire the great humanity of the physician in not tearing him piecemeal, for this will be the ruin of them all; to take the fever out of their hands, is to take the bread out of their mouths. Du Chêne is very easy about the matter, but all the others are stark mad.

LETTER LXXIX.

PARIS, Sunday, March 17, 1680.

Though this letter will not go till Wednesday, I can not help beginning it to-day, to inform you that M. de la Rochefoucault died last night. I am so much engrossed with this misfortune, and with the extreme affliction of our poor friend,* that I must relieve my mind by communicating the painful event to you.

Yesterday, which was Saturday, the Englishman's medicine had done wonders; all the favorable symptoms of Friday, which I mentioned to you, were increased; his friends began to sing Te Deum in their hearts; his lungs were clear, his head free, his fever less, his evacuations such as indicated a salutary crisis: in this state yesterday, at six o'clock in the evening, he relapsed, so as to leave no hopes of recovery; his fever redoubled in an instant, with an oppression of the chest and delirium; in a word, he was suffocated by the treacherous gout, and, notwithstanding he had a great degree of strength left even after all his bleeding, it carried him off in less than five hours, so that he expired at midnight in the arms of the Bishop of Condom. M. de Marsillac did not

* Madame de la Fayette.

leave him a moment; he is under inexpressible affliction: he will find, however, some consolation in the king and the court; and so will the rest of the family, from the place he enjoys: but when will poor Madame de la Fayette find again such a friend, such a companion, such kindness, such attention, such confidence, and such consideration for her and her son! She is infirm, confined to her room, and not like other people eternally from home. M. de Rochefoucault was also of a sedentary disposition; their situation rendered them necessary to each other; so that the mutual confidence and delightful friendship that subsisted between them was unequaled. Think of this, my child, and you will be convinced with me that no one could sustain a greater loss, for this is not to be repaired or obliterated even by time. I have never once quitted this disconsolate friend; she did not mix in the hurry and confusion of the family, so that she really stood in need of some pity. Madame de Coulanges has likewise acquitted herself very well on this occasion, and we shall continue to discharge our duty even at the hazard of our eyes, which are almost always filled with tears. You see how unluckily your letters came; they have hitherto had no admirers but Madame de Coulanges and myself; when the chevalier returns he may possibly find a proper season for presenting them; meantime you must write one out of condolence to M. de Marsillac; he does honor to filial affection, and is a living proof that you are not alone in this respect; but, in fact, I doubt that either of you will meet with many imitators. The melancholy that reigns around me has awakened all my sensibility, and makes me feel the anguish of separation in all its horrors.

LETTER LXXX.

Paris, Wednesday, April 3, 1680.

My dear child, poor M. Fouquet is dead,* and I am affected at the intelligence: I never knew so many friends lost in a

* Gourville affirms, in his Memoirs, that he was liberated before his

manner at once, and it overwhelms me with sorrow to see so many dead around me; but what is not around me pierces my heart, and that is the apprehension I suffer from the return of your former disorders; for though you would conceal it from me, I can perceive your flushings, your heaviness, and shortness of breath. In short, that flattering interval is now over, and what was thought a cure has turned out a mere palliative. I remember your words: that a flame half-quenched is easily revived. The remedies you treasure up against an evil day, and which you reckon infallible, ought to be used immediately. Has M. de Grignan no authority on this occasion? Is he not alarmed at your situation? I have seen young Beaumont; I leave you to guess whether I asked him any questions. When I recollected that he had seen you within a week, he appeared to me the most desirable companion in the world. He said you were not quite so well when he set out as you had been during the winter. He mentioned your supper and entertainment, which he praised highly; as also the kind attentions both of you and of M. de Grignan, and the care M. de Grignan's daughters took that you might not be missed when you retired to rest. He said wonders of Pauline and the little marquis; I should never have been the first to put an end to the conversation, but he wanted to go to St. Germain; for, as he said, he had paid me the first visit, even before that which he owed to the king his master. His grandfather had the same place which Marshal de Bellefond has had :* he was a very intimate friend of my father's; and instead of seeking out for relations, as is generally the custom, my father chose him, without further ceremony, to stand sponsor to his daughter; so that he is my godfather. I am perfectly acquainted with all the family. I think the grandson handsome, extremely handsome. You did well to say nothing

---

death, and Voltaire believed it, from the account of his daughter-in-law, Madame de Vaux. But Madame de Sévigné believed he died at Pignerol, and so did the public. Mademoiselle de Montpensier confirms the general opinion.   * Of steward of the household.

to him about your brother: I have myself mentioned it to no one, except to such persons as my son had previously informed of it, in order to find a purchaser.

I conclude you must by this time be at Grignan. I see with affliction the bustle of taking leave; I see, on your quitting your retirement, which appeared to you so short, a journey to Arles; another fatigue; and I see your journey to Grignan, where you may possibly be saluted on your arrival by a northeast wind; ah! I can not behold all these things for a person so delicate as you are, and not tremble.

You have sent me an account of Anfossi infinitely preferable to all mine. I do not wonder you can not think of parting with an estate where there are so many diverting gipsies. There could not be a more agreeable or novel reception; you are indeed so much a Stoic, and so full of reflections, that I should fear joining mine to yours, lest I should double the sorrow; but I think it would be prudent and reasonable, and worthy of M. de Grignan's affection, to use his utmost endeavors to be here about the beginning of October. There is no other place where you can think of passing the winter. But I will say no more at present; things urged prematurely lose all their force, and often create disgust.

There are no more long journeys talked of here; the only one spoken of is that to Fontainebleau. You will most assuredly have M. de Vendôme with you this year. For my part, I am preparing to set out for Brittany with inexpressible regret; but I must go in order to be there, stay a little while, and return. After the loss of health, which I always, with reason, place first, nothing gives me so much vexation as the disorder of my private affairs. It is to this cruel reason I sacrifice my ease and gratification; for I leave you to judge what a situation I am likely to be in, with so much time and solitude on my hands, to add new force to my anxiety at being separated from you. This cup, however, I must swallow, bitter as it is, in hopes of seeing you at my return; for all my movements tend to that point. And, however superior I may be to other things, that is always superior to me; it is my fate. And the sufferings which attend my affection for you, being offered to God, are a penance due for a love which I ought to bear for him alone.

My son is just arrived from Douay, where he commanded the gendarmerie during March. M. de Pomponne has spent the day here; he loves, honors, and esteems you perfectly. My being resident for you with Madame de Vins, occasions my being often with her; and, indeed, I could not wish to be better any where. Poor Madame de la Fayette is now wholly at a loss how to dispose of herself; the loss of M. de la Rochefoucault has made so terrible a void in her life, as to render her a better judge of the value of so precious a friendship. Every one else will be comforted in time; but she, alas! has nothing to occupy her mind, whereas the rest will return to their several avocations.

Mademoiselle de Scuderi is greatly afflicted with the death of M. Fouquet; that life is at length terminated, which so many pains have been taken to preserve. His illness was convulsions, and a constant retching, without being able to vomit. I depend on the chevalier for news, especially what relates to the dauphiness, whose court is composed exactly as you guessed; your notions are very just. The king is often there, which keeps the crowd somewhat at a distance. Adieu, my dear, affectionate child; I love you a thousand times more than I can express.

LETTER LXXXI.

Paris, Friday, April 12, 1680.

You mention the dauphiness to me; the chevalier can tell you more about her than I can. However, I think she does not seem to attach herself much to the queen. They have been to Versailles together, but on other days they generally make their separate parties. The king frequently visits the dauphiness in an afternoon, when he is sure not to be crowded She holds her circle from eight in the evening till half after nine; all the rest of the day she is alone, or with her ladies in waiting. The Princess of Conti almost always makes one of these private parties; for, as she is yet but very young, she stands in need of such a pattern to form her conduct by. The dauphiness is a miracle of wit, understanding, and good education. She frequently mentions her mother with great affection; and says, that she is indebted to her for all the prosperity and happiness she enjoys, by the pains she bestowed on her. She learns music, singing, and dancing; she reads, she works at her needle; in short, she is a complete being. I must own that I had a great curiosity to see her. Accordingly I went with Madame de Chaulnes and Madame de Carman; she was at her toilet when we came in, and engaged in a conversation in Italian with the Duke of Nevers. We were presented to her, and she received us very politely. It is easy to perceive that, if a moment could be found of putting in a word opportunely, it would not be difficult to engage her in conversation. She is fond of Italian, of poetry, of new publications, music, and dancing. You see that one need not be long dumb amid such a variety of topics for discourse; but it requires time—she was going to mass. Neither Madame de Maintenon nor Madame de Richelieu was in her apartment.

The court, my dear child, is by no means a place for me; I am past the time of life to wish for any settlement there. If I were young I would take pleasure in rendering myself agreeable to this princess; but what right have I to think of returning there? You see what my views are. As for those of my son, they seem to have become more reasonable; he will make a virtue of necessity, and keep his commission quietly. Indeed it is not an object for any one to give himself much trouble to gain, though Heaven knows it has cost us trouble enough; but the truth is, that money is very scarce, and he sees plainly that he must not make a foolish bargain. So, my dear, we must even wait for what Providence shall bring forth.

Yesterday the Bishop of Autun pronounced the funeral oration of Madame de Longueville,* at the church of the Carmelites, with all the powers and grace that man is capable of. Here was no *Tartuffe*,† no hypocrite; but a divine of rank, preaching with dignity, and giving an account of that princess's life with all the elegance imaginable, passing lightly over the most delicate parts of it, and dwelling upon or omitting all that should or should not be said. His text was these words, "Favor is deceitful, and beauty is vain; but a woman that feareth the Lord, she shall be praised." He divided his oration into two parts, equally beautiful; he spoke of the charms of her person, and of the late wars, inimitably; and I need not tell you, that the second part, which was taken up in giving an account of her exemplary penitence for the last twenty-seven years of her life, gave him an ample field to expatiate upon the virtues of her mind, and to place her in the bosom of her God.‡ He took occasion very naturally to praise

---

* Anne Genevieve de Bourbon, daughter of Henry Bourbon, second of the name, Prince of Condé, who died the 15th of April, 1679.

† It was imagined at that time, that the Bishop of Autun (Gabriel de Roquette) was the person whom Molière had in view in the character of Tartuffe.

We can not forbear adding an epigram of Boileau's upon him:

> On dit que l'Abbé Roquette
> Preche les sermons d'autrui ;
> Moi qui sais qu'il les achète,
> Je soutiens qu'il sont à lui.

Which may be Englished by a parody on a well-known epigram in our language:

> The sermons that Roquette pronounces
> Are his;—who 'd so have thought them?
> He swears they 're his; say not he bounces,
> For I know where he bought them!

‡ To estimate the skillfulness of the panegyrist, it is proper to know the soil on which he labored. The life of Madame de Longueville presented the Abbé Roquette with strange circuitous roads to measure, before he brought her to the way of salvation, whither he conducted

the king; and the prince was also compelled to digest a great many eulogiums; but as delicately prepared, though in a different manner, as those of Voiture. This hero was present, as were the duke, the Princess of Conti, and all the family, besides an infinite number of other persons; though, in my opinion, too few, for I think this respect was at least due to the prince, on occasion of an event he had not yet ceased to lament. You may perhaps ask me how I came there? Madame de Guénégaud offered the other day at M. de Chaulnes', to take me with her; as it was not inconvenient to me, I was tempted to embrace the offer; and I assure you I did not at all repent having done so. There were a great many women present, who had as little to do there as myself. Both the prince and the duke paid great attention to all who were there.

I saw Madame de la Fayette as we were coming out of the

her. She was one of the three ladies of whom Cardinal de Mazarin said to Don Louis de Haro: "We have three, among others, who create greater confusion than arose at the tower of Babel." Like Madame de Chevreuse and La Palatine, the part she took in the intrigues of the minority of Louis XIV. is notorious; like them, she united the triumphs of beauty to the success of factions, and the love of business to the love of amours. Voiture represents her as already serious and political, when, at an early age, she appeared at the Congress of Munster, where her husband presided over the French embassy. The Fronde began; her artifices and blandishments seduced the sage Turenne, when he came at the head of the Spaniards to give battle to the French. Beloved, not much in the style of a brother, by the Prince de Conti, she made him the chief of the Frondeurs, and general of the insurgents, thus opposing him to her other brother, the great Condé, who commanded the army of the court. It was she who afterward dragged this hero into the civil war, and joined him to the Spaniards. She long wandered as a heroine, or as Cardinal de Retz said, who had himself been her lover, as a fugitive adventurer. She went alternately, commanding or intriguing, to Holland, Flanders, Dieppe, Stenay, Montrond, Bordeaux. In 1649 she reigned in the Hôtel-de-ville of Paris, and did what no one had ever done before, nor will perhaps do after her, she lay-in there; and that at a time when this hotel served as a palace to the court, as the seat of government, and as the head-quarters of the church; she was bathed in tears; it seems that some of M. de la Rochefoucault's hand-writing had by accident fallen in her way, which had awakened all her sorrows. I had just parted from the Mesdemoiselles de la Rochefoucault at the Carmelites, who had been also weeping the loss of their father; the eldest, in particular, equaled M. de Marsillac in affectionate sorrow. I really do not think that Madame de la Fayette will ever be comforted; for my part, I am the worst of any of her acquaintance to be with her; for we can not help indulging ourselves in talking of that worthy man, and the conversation is death to her. She was certainly more deserving of his regard than any of those he had an affection for. She has read your little note, and thanks you warmly for the manner in which you seem to enter into her grief.

Have I told you of the reception Madame de Coulanges met with at St. Germain? The dauphiness told her that she already

army. Two of her lovers, the Count de Coligny and the Duke de Nemours, were killed in a duel. The first fought by her orders, in her quarrel, and under her inspection. The Duke de la Rochefoucault, who had long loved her, was betrayed by her, both as a friend and as a lover. When the peace of the Pyrénées had brought back the princes to France, it was found that age prescribed repose to her, at the same time that the state of affairs obliged her to it. She endeavored at first to escape it, by forming a party for Voiture's sonnet against Bense rades. But these little contests of wit were insipid, in comparison with those she had been engaged in. Nothing remained for her but devotion; and as a character and a party were always essential to her, she became the protectress of the Jansenists at court, and, what is more, mediatrix between them and Rome. For it was Madame de Longueville who in 1668 mediated the theological transaction which suspended the debates of the Formulary, and which was called *the peace of Clement IX.* Singular woman! who had the art of making herself conspicuous while working out her salvation, and of saving herself on the same plank from perdition and from ennui. It was asserted at the time, that she died for want of food, and there is no doubt she practiced the most rigid austerities. "Though naturally delicate," says Madame de Maintenon, "she never relaxed in the practice of self-denial." There is a life of this lady in two volumes by Villefore, which is said to be well written.

knew her by her letters; that her ladies had also told her a great deal of her wit, and that she wished to judge of it herself. Madame de Coulanges supported her character admirably upon the occasion; her repartees were brilliant, sallies of wit flew without number; in the afternoon she was invited to be of the princess's private party, with her three friends: all the ladies of the court would have strangled her. You see that by means of these friends she gets admittance to a private conversation; but what does all this tend to? She can not be one of their party in public, nor at table. This spoils the whole; she is fully sensible of the humiliation; and has been these four days tasting these pleasures and dissatisfactions.

LETTER LXXXII.

PARIS, Wednesday, May 1, 1680.

I know not what weather you may have in Provence, but we have had for these weeks past such horrible weather here that several journeys have been delayed by it, and mine among the rest. The good abbé had like to have perished in going and coming from La Trousse; so says M. de la Trousse—you would not have believed me. They had an architect with them, and went to give orders about some alterations, which will make this house, which we before thought so beautiful, hardly to be known again.

We have a new moon to-day, which I hope will bring fine weather with it, and let me set out; I have not yet fixed on what day I shall go. I can not express the concern this second parting gives me; I must surely be out of my senses to remove so much further from you, and to place a distance of a hundred leagues more between us than there is already. I have a mortal aversion to business; it takes up so great a portion of our time, and makes us run hither and thither just as it pleases. I shall be so affected when I am setting out, that those who hand me into my carriage may very naturally think it is at parting with them. I am certain I shall not be able to refrain from tears, and yet I must go, if it is only that I may come back again.

Mademoiselle de Meri is now in possession of your apartment; the noise of that little door opening and shutting, and the circumstance of not finding you there, have affected me more than I can express. All my people do their best to serve her. And if I were vain, I could show you a letter I received from her the other day, full of thanks for the assistance I have given her; but as I am very modest, you know, I will content myself with placing it in my archives.

I have seen Madame de Vins; she is buried in her law-suits. However, we find time to chat together, and express our mutual wonder at the odd medley of good and evil in this world, and the impossibility of being truly happy. You know all that fortune has hitherto done for the Duchess of Fontanges. What she has reserved for her is this: so violent a flux, with some degree of fever, that she is confined to her bed at Maubuisson, and her fine face already begins to swell. The Prior of Cabrières does not quit her for an instant; if he effects a cure, he will not make his fortune badly at court. Think whether her situation does not derogate somewhat from her happiness. Here is further room for reflection. But to another subject.

Madame de Dreux was liberated from prison yesterday; she was only *reprimanded*, which is a very slight punishment, and fined five hundred livres, which are to be distributed in alms. This poor lady has been confined a whole year in a room, where the light came in only by a small hole at the top, without tidings of any thing going on, or without comfort. Her mother, who doted on her, who was herself still young and handsome, and who was equally beloved by her daughter, died about two months ago, of grief at her child's situation. Madame de Dreux was ignorant of this event; and yesterday, when her husband and all the family went with open arms to the place where she was confined, to receive her, the first word she spoke on seeing them enter her room, was, "Where is my mother? Why is she not here?" M. de Dreux told her she was waiting for her at home. The poor creature could not, however, enjoy the satisfaction of being at liberty; but was incessantly inquiring what ailed her mother, that she was certain she must be ill, or she would have come to embrace her after so long a separation. At length she got home. "What! my mother not here? I do not see her, I do not hear her!" She flew up stairs. No one knew what to say to her; all were in tears. She ran into her mother's apartment, she looked about her, called, but received no answer; at length a Celestine friar, who was her confessor, appeared, and told her that she must not hope to see her mother again till they met in heaven, and that she must submit with resignation to the Divine will. Upon hearing this she fainted away, and when she recovered, burst into tears and lamentations, which pierced the hearts of all present, crying that it was she who had killed her mother; that she had rather have died in prison, than have been set at liberty to know the loss of so excellent a parent. Coulanges, who had run to M. de Dreux's, like many other friends, was witness to the whole of this affecting scene, which he related to us yesterday so naturally and pathetically, that Madame de Coulanges' eyes looked red, and I wept heartily, being wholly unable to suppress my tears. What think you, my child, of this bitter ingredient thrown into the cup of joy and triumph, to overpower the congratulations and embraces of a whole family and their friends? The poor soul is still in tears, notwithstanding all M. de Richelieu's endeavors to dry them for her. He has indeed done wonders in this affair.

I have been insensibly led into this long detail, which you will comprehend better than any one, and which has affected every heart. It is believed that M. de Luxembourg will be set at liberty upon as easy terms as Madame de Dreux; for some of the judges would have released her without even being *reprimanded*. And, upon the whole, the treatment of the accused persons has been shocking and scandalous, considering that nothing was proved against them. This, however, shows the integrity of the judges.

We all approve the discourses of your preacher; we have envied and admired him. The passion-sermon, which we heard not far from hence, was a most extraordinary one; I assure you the terms *rascal* and *scoundrel* were made use of, to express the humiliation of our blessed Saviour. Do not these terms convey noble and sublime ideas? Bourdaloüe preached like an angel from heaven, both last year and this, for it is the same sermon.

What you write me about this world appearing quite another world, if we could draw aside the curtain in every family, is both well expressed and perfectly true. Good heavens! who can tell whether even the heart of the princess, whom we praise so much, is thoroughly contented? She has appeared dull these three or four days past; who knows how things are with her? She would be with child, and she is not. Perhaps she wants to see Paris and St. Cloud, and she has not yet seen them. She is extremely affable; she studies to please. Who knows but this may cost her some uneasiness? Who knows whether she is pleased alike with all the ladies who have the honor of attending upon her? And lastly, who knows but she may be weary of so retired a life?

I have this very moment received your amiable melancholy letter of the 24th. Believe me, my dear child, it sensibly affects me. I am not yet set out, the bad weather detains me, for it would have been folly to expose myself in such a season. This has unhinged every thing. I shall write to you from Paris again, on Friday, and will tell you about the alterations that are going on: I gave my opinion first, and am not so silly as you think, when you are in the case. We read in history*

---

* Every one knows that painting and sculpture took their rise from love, and that a marshal, who fell in love with a painter's daughter, became an excellent painter, merely by endeavoring to please his mistress.

of greater miracles: there are *affections* which do not yield to the *other* passion; hence I am become an architect.

I admire extremely what you say respecting devotion. Good heavens! how truly may it be said that we are all like Tautalus with water close to our lips, and unable to drink! Let the heart be cold, the understanding enlightened, it is just the same. I have no need of the dispute between the Jansenists and Molinists to decide this matter. What I feel myself is sufficient, and how can I doubt it, if I observe myself an instant? I could talk a long time, and with infinite pleasure on this subject, if we were together, but you stop short, and I am silent. Corbinelli had his share of your letter, for I am fond of his frank truths. He has just heard a sermon of the Abbé Flechier's,* at the taking the vail of a young Capuchin nun, which has charmed him. The subject was the freedom of the children of God, which he explained in a bold and masterly style. He showed "that this young person alone could be called free, because she partook of the freedom of Christ and his saints; and she was released from the slavery in which we are held by our passions; that it was she who was free, and not we; that she had but one master, whereas we had a hundred; and that instead of lamenting for her, as we did, with a worldly sorrow which was blamable, we ought to consider, respect, and even envy her, as a person chosen from all eternity to be of the number of the elect." I have not repeated the tenth part of what he said on this subject; but it was altogether a finished piece. The funeral oration on Madame de Longueville is not to be printed.

You ask me why I do not take Corbinelli with me? He is going into Languedoc, loaded with the favors and civilities of M. de Vardes, who has accompanied his pension of 120 francs with so excellent a seasoning, I mean so many kind and affectionate sentiments, that our friend's philosophy could not withstand it. Vardes is always in extremes; and as I am

* Esprit Flechier, made Bishop of Lauvar in 1685, and removed from thence to Nimes in 1687.

persuaded that he formerly hated him, because he had used him ill, he now loves him, because he uses him well: this is the Italian proverb and its reverse.* I am going there with only the good abbé, and a few books, and your idea, which will prove the source of all my pleasure or pain. I assure you it will keep me from staying out in the evening dews: I shall recollect that it would displease you; and this will not be the only time you have prevented me from continuing my evening walk, and made me return home. I promise to consult you, and to follow your advice at all times; do the same by me, and be under no alarms; rest assured that I will take care of myself; I wish I could put the same confidence in you; but I have many subjects of complaint against you on this score; and without going further than Monaco, have I not the banks of the Rhône, whither you forced the stoutest hearts in your family to accompany you, in spite of themselves? I repeat it, in spite of themselves; and be pleased to remember, on the other hand, that I should die with fear even to pass les vaux D'Olioules† on foot. This confession of my cowardice is sufficient to prove my apprehensions and ensure your confidence. Let then, my dear child, the remembrance of me govern you, in some degree, as yours always governs me.

I fancy my son will meet me at Orléans. I am aware of the attentions of M. de Grignan: he has politeness, nobleness, and even affectionate tenderness; but he has some points which are not so agreeable, and more difficult to be conceived; and as every thing is cut diamond-wise, he has many sides which are inimitable, so that we are at once tempted to love and to scold him, to esteem and to blame, to embrace and to beat him.

Adieu, my dear child; I must now leave you. Surely you mean to laugh at me when you express your apprehensions lest

---

* *Chi offende non perdona.* The offender never pardons.

† *Les vaux D'Olioules*, or, as it is called in the dialect of that country, *leis baous D'Oulioules*, is a narrow pass by the side of a river, about a league in length, running between two steep hills, in Provence.

I should write too much. My lungs are almost as delicate as Georget's:* excuse the comparison, it comes from hence. But for you, my child, let me conjure you not to write. Montgobert, pray do not abandon me, but step in and take the pen from her hand.

LETTER LXXXIII.

PARIS, Monday, May 6, 1680.

You observe with great humor, that, if the human heart is left to itself, it will always find something to comfort itself with, and that its disposition is to be happy. I hope mine will have the same disposition as others, and that time and the air will abate the uneasiness I at present endure. I think you borrowed from me what you say about the passion of separating ourselves from each other; it might be supposed that we thought ourselves too near neighbors, and that after mature deliberation it had been resolved on both sides to make a voluntary removal of three hundred leagues further asunder. You see I in a manner copy your own letter; the reason is, that you have given so agreeable a turn to my idea, that I take pleasure in repeating it. I hope at last, the sea will set bounds to our passion, and that after having retired, each to a certain distance, we shall return back, and advance toward each other as fast as we have receded. It is certain that for two persons who seek each other's company, and delight in being together, we have had the most singular destiny. Whoever were to seek to destroy my faith in Providence, would deprive me of my only comfort; and if I thought it was in our own power to settle or unsettle, to do or undo, to will one thing or another, I should never have a moment's peace. The Creator of the universe must be with me the director of every event that happens; and when I look to him as the cause, I blame no one, and submit with humility, though not without inexpressible

* A celebrated ladies' shoemaker at Paris.

grief of heart; at the same time I put my trust in Him, that He will again bring us together as he has done before.

LETTER LXXXIV.

THE ROCKS, Friday, May 31, 1680.

Notwithstanding this letter will not go till Sunday, I am resolved to begin it to-day, that I may date once more in the month of May. I fear that of June will appear still longer to me. I am certain, however, of not seeing so fine a country as the one I have left. There is a month in the year in which it rains every day; this is owing to your prayers; why will you not leave Providence a little to itself? sometimes too much rain, sometimes too great drought; you are never contented. God forgive me! but this puts me in mind of the story of Jupiter in Lucian, who is so wearied with the incessant importunities of mortals, that he sends Mercury to inquire into the matter, and, at the same time, orders ten thousand bushels of hail to fall upon Egypt, to stop their mouths.

I will no longer oblige you to answer me on the subject of the Divine Providence, which I so greatly revere; and which, in my opinion, commands and orders every thing in the world. I am persuaded you will not dare to treat this opinion as an inconceivable mystery, with the disciples of your Father Descartes; it would be indeed inconceivable, that God should have made the world, and not direct all that passes in it. Those who make such fine restrictions and contradistinctions in their writings, speak much more freely, and with greater truth on the subject, when they have no crooked policy to govern them. These *cutpurses* are very agreeable in their conversation. I shall not mention their names, because I fancy you guess the principal one: the others are the Abbé du Pile, and M. Dubois,* whom you are acquainted with, and who has an infinite

* Dubois, of the French Academy, who translated several works of Cicero and Saint Augustin.

share of wit. Poor Nicole is still in the Ardennes,* and M. Arnauld buried under ground, like a mole.† But whither is my pen running? This is not what I meant to say to you. I intended to tell you that I received your letters at the place where we dined the day I left Nantes, and that, having no other means of conversing with you at so great a distance, the reading of them forms an occupation preferable to every other.

We found the roads greatly improved between Nantes and Rennes, thanks to the care of M. de Chaulnes; but the incessant rains we have had of late have made them as if two winters had followed close upon each other. We were continually in sloughs, or rivers of water; we did not dare to cross over by Chateaubriant, for fear of being unable to get further. We arrived at Rennes on Ascension eve, and dear good Marbeuf was ready to devour me; nothing would satisfy her, but my taking up my abode for a time at her house, but I refused; I would neither sup nor sleep there: the next day she gave me a very elegant public breakfast, when the governor, and every person of note in the town, came to visit me. We set out again at ten o'clock, though every body assured me, that I had time enough before me, and that the roads were *like this room;* for that, you know, is the usual comparison: however, we found them so much *like this room*, that we did not get there till after midnight, and were all the way up to the axle-trees in water, and from Vitré to this place, a road I have passed a thousand and a thousand times, it was impossible to know it again; the causeways are become impassable; the ruts are sunk to a frightful depth; the little inequalities are perfect mount-

---

* The forest of Ardennes, in the Low Countries.

† After the death of Madame de Longueville, these able writers, fearing persecution, left France. Arnauld retired into the Low Countries, where he lived long unknown and in poverty. He remained there till his death. Nicole, more conciliating and less dreaded, returned to France. He figured in the quarrel of Bossuet and Fénélon. He supported the former, but with prudence and moderation.

ains and caverns; in a word, *finding* that we could no longer *find* our way, we sent to Pilois for help; he came accordingly bringing with him about a dozen stout country-fellows, some of whom held up the carriage, while others went before with wisps of lighted straw; and all spoke such jargon, that we were ready to die with laughing; at length, thus attended, we arrived here, our horses jaded, our people dripping, our carriage almost broken down, and ourselves tolerably fatigued; we made a very light supper, went to bed, slept heartily, and this morning, when we awoke, we found ourselves safe and sound at the Rocks, though very much out of sorts. I had taken the precaution to send a servant before us, that we might not come into the midst of a dust of four years standing; and we are tolerably decent at least. We have been entertained with a great number of visitors from Vitré, such as the Recollets, Mademoiselle du Plessis, still in tears for her mother, etc. etc., but I had not a moment's comfort till I had got rid of them all, which was about six o'clock in the evening, and had spent a little time in my woods, with honest Pilois. The walks and alleys are really enchanting; there are half a dozen new ones you have never seen. By the by, be under no apprehension about my exposing myself to the damps; I know it would make you angry if I did, and that is sufficient to deter me.

You always tell me that you are in good health, and so does Montgobert; and yet I can not help thinking that the plan of plunging twice a day into the Rhône can only suit a person whose blood is violently heated. I entreat you, my child, to consult a very grave and learned author in regard to the effects bathing may have on your lungs: you know I was witness to the evident injury you sustained from your half-baths, though they were advised by Fagon.*

You must certainly have stood in need of all your strength to support the numerous visitors you have had; twenty persons extraordinary at table makes me start a little. These are

---

* First physician to Louis XIV.

whole retinues, as Corbinelli used to call them, when he found himself so crowded in your drawing-room, and neither saluted nor took notice of any one; it must be owned that your house is the most frequented of any in the country; this is living at rack and manger. Do you remember when we had all the Fouesnels here, with what impatience we waited for the happy minute when they were to take their leave; how cheerfully we bid them adieu in our hearts, and how terrified we were lest they should yield to the false entreaties we made them to stay; how our hearts bounded when we saw them fairly gone; and our reflections how much bad company was preferable to good, the latter occasioning pain when they leave us, whereas the departure of the other takes a weight from the mind, and restores it to freedom? do you remember all this, and how perfectly we enjoyed ourselves upon the occasion?

Madame de Coulanges writes me word that Madame de Maintenon has lost a cane to the dauphin; Madame de Coulanges has ordered it to be made. The head is a pomegranate of gold, studded with rubies; it opens and discovers the miniature picture of the dauphiness, with these words underneath, *Il piu grato nasconde.** Clement formerly made this device for you; but that which seemed an exaggeration when applied to you, is perfectly true with regard to this princess. The beautiful Fontanges still continues very ill. My son tells me they pass their time very pleasantly at Fontainebleau. Corneille's comedies are the delight of the whole court; I have written to my son that it must be a great pleasure to be obliged to be there, to have a master, a place, and the favor of the great; and had it been my case I should have been extremely fond of that part of the world; that the contrary was the sole reason of my removing to such a distance from it; that this kind of contempt was, in fact, the result of disappointment and vexation, and that *I abused it out of pure revenge*, as Montaigne says of youth; in short, that I wondered how he could prefer passing his time as I do, with Madame du

---

* The greatest charms are concealed.

Plessis and Mademoiselle de Launay, to spending it in the midst of all that is gay and great.

What I say for myself, my child, I say in reality for you; for do not imagine, if M. de Grignan and you were situated agreeably to your merit, that you would have any dislike to such a life; but it does not please Providence that you should arrive at more greatness than you at present possess. As to myself, I have seen the day when little, very little, was wanting for fortune to have placed me in the most agreeable situation in the world; when, all of a sudden, the scene changed to imprisonment and exile.* Do you think my fortune has been the happiest in the world? yet I am content; or, if I have my moments of murmuring, it is not on my own account.

Your description of Madame D.'s conduct is very amusing; it is a sort of economy in love, worthy of Armida. You seem to believe that M. de Rouillé will not return; I am sorry for it, and I should be still more so were it not that I believe your stay in Provence almost at an end, and consequently that you can have little occasion for him. If any thing is to be done in the assembly, the coadjutor will give a good account of it, in the absence of M. de Grignan.

LETTER LXXXV.

The Rocks, Wednesday, June 5, 1680.

At length I have the pleasure, at this immense distance from each other, to receive your letters on the ninth day after they are written, with the prospect of happier times before me. I often admire the great kindness and civility of those gentlemen of whom the author of Moral Essays speaks so.

---

* Madame de Sévigné alludes to the banishment of M. de Bussy, the chief of her house, and the confinement of M. de Fouquet, her intimate friend. To which may be added, the exile of the Arnaulds, and, further back still, the misfortunes of Cardinal de Retz, her relation and friend.

humorously, and to whom we are so much indebted. What do they not do for us? To what offices do they not submit, to be useful to us? Some run four or five hundred miles to carry our letters; others, at the hazard of their necks, climb to the tops of our houses, to prevent our being incommoded by the rains; and others suffer still more. In short, this is an arrangement of Providence; and the thought of gain, which is in itself an evil, becomes converted into a source of good.

I have brought a number of the best authors with me, which I have been arranging this morning. There is no looking into them, whichever it may be, without a desire to read it through. Some are religious tracts that do honor to the faith they maintain; others books of history, the best of their kind; besides ethics, poetry, novels, and memoirs. The romances are in disgrace, and banished to a by-closet. When I enter this little library I wonder how I am able to leave it again. In short, my child, it is altogether worthy of your presence, and so are my walks; but, for the company, it is very far from being so. There is strange skimming of the pot on Sundays:* one good thing, however, is, that they sup at six o'clock, and leave me to fly to my lawns and groves for relief. Madame du Plessis, in her deep mourning, never quits me. I could well say of her mother as of M. de Bonneuil, she has left a very ridiculous daughter behind her: she is so impertinent too. I am really ashamed of her regard for me, and I sometimes say to myself, Is it possible there can be any sympathy between her and me? She talks incessantly; but by the grace of God, I am to her, as you are to many others, absolutely dead; I do not hear three words she says. She is at daggers drawn with all her family about her mother's will: this is a new embellishment to the former beauties of her mind: she confounds the meaning of every thing she says;

* On account of the number of visitors, which was always greatest on Sundays, and to whom Madame de Sévigné thought herself obliged to do the honors of her house, which she humorously called *skimming her pot.*

and when she is complaining of the ill-treatment she receives, she cries, They have used me *like a barbarity, like a cruelty.* You will have me entertain you with such trash, and now I hope you have enough for a time.

My letters are of such an enormous length that you ought, according to your rule, to make yours to me very short, and leave all the rest to Montgobert. Health is at all times a real and intrinsic treasure, that will serve us on every exigency. Madame de Coulanges has written me a thousand trifles, that I would communicate to you, but that I think it would be absolutely ridiculous. The favor of her *female friend* (Madame de Maintenon) still continues. The queen accuses her of the cause of the distance between her and the dauphiness. The king comforts her for this disgrace: she visits him every day, and their conversations are of a length that surprises every body, and gives occasion to numberless conjectures.

I consider futurity as a dark road, in which the traveler may find light and accommodation when he least thinks of it.

M. de Lavardin is going to be married* in good earnest; and Madame de Mouci† is said to be the person who inspires Madame de Lavardin with the idea of doing every thing that can prove advantageous to her son. This De Mouci must certainly have a most extraordinary soul. Young Molac is to marry the Duchess of Fontanges's sister; the king gives him to the value of 400,000 francs with her.

How just is your observation upon the death of M. de la Rochefoucault and so many other friends! "The ranks close, and he is seen no more." It is certain that Madame de la Fayette is overwhelmed with grief, and can not feel, as she would have done at another time, the good fortune of her son. The dauphiness was particular in her attentions to her: the Princess of Savoy has spoken of her as her best friend.

---

* To Louise-Anne de Noailles, sister to Anne Julius Duke of Noailles, and Marshal of France.

† Marie de Harlaie, sister to Achilles de Harlaie, at that time attorney-general, and afterward first president of the parliament of Paris.

I am very glad my letter pleased M. de Grignan: I spoke my mind with great sincerity. He must divest himself of all those ruinous whims, which take their turns with him by the quarter. They must not merely sleep, like the nobility of Lower Brittany, but be altogether extinct.

Adieu, my beloved child; I admire and love your letters, and yet I will have no more of them; cut short, and leave Montgobert to prattle in your stead. I will try to take from you the desire of writing much: by the length of my letters you shall find them beyond your strength to answer, which is just what I wish; so shall I be a shield to you. I am of opinion that you have a numerous correspondence upon your hands, say what you will; for my part, I only stand upon the defensive in my answers, I never begin the attack; but then, even these seem of such a bulk, that, on post-days, when I retire to my chamber at night, and see my writing-desk, I am ready to run under the bed to hide myself, like our late *madame's* little dog, whenever it saw a book.

LETTER LXXXVI.

THE ROCKS, Wednesday, June 12, 1680.

So, I have written a sermon without thinking of it! I am as much surprised at this as the Count de Soissons,* when he was told he had made prose. It is true, I feel myself disposed to do all honor to the grace of Christ. I do not cry out, as the queen-mother did in the excess of her zeal against those vile Jansenists, "Ah! fie, fie upon grace!" I say the contrary, and can bring good vouchers for it. Since you have imparted to me your visions, with regard to the fortunes of your brothers-in-law, I will tell you sincerely that I was afraid the air of a house, where saving grace was sometimes talked of, might

* It is singular that Molière should have found in a nobleman the most laughable instances of ignorance, with which he endows his *Bourgeois Gentilhomme.*

have injured the Abbé de Grignan. Thank heaven, I have done no more harm than yourself; and if I am silent for the future, as I ought, and certainly shall be, it will not be from the fear of injuring any one. Your young bishops are seldom suspected of this heresy. I have just been writing to the chevalier: he has absolutely forgotten me, and as he is not infected with the Grignan indolence, it may be a serious business.

Your great building, my dear, is begun to-day; Du Bût will do all he can to hasten the workmen. There was no possibility of commencing sooner, and there is time enough to complete every thing. I send you a letter of Madame de Lavardin's, by which you will see what are her sentiments. I am almost tempted to send you likewise a very long letter I have received from Madame de Mouci, in which she takes pleasure in acquainting me with every thing she has done relatively to this marriage; she has made choice of me, in preference to any other person, to communicate the whole of his conduct to. She is in the right; the second volume is worthy the admiration of any one who had read the first. She seems happy in taking every opportunity of loading M. de Lavardin with favors, by means of the influence she has over his mother. She has made her give a thousand pounds worth of pearls; she has made her give all the fire-irons, stoves, candlesticks, tables, and silver waiters, that were worth having; handsome tapestry, fine old furniture, with linen and dressing gowns, which Madame de Mouci selected herself. Her heart takes this method of avenging itself; but for her it would have been a mere village wedding. She has made her give considerable estates to her son, and, to crown all, she will manage so that the new married couple will not live in the same house with the mother, whose overbearing temper, and rigid observance of hours, would by no means suit the young couple. Madame de Mouci delights in displaying to me the liberality of her soul, and I am amazed to see the extraordinary manner in which she contributes to M. de Lavardin's happiness. The desire of being singular, and of distinguishing ourselves by stepping a little out of the common road, seems to me to be the source of many virtues. She writes me word that she should be very happy if I were at Paris, because I should understand her; no one else being able to comprehend what she is doing. She adds besides that I should die with laughing, to see the grimaces Madame de Lavardin makes, every time the devil of avarice is cast out of her by the power of her exorcisms. The poor lady seems perfectly exhausted, *like the nuns of Loudun.** It must certainly be a very comic scene.

I have also received some very entertaining letters from the Marchioness d'Huxelles. The fair widows do wonders. Madame de Coulanges assures me, that she is to set out on the 20th for Lyons; she writes me a thousand trifles. This city will become the source of all the private intelligence of the court; but do you suppose she will communicate any of this precious commodity to the inhabitants?

I had a visit the other day from an Augustin friar, a poor creature, a very poor creature indeed. He assumed the airs of a preacher, but I answered his pompous ignorance only with a smile of contempt; he still went on, till at last I was strongly tempted to throw a book at his head. I fancy Madame de Coulanges will be ready to reply in the same way to the ladies of Lyons. Young Coulanges will be with you; he has given up M. de Chaulnes and Brittany for Lyons and the Grignans. I am quite of his opinion, my dearest child, and my greatest joy would be to make one of your party. Ah!

---

* Alluding to the *Histoire des Diables de Loudun*, History of the Devils of Loudun. It is well known that the fierce hatred of Cardinal de Richelieu, the manœuvers of the Capuchin Joseph, and the cruelty of the judge, Laubardement, caused the unfortunate curé Urbain Grandier to perish in the flames, as convicted of the crime of magic, "upon the deposition of Ashtaroth, devil of the order of Seraphims, and chief of the possessing devils, and Eusas, Cham, Acaos, Zebulan, Nephthaim, Uriel, and Acas, of the order of the principalities." These are the terms of the sentence.

how I should like to sup in your delightful grotto! How pleased I should be with M. de Grignan's music, and those beautiful passages in the opera, which have often made my eyes glisten. Oh! it would be a charming party. Your house is a little town. Really, to reflect upon our situations and dispositions, it might be supposed some magic change had been wrought upon us. And yet, to the honor of both, you fill your exalted station admirably, and shine as in your proper sphere; while I and my humble fortune seem fitted for the woods, and the solitude I inhabit. The truth is, I am assured from whence all this comes; it is necessary to raise our eyes to Heaven, after having long kept them fixed upon the earth.

The other evening one of my people told me, "that it was very warm in the mall; that there was not a breath of air stirring, and that the moon shone with the finest effect imaginable." I could not resist the temptation, so on I put bonnets, cloaks, capuchins, and all the needless defenses you could wish; and forth I sallied to the mall, where the air was as mild as in my own room. I found there a thousand fantastic illusions of the night, black and white friars, linen scattered here and there, black men in one place, others buried upright against trees, little dwarfs who just showed their heads and concealed the rest of their bodies, priests who dared not approach me, etc., etc. After having laughed heartily at all these figures, and fully convinced ourselves of the true origin of what are called spirits, apparitions, that play their farces in the theater of our imaginations, we returned to the house without sitting down, or feeling the lest dew. I beg your pardon, my dear child, but I thought myself obliged, after the example of the ancients, as the foolish fellow we met in the gardens at Livri used to say, to show this mark of respect to the moon; I assure you I have sustained no injury from it.

There has fallen to me, out of the clouds, one of the prettiest calambour* chaplets in the world; this is doubtless because I tell my beads so well. The best ball to the best

---

* *Calembour, calambouc,* or *calambac,* are knots of the aloe-tree round

player, you know. This chaplet has a cross of diamonds hanging to it, with a death's head of coral;· *I have certainly seen that vile face somewhere.* Tell me, I beseech you, how it found its way to me at such a distance? In the mean time, I shall not tell my beads without considerable musings; I am of opinion that it will occasion greater distractions. I wait your answer on this subject.

Have you heard the story of Madame de Saint-Pouanges? They concealed it a long time from me, lest it should prevent me from returning to Paris in a carriage. This lady was going to Fontainebleau, for we should let no advantage slip, where she pretended she should be highly entertained; she had a very pretty place at court, was young, and had a taste for all the pleasures suitable to her years; she adopted the fashionable mode of setting out at six o'clock in the evening, and driving post, so as to get in about midnight. But, listen to the consequences: her carriage was overturned by the way, a piece of broken glass pierced through her stays into her body, and she died of the wound. They write me word from Paris that she lost her reason, between the pain the surgeons gave her and the mortification of dying in the bloom of youth. Is not this a curious adventure? If you know it already, it will be ridiculous to tell it you a second time; but it has made a strange impression on my brain. It seems Madame de Nevers* has made one, on the greatest head in the world, and has turned another smaller one quite topsy-turvy; but I do not find that this has been attended with any serious consequences.

---

which the resin collects and hardens by incorporation. This calembouc held to the fire emits a fine perfume. The aloe-tree grows in the woods of Cochin-China.

* Madame de Nevers, the daughter of Madame de Thianges, was a perfect beauty. The *greatest head* is the king; but it was not true that he had designs upon her, as it was said she had upon him. The ther *smaller head* was the duke, the son of the great Condé, who was really very much in love with her.

The king took the sacrament on Whitsunday. Madame de Fontange's influence still continues brilliant and solid; but what are we to think of this friendship? I have received a letter from M. Pomponne, in the midst of his retirement, of which I am more proud than if it had been from amid all the splendor of St. Germain. It is there he is again become as perfect as at Frêne. Ah! how excellent a use does he make of his disgrace, and what charming company he is in!

LETTER LXXXVII.

THE ROCKS, Saturday, June 15, 1680.

I shall make no answer to what you say of my letters. I am extremely happy that they please you; had you not told me so I should have thought them unbearable. I never can muster up courage enough to read one of them through, and I often say to myself, Good heavens! with what nonsense do I pester my poor child! Sometimes I even repent having written so much, lest I should lay you under a sort of obligation to answer me in the same way; but let me entreat you, my child, to indulge me in the pleasure of chatting to you without putting yourself to the trouble of answering. Your last letter exceeded all the bounds of prudence and the care you ought to take of your health.

You are too good in wishing me more society; but, in fact, I do not want it. I am accustomed to solitude. I have my workmen to amuse me, and the good abbé has his likewise. His taste for buildings and alterations gets the better of his prudence. It does not cost him much, indeed, but it would cost him still less to let it alone.

All my delight is in my wood: it is impossible to describe how beautiful it is. I often walk there with my cane and Louison, which is all I desire. In my closet I find such agreeable company that I often say to myself, This is worthy my daughter; she could not here lay her hand amiss upon a book, there is hardly room left for choice. I have taken up *Les Conversations Chrétiennes* (Christian Dialogues). They are written by an honest Cartesian, who seems to have all your *Récherche de la Vérité* (Inquiry after Truth, by heart); which treats of that philosophy, and of the supreme power of God over his creatures, who, as St. Paul says, "live, move, and have their being," in Him alone, and by him know all things. I will let you know if this book is within my comprehension, if not, I shall quit it it with all humility, renouncing the foolish vanity of appearing wise when I am not so. I assure you I think like *our brothers;* and were I to express myself in print, I should say so. I know the difference between the language of policy and that of the heart. God is omnipotent, and does what he pleases; that I understand. He wants our hearts, and we will not give them to him; there lies the mystery. But do not discover that of our sisters of Saint-Marie: they write me word that they are charmed with the book I lent them.*

You remind me of the foolish answer I made to excuse myself from going to Madame de Bret***,† "that I had but one son." This made your bishops start. I thought that it had been merely my *heretical air*. I mentioned it to you the other day. I think, however, there appeared something strange in the expression. Heaven be praised, my dear countess, we have done no harm; your brothers could not be better provided for than at present, even had we been *Molinists*. *Probable opinions*, and the *direction of purposes*, would not have been more advantageous to them in the Hôtel de Carnavalet than the libertinism of our conversations. I am delighted at it, and have often thought how unjustly we might have suffered on this occasion.

* See Letter, May 25.

† Apparently, Madame de Bretonvilliers, whom the Memoirs of the times represent as the over-officious friend of the Archbishop of Paris De Harlai, who was not so timid a priest as he was a rigid Molinist.

I can make nothing of the affair of M. de la Trousse or Madame d'Epinoi, or of the servant who robbed them. I will endeavor to get information on this subject, and will send you the letters. You find that poor Madame de Lavardin is quite unhappy. Who would have supposed that she would have been otherwise than rejoiced at her son's being married?* But I speak like a fool. It should be our invariable maxim, that human nature can never be happy. Young Chiverni seems to be as much so as any one: you see how he has extricated himself from his misery. Your poor brother, indeed, seems fated never to be happy in this world; as to the other world, if we may judge by appearances, I see no probability of his being in the right road. The Bishop of Chalons is certainly in heaven, for he was a devout prelate and a virtuous man. You see all our friends are lost to us one after another.

I wrote the other day to Madame de Vins that I would leave her to guess what sort of virtue I practiced most here; and informed her it was liberality. It is certain that I have given away very considerable sums since my arrival; eight hundred francs one morning, one thousand another, five hundred another, one day three hundred crowns; you may think I am jesting, but it is too true. I have farmers and millers who owe me these sums, and have not a farthing to pay me with. What is to be done in this case? Why I make a virtue of necessity, and forgive them the debts. You will readily believe that I make no great merit of this since it is forced liberality; but my head was full of it when I wrote to Madame de Vins, and so down it went on the paper. I endeavor to make the fines pay for it. I have not yet touched one of the six thousand francs from Nantes; money-matters are not soon settled. The other day I had a visit from a pretty little wife of a farmer of Bodégat, with sparkling eyes, fine person, and smartly dressed in a holland gown, with ruffled cuffs, and a long train. Good heavens! thought I, when I saw her, I am ruined; for you must know, her husband owes me eight thou-

---

* See the preceding Letter.

sand francs. M. de Grignan would certainly have fallen in love with this woman; she is the very image of one he admired at Paris. This morning a countryman came in with bags on all sides, some under his arms, some in his pockets, and some in his breeches, which he began to untie, for in this country they dress in a strange way; the fashion of buttoning the lower part of the jacket is not yet introduced here; they are very saving of the stuff of which their breeches are composed, and from the gentry of Vitré down to my clodpole, every thing is in the highest state of negligence. The good abbé, who, you know, loves the main chance, seeing the fellow so loaded, thought we were rich forever. "Upon my word, friend, you are bravely loaded, how much money do you bring us?" "Please your reverence," answered the man, "I think there is a matter of thirty francs." My dear child, I believe all the *doubles** in France were collected to fill these bags. In this manner do they abuse our patience and forbearance.

You give me great pleasure by what you say of Montgobert. I thought, indeed, what I wrote to you upon her account was superfluous, and that your excellent understanding would reconcile every thing. In this manner, my child, you ought always to act, in spite of momentary vexations. Montgobert has an excellent heart, though her temper is rather too hasty and impetuous; I always honor the goodness of her heart. We are frequently obliged to bear with the little dependencies and circumstances of friendship, though they may sometimes be disagreeable. I shall some day send her a bad cause to defend at Rochecourbiere; since she has a talent for these things, it ought to be exercised. You will have M. de Coulanges with you; who will be a capital performer. He will inform you of his views and expectations, I know nothing of them myself; he dreads solitude so much that he will not even write to any one who lives in it. Grignan, therefore, is a place perfectly qualified to charm him, as he himself is to

---

* Small pieces of money, of which about five are equal to an English penny.

charm others; I never met with such delightful society, it is the object of all my wishes; I think of you all incessantly; I read your letters over and over again, saying as at Livri: Let us see what my daughter said to me a week or ten days ago; for, in short, it is she who converses with me, and I thus enjoy "the ingenious art of painting language, and of talking to the eyes."

You know it is not the retired groves at the Rocks that make me think of you; I thought of you as much in the midst of the bustle of Paris. You are fixed in the center of my heart; every thing else is transient; it passes and is forgotten. I have forgotten even my Agnes, and yet she is very amiable; her wit has something of the simplicity of the country in it; but that of Madame de Tarente is still in the high courtly taste. The roads from hence to Vitré are grown so intolerably bad, that the king and M. de Chaulnes have ordered them to be repaired. All the peasants of that barony will be assembled there on Monday next.

Adieu, my dearest! when I tell you that my affection is of no use to you, do you not understand in what way I mean, and to what my heart and imagination tend? Pray tell me if you intend to place our little girl at Aix with her aunt,* and to send Paulina away. The dear child is a perfect prodigy; her understanding and wit are a sufficient portion for her; will you then place her on a level with a common person? I should always take her with me wherever I went, and should never think of sending her to Aix with her sister.† In short, I should treat her, as she merits, extraordinarily.

---

* Marie Adhémar de Monteil, sister of M. de Grignan, and one of the nuns of Aubenas, a town and convent of the Lower Vivares. See the letter of 9th of June.

† Marie Blanche, the eldest sister of Paulina, was in the nunnery of St. Marie of Aix, where a short time afterward she took the vail.

LETTER LXXXVIII.

THE ROCKS, Sunday, Sept. 15, 1680.

What infinite obligations does my heart owe you, and how happy have you made it, by permitting me to hope for your presence this winter! I have read over and over again the delightful letter I so fondly and impatiently expected. I said to myself, "Yes, this is the voice of my child, who assures me she shall come to Paris soon after All-Saints." Oh, how great the joy to have such comfortable assurance in my possession!

You surprise me at the profound secrecy that our lovely saint observes of her noble and pious intentions to Madame du Janet. It is so natural to talk of what we ardently wish, of what the heart is full of, that it is doing penance beforehand to keep silence on such occasions; but such is her disposition; she speaks on this subject only to her holy father alone, as it is he alone who is to determine the duration of a residence which she would be sorry to have protracted. By depriving herself of the pleasure of communicating her intentions, she finds them more strongly confirmed in her breast.

I can not at this distance discover what is become of the crowd that so lately swarmed in your castle. I left you, I thought, in the midst of a fair; but since I now find you reposing on your little bed, you must certainly have found means to escape from the throng. Montgobert has not written to me, and you mention your health very slightly; you ought to have informed me whether the medicines you are taking have the desired effect, and whether this thinness upon thinness is likely to reduce you to your former state. It is a sad misfortune that what does you service in one way, should injure you in another; it throws a damp upon the satisfaction we should otherwise feel.

We are at present among a set of persons with whom we make great use of both our reason and reasoning. You know, my child, what a good hearer I am, *thanks to God and you*, as they say in this country; I have lost, by dint of listening to you, the gross ignorance I possessed on many subjects; this is a pleasure I now feel the advantage of. We have had here a party or two at ombre and reversis, and the next day *altra scena* (a change of scene). M. de Montmoron came, you know he has a great deal of wit; Father Damaie, who does not live quite a hundred miles from this place; my son, who you know is perfect master of disputation, and Corbinelli's letters, making four, and I am audience for them; they entertain me exceedingly. M. de Montmoron perfectly understands your philosophy, and controverts it stoutly. My son maintains the cause of *your father;* as also Damaie; and Corbinelli, in his letters, takes the same side; but they are not all more than a match for Montmoron. He insists that we can have no ideas but what are imparted through the medium of the senses. My son contends that we think independently of our senses; for instance, *we think that we think :** this is in general the subject of our disputations, which have been carried on with great spirit, and have delighted me extremely. Could you, my child, have made a party in this conversation, by your letter, as Corbinelli has done, you would have strengthened a little our Sévigné. And now I mention him, I must acquaint you that he is still very far from being well, though he thinks himself out of danger, as indeed I do also;

---

* We are agreeably surprised to see at this era, in the heart of Brittany, a gentleman who so ably refuted the system of *innate ideas*, and already exhibiting the theory of Locke. For though the English philosopher was in Paris in 1675, I do not think his opinions were ever promulgated there, or that they were even at that time published. But Hobbes, and particulary Gassendi, had raised objections to the meditations of Descartes, of which the principles had sprung up in able heads.

But what deceives Madame de Sévigné here, is the word to *think*, ill understood, and applied to many secondary operations of the understanding. Its too general signification disguises its origin. Descartes himself was mistaken by not submitting this word sufficiently to the analysis which he himself invented.

but he is tired of doctors as well as you; he has taken more medicines than were necessary; they have acted upon his blood, and heated it to such a degree that every day some of those horrible eruptions appear which are so very disagreeable both to those who suffer and those who see them; thus the poor fellow is happy to have a little respite, that he may repose himself.

Yesterday I observed, with admiration, how very easy it is to console ourselves for the want of play by a better avocation; and how patient we are while we are squandering our money in farthings, as I said the other day at Rennes. But without imitating you, for I hate a bad copy of a good original, I shall tell you that my age and experience make me wish not to have always such demands upon me, and that I could now and then put a little wit into my poor head; indeed it is what I am every day endeavoring to do when in my closet or my wood. You will not perhaps be displeased to know the person who has engaged us in play of late. It is a tolerably pretty woman from Vitré, who has been here three nights, and during her stay we have hardly had the cards out of our hands, she is so passionately fond of them. How much better does Mademoiselle de Grignan spend her time, happy creature! In reading your letters over more carefully, I find she speaks without reserve of her intentions to Madame du Janet, and that is the only conversation she had with M. de Grignan that she conceals from her; but still I can not help wondering that she should mention the one without the other. It must be no small satisfaction to her to have the conversation of so prudent and good a person. I reverence more than ever the wise dispensations of Providence when I reflect how it turns the steps you are about to take to my advantage; and I already begin to enjoy, in imagination, the pleasure I am to receive.

I ask a thousand pardons: I have met with a little book of madrigals,* containing the prettiest things in the world. I

---

* By La Sablière.

must endeavor to bring them into favor with you this winter. It is a pleasure to have a bad memory; we are reading Sarasin again, and I am as much delighted with him as at first; this is the case also with *Les Petites Lettres;* we find something new in these, and we add others according to our fancy: your brother has an excellent knack at furnishing these amusements. I had a mind to dip again into the Prejudices.* I think them admirable: but what crowns the whole, my dearest child, is, that these things all lead directly to you. Oh, how sweet the consolation, to think that we shall meet once more! Alas, a whole year has passed in continual adieus; mortifying occupation! I can not look upon the past with so much tranquillity as you do. It is to me a source of the bitterest uneasiness, at least it has been so till I read the pleasing assurance of your return; now I forgive it in consideration of the future, which offers itself to my imagination fraught with hopes that make amends for all.

LETTER LXXXIX.

THE ROCKS, Sunday, Sept. 22, 1680.

You are so much of a philosopher, my beloved child, that there is no such thing as giving vent to the transports of the heart with you. You are continually anticipating hopes; and you pass over the joy of possession, to contemplate the hour of separation. Believe me, we ought to manage differently the blessings which Providence has in store for us. After having made you this reproach, it remains with me honestly to confess that I deserve it as much as you do, and that it is impossible for any one to be more alarmed at the cruel rapidity of time, or to have a stronger foretaste of those sorrows which generally follow in the train of pleasures. In short, my child, this life is a perpetual checker-work of good and evil, pleasure

---

* A work of M. Nicole's, entitled, *Préjugés légitimes contre les Calvinistes* (Well-founded Prejudices against the Calvinists).

and pain. When in possession of what we desire, we are only so much the nearer losing it; and when at a distance from it, we live in the expectation of enjoying it again. It is our business, therefore, to take things as God is pleased to send them. For my part, I am resolved to indulge myself in the delightful hope of seeing you, without any mixture of alloy.

You are very unjust, my love, in the judgment you pass upon yourself; you say, that though people at first think you agreeable, upon a longer acquaintance they cease to love you; it is precisely the reverse; you have a certain air of superiority that makes people afraid of you, and despair of ever being admitted into the number of your friends; but when once they know you, it is impossible not to be attached to you; and if any of your acquaintance seem to shun you, it is only because they love you, and can not bear the thought of not being so much loved in return as they wish. I have heard many persons extol the charms of your friendship to the skies, and afterward reflect on their own want of merit, which prevented them from preserving that happiness; thus each blames himself for a degree of coldness; but where there is no real cause of complaint on either side, it seems only to require a little leisurely conversation to be good friends again.

I have a great desire to read Terence; nothing could give me greater pleasure than to see the originals, of which the copies have afforded me so much pleasure. My son will translate to me satire against foolish amours;* he ought to be able to write one himself, or at least to profit by this; if the situation he is in at present does not correct him, I know not what will. We read books of controversy; one has lately been published† in answer to the Prejudices, to which I wish M. Arnauld had

---

* She, no doubt, alludes here to the well-known description of the extravagance of lovers, which is to be found in Terence's Eunuch, Scene I. beginning in these words:

In amore hæc omnia insunt vitia, etc.

† Written by the Protestant minister Claude, entitled, "A Defense of the Reformation against the 'Well-founded Prejudices' of M. Nicole."

replied; but I fancy that he has been forbidden; and it is thought more advisable to leave this book unanswered, though it may do injury to religion, than to permit the publication of another that may serve to justify the Jansenists from the errors with which they have been reproached; but more of this another time. I have been promised the coadjutor's speech, but I have not yet had it; my son and several others speak highly in its praise.

LETTER XC.

The Rocks, Wednesday, November 26, 1684.

So much the worse for you, my dear child; if you do not read over your letters, your indolence robs you of a great pleasure, which is not one of the least of the evils it may occasion you; for my part, I read them over and over again; they constitute all my joy, all my sorrow, all my occupation, so that you are the center and cause of all. I shall begin this letter with you.

Is it possible that what you tell me can be true, that when you spoke to the king you were like a person beside yourself, and so lost, to use your own expression, in the blaze of majesty, that you knew not what you said, nor could recollect any of your ideas. Never, never can I believe that my beloved daughter, always so remarkable for her ready wit and happy presence of mind, should have been in such a situation. I must confess, that from what his majesty said to you—"that he would do something for M. de Grignan"—I by no means understand that he merely alluded to the great expense M. de Grignan had lately incurred: no, the king's answer appeared to me to bear this construction, "Madam, the favor you ask of me is a trifle, I will do something more for Grignan;" meaning, I suppose, the affair of the survivorship, which he knew would be a capital point for your family. I had no idea of the little present in question, and you know what I said upon that subject in my last letter. It rests with you, my dear, to set me right, and I beg you will do so, for I do not love to view things in a wrong light.

Madame de la Fayette has written me word that you were an angel of beauty at court, that you spoke to the king, and that it was thought you were soliciting a pension for your husband. I returned a slight answer, "that I believed it was to entreat his majesty to consider the great expenses M. de Grignan had been obliged to incur in Provence," and that was all.

You relate inimitably the story of M. de Villequier and his mother-in-law. There seems no danger of her proving a Phædra to him. Had you read that part of your letter over, you would easily have conceived the manner in which it struck me. It is not unlike the story of Joconde; and the chambermaid yawning with fatigue at her long waiting is admirable. I think Madame d'Aumont's conduct very praiseworthy: it ought to silence the world, and satisfy her husband. What great doings in Savoy! I can not believe the king will withhold his pity and assistance from the young Princess of Baden, when she represents to him the situation of her mother, abandoned by all her children. I do not believe she will set out till her mother is gone. This good mother, it is true, has so much fire about her, that it is difficult to persuade one's self she is not still in the prime of her youth. The Princess de Tarente intends to receive her at Vitré. As for Madame de Marbeuf, she is one of her old acquaintance; they have spent whole winters together in supping and playing at the Palace of Soissons; you may judge how readily this will be renewed at Rennes. I have told my son the story of the Chevalier de Soisson's engagement: we could neither of us have believed the eyes of a grandmother retained still so much power. I do not think the raising of the siege of Buda* worth mentioning

---

* After having beaten the Turks, and repulsed the troops they were leading to the assistance of Buda, the Duke of Lorraine was at length obliged to raise the siege, which had lasted for nearly four months.

to you; it is a piece of news hardly of sufficient consequence to obtain a place in my letter. I fancy the dauphiness,* however, will take the pains to be sorry: her brother has exposed himself so much, and acquitted himself so well in this expedition, that it is a pity such an elector should be obliged to return from it.

Our *worthy* is very ill with one of those bad colds and coughs which you have seen him afflicted with. He is in his little closet. We take better care of him here than could be done at Paris. My daughter-in-law has gone through all the hot and cold regimen of the Capuchins, without being affected either one way or the other by them. When the weather is fine, as it has been for the last three days, I venture out about two o'clock, and walk backward and forward before the gardeners, who are cutting wood, and representing the picture of winter, but without stopping to contemplate the scene; and after I have enjoyed all the heat of the sun, I return to the house, leaving the evening to those of a more hardy constitution. In this way do I govern myself to please you, and very often I do not stir out of the house at all. Coulanges' chair, a few books that my son reads admirably, and now and then a little conversation, will compose the whole of my occupation during the winter, and the subject of your anxiety; for I shall exactly follow your orders in all points, and every where.

My son understands perfectly well what *Wednesday* means.† To say the truth, we would be very dull without him, and he without us; but he manages matters so well that there is generally a party of ombre in my apartments, and at intervals we read, and make comments on what we read; you know what sort of place the Rocks is. We have read a folio volume through in little more than a week. We have been engaged

---

* The dauphiness was always a German in her heart; this partiality, which the subsequent war increased and rendered more offensive, contributed, with other eccentricities of character, to alienate the affections of her husband, the king, and the whole court.

† This was one of Madame de Sévigné's post-days.

with M. Nicole, the Lives of the Fathers of the Desert, and the History of the Reformation in England; in short, those who are happy enough to have a taste for reading never need be at a loss for amusement.

LETTER XCI.

THE ROCKS, Sunday, February 27, 1685.

Ah, my child! was ever any thing so ill-timed as the death of the King of England,* just at the eve of a masquerade? My poor little marquis† is very unfortunate to have such an unexpected event thrown in the way of his pleasure. I know nothing that can comfort him for this disappointment but the universal encomiums that have been given to his charming dress, and the hope that the masquerade is only put off for a time.

My dear child, I make you my compliments of condolence on these great occurrences, and expect yours in return upon my mistaken ideas; for I was at the masquerade, the opera, and the ball, snug in a corner, contemplating you with admiration; in short, I was in as great an agitation as you may suppose your poor mother to experience on such an occasion; and, after all, there was no entertainment of any kind.

I enter into your sentiments, my beautiful dear, better than any one. Yes, yes, I can very well conceive that we are transfused into our children, and, as you say, feel more keenly for them than for ourselves. I have sufficiently experienced these emotions, which are not without their pleasure when the object is deserving of them and of the admiration of every one besides. Your son pleases extremely; there is something inexpressibly smart and agreeable in his countenance; the eye does not pass lightly over him as over others in general, but

* Charles II., who died 16th February, 1685.
† Louis-Provence, Marquis de Grignan, Madame de Sévigné's grandson.

rests attentively. Madame de la Fayette tells me she has written to Madame de Montespan that she had engaged her honor that you and your son would have reason to be satisfied with her. I know no one who would be more happy to serve you than Madame de la Fayette.

But is it not extraordinary that we have not yet had a word together on the death of the King of England? He was by no means an old man, and he was a monarch; this shows that death spares no one. It will be a great happiness if he was a Catholic in his heart, and died in the faith of our holy religion. England appears to me a theater that is about to furnish some very extraordinary scenes: the Prince of Orange, the Duke of Monmouth, an infinite number of Lutherans, and a confirmed aversion to all Catholics; but time will discover in what way Providence will direct the performance, after this tragical event;* however, it seems it will not put a stop to the diversion at Versailles, since I find you are to return there

---

* Charles II. was sixty-five years of age, and had reigned about twenty-five years, reckoning from the restoration of the Stuarts. He received the sacraments agreeably to the rites of the Church of Rome, but more, it is said, in compliance with the entreaties of his brother than the dictates of his conscience. He had some good private qualities. But, as a prince, his character, says the impartial Hume, was "dangerous to his subjects, and dishonorable to himself." To rid himself of his parliament, he had placed himself in a state of disgraceful independence on Louis XIV. It has been said of him that he never said a foolish thing, and never did a wise one. Judging by the following anecdote, he carried further even than policy required, the practice of dissimulation, which would be, as it is declared, the necessary virtue of kings, if it be true that weakness and indolence are their natural vices. It is said that Charles II. having reproached his minister Shaftesbury with being "the greatest knave in the three kingdoms," he replied, "Apparently your majesty only includes subjects."

Madame de Sévigné speaks of the state of England in the character of a well-informed person. The rebellion of Monmouth and his tragical end in the same year, and James II. dethroned and driven out of the kingdom three years afterward by his son-in-law, justified but too well her predictions.

on Monday. You say a thousand kind things of the concern it would give you to leave me behind at Paris, if I were there; but as this, to my great regret, is not the case, make the most of this opportunity, follow the court: no one is formed to make a better figure there, and I think every thing seems to tend toward the completion of your wishes. Mine, though made at such a distance, are not less ardent and sincere than if I were with you. I feel, though less delicately, the truth of a remark you made to me one day, and which I then laughed at: that you were so much mistress of my imagination and my heart that I had you always present with me; this is very true, my child, but I must own I had rather enjoy a little more of reality.

LETTER XCII.

The Rocks, Wednesday, Aug. 11, 1685.

You see, my dear, that we are now come to reckon by days only, not by months! not even by weeks! But, alas! what you say is very true: there could not be a more cruel damp to our pleasures than the thought that we might be obliged to part again almost as soon as we met; this is a painful idea; it occurs to me but too often; day or night I am not free from it; it came in my head the last time I was writing to you, and I could not forbear saying to myself, Surely this evil ought to be sufficient to secure me from the danger of experiencing a greater; but I dare not dwell upon this melancholy reflection, and shall now divert it by the thought that I am soon to see you at Baville. I shall not be at all ashamed of my equipage; my children have very elegant ones, and I have had the same; but now the times are altered; I have only two horses of my own, and shall hire four horses from the postmaster of Mans; and in that manner I shall make my entrance into Paris without the least concern. You will find my leg in a state of perfection, which will make you love

Charlotte all your life; she has fancied you from hence more beautiful than the day, and this idea has given her an extreme desire to restore this leg to you, worthy of your admiration, when you know from what a situation it has been extricated. All this is past, and so is the visit of little Coulanges; he set out on Monday morning with your brother. I accompanied them as far as the gate that leads to Vitré; there we stopped to await the arrival of your letters from Paris, which came as expected, and were read with the usual pleasure. As you only mentioned that M. d'Ormesson's wife was at the point of death, I have not dared to write to him; but as soon as you let me know she is buried, I will venture to send him a line or two by way of condolence and comfort; but indeed, considering the state she was in, what could be more desirable for herself and her family than her death? Ah, my dear child, how humiliating it is to be obliged to drag about the lees of life and understanding! how much preferable would it be, could we have our wish, to leave behind us a remembrance worthy of being preserved, rather than spoil and disfigure it by the infirmities and weakness of old age! I should like to be an inhabitant of that country where they kill their parents out of kindness, when they become old and helpless, if such a practice could be reconciled to Christianity.

Our gentlemen sung *Guadeamus* on Monday evening at Marbeuf's. Your brother is not quite recovered of his slight disorder. I have had some delightful conversations with Coulanges on the subject he is so much at a loss to comprehend: scenes have passed between us not inferior to some of Molière's. When do you expect *Saint Grignan?*

N.B. No more letters are found from Madame de Sévigné to her daughter till toward the end of 1688, both having passed the intermediate time together at Paris.

LETTER XCIII.

PARIS, Friday, October 8, 1688.

What a tremendous rain, just, my child, as you are going to descend that frightful mountain of Rochepot! How numberless are the vexations of those who love with any degree of fervor! We know not how to love heroically, notwithstanding the example of heroism below :* but there is no knowing you without being attached to you with the greatest tenderness. Our poor hero is still dreadfully afflicted with the gout; it is a perfect martyrdom. There are several persons of wit and learning, as St. Romain,† the Abbé Bigorré, Crosailles,‡ who visit him with a view to divert his painful moments with the news of the day, and other topics; but still he suffers greatly.

Our young marquis could not have been at the opening of the trenches, for M. de Vauban could not wait the arrival of the dauphin on account of the rains; we are still persuaded that in a very few days your mind will be at ease.

The Prince of Orange has declared himself protector of the religion of the Church of England, and has demanded the young prince,§ that he may be brought up in that faith. This is a great event: several of the English nobility have joined him. You know that La Trousse has taken Avignon.‖ Madame de Coulanges, who overflows with money, has lent

---

* Meaning the Chevalier de Grignan, who had an apartment in the Hôtel de Carnavalet, Madame de Sévigné's house at Paris.

† St. Romain had been embassador in Switzerland.

‡ Brother of Marshal de Catinet, and a man of great merit. He had been captain of the French guards, but had quitted the service on account of ill health.

§ James, Prince of Wales, son of James II., born the 20th June, 1688; but better known afterward by the name of the Pretender.

‖ Some disputes that had happened between the court of France and that of Rome had obliged Louis XIV. to sieze upon the county of Venaissin, belonging to the pope.

Mademoiselle de Méri a thousand francs; we expect that lady here every day. M. de la Trousse (her brother) will very readily repay the loan.

I am much pleased, my dear child, that you approve the coming of the good Abbé de Bigorré; his company will prove no small amusement to me. We entertain ourselves below stairs with frequent conversations upon the state of our affairs; I find there all the consolation that a sound understanding and a generous heart can afford me; for the more the chevalier is known the more he must be esteemed and loved. I have no need to ask him if you love me; for I am convinced of it by a thousand instances: but without questioning him upon the subject, he gave me the most charming proofs of it. We eat together, and keep a very good table. The philosophy of Corbinelli is to come to-night. We have written in all our apartments, *Fais ce que tu voudras; vive la sainte liberté!**

I have seen Madame de Fontenilles: she has lately lost her mother, and seems overwhelmed with grief. You will judge what impression this made upon me. Her mother died in a shocking way, crying out in all the agonies of despair, and terrified with the thought of taking the last sacraments: she received them, however, but with a gloomy and dreadful silence. Her son and Alliot arrived just two hours after her death.

LETTER XCIV.

Paris, Tuesday, October 26, 1688.

Oh! what a letter, my child! It well deserves that I should come here on purpose to receive it, as I did. At length, then, you are arrived safe at Grignan, and are in perfect health; and such is my fate that, though you are removed at the distance of half the globe from me, I must rejoice at it. Perhaps it may

---

* Do as you like: reign, sacred Liberty!

please Heaven that ere long I shall embrace you again: let me live in that hope. You make a very pleasing portrait of Paulina. I know her again; she is not at all altered, as M. de Grignan would have made us believe she was. She is a sweet creature, and worthy of being loved. She adores you, and her absolute submission to your will, even in the midst of her joy at seeing you, if you decide that she should leave you again, at once engages my pity and concern; nor can I help admiring the power she has over herself. Were I in your place I should be loth to part with such an agreeable companion, who will at once furnish you with amusement and occupation. I would make her work at her needle, and read works of taste: I would argue with her, and sound the depth of her capacity. I would talk to her with affection and confidence; for, believe me, you will never be tired of her society, on the contrary, she may be of great use to you. In short, I would make the most of her, and would not punish myself by depriving myself of such a comfort.

I am very glad the chevalier speaks well of me; my vanity is concerned in preserving his good opinion. If he is fond of my company, I, in return, can never have too much of his, and I think it a proof of good taste to be desirous of cultivating his esteem. I know not how you can say that your humor is a cloud which hides or obscures the affections you have for me. If such may have been the case formerly, you have for many years past totally removed the vail, and you no longer conceal from me any part of the most perfect and tender affection that one person can entertain for another. Heaven will reward you for it in your own children, who will love you, not in the same way, as perhaps they may not be capable of it, but at least to the utmost of their abilities, and we can desire no more.

LETTER XCV.

PARIS, All-Saints' day, 1688, nine o'clock at night.

Philipsburg is taken, and your son is well! I have only to turn this phrase in every possible way, for I will not change my text. Learn then again from this note, that *your son is well, and that Philipsburg is taken!* A courier is just arrived at M. de Villacerf's, who says that the dauphin's courier reached Fontainebleau while Father Gaillard was preaching; and that the sermon was immediately interrupted, and thanks returned to God for this brilliant achievement. No further particulars are known, except that there was no assault, and that M. du Plessis was right when he said the governor had ordered wagons to carry away his equipage. Recover your breath, then, my dear child, and let the first thing you do be to return thanks to God. No other siege is talked of; rejoice that your son has witnessed that of Philipsburg; it is an admirable period for him; it is the dauphin's first campaign. Would you not have been grieved if he was the only person of his age who was not present on the occasion, in which all the rest glory? But let us not look back; every thing has happened as we could have wished. It is you, my dear count, we may thank for it. I congratulate you on the joy you must experience, and beg my compliments also to the coadjutor; you are all relieved from great anxiety. Sleep soundly, then, my dearest, sleep soundly on the assurance we give you; if you are covetous of grief, as we formerly said, seek some other occasion, for God has preserved your dear child to you. We are in raptures, and in this feeling I embrace you with an affection that I believe you can not doubt.

LETTER XCVI.

PARIS, Monday, November 8, 1688

THIS is the day, my dear child, on which you are to begin your journey; we follow you step by step. The weather is delightful; the durance will not be so terrific as it sometimes is. It looks as if you were resolved to remove further and further from us out of mere spite; you will find yourself at last on the sea-shore. But it is the will of God that we should meet with periods in our life which are difficult to bear; and we must endeavor to repair, by a submission to his will, the too great sensibility we feel toward earthly things. In this respect it is impossible to be more culpable than I am.

The chevalier is much better. It is painful to reflect that the weather which agrees with him is precisely what may dethrone the King of England; whereas he suffered dreadfully a few days ago, when the wind and tempests were dispersing the fleet of the Prince of Orange: he is unhappy at not being able to make his health accord with the good of Europe; for the sentiment of joy is universal at the failure of the prince, whose wife* is a perfect Tullia; ah, how boldly would she drive over the body of her father! She has empowered her husband to take possession of the kingdom of England, of which she calls herself the heiress; and if her husband is killed, for her imagination is not very delicate, M. de Schomberg† is to take possession of it for herself. What say you to a hero, who so sadly disgraces the close of a glorious life? He saw the admiral's ship sink in which he was to have em-

---

* Mary Stuart, daughter of James II., king of England, and wife of William Henry of Nassau, Prince of Orange, afterward king of England by the name of William III. Tullia, the daughter of Servius Tullius, king of Rome, caused her chariot to drive over the bleeding body of her father, who had just been assassinated.

† Frederic Armand, Count de Schomberg, marshal of France, obtained permission to retire from the king's service in 1685, on account of his having embraced the Protestant religion. He was minister of state, and generalissimo of the armies of the Elector of Brandenbourg, and went over to England in 1688 with the Prince of Orange.

Marshal de Schomberg had ancient leagues with the Princes of Orange. He had, besides, much cause to complain of the court, and even of Turenne, during the war with Holland. See a curious account of this general in the *Fragmens Historiques de Racine.*

barked; and as the prince and he were the last in following the fleet, which was under weigh in the finest weather possible, they were obliged, by a tremendous storm that suddenly arose, to return to port, the prince being very much indisposed with his asthma, and M. de Schomberg as much vexed. Only twenty-six sail returned with them; the rest were all dispersed, some toward Norway, others toward Boulogne. M. d'Aumont has sent a courier to the king, to inform him that vessels had been seen at the mercy of the winds, and that there were many appearances of shipwreck. A vessel armed *en flute*, in which were nine hundred men, sunk in sight of the prince of Orange. In short, the hand of God is visible upon this fleet: many ships may return, but it will be long before they will be able to do any mischief, for the dispersion has certainly been great, and has happened at a time when it was least expected: this is certainly a stroke of Providence. I need not say so much to you of this great news, for the papers are full of it; but as we are so too, and as we can talk of nothing else, it flows naturally from my pen.

Shall I give you another instance of wounds that were not received at the siege of Philipsburg? It relates to the Chevalier de Longueville: the town was taken; the dauphin had just inspected the garrison, the little chevalier mounted the back of the trenches to look at something, when a soldier, aiming at a woodcock, shot this poor child, and he died in consequence the next day: his death is as singular as his birth.*

LETTER XCVII.

PARIS, Friday, December 3, 1688.

I HAVE to inform you to-day that the king made yesterday seventy-four knights of the order of the Holy Ghost,

* Charles-Louis d'Orleans, natural son of Charles Paris d'Orleans, Duke of Longueville, killed in crossing the Rhine in 1672.

of which I send you the list. As he has done M. de Grignan the honor to include him, and as you will receive a hundred thousand congratulations upon the occasion, wiser heads than mine advise you neither to say nor write any thing that may give offense to any of your companions in this honor. The best way, perhaps, would be to write to M. de Louvois, and to say that the honor he had done you of inquiring after you by your courier gives you the privilege of thanking him; and that wishing to believe, on the subject of the favor the king has just granted to M. de Grignan, that he has contributed toward it by his approbation at least, you return him thanks also for this. You will give this a better turn than I can do; and it will do no injury to the letter M. de Grignan should write. The particulars of what passed are these: The king said to M. le Grand :* "The count de Soissons† and you must agree among yourselves with respect to rank." You must know, that M. le Grand's son is in the promotion, which is contrary to the general rules. You must know, also, that the king said to the dukes that he had read their memorial, and that he found that the house of Lorraine had taken precedence of them on several occasions; and so it is decided.‡ M. le Grand then spoke to the Count de Soissons; they proposed to draw lots, "provided," said the count, "that if you win I pass between you and your son."§ M. le Grand would not consent to this, and so the Count de Soissons is not a chevalier. The king asked M. de la Tremouille how old he was? he replied that he was thirty-three; the king excused him two years. This favor, it is said, which has given some offense to the principality, has not been estimated as it ought

---

* Louis de Lorraine, Count d'Armagnac, first equerry of France.

† Louis Thomas de Savoy, Count de Soissons.

‡ It is related that the Duke of Luxembourg said aloud upon this subject: "There is one thing I can not comprehend." "And what is that?" said the king. "How a Bourbon can look upon a Guise."

§ Henry de Lorraine, Count de Brionne.

to have been. However, he is the first duke, according to the precedence of his dukedom.*

LETTER XCVIII.

PARIS, Monday, December 6, 1688.

Your last letter has an air of gayety and expansion of heart which convinces me that Franckendal is taken, and that he is safe, I mean the marquis. Enjoy this pleasure, my beloved child; your son sleeps to-night at Claie; you see he will pass through Livri, and to-morrow he will sup with us. The chevalier, who is indeed an excellent creature in all respects, is returned from Versailles; he has thanked the king, and it has all passed off well. You will assume the blue ribbon on the second of January in the midst of Provence, over which you have the command, and where there are only you and M. d'Arles your uncle. This distinction and remembrance of his majesty, when you the least expected it, are highly gratifying; even the compliments you receive on all sides are not like those which are paid to others; it is to little purpose to say, "Ah this! ah that!" for my part, I say on this subject, as on many others, "What is good, is good;" you will lose nothing; and when we think of those who are in despair, we consider ourselves very fortunate to be in the recollection of a master who does not forget the services that are rendered him both by ourselves and our children. I own to you I feel this joy thoroughly, without appearing to do so. The chevalier has a great desire to send word of it this evening to our marquis at Claie, who will not be insensible to it. He wishes also to send you your blue ribbon with two Saint Esprits, because the time draws on: he believes you to have your grandfather's† cross

---

* Messieurs de la Tremouille had the highest rank at court, as being the eldest dukes, and Messieurs d'Usez the highest rank in the parliament as being the eldest peers.

† Louis Castellane de Adhémar de Monteil, received knight of the

at Grignan; if you have not, you would be at a loss for one. I own that if the chevalier had not forestalled me, I should have made you this pretty little present; but I give place to him in every thing. The favor is complete by the permission of not attending the installation. I am charged with a hundred compliments; Madame de Lesdiguières, Madame de Mouci, Madame de Lavardin, M. de Harlai, and I know not how many others I could name; for they are in long lists, as when you gained your lawsuit. Think not, my dear child, that you have been out of luck for the last three months; I begin with your gaining your cause; then the preservation of your son; his early reputation; his contusion; the beauty of his company, to which you contributed; and I conclude with the business of Avignon and the blue ribbon: think well of this, and be thankful to God.

LETTER XCIX.

PARIS, Friday, December 10, 1688.

I can not answer your letters to-day, as they came so late, and I answer two on a Monday. The marquis* is a little rustic, but not enough so to render him ridiculous; he will not have so fine a figure as his father, nor is it to be expected; in other respects he does very well, answering pertinently to every thing that is asked him, like a man of good sense, who has made observations and sought information during his campaign; his conversation is tinctured with modesty and rectitude that charm us. M. du Plessis is worthy of the esteem you bear him. We take our meals together very socially, amusing ourselves with the unjust proceedings we sometimes adopt against one another; make yourself easy upon this score, and think no more about it; let it be my part to blush

---

king's orders in 1584, lieutenant-general of the government of Province, was M. de Grignan's great-grandfather.

* The son of Madame de Grignan.

at thinking that a wren is a heavy burden to me : I own I am grieved at it, but we must submit to the great justice of paying our debts : no one understands this better than yourself ; you have also kindness enough for me to believe that I am not naturally avaricious, and that I have no intention to hoard. When you are here, good madam, you tutor your son so well, that I am compelled to admire you ; but, in your absence, I undertake to teach him the common rules of conversation, which it is important to know; there are some things of which we ought not to be ignorant. It would be ridiculous to appear astonished at certain events which are the topics of the day; I am sufficiently acquainted with these trifles. I also strongly recommend to him attention to what others say, and the presence of mind by which we quickly comprehend and answer; this is a principal object in our intercourse with the world. I repeat to him instances of miracles of this kind which Dangeau related to us the other day; he admires them, and I lay great stress upon the charms, and even utility, of this sort of alertness of mind. In short, I obtain the chevalier's approbation: we converse together on books, and the misfortune of being troubled with listlessness and want of employment : we call this laziness of the mind, which deprives us of a taste for good books and even romances; as this is an interesting subject, we frequently enter upon it. Little Auvergne* is very fond of reading ; he was never happy, when with the army, unless he had a book in his hand. God knows whether M. du Plessis and we can turn this fine and noble passion to account ; we are willing to believe the marquis susceptible of the best impressions ; we suffer no opportunity to pass unimproved that can tend to inspire him with so desirable a taste. The chevalier is of more use to this dear boy than can easily be imagined ; he is continually striking the full chords of honor and reputation, and takes an interest in his

* Francis-Egon de la Tour, Prince of Auvergne, who quitted the French army in 1702, in which he served in Germany, to enter into the service of the emperor.

affairs, for which you can not sufficiently thank him: he enters into every thing, attends to every thing, and wishes the marquis to regulate his own accounts and incur no unnecessary expenses; by this means, he endeavors to give him a habit of regularity and economy, and to make him lay aside the air of grandeur, of "what does it signify," of ignorance, and indifference, which is the direct path to every kind of injustice, and, at length, to the workhouse: can there be any obligation equal to that of training up your son in these principles? For my part, I am charmed with it, and think this sort of education far more noble than any other. The chevalier is a little afflicted with the gout: he will go to-morrow, if he can, to Versailles, and will inform you of the situation of his affairs. You already know that you are a knight of the order, which is a very desirable thing in the center of your province, and in actual service, and will admirably become M. de Grignan's fine figure: there will, however, be no one to dispute it with him in Provence, for he will not be envied by his uncle,* as this title does not go out of the family.

La Fayette is just going from hence; he has been holding forth a full hour about one of the little marquis's friends. He has related so many ridiculous things of him that the chevalier thinks himself obliged to mention them to his father, who is his friend; he thanked La Fayette for his intelligence, for, in fact, there is nothing of so much consequence as being in good company, and it often happens that, without being ridiculous ourselves, we are rendered so by those we associate with. Make yourself easy upon this subject, the chevalier will set matters right. I shall be very much mortified if he can not present his nephew on Sunday; this gout is a great drawback upon our happiness. With respect to Paulina, can you, my dear child, expect her to be perfect? She is not mild in her own apartment; many persons who are very much beloved and respected, have had the same fault. I think you

* The archbishop of Arles was commander of the royal orders of knighthood.

may easily correct it; but take particular care not to scold and humiliate her. All my friends load me with a thousand compliments and a thousand regards to you. Madame de Lavardin called upon me yesterday, to tell me she esteemed you too highly to send you *compliments;* but that she embraced you with all her heart, and the great Count de Grignan—these were her words. You have great reason to love her.

What I am going to relate is a fact. Madame de Brinon, the very soul of St. Cyr, and the intimate friend of Madame de Maintenon, is no longer at St. Cyr;[*] she quitted that place four days ago; Madame Hanover, who loves her, brought her back to the Hôtel de Guise, where she still remains. There does not seem to be any misunderstanding between her and Madame de Maintenon, for she sends every day to inquire after her health; this increases our curiosity to know the subject of her disgrace. Every one is whispering about it without knowing more. If this affair should be cleared up, I will inform you of the circumstances.

LETTER C.

Paris, Friday, December 31, 1688.

Per torner dunque al nostro proposito,[†] I must tell you, my child, that all the uncertainties of the day before yesterday,

---

[*] Madame de Brinon, at that time of the first establishment of St. Cyr, was placed at the head of that house. She had great learning and talents, but an equal portion of pride and ambition. The superior only of the house, she assumed the airs of an abbess. She displayed the most offensive ostentation; she held a court; she opposed Madame de Maintenon, whose dependent she was. These things offended the king, as well as her benefactress. A *lettre de cachet* obliged her to leave St. Cyr in twenty-four hours.

The Duchess of Hanover, who received her, and who was the daughter of the celebrated princess palatine, was soon disgusted with Madame de Brinon, who retired to the Abbey of Maubuisson, and died there, regretting the world, regretting St. Cyr, and regretting life.

[†] To return then to our proposition.

which seemed to be fixed by the assurances M. de Lamoignon gave us that the King of England was at Calais, are now changed into the certainty that he is detained in England; and that if this ill fortune has not befallen him, he has perished; for he was to make his escape, and embark a few hours after the queen. So, that though we have no certain intelligence of his being arrested, there is not a single person who does not now credit it. Such is our situation; and such the way in which we are closing the present year, and entering upon that of '89; a year marked out by extraordinary predictions, as pregnant with great events. Not one, however, will take place that is not agreeable to the order of Providence, like all our actions, and all our journeyings. We must submit to every thing, and look boldly in the face of futurity; this is going a great way.

In the mean while, count, I address myself to you. Yesterday the Knights of St. Michael went through the ceremony with several of those of the order of the Holy Ghost, at the hour I mentioned to you after vespers, and to-morrow the rest will do the same. The chevalier will inform you how it is managed with respect to the absentees. You must make your profession of faith, and give an account of your life and manners. Of this you will be duly informed; you are not the only one; and in the mean time *hold off, fair and softly*. Yesterday, M. de Chevreuse, of the order of St. Michael, passed before M. de la Rochefoucault, who said to him, "Sir, you pass before me, which you have no right to do." M. de Chevreuse replied, "Sir, I have a right, for I am Duke de Luynes." "Oh, sir," rejoined the other, "in this respect I yield to you." The gazette will inform you, my dear count, that M. de Luynes has given this duchy to his son, with the king's permission; and M. de Chevreuse, who will henceforward be called M. de Luynes, the duchy of Chevreuse to his son, who will be styled Duke de Montfort. Your son's comrades are highly distinguished by titles. It is said that some troops are to be sent into Brittany with M. de Momont, Major-

General, to be under the command of M. de Chaulnes; there will be encampments in all the provinces. You need only refer to the map, to judge whether we have occasion to be on our guard on all sides; cast your eyes for a moment over all Europe. Madame de Barillon is very uneasy respecting her husband;* but it is said at random, for no letters arrive, that he is safe, though the chapel of the King of England has been pulled down, as well as that belonging to the embassador's household. Time will clear up all this. But who am I speaking to? is it still to this count? My dear child, your good lady, who swore she would not touch a card till the King of England had won a battle, will not probably play again for a long time. Poor woman! The Prince of Orange is in London—this is still the subject of my letter, as it is of all conversation, for every one considers himself as concerned in this great scene. The queen is still in a convent at Boulogne, always in tears at the absence of her husband, whom she passionately loves.

Madame de Brinon is quite forgotten. A new comedy is said to be in rehearsal, which is to be represented at St. Cyr, and is called Esther. The carnival does not promise to be very gay. My son's letters are constantly filled with the most affectionate sentiments for you and M. de Grignan. We expect your letters, but probably shall not answer them till Monday. The chevalier and I have very long conversations about you; he is tolerably well, and when your son returns from Chalons, he intends to accompany him to Versailles. The good Corbinelli exhausts his rhetoric upon the present situation of affairs, and at the same time adores you. Adieu, my lovely child; I embrace you a thousand times, and wish you a happy year in that of 1689.

* M. de Barillon was the French Embassador to England.

LETTER CI.

PARIS, Monday, January 3, 1689.

Your dear son arrived this morning. We were delighted to see him and M. du Plessis; we were at dinner when they came, and they ate very heartily of our repast, which was already somewhat impaired. Oh, that you could have heard all the marquis said of the beauty of his company! He first asked if the company was arrived; and on the question, whether it was a fine one, this was the answer he received: "Indeed, sir, it is; it is one of the finest that ever was seen; *it is an old company*, and more to be prized than the *new ones*." You may guess the effect such an encomium must have on a person who was not known to be the captain. Our boy was in raptures the next day at the sight of his noble company mounted; the men, made on purpose, as it were, and selected by you, and the horses cast in the same mold, gave him such high spirits, that M. de Chalons* and Madame de Noailles (his mother) entered into his feelings of joy. He has been received by these pious persons as the son of M. de Grignan; but why do I tell you all this? it is the marquis' business.

LETTER CII.

PARIS, Wednesday, January 5, 1689.

I took the marquis with me yesterday; we began by visiting M. de la Trousse, who was so obliging as to put on the dresses of the novice and professor, as on the ceremonial day; these two habits set off a fine figure to advantage. A foolish thought, without considering consequences, made me regret that the fine shape of M. de Grignan had not shone upon this occasion. The page's dress is very becoming; and I am not

---

* Louis Antoine de Noailles, Bishop de Chalons sur Marne, afterward Archbishop and Cardinal of Paris.

at all surprised that the Princess of Clèves should fall in love with M. de Nemours and his handsome legs.* The mantle has all the magnificence of royalty; it cost La Trousse 800 pistoles, for he purchased it. After having viewed this pretty masquerade, I took your son to all the ladies in the neighborhood. Madame de Vaubecourt and Madame Ollier received him with great politeness; he will soon pay visits upon his own account.

The Life of St. Louis has induced me to read Mézerai; I was willing to take a view of the last kings of the second race, and I want to unite Philip de Valois with King John; this is an admirable period of history, upon which the Abbé de Choisi has written a book that may be read with interest. We endeavor to beat into your son's head the necessity of being a little acquainted with what has passed before his time; and it will have effect; but, in the mean while, there are many reasons for paying attention to what is passing at present. You will see by the news of to-day how the King of England escaped from London, apparently with the consent of the Prince of Orange. Politicians reason upon this subject, and ask if it be more advantageous for this king to be in France; some say Yes, because he is here in security, and will not run the risk of being compelled to give up his wife and child, or lose his head; others say No, because he leaves the Prince of Orange to enjoy the protectorship, and be adored, having made his way to it naturally, and without bloodshed. It is certain that war will soon be declared against us, or perhaps, even we may declare it first. If we make peace in Italy and Germany, we may apply ourselves with greater attention to the English and Dutch war; this is to be hoped, for it would be too much to have enemies on all sides. You see whither my rambling pen leads me; but you may easily suppose that all conversations turn upon these great events.

* Allusion to Madame de la Fayette's romance.

LETTER CIII.

PARIS, Monday, January 10, 1689.

We often stumble upon the same ideas, my dear child; I even think that I wrote to you from the Rocks what you say in your last letter respecting time. I now consent that it should fly; the days have no longer any thing so dear and precious for me as I found them to contain when you were at the Hôtel de Carnavalet. I enjoyed, I made the most of every hour; I treasured it as a miser does his gold; but in absence, the case is different; time can not fly fast enough till the wished-for period arrives; we hurry it along, and would willingly dispose of all the intermediate space in favor of the days to which we aspire; it is a piece of tapestry which we are eager to finish; we are lavish of hours, and bestow them on any one. But I own that when I reflect on the point to which this profusion of hours and days leads me, I tremble. I am no longer certain of any, and reason presents me with the image of what I am certain to find in my way. My child, I will put an end to these reflections with you, and endeavor to turn them to my own advantage.

The Abbé Têtu is in an alarming way for want of sleep. The physicians would not answer for his intellects. He is sensible of his situation, which is an additional calamity: he is kept alive merely by opium: he seeks for diversion and amusement, and accordingly frequents public places. We want him to go to Versailles to see the King and Queen of England, and the Prince of Wales. Can there be a grander spectacle, or one more capable of affording the highest interest? It appears that the Prince of Orange favored the king's flight. The king was sent to Exeter, where it was his intention to go; the front of his house was well guarded, and all the back doors left open. The prince was not inclined to sacrifice his father-in-law. He remains in London in the place of the king, without taking upon himself the title, being only desirous of restoring what he thinks the true religion, and supporting the laws of the country, without spilling a drop of blood : this is precisely the reverse of what we thought of him ; we see him in a very different point of view. Our king, however, acts in a manner almost divine with respect to their Brittanic Majesties ; for is it not being the representative of the Almighty to support a king banished, betrayed, and abandoned ? The noble ambition of our sovereign is gratified by acting this part. He went to meet the queen, with all his household, and a hundred coaches and six. When he perceived the Prince of Wales's carriage, he alighted and affectionately embraced him ; he then ran to the queen, who was by this time alighted ; he saluted her, talked with her some time, placed her at his right hand in his carriage, and presented the dauphin and monsieur to her, who were also in the carriage, and conducted her to St. Germain, where she found every thing prepared for her like a queen—all sorts of apparel, and a rich casket containing six thousand louis-d'ors. The King of England was expected the next day at St. Germain, where the king waited for him. He arrived late. His majesty went to the end of the guard-room to meet him ; the King of England made an inclination as if to embrace his knees, but the king prevented him, and embraced him three or four times very cordially. They talked together in a low voice for nearly a quarter of an hour ; the king presented the dauphin and monsieur to him, the princes of the blood, and Cardinal de Bonzi. He conducted him to the queen's apartment, who could scarcely refrain from tears. After a conversation of a few minutes his majesty led them to the apartment of the Prince of Wales, where they again conversed for some time, and he then withdrew, not choosing to be attended back, saying to the king, " This is your house; when I come you will do the honors of it, and I will do the honors of mine when you come to Versailles." The next day, which was yesterday, the dauphiness went there with all the court. I know not how they regulated the chairs, for they had those belonging to the Queen of Spain ; and the Queen-mother of England was treated as a daughter of France : I shall hereafter send you these particulars. His majesty sent the King of England ten thousand louis-d'ors; the latter looks old and fatigued; the queen is thin, with fine black eyes swelled with weeping; a fine complexion, but rather pale; a large mouth, beautiful teeth, a fine figure, and a great share of sense; no wonder if with all these she pleases every one who beholds her. Here is matter for general conversation that will not soon be exhausted.

The poor chevalier can neither write nor go to Versailles, which grieves us sadly, as he has a thousand things to do there; but he is not ill: on Saturday he supped with Madame de Coulanges, Madame de Vauvineux, M. de Duras, and your son, at the lieutenant's, where the healths of the first and second were drank, that is to say, Madame de la Fayette's and yours, for you have yielded to the date of friendship. Yesterday Madame de Coulanges gave a very pretty supper to the gouty gentlemen, the Abbé de Marsillac, the Chevalier de Grignan, and M. de Lamoignon, whose nephritic complaints stood him in stead of the gout; his wife and the *divinities* were admitted in consequence of colds which they are never without; I in consideration of the rheumatism I had twelve years ago, and Coulanges, for deserving to have the gout. There was no scarcity of conversation; the little man sung, and gave the Abbé de Marsillac great pleasure, which he expressed by his admiration, and by imitating the tones and manners, which reminded me so strongly of his father that I could not help being affected. Your son was at the Mesdemoiselles de Castelnau's. There is a younger sister, very pretty and very agreeable, who is quite to your son's taste, and he leaves the squint-eyed girl to Sanzei; he took a hautboy with him, and they danced till midnight. This society is very pleasant to the marquis, as he meets St. Hérem, Janin, Choiseul, and Ninon there; so that he is not in a foreign country. The chevalier does not seem to be in haste to marry him, nor does M. de Lamoignon seem very desirous of marrying his daughter. We can say nothing with respect to the marriage of M de Mirepoix,* this is the work of M. de Montfort: people seem to be infatuated, or else their heads are turned, for they do not think as they used to do; in short, this man seems impelled by his destiny, and what can be done in such a case?

M. de Lauzun is not gone back to England; he has an apartment at Versailles, and is perfectly satisfied; he has written to Mademoiselle to have the honor of seeing her, which has given her great offense. I have performed a master-piece; I have been to visit Madame de Ricouart, who is lately returned, very well pleased at being a widow. You have nothing to do but appoint me to complete your acknowledgments, like your romances, do you recollect? I thank the amiable Paulina for her letter; I am confident her person would please me; so she could then find no appellation for me but that of *madam?*† this is being very serious. Adieu, my dear child; preserve your health, in other words, your beauty, which I so much admire.

LETTER CIV.

PARIS, Wednesday, January 12, 1689.

You retired then at five o'clock in the afternoon; you drew king and queen at dinner; you were in as good company as

---

* Gaston John Baptist de Levis, Marquis de Mirepoix, married, January 16, 1689, to Anne Charlotte Maria de Saint Nectaire, daughter of Henry Francis, Duke de la Ferté, and of Mary Gabriel Angelica de la Mothe Houdancourt.

† It must have been observed that the Marquis de Grignan followed this etiquette with his mother, which was the custom among persons of high rank, and particularly in the southern provinces, where the Roman laws gave fathers an absolute power over their children, which inspired children with more respect than love, and exacted the forms of submission, even in the overflowings of the heart. Madame de Sévigné was averse to this false dignity, the most gloomy mask that love can assume; and it has been seen that she even laughed at her daughter, who, in speaking of her grandfather, had written to her, *monsieur votre*

at Paris. It will not be my fault if the archbishop (of Aix) does not know that you are satisfied with him; I informed Madame de la Fayette of this the other day, who was much pleased with the information; she enjoins you both to lay aside the spirit and way of thinking of Provence. But to come to the King and Queen of England. It is so extraordinary to have this court here, that it is the constant subject of conversation. The regulation of rank and precedency is to be attended to, in order to render life agreeable to those who are so unlikely to be restored. This the king said the other day, adding that the English king was the best man in the world; that he should hunt with him; that he should come to Marli and Trianon; and that the courtiers should habituate themselves to him. The King of England does not give his hand to the dauphin, and does not reconduct him. The queen has not kissed monsieur, who is offended at this; she said to the king, "Tell me what you wish me to do; if you would have me follow the French fashion, I will salute whom you please; but it is not the custom in England to salute any one." She paid a visit to the dauphiness, who was ill, and who received her in bed. No one sits in England; I believe the duchesses will follow the French fashion, and behave to her as they did to her mother-in-law.* We are greatly taken up with this new court.

In the mean time, the Prince of Orange is in London, where he has imprisoned several lords; he is severe, and will soon make himself hated. M. Schomberg is commander-in-chief in Holland, in the room of this prince, and his son is to have the reversion: so the mask is now completely thrown off.

---

pere. Every one knows the humorous speech of the great Condé, before a man who affected to say Monsieur and Madame in speaking of his relations: "Monsieur my groom, go and tell monsieur my coachman, to put messieurs my horses to monsieur my coach."

* Henrietta of France, daughter of Henry IV., and wife of Charles I. King of England.

LETTER CV.

PARIS, Friday, January 14, 1689.

I have dined, my dear child, and am now in the chevalier's apartment; he is in his chair, with a thousand little aches and pains that fly about him. He has slept well; but this confinement affects his spirits, and vexes him exceedingly; I too am grieved at it, as I know the ill consequences better than any one. It is very cold; the thermometer is at the lowest degree; our river is frozen; it snows, freezes, and thaws at the same time; there is no walking in the streets; I keep to the house, and to the chevalier's chamber. If I could have an answer from you before the end of a fortnight, I would desire you to tell me whether I do not incommode him, by staying with him all day; but as I have no time to lose, I put this question to himself, and I fancy he is not displeased at it. The weather is an additional cause of his illness; it is not the sort he likes; it is always unfavorable when it is extreme.

M. de Gobelin is still at St. Cyr; Madame de Brinon is at Maubuisson, where she will soon be tired; she can never remain long in a place; she has made many agreements, and been in several convents; her good sense does not screen her from this error. Madame de Maintenon is much pleased with the comedy* which she has made her young ladies of St. Cyr

---

* It was the Supérieure Brinon who first made the pensioners of St. Cyr perform pieces of her selection. They were ill chosen. Cinna, and afterward Andromache, were substituted in their room. But there was so much love in this last tragedy, and the young ladies played it so well, that it was not judged proper for their representation. This was what Madame de Maintenon wrote herself to Racine, at the same time desiring him to supply another poem, moral or historical. Racine hesitated: he wished to please the court, but the public and posterity withheld him. He deemed it impossible to fill the frame that was given him, by a performance worthy of his music. Boileau, too, despaired of it. Racine thought of the subject of Esther; and his friend considered it well judged, as it really was. This very Boileau, the severity of whose taste and character made him so much aspersed, gave, in his

perform; it will be a very fine piece according to report. She has paid a visit to the Queen of England, who, having made her wait a moment, said she was very sorry she had lost any time in seeing and conversing with her, and received her extremely well. Every one is pleased with this queen; she has an excellent understanding. She said to the king, on seeing him caress the Prince of Wales, who is a lovely child, "I formerly envied the happiness of my son, in not feeling his misfortunes; but I now pity him, for being insensible to your majesty's caresses and kindness." All she says is proper and to the purpose; but this is not the case with her husband: he has a great share of courage, but his understanding is not above the common standard; he relates what has passed in England with an insensibility that excites the same feeling for himself. He is a good man,* and partakes of all the amusements of Versailles. The dauphiness does not intend to visit this queen; she wants her right hand seat and chair of state, which can not be; she will therefore be always in bed, when the queen visits her. Madame is to have an armchair upon the left hand, and the princesses of the blood are to visit with her; before whom they have tabourets only. The duchesses will be upon the same footing as at the dauphiness's; this is settled. The king, knowing that a king of France gave a Prince of Wales only a chair on the left hand, chooses that the King of England should treat the dauphin in the same manner, and precede him. He is to receive Monsieur without chair or ceremony. The queen has saluted him, saying to our sovereign what I told you. It is not yet certain that M. de Schomberg is to succeed the Prince of Orange in Holland. This is a year of falsehood.

regard for Racine, the most perfect example of friendship—an example perhaps, that will never again be met with between two men gifted with the same kind of superiority.

* The Archbishop of Rheims, brother of M. de Louvois, seeing him come out of the chapel of Versailles, said: "What a good man! he has given up three kingdoms for a mass."

LETTER CVI.

PARIS, Monday, January 17, 1689.

My letter, then, is dignified with a title; this is a proof of its singular merit. I am glad my story amused you. I can never guess at the effect my letters will produce, but this has been a happy one.

If you sought an opportunity of coming to an explanation with the archbishop, instead of suffering the misunderstanding which people endeavor to create between you to ferment, a short time would clear up the whole, or you would silence chatterers; either of these is desirable, and you will find good result from it; you will put an end, it is true, to the amusements of the Provençals; but it is only silencing ridiculous impertinence. M. de Barillon is arrived; he has found a family group, with many of whose faces he was not acquainted. He is grown very fat, and said to M. de Harlai, "Sir, do not remind me of my fat, and I will say nothing to you of your lean." He is very lively, and much of the same disposition as his namesake whom you know. I will pay all your compliments to him, when they will not appear forced; I have done so with regard to Madame de Sully, who returns you a thousand with a very good grace; and to the countess,* who is too witty upon M. de Lauzun, whom she wished to raise to the pinnacle of honor, and who has neither an apartment at Versailles, nor the free admittance he formerly had. He is merely returned to court, and his exploit does not appear so extraordinary, though a very pretty romance was at first made out of it.

The English court is quite established at St. Germain; they would not accept more than 15,000 livres a month, and have regulated their court upon that foundation. The queen is very much liked; our king converses very pleasantly with

---

* The Countess de Fiesque, the constant friend of M. de Lauzun, and who often performed the part of mediatrix between him and mademoiselle.

her; she has good sense without affectation. The king wished the dauphiness to pay her the first visit, but she was always so conveniently indisposed, that this queen paid her a visit three days ago, admirably dressed; a black velvet robe, a beautiful petticoat, her hair tastefully disposed, a figure like the Princess de Conti's, and great dignity of manner. The king received her as she alighted; she went first into his apartment, where she had a chair below the king's; here she remained half an hour; he then conducted her to the dauphiness, who was up; this occasioned a little surprise; the queen said to her, "I expected to have found you in bed, madam." "I wished to rise, madam," replied the dauphiness, "to receive the honor your majesty does me." The king left them, as the dauphiness has no chair in his presence. The queen took her place, with the dauphiness on her right hand, madame on her left, and there were three other chairs for the three young princes. They conversed together for upward of half an hour; several duchesses were present, and the court was very numerous. At length she retired; the king gave orders to be informed of it, and handed her back to her carriage. I do not know how far the dauphiness went with her, but I shall hear. The king, upon his return, highly praised the queen; he said, "This is how a queen ought to be, both in person and mind, holding her court with dignity." He admired her courage in misfortunes, and her affection for her husband; for it is certain that she loves him, as that hateful woman, Madame de R***, told you. Some of our ladies who wished to assume the airs of princesses, did not kiss the queen's robe, some of the duchesses wished to avoid it also; but the king was displeased at this, and they now pay her homage. Madame de Chaulnes has been informed of these particulars, but has not yet performed this duty.

LETTER CVII.

Paris, Wednesday, February 16, 1689.

The chevalier is still at Versailles, but I expect him this evening. The marquis dined with me the other day; I conversed a good deal with him, and I can assure you, with much satisfaction. There is an air of truth and modesty in all he says, which does not in the least resemble the style of these thoughtless youths who always appear fools or liars. He related to me all the fatigues of his journey to Philipsburg, which were very great; little D'Auvergne had the fever for four days, from mere weariness; the marquis is strong, and bears this first trial with great courage; he told me his other adventures, gave me an account of all the blows that were given on each side of him, and the contusion he received; and this, without ostentation, with a cool composed air of veracity, which is highly pleasing. I love to converse with him, and lose no opportunity of doing it; he supped yesterday with M. Turgot, and some young folks, at the rich little La Martillière's; he returned at midnight. He is gone to the horse-market, being wholly taken up with his company; he will write to you to-night: he loves you, and knows your extreme affection; you do nothing for him to which he is not as sensible as you can possibly wish: it is not even necessary to rouse him upon this subject.

I dined yesterday with Mademoiselle de Goileau; it was a company of wits; the Abbé de Polignac, the Abbé de Rohan, his doctor, Abbé David, and Corbinelli. After dinner they discussed, very pleasantly, the philosophy of your Father Descartes; it was with great difficulty they could comprehend the motion God gives to a ball that is pushed by another; they would have it that the first communicated its motion, and you know how the Abbé Polignac and Corbinelli exclaimed upon the occasion: this diverted me, and brought my dear little Cartesian to my remembrance, whom even I could understand so readily. From thence I went to Madame de la Fayette's where, by good fortune, I found only M. de Pomponne and M. de Barillon: we spent two hours very agreeably, and the more so as we are seldom so fortunate. They say that the English parliament has made the Prince of Orange king, because the former king has deserted his kingdom, *and broken the treaty between sovereign and subjects;* that his flight is an *abdication;* that they are determined to render the throne elective; and that the parliament would not allow the Princess of Orange to be queen: these were the reports of yesterday, The chevalier will bring us news from Versailles. Some say with regard to the King of England's apathy, that by hearing him talk, it is easy to guess why he is here.

LETTER CVIII.

PARIS, Monday, February 21, 1689.

It is certain that we are separated from each other by a grievous distance: this is enough to make us shudder; but what would it have been if I had added to it the road from hence to the Rocks or Rennes? This, however, will not take place so soon. Madame de Chaulnes wishes to see the termination of several affairs, and I am only afraid that she will set out too late, considering my intention of returning next winter, which I must do for several reasons; the first of which is that I am convinced M. de Grignan will be obliged to return on account of his knighthood, and you can not take a better opportunity to escape from your falling, uninhabitable castle, and come and pay your court a little with the knight of the order, who will not be a knight till that time. I paid mine the other day at St. Cyr much more agreeably than I expected. We, that is, Madame de Coulanges, Madame de Bagnols, the Abbé Têtu, and I, went on Saturday. We found our places kept; an officer told Madame de Coulanges that Madame de Maintenon had ordered a place for her next herself; you see what honor is paid her. "You, madam," said he, "may choose."

I placed myself with Madame de Bagnols in the second row behind the duchesses. Marshal de Bellefond came, and placed himself by choice at my right hand, and before us were the Duchesses d'Auvergne, De Coislin, and De Sully. The marshal and I listened to the tragedy with an attention that was remarked, and bestowed some praises in a low voice that were very well placed. I can not tell you the extreme beauty of this piece: it is a performance not easy to represent, and is inimitable: it is the union of music, poetry, singing, and character, so perfect and complete that there is nothing we wish to alter. The young ladies who represent kings and great personages seem to be made on purpose. It commands attention, and the only unpleasant circumstance attending it is, that so fine a production should at last end. Every thing in it is simple and innocent, sublime and affecting: the sacred history is so faithfully adhered to as to create respect; all the airs corresponding with the words, which are taken from the Psalms or Ecclesiastes, and interwoven with the subject, are singularly beautiful; the taste and attention of the audience are the criterions of the merit of the piece. I was delighted with it, and so was the marshal, who left his place to inform the king how much he was gratified, that he was seated next to a lady who was very worthy of seeing Esther. The king approached our seat, and having turned round, addressed himself to me: "I am told, madam," said he, "that the piece has given you satisfaction." I replied, with perfect self-possession, "Sire, I am delighted; what I feel is beyond the power of words to describe." The king continued, "Racine has great talents." I replied, "Sire, he has indeed; and so have these young people: they enter into the subject as if it had been their sole employment." "Ah! that is very true," he rejoined. And then he retired, leaving me the object of universal envy. As I was almost the only new spectator, the king took pleasure in observing my genuine admiration, which was without noise or parade.* The prince and princess came

* By mentioning the circumstance to which she believed she was

and spoke a word to me; Madame de Maintenon flashed upon me like lightning, and then retired to the king. I answered every one, being in one of my happiest moods. We returned at night with flambeaux. I supped at Madame de Coulanges', to whom the king had also spoken with an air of affability that made him appear fascinating. I saw the chevalier at night. I related to him very naturally my little good fortune, being unwilling to conceal it without a reason, as some people do. He was pleased, and here I conclude upon this head. I am sure he did not afterward find in me any ridiculous vanity, or the transports of a vulgar country bumpkin. Ask him. M. de Meaux talked to me a good deal about you, and so did the prince. I pitied you for not being present; but how was it possible? one can not be every where. You were at the opera at Marseilles. As Atys is not only too happy, but too charming, it is impossible you could have been tired with it. Paulina must have been surprised at such a spectacle; she has no right to wish for a more perfect one. I have so pleasing an idea of Marseilles, that I am persuaded you are amused there; and I will back the dissipations of that place against those of Aix.

But on that very Saturday, after the representation of Esther, the king was informed of the death of the young Queen of Spain,* who was carried off in two days by a violent vom

indebted for this little favor of the king, she proves sufficiently that she was not so much elated with it as has been pretended.

* Maria-Louisa of Orléans, daughter of monsieur, and of Henrietta-Anne of England, his first wife.

Madame de la Fayette says in her Memoirs, that the Queen of Spain was poisoned by a cup of chocolate. Dangeau affirms that it was by an eel pie. Madame, in her *Lettres Originales*, maintains that the poison was communicated by raw oysters.

Voltaire has denied this poisoning, as well as several others. It was a system of the historian. But he only confutes Dangeau's account, who had said that three of the queen's women had died in consequence of eating of the same dish. Against this detail he brings forward respectable authority.

Madame de la Fayette, who, in the life of Madame (Henrietta of

iting: this has very much the air of foul play. The king informed monsieur of it next day, which was yesterday; great was the grief upon the occasion; madame wept bitterly, and the king retired in a flood of tears.

It is said there is good news from England; not only the Prince of Orange is not elected king or protector, but he is given to understand that he and his troops have nothing to do but return: this shortens our solicitude. If this news should gain ground, our Brittany will be in less agitation, and my son will not have the mortification of commanding the nobility of the viscounty of Rennes, and the barony of Vitré. They have chosen him, against his will, to be at their head. Any one else would be greatly elated with this honor, but he is vexed at it, not liking, under any title whatever, to take the field in that way.

England), had not dared to confirm the opinion of her having died by poison, joined with Voltaire in that of the Queen of Spain, daughter of this princess.

The evidence of Madame (De Bavière) would be stronger if she were not so partial, and did not show herself so ready to give credit to every crime. What she adds, that it was two of the queen's French waiting women who poisoned her, is very improbable.

She says, however, that it was the Earl of Mansfield who procured the poison, a circumstance which agrees with the common report of that period.

In fact, all the letters and memoirs of cotemporary writers agree in saying that the Council of Spain, devoted to the emperor and the Prince of Orange, and resolved to enter into the league against France, wished to remove a queen who was too good a Frenchwoman, and who, governing her husband, was too great an obstacle to the projects of war that had been formed.

It is true that such a report, at the moment of the breaking out of hostilities, can not pass for an historical proof; but it must be owned that it very nearly resembles truth.

LETTER CIX.

PARIS, Ash-Wednesday, February 23, 1689.

My dear child, the life you lead at Marseilles delights me. I love that city, which resembles no other in the world. Ah! how well I understand Paulina's admiration! How natural, how just, how novel all her surprise must be! How pretty I think her! how pleasing to me is the mind which my fancy gives her! It seems to me that I love her, and that you do not love her enough. You want her to be all perfection. Did she engage for this when she left her convent? You are not just. Who is there without faults? Do you, in conscience, expect her to be free from them? Whence can this hope arise? It is not in nature. You wish her then to be a *prodigious* prodigy, such as was never before seen. If I were with you, I think I should do her some good offices, merely by correcting your imagination a little, and by asking you, if a young girl, who thinks of nothing but pleasing you and improving herself, who loves and fears you, and who has a great share of understanding, is not in the first rank of excellence? These are the dictates of my heart in favor of my dear Paulina, whom I love, and whom I entreat you immediately to embrace for my sake. Add to this her good conscience, which makes her renounce the compact, when she sees the jugglers perform their necromancies. This life, though agreeable, must have fatigued you; it is too much for you, my dear child; you go to bed late, and you rise early, I have had apprehensions for your health. The reason I do not talk to you of mine is, that it is as I wish yours to be, and that I have nothing to say upon the subject.

LETTER CX.

PARIS, Monday, February 28, 1689.

The chevalier went yesterday to Versailles to know his fate; for, not finding himself in the lists that have appeared, he is anxious to know whether he is reserved for the dauphin's army, which has not yet been mentioned. As he has said that he was capable of serving, he has a right to think that he has not been forgotten; at all events it will not be his fault; he is one of the best. It is certain that the King of England set out this morning for Ireland, where he is expected with impatience; he will be better there than here. He will traverse Brittany with the swiftness of lightning; and go straight to Brest, where he will find Marshal d'Estrées, and ships and frigates ready; he takes with him 50,000 crowns. The king has given him sufficient arms for 10,000 men. As his Britannic majesty took leave, he said with a smile, "That arms for himself were the only things that had been forgotten;" our king gave him his; the heroes of romance never did any thing more gallant than this action. What will not this brave but unhappy king do, with arms that have ever been victorious? Behold him then with the casque and cuirass of Rinoldo and Amadis, and all our most celebrated knights-errant; I will not say of Hector, for he was unfortunate. There is not an offer that can be suggested, that our king has not made him; generosity and magnanimity have been carried to their height. M. d'Avaux* is to go with him; he set out two days ago. You will ask why M. de Barillon† was not the person. The reason is, that M. d'Avaux, being perfectly acquainted with the affairs of Holland, will be more useful, than he who is acquainted only with those of England.‡ The queen has shut herself up at Poissi with her son; she will be near the king, and the fountain-head of intelligence. She is overwhelmed

---

* John-Anthony de Mesmes, Count d'Avaux, nephew of Claudius de Mesmes, also Count d'Avaux, both celebrated for their superior talents in negotiation, and for uncommon qualities of heart and mind.

† M. de Barillon had been embassador to England.

‡ The reason assigned here for the preference that was given to M. d'Avaux, is not the true one: d'Avaux had the merit of having foreseen and announced every event that happened, whereas De Barillon had the misfortune to be wrong in every thing; this was the real cause of the preference.

with grief, and suffers from a nephritic complaint, that makes it feared she has the stone; she is really to be pitied. You see, my dear child, it is the rage of talking that makes me write all this; the chevalier and the gazette will give you better information than I can do. Your son has lived with me; I never leave him, and he is satisfied. He is going to take leave of the little Mesdemoiselles Castelnau; but his heart has yet no attractions. His duty and his regiment take up all his time. He is delighted at the thoughts of going, and of setting the example to others.

LETTER CXI.

PARIS, Wednesday, March 2, 1689.

Shrove-Tuesday is not an indifferent day to Paulina. I cannot help scolding you, my dear child, for not having sent her prettily to the good Langlée's, to dance a little with Mademoiselle d'Oraison; what harm would there have been in allowing her this little pastime? I am sure this dear child is interesting, that she has a good air, a good carriage, and even eclipses more regular beauties. I scold you also for reading all your letters before you go to bed. I know it is scarcely possible to keep them till the next day; but you must calculate upon not sleeping, for there will often be many things in them that will create disagreeable thoughts; nor would it be a whit better if they contained nothing but reflections and news. Before the imagination has sifted the contents, the night is gone. As you know all this to be true, settle the matter for the benefit of your health. I took my marquis yesterday to Madame du Pui-du-fou's; she grows very old. M. de Mirepoix, who had been there once before to see me, came a second time, and each time his whole conversation turned upon his condescension in marrying to please his family. The little puppet is dying of the spleen in this dreary abode. I afterward went to Madame de Lavardin's, to whom I remembered

you. She embraced your son several times. She loves you
dearly, and so does Madame de Mouci; but this last is in the
third heaven; she has lost a sister, who was a nun, for whom
she had very little regard: I shall make your compliments to
her and her learned brother.* The chevalier arrived last night,
and is very well; he will be employed, but he knows not yet
in what country; I admire his courage. Your son is a very
agreeable and a very pretty fellow; he already manages all
his affairs, gives orders, makes purchases, and keeps his accounts; it is a pity his father had not done the same. The
chevalier will inform you what our king said to the King of
England at his taking leave: "Sir, it is with grief I see you
depart, yet I never wish to see you again; but if you return,
be assured you will find me the same as you leave me." Could
any thing better have been said? He has loaded him with
every thing, great and small; two millions of money, ships,
frigates, troops, officers, and M. d'Avaux, who makes, upon
the occasion, one of the most brilliant figures in the world. I
will venture to say that there is no one who would not be
proud of the employment, who would not think it worthy of
a man thoroughly acquainted with business, and capable of
giving advice: if M. de Barillon is not sensible of this he is
very happy. I now come to the minutiæ, such as toilets,
camp-beds, services of plate, plain and gilt, arms for his person, which are the king's; arms for the troops in Ireland, and
those who go with him, who are very numerous; in short,
generosity, magnificence, and magnanimity were never so
strikingly displayed as upon this occasion. The king is not
willing that the queen should go to Poissi; she will see very
little company, but the king will take care of her, and she
will receive news without intermission. The parting of the
King and Queen of England rent the hearts of all the specta-
tors; nothing but tears, sighs, lamentations, and swoonings
were to be seen or heard, which is very easy to be compre-

* Achilles de Harlay, then attorney-general, and afterward first
president in the parliament of Paris, in November, 1689.

hended. Such is his destiny. He has a good cause; he is the protector of the true religion, and his courage will allow him no other alternative than conquest or death.

LETTER CXII.

PARIS, Wednesday, March 23, 1689.

I shall not retract the praises I have bestowed on the tragedy of Esther; I shall be delighted with the harmony and novelty of this spectacle as long as I live; I was in raptures with it; I found in it a thousand things so just, so well introduced, and so important to a king, that I entered with uncommon spirit into the pleasure arising from the utterance, in fiction and song, of the most solid truths; I was affected with these various beauties, and am very far from changing my opinion. But I told you that the impression of this piece has produced its usual effect, and has brought forth a *civil demur* against excessive applause. I, who have read it again with pleasure, suppose that the critics are routed, as M. d'Aiguebonne will be with his *demur*, if the chevalier has time to press the point. The victory of the grand council has been brilliant and gratifying, and I doubt not that it will give you ample satisfaction; I am impatient to receive your letter upon this subject. M. de Lamoignon told me again to-day, that this advantage, gained sword in hand, was greater than we supposed. I told him he was mistaken, as we had felt the pleasure in its fullest extent. He is very much engaged in the great cause between mademoiselle, the prince, and the whole house of Lorraine, who have recourse to law in the same way we have. M. de Lamoignon is to plead on Thursday, and the affair will be determined upon hearing.

The King of England set sail on the 17th, and arrived in Ireland on the 19th. Little Mailly, who accompanied him to Brest, is returned. Adieu, my beloved child; I dread an increase of distance from you; it makes me ill. I swallow this journey like a dose of medicine; but the worst is, that I have no time to lose; in truth, my reflections are often of the most melancholy cast; for, though I submit to that Providence which separates us, what would become of me if I had not the hope of seeing you again?

LETTER CXIII.

The Rocks, Wednesday, June 1, 1689.

Paulina is too fortunate in being your secretary; she learns, as I told you, to think, and express her thoughts, by seeing how you express yours. She is learning the French language, which most women are ignorant of, but you take the trouble of explaining words to her, which she would not understand; and by instructing her in so many subjects, you relieve your own head and mine. The tediousness of dictating is not equal to the fatigue of writing; and my mind is never at rest, but when I know yours is so. Persevere, then, in instructing your daughter so properly, and in affording so great a relief to yourself and to me.

When you are assured of my being in perfect health, you do every thing that can be done, which is to dread its interruption. This too sometimes engages my thoughts, and not finding any of those little inconveniences with which you are acquainted, I say with astonishment, I must, however, expect that this happy state will change; and I conclude, that I ought, as upon all other occasions, to submit to the will of God, and believe, that in inflicting ills upon me, he will give me patience. I will therefore enjoy my present lot.

LETTER CXIV.

The Rocks, Sunday, July 3, 1689.

It is nine months this third of July, reckoning from day to day, and from Sunday to Sunday, since I left you with a deluge of tears, and more than you perceived, at Charenton. Such partings are grievous and bitter, particularly when we have not much time to lose. But to turn them to our advantage, we ought to make them a period of abstinence and penance, which would be the sure means of making them salutary; it is certain that this holy economy is a favor from heaven, like all others, which we do not deserve to obtain. Nine months, then, have passed, in which I have neither seen nor embraced you, nor even heard the sound of your voice. I have not been ill, I have had no particular uneasiness; I have seen fine houses, fine countries, and fine cities. Nevertheless, I must acknowledge that it appears to me nine years since I left you. I have had no letter from you this post; the delay is always a disappointment to me. Madame de Lavardin tells me that she said to Madame de Buri, with regard to Chabrilland's cause, which the last expects to gain, "You have always great expectations; but one of your friends, who understands these things, is not of the same opinion." "Ah!" said she, "you mean M. de Fieubet, but I do not believe him." And Madame de Lavardin afterward told me that M. d'Arles is to have the honor of the civil petition. It is he, then, who is to be the solicitor; but I would not, I think, solicit with beat of drum in open court, where people are convinced you have already but too much credit. We lead here, my dear countess, the life I described to you. It is very fine weather; we are so perfumed at night with jasmines and orange-flowers, that in this respect I think I am in Provence. M. and Madame de Chaulnes have written to me from St. Malo, and constantly mention you. Write to La Troche; she can not be consoled for your forgetfulness of her. I know not how it has happened, for you are punctual. It is not possible that I have not informed you of the death of her husband. I expect your answer.

LETTER CXV.

The Rocks, Wednesday, October 5, 1689.

It had never entered my brain to accuse certain iron wires in the head-dress of being the cause of long faces; this hint would be very useful to certain persons of our acquaintance. I had heard they were very friendly; but no, quite the contrary. These two little wires press against the temples, prevent the circulation of blood, and cause abscesses. Some die in consequence. They may consider themselves fortunate whose faces are only lengthened an ell, and who become as pale as death; but young people, who are more hardy, may recover in time. I am very much inclined to place this story in the class with some others, formerly related to me by the good Princess de Tarente; however, it is not amiss to know every thing.

I do not in the least doubt that M. de la Garde, who never refused a remedy, will avail himself of that of the lady you mention. You will see him with his head upon the ground, and his heels in the air, *turning an affair**** like her; I really believe that if we were to pursue this regimen for any length of time, we should no longer have sore eyes. I have nothing to give you in return for your account of this visit.

We have had a very worthy, sensible, agreeable, unaffected, learned, and every way desirable, visitor with us; a man of great endowments, and capable of entering upon every subject of conversation; he has been here for a week. One of his brothers-in-law is arrived, the Abbé de Marbeuf, who spoils nothing; and a brother-in-law of the Count de Lis, who would spoil every thing if he opened his lips; this is a secret misanthropist, for he keeps his chagrin to himself; he is very well made, and sings so much like Beaumaviel, that he might be mistaken for him. When our worthy friend departed, every

---

* It has already been observed that this was a favorite expression of M. de la Garde.

thing was comparatively flat and insipid; we renewed the just observations we made in this country with you, on pleasant and disagreeable company; and fixed that the disagreeable was the most desirable; their absence is a relief; whereas pleasant society leaves us dull and dejected; we can not easily pursue the old track; in short, it is a great misfortune to associate with sensible people, but it is a misfortune that does not often happen to us

---

LETTER CXVI.

The Rocks, Sunday, November 13, 1689.

Your letter is not yet arrived; this is always a grief to me; though I have in some degree got the better of the apprehensions I formerly suffered from the delay; it is the whim of the post, and we must endure it; but as I am constantly with you at Grignan, I lose the thread of the conversation; this it is that vexes me. I know not whether you go to the assembly with M. de Grignan, or remain at your château. I am very uneasy about the chevalier's health, and the effects of the bark, repeated in its usual dose; its heat operating upon that of the chevalier's blood, brings to my mind an old saying, *When the brave meets the brave, they remain brave.* We hope, therefore, that this brave bark will make the blood remain brave; God grant it may; it is very difficult to subdue.

I have received a long letter from my new friend, the *man-wolf* Guébriac; I would have sent it to you, as his style, which is very easy, would be agreeable enough, if he did not praise me so extravagantly; in fact, my modesty will not suffer it; he is so astonished to find a woman with a few good qualities and good principles, who in her youth had some charms, that he seems to have passed his life in a whirlwind of passions, among a banditti equally devoid of faith and law, where love reigned alone, despoiled of every kind of virtue; this has given rise to some very pleasant things.

We are reading the History of the Church by M. de Godeau;* it is really a very fine work; in what a respectable light does it place religion! we are ready to suffer martyrdom with Abbadie. Every thing has its turn; Corisca is very pretty and very roguish; *altri tempi, altre cure.* Love me always, my dear child, but never weigh other love in the same scale with yours; your heart is of the first order, and no one resembles it.

LETTER CXVII.

The Rocks, Wednesday, January 11, 1690.

Good heavens! what a new year's gift! what wishes! what could be more calculated to charm me? I will tell you a feeling I have just discovered in myself; if it could repay yours I should be satisfied, for I have no other coin: instead of the kind fears which the frequent deaths that surround you occasion, and which make you think of others, I offer you the real consolation, and even the joy, which frequently arise to me from my being older than you. The thought that the oldest goes first, and that I shall probably and naturally keep my rank with my dear child, constitutes the true charms of this feeling. What have I not suffered, when your ill state of health made me dread a reverse of the order of nature? These were trying times; let us talk no more of them; you are well, God be praised; and every thing has resumed its natural course. *God preserve you;* I believe you hear my tone of voice, and know me.

I now come to the chevalier; I have no hesitation in believing that the climate of Provence would agree with him better in winter than that of Paris. All those who, like swallows, fly to your sunshine, afford sufficient testimony of this. But, while I rejoice at his being sensible of the difference, I am grieved at his having lost a thousand crowns of his income;

---

* Antony Godeau, Bishop of Grasse and Vence.

and by what means? was his regiment worth so much to him? He will sell it then to the marquis;* but will not the money arising from it, in payment of debts, diminish the interest of loans? Settle this account for me, which makes me uneasy; I can not figure to myself the Chevalier de Grignan at Paris without his genteel and neat little equipage; I can not see him walking on foot, nor inquiring for places to Versailles; such an idea can not enter my head; this article is interlocutory; ah, how happily this term of chicanery finds admittance here! Neither do I comprehend your sixty-four people, besides guards; you deceive me, this can not be your meaning, you must give me a mathematical demonstration.

With regard to Paulina, you can not surely hesitate respecting the choice you have to take, between good and evil. The superiority of your understanding will easily point out to you the true road; every thing leads you to your duty; honor conscience, and the power you possess. When I consider how much she has corrected herself in a short time to please you, and how much she is improved, you will be answerable for all the good she neglects. As to reading, you are too much engaged in conversation and discussion to attend to it: we are most quiet here, and therefore have leisure for it. I even read works I had slightly run over at Paris, and which appear quite new to me. We also read, by way of interlude to our grand lectures, scraps that we meet with, such as the fine funeral orations of M. de Bossuet,† M. Fléchier,‡ M. Mascaron,§ Father Bourdaloue: we pay a fresh tribute of tears to M. de Turenne, Madame de Montausier, the Prince, the late Madame, and the Queen of England; we admire the portrait of Cromwell: these are master-pieces of eloquence, which charm the mind. You must not say, "These are old;" they are not old,

---

* The Chevalier de Grignan, attaining the rank of field marshal in 1688, had leave to keep his regiment, that he might afterward resign in favor of the Marquis de Grignan his nephew.

† The Bishop of Meaux.   ‡ The Bishop of Nismes.
§ The Bishop of Agen.

they are divine. Paulina should be made acquainted and delighted with them; but this is calculated solely for the Rocks. I know not what book to recommend to Paulina: Davila is fine in Italian, we have read it; Guicciardini is very long; I should like the anecdotes of Medicis, which are an abridgment, but they are not in Italian. I will not name Bentivoglio again;* let her confine herself to poetry, I do not like Italian prose; to Tasso, *Aminto*, *Il Pastor Fido*, etc. I dare not add Ariosto, there are some bad passages in it; let her also read history; let her cherish this taste, which may long preserve her from idleness; it is to be feared that if this part of reading were suppressed there would be scarcely any thing to read; let her begin with the life of Theodosius the Great, and let her tell me how she likes it. This, my child, is a letter of trifles; we set apart some days for chatting, without offense to serious matters, in which we always take true interest.

LETTER CXVIII.

The Rocks, Sunday, January 15, 1690.

You are right, I can not reconcile myself to the date of this year; it has, however, been already begun for some time; and you will find, that, let us pass it as we may, we shall soon find the bottom of the bag that contained the thousand livres.†

You really spoil me, and so do my Paris friends; the sun has scarcely gained upon us a barley-corn before you tell me when you shall expect me at Grignan; and my friends desire me to fix from that hour the time of my departure, in order to hasten their joy. Such pressing civilities flatter me highly, and particularly yours, which admit of no comparison. I will, then, sincerely confide to my dear countess, that between this

---

* Gui Bentivoglio, cardinal, and author of the Civil Wars in Flanders, and several other works.

† Madame de Sévigné compared the twelve months of the year to a bag with a thousand livres, which is exhausted almost as soon as it is opened.

and September, I can not entertain a thought of leaving this country; this is the time when I send my little means to Paris, of which only a very small part is gone. This is the time when the Abbé Charier is treating for my fines and sales, which amount to ten thousand livres; but more of this hereafter; let us content ourselves with driving away every hope of taking the least step before the time I have mentioned. I will not, however, say that you are my goal, my perspective; you know it well, and that you are so firmly rooted in my heart that I fear M. Nicole would find much difficulty to prune you away; this, in short, is my disposition. You use the most affectionate expression possible to me, in hoping you may never see the end of the happy years you wish me. We are very far from agreeing in our wishes; for I have informed you of a very just and very proper truth, which God will doubtless grant, and which is to follow the natural order of providence; this is my comfort through the thorny road of old age: mine is a rational feeling, and yours too extraordinary and too kind a one.

As to Paulina, that devourer of books, I had rather she should swallow bad ones, than have no love for reading; romances, plays, Voiture, Sarrasin, have all been exhausted; has she dipped into Lucian? is she capable of enjoying *Les Petites Lettres?* History should come next, and if she does not find her account in this, I pity her. If she does not like the finest works of devotion, so much the worse for her, for we know but too well that even without devotion ourselves, they are charming. With respect to ethics, as she would not make so good a use of it as you, I would not have her meddle either with Montaigne, Charron, or any others of his stamp; she is too young. The true morality of this age, is what we learn in conversation, fables, history, and example. If you were to bestow a little of your time upon her in conversation, she would reap greater benefit from this than from all the rest. I know not whether what I say is worth your reading, I am very far from being wedded to my opinion.

LETTER CXIX.

The Rocks, Sunday, January 22, 1690.

Good heavens, what a situation you are in! how pressing a one! and how much and sensibly I am grieved at it! But, my child, how weak and futile are wishes upon such occasions! and how needless it is to tell you that if I had now, as I have had, some portable sum which depended on me, it should soon be yours! I am overwhelmed with a host of little creditors who dun and threaten me, and I do not know whether I shall be able to satisfy them, as I had hoped to do; for I am quite suffocated by the obligation I am under of paying immediately 5000 livres by way of fine, and the price of the estate of Madame d'Acigné, which I have purchased, to avoid paying 10,000 if I had waited two years longer. Such, then, is my situation; but this is only to acquaint you with the utter impossibility of my assisting you. Your brother appears to me to feel for you, and I am persuaded he would perform his duty better than your rich prelates, if the times were as they have been, that is, if it were possible to borrow. He will talk to you himself, and tell you his opinion of your affairs. I have also set forth to him the embarrassments of your little colonel; he mentioned the subject to me the first, some time ago, pitying and regretting, like us, that the chevalier had not the management of him for the first year or two; nothing could have been of so much service to him as such a master; in short, my dearest child, no one but God can confine so great a number of disagreeable things within the bounds of resignation, in which you appear to me. To return to my son; he had some anxiety on seeing a stripling of seventeen or eighteen at the head of such a troop. He remembers enough of past times to know how difficult it is at that age to command old officers; and this difficulty would have been removed, if he could have had his uncle to establish him; this is a very disagreeable and delicate time for him. Can not you assist him with some prudent counselor, to advise him a little? For, in short, he is alone, and can not at his age know a profession that requires more experience than any other. I have conjured you to send for the marquis to Grignan; what will he do during the carnival at Paris and Versailles? do you think he will acquit himself well of the duty and compliments he has to go through? I perhaps do him wrong; but he is very young, and little accustomed to this business; in short, I think he has more to perform than he is equal to. I resign the pen to my son; I will resume it again presently.

LETTER CXX.

The Rocks, Sunday, February 26, 1690.

I could not have believed that I should have wept so much for La Chau; but it is impossible to read your account of his poor wife's unfeigned and violent affliction without being affected to tears. This is, indeed, a peculiar misfortune, and a fate which nothing could prevent. The man is in haste, he wants to get to his journey's end; he is advised, for very weighty reasons, not to expose himself, or, at least, not to go into the little boat; but he will listen to no one, he must go, he must be punctual to his appointment; Death is waiting for him at a particular spot upon the Rhone; he must meet him there, and perish. Good heavens, my dear child, how all this is arranged! Every one sees his own fate in this accident, and his wife's grief becomes ours; as we are exposed to similar perils, it is our own interest that makes us weep, when we suppose we are lamenting the misfortunes of others. Christianity dictates to us that we should think first of this poor man's salvation; but his wife afterward claims our pity for the loss of 4000 livres; if the dead body should not float, or the violence of the Rhone should throw it beyond Arles upon some unfrequented shore, Providence will dispose of this gold, sewed up in his wet coat, as of the rest.

I highly approve the resolution of not sending for the marquis, this is the surest way; the journey would be both expensive and fatiguing, and productive of no good but the mere gratification of your affection; bear this like many other things, and rather wait till he is a brigadier or major-general, than make him lose his time now. Beaulieu informs me, that he is quite overwhelmed with business, and that he attends to nothing else. Is it possible, that he should have visited Madame de la Fayette before Madame de Vins? I blame him; I am as jealous upon this occasion as you are, for I frequently put myself in your place; every reason should have induced him to have flown to Madame de Vins; she wrote to me the other day that she longed to see him, and to observe the difference and transition from infancy to youth. He has waited upon Madame de Lavardin, and will have time to pay her another visit.

M. de Grignan has resolved upon a very precipitate journey; it is difficult to avoid such courses, when we command singly in a province, whether for the service of the king, or the honor of the post. You never examine thoroughly into this business, except for M. de Grignan; this is natural enough; but the example should extend further. *No enemies*, my dear child; let this be your maxim, it is equally Christian and politic: I not only say *no enemies*, but also *many friends;* you have felt the good effects of these in your law-suit; you have a son; you may stand in need of those who you may now think can never be of service to you. We are deceived; see how Madame de la Fayette abounds with friends on every side, and of all ranks. She has a hundred arms, and they all serve her; her children feel it, and thank her daily for her courteous disposition; an obligation which she owes to M. de la Rochefoucault, and of which her family reaps the benefit. I am certain that you have been of this opinion for many years.

You explain Madame Reinié's conduct very well; it is droll to think of her leaving Paris, her husband, all her business, to fly for three or four months *all over* Provence asking for money, without getting any, fatiguing herself, returning after being at great expense, and getting the rheumatism into the bargain! for recollect that she has pains *all over* her; and such as at length have defeated you.

I am delighted at Paulina's partiality to M. Nicole; it is a proof that she reads him with attention; this taste gives me the highest opinion of her understanding; I also like her anger that the bishops do not fight for promotion. But, my dear, on your honor do you believe it right to give us only the first volume of the romance of the *Princess*, the *Infanta*, or the *First Minister*, so charming as we thought it?* I will not allow you to stop here; I insist upon knowing what is become of the princess's good and just resolution? I am afraid it has vanished, by the necessity of the times, the want of a *minister*, the sudden journey, the impossibility of collecting *the leaves of the Sibyl*, idly and incautiously scattered to the winds for ten years. In short, I fear your good intentions will come to nothing, as I have so often found during the last twenty years: this story, however, requires a continuation, but it should not be too serious with regard to your affairs. I wish also to be informed of the success of M. Prat's journey to the enraged lover of the Princess *Truelle*. I should like to know who were the confidants of the *first minister* and *the favorite*; and who received the couriers. Tell me if you are still satisfied with *Flame*;† he is a very considerable personage in your household. I want to know some particulars respecting the count's journey, and if the treasurer will do as he wishes: here are a number of questions, my dearest child, for which I apologize. It is kind of you to love my letters; when you receive three at a time you say you are rich; but what fatigues do they not occasion you! They are so very long that you should not answer them minutely. Adieu, my love; how does Lent agree with you? for my part I like it

---

* This was an account, in the form of a romance, of what passed in M. de Grignan's family.

† M. de Grignan's house-steward.

extremely. I took a mess of milk-coffee this morning: I am not yet surfeited with it, nor with sermons, for we read none but those of M. le Tourneux and St. John Chrysostom. It is delightful weather, the winter is past, and we have a prospect of spring that is superior to spring itself.

N.B. This letter is the last from the mother to the daughter.

LETTERS TO M. DE POMPONNE.

THE following Letters, relating to the trial of M. Fouquet, were addressed to the Marquis de Pomponne, who was afterward Minister of Foreign Affairs.

The trial of Fouquet was not the least curious and least interesting event of the reign of Louis XIV. The plan of ruining him was laid with such odious art, and the conduct of his enemies, many of whom were his judges, was so inveterate, that it would have been impossible not to have been interested for him, even had he been more criminal than he really was. Accused and tried for financial peculations, he was sentenced to banishment for a crime against the state. His crime was a vague plan of resistance and flight into a foreign country, which he had thrown upon paper five years before, when the factions of the Fronde divided France, and when he thought he had reason to complain of the ingratitude of Cardinal Mazarin. This plan, which he had wholly forgotten, was found among the papers that were seized at his house.

It is well known that Louis XIV. was led to believe that Fouquet was a dangerous man. A guard of fifty musketeers were appointed to conduct him to the citadel of Pignerol, the king having changed the sentence of banishment into perpetual imprisonment. It was still apprehended that he had formidable friends. Among these were Pelisson and Lafontaine; one defended him eloquently, and the other bewailed his misfortunes in a very beautiful and pathetic elegy, in which he went so far as to ask the king to pardon him.

LETTER I.

To-day, Monday, November the 17th, 1664, M. Fouquet was brought a second time before the chancellor. He seated himself without ceremony upon the sellette,* as he had done the first time. The chancellor began by bidding him hold up his hand. He replied, that he had already assigned the reasons which prevented him from taking the oath. The chancellor then made a long speech to prove the legal authority of the court, that it had been established by the king, and that the warrants had been confirmed by the parliament.

M. Fouquet replied, that things were often done under the name of legal authority which were found upon reflection to be unjust.

The chancellor interrupted him : " What! do you mean to say that the king abuses his power ?" M. Fouquet replied, " It is you, sir, who say it, not I; this was not my idea, and, in my present situation, I can not but wonder at your wishing to implicate me still further with his majesty ; but, sir, you yourself well know that we may be mistaken. When you sign a sentence, you believe it just, yet the next day you annul that sentence ; thus you see it is possible to change our opinion."

" But," said the chancellor, " though you will not acknowledge the power of the court, you answer and put interrogatories, and you are now upon the sellette." " It is true, I am so," he replied, " but it is not voluntarily ; I am brought here against my will ; it is a power I must obey, and a mortification which God has inflicted upon me, and which I receive from his hands; after the services I have rendered, and the offices I have had the honor to bear, I might have been spared this humiliation.

The chancellor then continued the examination respecting the pension of the gabelles, to which the replies of M. Fouquet were extremely satisfactory. The examination will pro-

* Stool on which a prisoner sits.

ceed, and I shall send you a faithful account of it; I am anxious to know whether my letters come safely to your hands.

Your sister, who is with our ladies at the Faubourg, has signed; she is now with the community, and seems perfectly satisfied.

Your aunt does not appear at all displeased with her; I did not think it was she who had taken the leap, but some other person. You know, of course, of our defeat at Gigeri,* and as those who formed the plan wish to throw the failure upon those who executed it, they intend to bring Gadagne to trial. There are some who will be satisfied with nothing less than his head; but the public is persuaded that he could not have advised otherwise than he did. M. d'Aleth, who excommunicated the subaltern officers of the king, who were for compelling the clergy to sign, is very much talked of here. This will ruin him with your father, while it will bring him into favor with Père Annat.†

Adieu! The desire of gossiping has seized me, but I must not yield to it; the narrative style should be concise.

LETTER II.

Friday, November 20, 1664.

M. Fouquet was examined this morning respecting the gold mark; he answered extremely well; several of the judges bowed to him; the chancellor reproved them and said that, as he was a Breton, it was not the custom. "It is because you are Bretons that you bow so low to M. Fouquet." In returning on foot from the arsenal, M. Fouquet asked what the workmen were doing; he was told they were making the vase of a fountain; he went to them, and gave his opinion, and after-

---

* The first expedition against Algiers.
† A jesuit, confessor of Louis XIV.

ward returned smiling to Artagan. "You wonder, no doubt," said he, "at my interfering, but I formerly understood these things well." The friends of M. Fouquet, and I among the rest, are pleased at this delightful composure; others call it affectation; such is the world. Madame Fouquet, his mother, has given the queen a plaster that has cured her convulsions, which, properly speaking, were nothing but the vapors.

Many, believing what they wish, imagine that the queen will, on this account, intercede with his majesty to pardon the unfortunate prisoner; but I, who hear a great deal of the kindness of this country, do not believe a word of it. The noise the plaster has made is wonderful; every body says that Madame Fouquet is a saint, and has the power of working miracles.

To-day, the 21st, M. Fouquet has been questioned respecting the wax and sugar taxes. At certain objections that were raised, and which appeared to him ridiculous, he lost his temper. This was going a little too far, and there was a haughtiness in his manners that gave offense. He will correct himself; for this mode of proceeding is by no means advisable; but patience will sometimes escape; it seems to me as if I should have done the same.

I have been at Sainte-Marie, where I saw your aunt, who appeared to be swallowed up in devotion; she was at mass, and in quite a religious ecstasy. Your sister was looking very pretty; fine eyes, and great animation; the poor child fainted this morning; she is very much indisposed; her aunt is uniformly kind to her. M. de Paris has given her a sort of defeasance, which gained her heart, and induced her to sign the wicked formulary.* I have not mentioned the subject to either of them; M. de Paris† has forbidden it. But I must give you

---

* This relates to the condemnation of the five propositions of Jansenius; the clergy of France protested against them, and drew up a formulary, which the nuns of Port Royal and many others refused to sign; this refusal, in the end, caused their dispersion.

† The then archbishop of Paris was the sage Péréfixe.

an idea of prejudice; our sisters of Sainte-Marie said to me, " God be praised, who has at length touched the heart of this poor child! she is now in the way of obedience and salvation." From thence I went to Port Royal, where I found a certain great recluse* of your acquaintance, who accosted me with, " Well, this silly goose has signed; God, in short, has abandoned her; she is lost." I thought I should have died with laughing, when I reflected on the different effects of prejudice; in this, you see the world in its true mirror. I think extremes should always be avoided.

Saturday evening. M. Fouquet entered the chamber this morning, and was interrogated upon the subject of grants; he was attacked weakly and defended himself ably. Between you and me, this is not the worst part of the business. Some good angel must have informed him that he had carried himself too proudly; for he altered his manner to-day, and the judges altered theirs, by not bowing to him. The examination will not be resumed till Wednesday; and I shall not write to you till then. I have only to add, that if you continue to pity me so much, for the trouble I take in writing to you, and desire me not to go on, I shall think my letters tire you, and that you do not like the fatigue of answering them; but I promise not to write such long ones in future, and I absolve you from answering them, though I prize your letters highly. After these declarations, I should think you would not attempt to interrupt the course of my gazettes. In flattering myself that I contribute a little to your pleasure, I add greatly to my own. I have so few opportunities of proving my friendship and esteem for you, that I must not neglect such as present themselves. Pray make my compliments to your family and your neighbors. The queen is much better.

* No doubt the celebrated Doctor Arnauld d'Andilly.

LETTER III.

Monday, November 24, 1664.

If I know my own heart, it is I who am the party obliged, by your receiving so kindly the information I send you. Do you think I have no pleasure in writing to you? Believe me, I have a great deal, and am as much gratified in writing, as you can be in reading what I write. The sentiments you entertain upon the subject of my letter are very natural; hope is common to us all, without our knowing why; but it supports the heart. I dined at Sainte-Marie de Sainte-Antoine two days ago; the lady abbess related to me the particulars of four visits she has received from Puis * * *,* within the last three months, at which I am very much astonished. He came to tell her that the now blessed Bishop of Geneva (François de Sales) had been so extremely kind to him during his illness last summer, that he could not help feeling most strongly the obligations he owed him; and he requested her to obtain the prayers of the community for the deceased. He gave her, for the accomplishment of his holy purpose, a thousand crowns, and entreated her to show him the bishop's heart. When he was at the grate, he fell upon his knees, and remained full a quarter of an hour, bathed in tears, apostrophizing this heart, and praying for a spark of the divine fire which had consumed it. The lady abbess also melted into tears; and gave him the relics of the deceased, with which he hurried away. During these visits, he appeared so earnest about his salvation, so disgusted with the court, so transported with the idea of his conversion, that a person more clear-sighted than the abbess would have been deceived. She contrived to introduce the subject of Fouquet; he answered her as a man who was interested in nothing but religion; that he was not sufficiently known; that justice would be done him, agreeably to the will of God,

---

* This name appears to be altered. and ought, as will be seen further on, to be Puissort.

if from no other consideration. I never was more surprised than at this conversation. If you ask me what I think of it, I must answer, that I do not know; that it is perfectly unintelligible to me; that I can not see the drift of this comedy, nor, if it is not a comedy, how the steps he has since taken are to be reconciled with his fine speeches.

Time must explain all this, for it is at present perfectly enigmatical. Do not mention it, for the lady abbess desired me not to make the circumstance known.

I have seen M. Fouquet's mother. She told me she had sent the plaster to the queen by Madame de Charost.* The effect was certainly wonderful: in less than an hour the queen felt her head relieved, and so great a discharge of offensive matter took place, that had it remained it might have suffocated her in the next fit. The queen said aloud that it was this matter which had occasioned the convulsions of the preceding night, and that Madame de Fouquet had cured her. The queen-mother thought the same, and said so to the king, who did not attend to her. The physicians, who had not been consulted in applying the plaster, withheld their sentiments on the subject, but made their court at the expense of truth. The same day, these poor women threw themselves at the feet of the king, who took no notice of them. Every body is acquainted with the circumstance of the cure; but no one knows what will come of it: we must wait the event with patience.

M. Fouquet was interrogated again this morning, but the chancellor's manner was changed; it seems as if he were ashamed of receiving his lesson every day from Boucherat.† He told the reporter to read the article, upon which he wished to examine the accused; and the reading lasted so long, that it was half-past ten o'clock before it was finished. He then

---

* Fouquet's daughter.

† Boucherat, then master of requests, and afterward chancellor, had been appointed to put the seals on the papers of the superintendent. He was on the commission charged with the prosecution.

said, "Let Fouquet be brought in;" but corrected himself immediately by saying "M. Fouquet;" as, however, he had not directed the prisoner to be sent for, he was still at the Bastille. A messenger was then dispatched for him, and he arrived at eleven o'clock. He was questioned respecting the grants, and answered extremely well; but he was a little at a loss as to certain dates, which would have injured him considerably, if the examiner had been skillful and awake; but, instead of this, the chancellor was asleep. This was observed by M. Fouquet, who would have laughed heartily, if he had dared. At length the chancellor roused himself, and continued the examination; and though M. Fouquet rested too much on a prop that might have failed him, the event proved that he knew what he was about; for, in his misfortune, he has certain little advantages that belong exclusively to himself. If they go on slowly every day, the trial will last a long time.

I shall write to you every evening; but I shall not send my letter till Saturday or Sunday evening: it will give you an account of the proceedings of Thursday, Friday, and Saturday, and I will contrive that you shall receive one on Thursday, informing you of the proceedings of Monday, Tuesday, and Wednesday: in this way your letters will not be long detained. I beg my compliments to your recluse, and to your better half. I say nothing of your dear neighbor; it will soon be my turn to give you news of her myself.

LETTER IV.

Thursday, November 27, 1664.

The examination upon the subject of the grants was resumed to-day. The chancellor kindly endeavored to drive M. Fouquet to extremities, and to embarrass him, but he did not succeed. M. Fouquet acquitted himself admirably; he did not come into the chamber of justice till eleven o'clock, because the chancellor made the reporter read as before; but in spite of this parade of justice, he said the worst he could of our poor friend. The reporter* always took his part, because the chancellor evidently leaned to the other side of the question. At last he said, "Here is a charge to which the accused will not be able to answer." "And here, sir," said the reporter, "is a plaster that will cure the weakness;" he made an excellent justification of him, and then added: "In the place in which I stand, sir, I shall always speak the truth, in whatever form it presents itself to me."

This allusion to a plaster called forth a smile from the audience, as it reminded them of the one that has lately made so much noise at court. The accused was then brought in; he only remained an hour in court; and, on his leaving it, M. d'Ormesson was complimented by several persons upon his firmness.

I must relate to you what I myself did. Some ladies proposed to me to accompany them to a house exactly opposite the arsenal, where we could see the return of our poor friend. I was masked,† but my eye caught him the moment he was in view. M. d'Artagan was at his side, and fifty mousquetaires about thirty or forty steps behind him. He appeared thoughtful. The moment I saw him my legs trembled, and my heart beat so violently that I could scarcely support myself. In approaching us to re-enter his dungeon, M. d'Artagan pointed out to him that we were there, and he saluted us with the same delightful smile you have so often witnessed. I do not believe he recognized me; but I own I was strangely affected when I saw him enter the little door. If you knew the misfortune of having a heart like

---

* The reporter was M. d'Ormesson, one of the most respectable magistrates of his time.

† It was still the custom for ladies to wear masks when they went abroad; a custom which is retained in Corneille's plays, and which was brought from Italy by the Medicis, with many other customs equally disagreeable. These masks of black velvet, to which the *loups* succeeded, were intended as a preservative to the complexion.

mine, I am sure you would pity me; but from what I know of you, I do not think you have much the advantage of me in this point. I have been to see your dear neighbor. I pity you as much at losing her as I rejoice at her being with us. We have had a good deal of conversation upon the subject of our poor friend; she has seen Sappho,* who has considerably raised her spirits. I shall go there to-morrow, to recruit my own; for I often feel the want of consolation; it is not that I do not hear a thousand things, that should inspire hope; but alas! my imagination is so lively, that every thing which is uncertain destroys me.

Friday, November 28.

The court opened early this morning. The chancellor said he had now to speak of the four loans: D'Ormesson observed, that it was a very unimportant affair, and one upon which no blame could be attached to M. Fouquet, as he had declared from the beginning. An attempt was made to contradict him: he begged leave to explain the matter according to his own view of it, and desired his colleagues to listen to him. The court was attentive, and he convinced them that it was a very trifling business. The accused was then ordered to be brought in; it was eleven o'clock. You will remark that he has never been more than an hour upon the sellette. The chancellor still wished to speak of the loans. M. Fouquet requested he might be allowed to state what he had omitted the day before, respecting the grants; leave was given him, and he said wonders. The chancellor asked him, "Have you had your acquittance for the employment of this sum?" He replied that he had, but that it was conjointly with other things which he had marked, and which will come in their course. "But," said the chancellor, "at the time you received these acquittances you had not incurred the expenses?" "True," replied M. Fouquet, "but the sums were set apart

---

* Mademoiselle Scudery, sister of the author, known under this name by an unfortunate fertility of imagination; a woman who had more wit than her writings display, though they display a great deal.

for the purpose." "This is not enough," said the chancellor. "Pardon me, sir," said M. Fouquet; "when I gave you your appointments, for instance, I sometimes received the acquittance a month beforehand, and as the sum was set apart, it was exactly the same as if it had been paid." "That is true," said the chancellor; "I was much indebted to you." M. Fouquet replied that he had no intention to reproach him, and that he was at that time happy to serve him; but the circumstance had occurred to his mind, as an instance in point, and he could not help making use of it.

The court has closed till Monday. They seem determined to prolong the affair as much as possible. Puis*** has promised to give the accused as few opportunities of speaking as he can. The fact is, they are afraid of him. They would, therefore, interrogate him summarily, and even pass over some of the articles; but he is determined they shall not do this, nor will he suffer them to judge his cause without his being permitted to justify himself upon every separate head of accusation. Puis*** is in continual apprehension of offending Petit. He excused himself the other day by saying that M. Fouquet had certainly spoken too long, but that he had no means of interrupting him. Ch*** is constantly behind the screen whenever the examinations take place; he hears all that is said, and offers to go to the judges and explain the reasons by which he is led to draw such opposite conclusions. All this is irregular, and shows a great inveteracy against the unfortunate prisoner. I own I have no longer any hope. Adieu, sir, till Monday. I wish you could see my heart, you would then be convinced of the sincerity of a friendship which you profess to prize.

LETTER V.

Two days ago every one believed that it was intended to protract M. Fouquet's affair as much as possible; but now the reverse of this appears to be the case, and the interrogations are hurried over in a most extraordinary manner. This morning the chancellor took his paper and read; as he would an inventory, ten heads of accusation, without giving the accused time to reply. M. Fouquet said, "I do not wish, sir, to prolong the business, but I entreat you to give me time to answer the charges that are brought against me. You question me, and it appears as if you did not wish me to reply; but it is of consequence to me to speak. There are many articles I must explain; and it is but justice that I should answer to all those which are formally alleged against me." The court was then obliged to attend, contrary to the wishes of the ill-disposed, who could not bear to hear him defend himself so ably. He answered extremely well to every accusation. The trial will now go on, but will be conducted so rapidly that I expect the examination will close this week. I have just been supping at the Hôtel de Nevers; the mistress of the house and I conversed a good deal upon this subject. We are uneasy to a degree, which you only can comprehend, for I have just received your letter; it surpasses even my own feelings upon the subject. You put my modesty to too great a trial in asking me upon what terms I am with you and your dear recluse. It seems to me that I see him and hear him say what you tell me. I am quite piqued that it was not I who metamorphosed Pierrot to Tartuffe;* it was so natural that if I had half the wit you ascribe to me, it would have flowed mechanically from my pen.

I must relate to you a little anecdote, which is perfectly true, and which can not fail to amuse you. The king has lately employed himself in making verses; Messieurs de Saint Aignan and Dangeau put him in the way of it. He wrote a little madrigal the other day with which he was not much pleased. One morning he said to Marshal de Grammont, "M. le maréchal, read this little madrigal, if you please, and tell me if you ever saw so silly a one; because it is known that I have lately

* The Chancellor Seguier's name was Pierre.

been fond of poetry they bring me all the nonsense that is written." The marshal having read it, said to the king, "Your majesty is an excellent judge of every thing: this is certainly without exception the most silly and ridiculous madrigal I ever read." The king laughed, and continued, "Must not the writer be a great fool?" "There is no other name for him," said the marshal. "O!" said the king, "how delighted I am that you have spoken your sentiments so freely! I am myself the author of it." "Ah! sire, what treason have I uttered! I entreat your majesty to give it me again. I read it hastily." "No, M. le maréchal; the first sentiments are always the most natural." The king was very much entertained at this little frolic; but those about him thought it the most cruel thing that could be done to an old courtier. For myself, I love to make reflections, and I wish the king would reflect in like manner on this adventure, that he might see how far he is from knowing the truth. We are upon the point of experiencing a still more painful instance of royal delusion, in the repurchase of our rents, at an expense that will send us all to the workhouse. The emotion it occasions is great, but the hardship is greater. Do you not think this is undertaking too much at once? The loss of a part of my income is not the point that affects me the most.

Tuesday, December 2.

Our dear unfortunate friend spoke for two hours this morning, but so uncommonly well that several persons could not help expressing their admiration. Among others, M. de Renard said, "This man, it must be owned, is incomparable; he never spoke so well in the parliament; he maintains his self-possession better than he has ever done." The subject was the six millions, and his own expenses. Nothing could exceed what he said. I shall write to you on Thursday and on Friday; these will be the last days of the examination, and I shall go on to the end.

God grant my last letter may contain the information I so

ardently wish. Adieu, my dear sir; desire our recluse (Arnauld) to pray for our poor friend. I heartily embrace you both, and, for modesty's sake, I include your wife.

IN CONTINUATION.

Tranquillity reigns throughout the family of the unfortunate Fouquet. It is said that M. de Nesmond declared on his death-bed, that his greatest sorrow was that he had not excepted to these two judges; that if he had lived to the end of the trial he would have repaired his fault, and that he prayed God to pardon his error.

M. Fouquet, as I observed before, spoke to-day two complete hours, upon the subject of the six millions; he commanded attention, and performed wonders. Every one was affected in his way. Puissort made gestures of disbelief and disapprobation, that shocked every honest man in court.

When M. Fouquet had done, M. Puissort rose impetuously, and said, "Thank God, it can never be said that he has not had his bellyful of speaking." What say you to this speech? Was it not worthy of a judge? It is said that the chancellor is very much alarmed at the erysipelas that occasioned the death of M. de Nesmond, fearing there may be a repetition of the judgment in store for himself. If the apprehension could inspire him with the sentiments of a man about to appear before God, it would be something; but it will be said of him, I fear, as of Argante, *e mori come visse:** he died as he lived.

Wednesday, December 3.

I have received your letter; it has proved to me that I have not obliged a person who is ungrateful; nothing can be more kind, nothing more gratifying. I must be wholly exempt from vanity to be insensible to such praises. I assure you, I am delighted at the good opinion you entertain of my

---

* Gerusalemme Liberata, canto 19; the verse runs thus:
Moriva Argante, e tal moria qual visse.

heart, and I further assure you, without meaning compliment for compliment, that my esteem for you infinitely surpasses the power of ordinary language to express, and that I experience real pleasure and consolation in being able to inform you of events in which we are both so much interested. I am very glad your dear recluse takes her part in them; I supposed you would make them known also to your incomparable neighbor. You gratify me extremely in telling me that I have made some progress in her heart; there is no one in whose affections I would more gladly establish myself, and when I would indulge in a little gayety, I think of her and her enchanted palace. But I return to business, from which I have been insensibly led, to tell you of the sentiments I entertain for yourself and your amiable friend.

M. Fouquet was upon the selette again to-day. The Abbé d'Effiat bowed to him, as he passed. In returning his bow, he said to him, with the same enchanting smile we have so often observed, "Sir, I am your very humble servant." The abbé was so much affected that he could not speak.

As soon as M. Fouquet was in the chamber, the chancellor desired him to be seated. He replied, "Sir, you took advantage, yesterday, of my placing myself upon the sellette: you infer from my doing so that I acknowledge the authority of the court; as that is the case, I beg leave to stand." The chancellor then told him he might withdraw. M. Fouquet replied, "I do not mean by this to advance any new objection; I only wish to make my protestation, as usual, and, the charge being cited against me, to be permitted to reply."

This was agreed to. He then seated himself, and the examination respecting the pension of the gabelles was resumed, to which he replied admirably. If this mode continue, the interrogations will be favorable to him. The spirit and firmness he displays are the subject of general conversation at Paris. He has asked one thing of a friend which makes me tremble: he has entreated him to let him know his sentence, whether favorable or otherwise, in some private way, by signal, the instant it is pronounced, that he may have time to reconcile himself to his fate before it be announced to him officially; adding, that if he has half an hour to prepare himself, he shall hear without emotion the worst that can be told him. This has made me weep, and I am certain it will affect you also very painfully.

There were few persons at the examination, on account of the queen's illness; she was supposed to be dying, but is now somewhat better. Yesterday evening she received the viaticum. It was the most affecting and solemn spectacle that can be imagined, to see the king and the whole court going for the holy sacrament, and conducting it to the palace. It was received with a profusion of lights. The queen made an effort to rise, and took it with a devotion that reduced every one to tears. It was not without difficulty that she had been brought to consent; the king was the only one who could make her listen to reason; to every other person she said that she was very willing to receive the communion, but not the viaticum; it was full two hours before she could be prevailed upon.

The general approbation that is given to M. Fouquet's answers, is very grating to Petit.* It is even thought he will engage Puis*** to feign illness, in order to interrupt the torrent of admiration, and to have time himself to take breath at

---

* Petit is a feigned name, meant either for Le Tellier or Colbert. With regard to Puis***, as, from the sense of the expressions, he must be one of the judges against Fouquet, there is little doubt that Puissort is the person alluded to; and what is said of him in the preceding Letters must be so understood.

It may further be remarked that the conduct of Colbert and Le Tellier, in this business, was extremely well characterized by a criticism of the great Turenne, who interested himself warmly for Fouquet. To some one who blamed the violence of Colbert, and praised the moderation of Le Tellier, Turenne replied, "True, sir; M. Colbert has most desire that he should be hanged, and M. Le Tellier most fear lest he should not be."

this, and other instances of his ill success. I am the most obedient servant of the dear recluse, of your lady, and the adorable Amalthée.

LETTER VI.

Thursday, December 4, 1664.

At length the examinations are over. M. Fouquet entered the chamber this morning. The chancellor ordered his *project against the state* to be read throughout. M. Fouquet spoke first upon the subject. "I believe, sir," said he, "you can derive nothing from this paper, but the effect it has just produced, of overwhelming me with confusion." The chancellor replied, "You have yourself heard and seen by it that your regard for the state, which you have so much insisted upon in court, was not so considerable but that you would have embroiled it from one end to the other." "Sir," replied M. Fouquet, "this idea occurred to me only in the height of the despair in which the cardinal often placed me; especially when, after contributing more than any man in the world to his return to France, I found myself repaid by the basest ingratitude. I had a letter from himself, and one from the queen-mother, in proof of what I say; but they have been taken away with my papers, as have several letters. It is to be lamented that I did not burn this unfortunate paper which had so completely escaped my mind and my memory that I have been nearly two years without thinking of it or knowing even that it existed. However this affair may terminate, I disown it with my whole heart, and I entreat you, sir, to believe, that my regard for the person and the service of the king has never been in the slightest degree diminished." "It is very difficult to believe this," said the chancellor, "when we see such contrary sentiments expressed at a different period." M. Fouquet replied, "At no period, sir, even though at the hazard of my life, have I ever abandoned the king's person; and at the time in question, you, sir, were at the head of the council of his enemies, and your relations gave free passage to the army against him."

The chancellor felt this stroke; but our poor friend was irritated, and therefore not quite master of himself. The subject of his expenses was afterward introduced. "I undertake," said he, "to prove that I have not incurred a single expense which, either by means of my private income, with which the cardinal was well acquainted, or my appointments, or my wife's fortune, I was not able to afford; and if I do not prove this satisfactorily, I consent to be treated with the utmost ignominy." In short, this interrogation lasted two hours; M. Fouquet defended himself ably, but with a degree of warmth and petulance; the reading of the project having ruffled him exceedingly.

When he had left the court, the chancellor said, "This is the last time we shall interrogate him." M. Poncet then went up to the chancellor, and said, "You have made no mention, sir, of the proofs there are that he had attempted to put his project against the state into execution." The chancellor replied, "They are not, sir, sufficiently strong; he would have refuted them too easily." Upon which Saint Hélène and Puissort said, "Every one is not of that opinion." This is a subject to muse upon. The rest to-morrow.

Friday, December 5.

This morning the subject of the requests was mentioned, which are of little importance except that there are persons, not ill disposed, who wish the sentence to refer to them. The business on the side of the prosecution is at an end. It is now M. d'Ormesson's turn to speak; he is to recapitulate the several matters. This will occupy the whole of the next week, during which the time we shall pass can scarcely be called living. For myself, you would hardly know me, and I do not think I can hold out so long. M. d'Ormesson has desired me not to see him again till the business is over: he is in the conclave, and will have intercourse with no one. He affects great reserve; he listens to me, but does not answer. I had the pleasure, in bidding him adieu, to acquaint him with my sentiments. I will inform you of all I hear. God grant my last tidings may be good; I desire it fervently. I assure you we are all very much to be pitied. I mean you and I, and all who, like ourselves, are interested in the event. Adieu, my dear sir: I am so dull this evening, and my heart is so much oppressed that I must conclude.

LETTER VII.

Tuesday, December 9, 1664.

I assure you the days pass very tediously; suspense is extremely painful: but it is an evil to which the whole family of the unfortunate prisoner is habituated. I have seen, and can not sufficiently express my admiration of them. It seems as if they had never known, never read, the events that have taken place in former times. What surprises me most is, that Sappho is just like the rest; she, whose understanding and penetration are unlimited. When I reflect upon this circumstance, I persuade myself, or, at least, I wish to persuade myself, that they know more of the matter than I do. When I reason too with others, on whose judgment I can rely, and who are less prejudiced, because less interested, I find all our measures so just that it will be really a miracle if the business does not terminate according to our wishes. We are sometimes only lost by a single voice, but that voice is every thing. I remember, however, the recusations, respecting which these poor women thought themselves so sure, and we lost them by five to seventeen; since that time their confidence has been my distrust. Yet I have a little spark of hope in my heart; I hardly know from whence it comes, nor whither it would lead, nor is it sufficient to make me sleep in peace. I talked over this affair yesterday with Madame du Plessis;* I can see

* Madame du Plessis Belliere, the intimate friend of Fouquet. He

nobody; but those who will converse with me on the subject, and who are of the same opinion as myself. She hopes, as I do, without knowing the reason. "Why do you hope?" "Because I do;" this is our answer; a notable one, it must be confessed. I told her, with the greatest sincerity in the world, that if the sentence should be in conformity to our wishes, the height of my joy would be to dispatch instantly a man on horseback with the pleasing intelligence to you; and that the pleasure of picturing the delight I should give you, would render my own delight complete. She perfectly agreed with me; and our imagination gave us more than a quarter of an hour's holiday on the occasion. I must correct my last day's report of the examination respecting the project against the state. I related it to you exactly as I heard it; but the same person has since tasked his memory, and told it to me over again more accurately. Every body has heard it from the different judges. After M. Fouquet had said that the only effect that could be drawn from this project was the confusion the reading it had occasioned him, the chancellor observed, "You can not deny that this is a crime against the state." "I confess, sir," he replied, "that it is a foolish and extravagant thing, but not a crime against the state. I entreat you, gentlemen," said he, turning toward the judges, "to suffer me to explain what constitutes a state crime; not that I consider you less capable of defining it than myself, but I have had more time perhaps than you to examine the question. A crime against the state, is when a person, holding an important office, and being in the secrets of a prince, suddenly goes over to the side of his enemy, engages his whole family in the same interests, opens the gates of a city, of which he is the governor, to the foe, shuts them against his lawful sovereign, and reveals to his enemy the secrets of the state. This, gentlemen, is what is called a state crime." The chancellor did not know which way

had commissioned her to take his papers from his house at St. Mandé. She was not in due time to execute it. She was at first exiled, and afterward recalled. She died in 1705, aged 100 years.

to look, and the judges could scarcely refrain from laughter. This is the truth without any embellishment. You will agree with me, that nothing could be more spirited, more delicate in its satire, and at the same time more diverting.

The whole kingdom knows and admires the prisoner's reply on this occasion. He afterward entered minutely into his defense, and said what I told you before. I should have been quite unhappy if you had not known this circumstance, and our dear friend would have lost much by it. This morning M. d'Ormesson began the recapitulation. He spoke well and clearly. On Thursday he will give his opinion; his colleague will then speak for two days; it will take several more for the rest to give their opinions. Some of the judges say that they shall enlarge a great deal upon the subject, so that we have to languish in expectation till next week. In this state of suspense we can scarcely be said to live.

Wednesday, December 10.

M. d'Ormesson has continued the recapitulation; he has done wonders, that is, he has spoken with extraordinary clearness, intelligence, and ability. Puissort interrupted him five or six times, with no other intention than to embarrass him, and prevent his speaking so well: he said to him in one instance, where his argument went strongly in favor of M. Fouquet, "Sir, we shall speak after you, we shall speak after you."

LETTER VIII.

Thursday, December 11, 1664.

M. d'Ormesson has not yet finished. When he came to the article of the gold mark, Puissort said, "This speaks strongly against the accused." "It may be so," said M. d'Ormesson, but there are no proofs." "What!" said Puissort, "have not the two officers been examined?" "No," replied M. d'Ormesson. "It can not be," said Puissort. "I can find no such thing in the proceedings," said M. d'Ormesson. Upon this, Puissort rose in a fury, and said, " Sir, you ought rather to say, I find here a very gross omission." M. d'Ormesson made no answer, but if Puissort had addressed another word to him, he would have replied, " I am here, sir, as a judge, and not as an informer." You may remember what I once said to you at Fresne, that M. d'Ormesson would not discover the omission till there was no remedy. The chancellor also interrupted M. d'Ormesson several times; he told him it was not necessary to speak of the project. This must be from malice; for many will suppose it a great crime, and the chancellor would be glad that the proofs, which are truly ridiculous, should be withheld, that the idea which prevails might not be weakened. As, however, it is one of the articles of the indictment, M. d'Ormesson will not omit it. He will finish to-morrow. Sainte-Hélène will speak on Saturday. On Monday the two reporters will give their opinion, and on Tuesday, the whole committee will assemble early in the morning, and not separate till judgment be passed. I tremble when I think of this day. The hopes of the family are very sanguine. Faucault goes about every where, and shows a writing of the king's, in which he is made to say that he should think it very improper if any of the judges leaned toward the prisoner, from the circumstance of his papers being taken away; that it was he who ordered it to be done; that there is not one that can be of use to the prisoner in his defense; that they are papers that relate merely to his office; and that he makes this known that the judges may not draw improper inferences. What say you to this magnanimous proceeding? Are you not grieved that a prince, who would love justice and truth if he were left to himself, should be prevailed upon to act thus? He said the other day at his levee, that Fouquet was a dangerous man; this has been put into his head by some one. In short, our enemies no longer keep within bounds; they run at full speed; threats, promises, every thing is resorted to; but if God be on our side, we shall be stronger than they. You will perhaps have another letter from me; if we have good news, I shall dispatch an express to you, with all possible expedition; but how I shall act, or what will become of me, in any other case, I am at a loss to conjecture. A thousand compliments to our recluse, and to your better half. Pray earnestly to God for our friend.

Saturday, December, 13.

After having fixed and changed, and fixed and changed again, it was at length resolved that M. d'Ormesson should give his opinion to-day; that Sunday might pass over, and Sainte-Hélène begin anew on Monday, which would make a stronger impression. M. d'Ormesson's opinion was, that the accused should be sentenced to perpetual banishment, and his property confiscated to the king. M. d'Ormesson has by this means established his reputation as a judge. The sentence is a little severe,* but let us pray that no worse counsel may be given; it is always glorious to be the first in an assault.

LETTER IX.

Wednesday, December 17, 1664.

You languish, my dear friend, after intelligence, and so do we. I was sorry I sent you word that judgment would be pronounced on Tuesday; for, not hearing from me, you must have thought it was all over; but our hopes are as strong as ever. I informed you, on Saturday, in what way M. d'Ormesson had reported the cause, and how he had voted, but I did not sufficiently express the extraordinary esteem he has acquired by his conduct in this business. I have heard several of this profession say that his speech was a master-piece; that he ex-

---

* Severe as it was, the king aggravated the punishment still more. Fouquet's dilapidations were certainly criminal, but Cardinal Mazarin gave less and took much more. The licentiousness of the times, and the force of example, were an excuse, if any excuse could be made.

plained himself with great clearness, and rested his opinion upon the most convincing arguments: it was eloquence and grace combined. In short, no man had ever a finer opportunity of making himself known, and no man ever made a better use of it. If he had wished to open his door to congratulations, his house would have been crowded; but he was too modest for this, and kept out of the way. His colleague, Sainte-Hélène, indignant at his success, spoke on Monday and Tuesday. He resumed the affair weakly and miserably, reading what he had to say, without adding any new circumstance or giving a different turn to it. He voted, but did not assign his reasons, that M. Fouquet should lose his head for his crime against the state; and to gain votes on his side, he played the Normand, and alleged that it was probable the king, who alone could do it, would remit the sentence and pardon him. It was yesterday he performed this brilliant action, at which we were as much grieved as we had before been satisfied with the conduct of M. d'Ormesson.

This morning Puissort spoke for four hours, but with so much vehemence, fury, rage, and rancor, that several of the judges were shocked; and it is thought his intemperance will do more good than harm to our poor friend. He even redoubled his violence toward the end, and said, upon the subject of the crime against the state, that the example of a certain Spaniard, who had so great a horror for a rebel that he ordered his house to be burned, because Charles of Bourbon had passed through it, ought to make us blush at our moderation; that we had much greater reason to hold in abhorrence the crime of M. Fouquet; that the halter and the gibbet were the only proper punishments for him; but that, in consideration of the high offices he had held, and the noble families to which he was related, he would relax his opinion, and vote with M. de Sainte-Hélène, that he be beheaded.

What say you to this moderation? Is it because he is the uncle of M. de Nesmond, and was excepted against, that he conducts himself so generously? For my part, I can scarcely contain myself when I think of this scandalous proceeding. I do not know whether judgment will be pronounced to-morrow, or the business be protracted to the end of the week. We have still many difficulties to encounter: but perhaps some one will side with M. d'Ormesson, whose opinion at present stands alone.

But I have to beg your attention to two or three little incidents, which are no less extraordinary than true. In the first place, then, a comet made its appearance about four days ago. It was announced, at first, by some women only, who were laughed at for their pains; but it has now been seen by every one. M. d'Artagan sat up last night, and saw it very distinctly. M. de Neuré, a great astronomer, says it is of considerable magnitude. M. du Foin has seen it, with three or four other learned men. I have not seen it myself, but I intend sitting up to-night for the purpose: it appears about three o'clock. I tell you of this, ignorant whether you will be pleased or displeased with the intelligence.

Berrier, in the literal sense of the word, is become mad; he has been bled profusely, and is in a perfect frenzy. He raves of wheels and gibbets, and has even mentioned particular trees; he declares he is going to be hanged, and makes so dreadful a noise that his keepers are obliged to chain him. This is evidently a judgment of Providence, and a very just one. A criminal of the name of Lamothe, who was in prison and about to be tried, has deposed that Messrs. de B***,* C***, and B*** (they add also Puissort, or Poncet, but of him I am not so certain) urged him several times to implicate M. Fouquet and Lorme, promising if he would do so that they would obtain his pardon; but he refused, and published the circumstance in court, before his trial took place. He was condemned to the galleys. The wife and mother of M. Fouquet have procured a copy of the deposition, and will present it to-morrow at the chamber. Perhaps it will not be received,

* M. de Boucherat was one of the commissioners: the other, B***, is, no doubt, Berrier.

because the judges are now giving their opinions; but it may be made known, and must produce a strong impression on the court. Is not all this very extraordinary?

I must tell you, also, of a heroic act of Masnau. He had been dangerously ill, for a whole week, of a bladder complaint; he took a variety of medicines, and was at last bled, at midnight. The next morning, at seven o'clock, he insisted on being carried to the chamber of justice, where he suffered the most excruciating pain. The chancellor saw him turn pale, and said, "This is not a fit place for you, sir; you had better retire." "True, sir," he replied, "but I may as well die here." The chancellor perceiving him ready to faint, and finding him bent upon remaining, said, "Well, sir, retire; we will wait for you." Upon this he went out for a quarter of an hour, during which time he passed two stones, of so enormous a size, that it might be considered as a miracle, if men were deserving that God should work miracles in their favor. This worthy man then returned into court, gay and cheerful, every one astonished at the adventure.

This is all I know. Every body is interested in this weighty affair. Nothing else is talked of. Men reason, infer, calculate, pity, fear, wish, hate, admire, are overwhelmed; in short, my dear sir, our present situation is a most singular one; but the resignation and firmness of our dear unfortunate friend is perfectly heavenly. He knows every day what passes, and every day volumes might be written in his praise. I beg you to thank your father* for the gratifying note he has written me, and the charming works he sent me. I have read them, though my head feels, alas, as if it were split into pieces. Tell him I am delighted he loves me a little—a great deal, I mean—and that I love him still more. I have received your last letter; alas! you overpay so abundantly the trifling services I render you, that I remain your debtor.

* Arnaud d'Andilly, the translator of Josephus.

LETTER X.

Friday, December 19, 1664.

This is a day which gives us great hopes; but I must go back in my story. I told you that M. Puissort had, on Wednesday, voted for the death of our friend; on Thursday, Nogués, Gisaucourt, Feriol, and Péraut, voted in the same way. Roquesante concluded the day, and, after speaking well for an hour, sided with M. d'Ormesson. This morning our hopes have sailed before the wind, for several votes that were doubtful have been given: Toison, Masnau, Verdier, La Baume, and Catinet, and all in favor of M. d'Ormesson's opinion.* It was then Poncet's turn to speak; but, thinking that those who remained were almost all disposed to be lenient, he would not begin, though it was only eleven o'clock. It is thought he wishes to consult with some one what he shall say, and that he is not willing to bring disgrace upon himself, and consign a man to death unnecessarily. Such is our present situation, and, though so favorable a one, our joy is not complete; for you must know that M. N. is so enraged, that we expect some unjust and atrocious proceeding in consequence, that will plunge us again into despair. But for this, my dear sir, we should have the satisfaction of seeing our friend, though unfortunate, yet safe, as far as his life is concerned, which is a great thing. We shall see what will happen to-morrow. We are now seven to six. Le Feron, Moussy, Brillac, Bénard, Renard, Voisin, Pontchartrain, and

---

* Names of the committee who judged Fouquet:

FAVORABLE.

D'Ormesson,	Le Feron,	Moussy,	Brillac,	Renard,
Bénard,	Roquesante,	La Toison,	La Baume,	Verdier,
	Masnau,	Catinet,	Pontchartrain.	

ADVERSE.

| St. Hélène, | Piussort, | Gisaucourt, | Feriol, | Nogués, |
| Heraut, | Poncet, | Père Seguier, | The Chancellor. | |

the chancellor, have not yet voted; but of these, we shall have by far the greater number.

Saturday.

Fall on your knees, sir, and return thanks to God; the life of our poor friend is saved. Thirteen were of M. d'Ormesson's opinion, and nine of Sainte-Hélène's. I am almost wild with joy.

Sunday evening.

I was sadly afraid some other person would have the pleasure of communicating to you the joyful tidings. My courier was not very diligent; he said, on setting out, that he would sleep no where but at Livri; he assures me, however, he was the first that arrived. Heavens! how gratifying must the intelligence have been to you! How inconceivably sweet are the moments that relieve the heart on a sudden from the anguish of so painful a suspense! It will be a long time before I shall lose the joy I received yesterday. It was, in reality, too great—too much, almost, for me to bear. The poor man learned the news by signals, a few moments after judgment was pronounced, and I dare say felt it in all its extent. This morning the king sent the Chevalier du Guet to the mother and wife of M. Fouquet, recommending them both to go to Montluçon in Auvergne, the marquis and Marchioness of Charost to Ancenis, and the young Fouquet to Joinville in Champagne. The good old lady sent word to the king that she was seventy-two years of age; that she besought his majesty not to deprive her of her only remaining son, the support of her life, which apparently was drawing near its close. The prisoner does not yet know his sentence. It is said he will be taken, to-morrow, to Pignerol, for the king has changed his banishment into imprisonment. His wife, contrary to all rule, is not permitted to see him. But let not this proceeding abate the least particle of your joy; mine, if possible, is increased; for I see in this more clearly the greatness of our victory. I shall faithfully relate to you the sequel of this curious history. I have given you what has passed to-day; the rest to-morrow.

Tuesday evening.

This morning, at ten o'clock, M. Fouquet was conducted to the chapel of the Bastille. Foucault held the sentence in his hand. "You must tell me your name, sir," said he, "that I may know whom I address." M. Fouquet replied, "You know very well who I am; and as for my name, I will not give it here, as I refused to give it at the chamber of justice; by the same rule, also, I protest against the sentence you are going to read to me." What passed being written down, Foucault put on his hat and read the sentence; M. Fouquet heard it uncovered. Pecquet and Lavalée* were afterward separated from him, and the cries and tears of these poor men melted every heart that was not of iron; they made so strange a noise that M. d'Artagnan was obliged to go and comfort them; for it seemed to them as if a sentence of death had just been read to their master. They were both lodged in the Bastille, and it is not known what will be done with them.

M. Fouquet went to the apartment of M. d'Artagnan: while he was there, he saw M. d'Ormesson, who came for some papers that were in the hands of M. d'Artagnan, pass by the window. On perceiving him, M. Fouquet saluted him with an open countenance, expressive of joy and gratitude; he even cried out to him that he was his humble servant. M. d'Ormesson returned the salutation with very great civility, and came with grief of heart to tell me what had passed.

At eleven o'clock a coach was ready, into which M. Fouquet entered, with four guards. M. d'Artagnan was on horseback with fifty musqueteers; he will escort him to Pignerol, where he will leave him in prison, in the care of a man of the name of St. Mars, who is a very honest fellow: he will have fifty soldiers to guard his prisoner. I do not know whether an-

* His physician and his servant.

other servant has been allowed our friend; you can form no idea how cruel the circumstance of taking Pecquet and Lavalée from him appears to every one: some even go so far as to draw dreadful inferences from it. May God preserve him, as he has hitherto done: in him we must put our trust, and leave our friend to the protection of that Providence which has been so gracious to him. They still refuse him his wife, but have permitted the mother to remain at Parc, with the abbess her daughter. L'Ecuyer will follow his sister-in-law; he has declared that he has no other means of subsistence. M. and Madame de Charost are going immediately to Ancenis. M. Bailly, the attorney-general, has been turned out of office, for having said to Gisaucourt, before judgment was pronounced, that he ought to retrieve the honor of the Grand Council, which would be disgraced if C***, Poncet, and himself acted together in the business. I am sorry for this upon your account: it is a rigorous measure. *Tantœne animis cœlestibus iræ?**

But no, it does not mount so high as that. Such harsh and low revenge can not proceed from a heart like that of our monarch's. His name is employed, and, as you see, profaned. I will let you know the rest: how much better could we converse upon these things! it is impossible to communicate by letter all we have to say. Adieu, my dear sir, I have not so much modesty as you, and, without taking refuge in the crowd, I assure you I love and esteem you highly. I have seen the comet; its train is of a beautiful length. I partly found my hopes on it. A thousand compliments to your dear wife.

Tuesday.

I send you something to amuse you for a few minutes. You will certainly find it worth reading. It is charity to entertain you both in your solitude. If the friendship I bear the father and the son were a remedy against dullness, it is an evil of which you would never have to complain. I am just come

---

* Virgil's Æneid, lib. i.

from a place where, it seems, I have renewed this sentiment, by talking of you with five or six persons, male and female, who, like me, rank themselves among your friends; it was at the Hôtel de Nevers. Your wife was of the party; she will tell you of the delightful little comedians we met there. I believe our dear friend is arrived, but I have had no certain intelligence. It is only known that M. d'Artagnan, continuing his obliging manners, gave him the necessary fur clothing, that he might pass the mountains without inconvenience. I know also that M. d'Artagnan has received letters from the king, and that he told M. Fouquet to keep up his spirits and his courage, and that every thing would go well. We are always looking forward to some mitigation, and I in particular: hope has been too kind for me to abandon it. Whenever I see the king at our ballets, these two lines of Tasso come into my head:

> Goffredo ascolta, e in rigida sembianza
> Porge piu di timor che di speranza.*

But I care not to despond: we must follow the example of our poor prisoner; he is tranquil and gay; let us be so too. It will give me real pleasure to see you here. I can not think your exile will be of long duration. Assure your good father of my affection; I can not help expressing myself thus; and let me know your opinion of the stanzas. Some of them are admired, as well as some of the couplets.

LETTER XI.

Thursday Evening, January, 1665.

At length, the mother, the daughter-in-law, and the brother have obtained leave to be together; they are going to Mont-

---

* Godfrey attends, and with a brow severe
But little gives to hope, and much to fear.
       Hoole's Translation.

luçon in the heart of Auvergne. The mother had permission to go to Parc-aux-Dames to her daughter, but her daughter-in-law has prevailed on her to accompany her. M. and Madame de Charost are on their way to Ancenis. Pecquet and Lavalée are still in the Bastille. Can any thing be more dreadful than this injustice? They have given M. Fouquet another servant. M. d'Artagnan was his only comfort in his journey. It is said that the person who is to have the care of him at Pignerol is a very worthy creature. God grant he may be so! or rather, God protect our friend! He has already protected him so visibly that we ought to think he has an especial care of him. La Forêt, his old esquire, accosted him as he was going away. "I am delighted to see you," said Fouquet to him; "I know your fidelity and affection: tell my wife and mother not to despair, that my courage remains, and that I am in good health." Is not this admirable? Adieu, my dear sir; let us be like him; let us have courage, and dwell on the joy occasioned by the glorious sentence of Saturday.

Madame de Grignan is dead.*

Friday Evening.

It seems, by your thanks, as if you were giving me my dismissal; but I will not receive it yet. I intend to write to you whenever I please, and as soon as I have the verses from Pontneuf, I shall send them to you. Our dear friend is still upon the road: it was reported that he had been ill; every body exclaimed, "What! already?" It was reported also that M. d'Artagnan had sent to court to know what he was to do with his sick prisoner, and that he had been answered unfeelingly, that he must proceed with him, however ill he might be. This is all false: but it shows the general feeling, and the danger of furnishing materials with which to build whatever horrid castles we please. Pecquet and Lavalée are still in the Bastille: this conduct is truly unaccountable. The chamber will be resumed after the Epiphany.

* Angélique Claire d'Angennes, M. de Grignan's first wife.

I should think the poor exiles must be arrived ere this at the place of their destination. When our poor friend has reached his, I will inform you; for we must follow him to Pignerol: would to God we could bring him thence to the place we wish!* And how much longer, my dear sir, will be your exile? I often think of this. A thousand compliments to your father. I have been told your wife is here: I shall call upon her. I supped last night with one of your lady friends, and we talked of paying you a visit.

* It was the general opinion that Fouquet died in prison in the year 1680. See *Le Siècle de Louis XIV.*, and the note at the beginning of the letter dated April 3, 1680.

LETTERS TO HER SON THE MARQUIS DE SEVIGNE.*

LETTER I.

PARIS, August 5, 1684.

WHILE I am expecting your letters, I must relate to you a very amusing little history. You remember how much you regretted Mademoiselle de ***, and how unfortunate you thought yourself in having missed her for a wife: "Your best friends had all conspired against your happiness; Madame de Lavardin and Madame de la Fayette had done you irreparable injury! A young lady of noble birth, great beauty, and ample fortune, was lost to you; surely a man must be doomed never to marry, and to die like a beggar, to let such an opportunity escape him, when it was in his own power! The Marquis de *** was not such a fool; he has made his fortune, and is settled. You must certainly have been born under an unlucky planet to miss such a match! Only observe her conduct; she is a saint; an example to all married women." You remember all this, I suppose, my dear

---

* This only son of Madame de Sévigné inherited neither her genius, her virtues, nor her energy of character. She treated him always with great kindness, but was never blind to his faults. Her judicious management seems to have had a salutary effect on him, after the follies of his youth were over. He reformed in a measure, and, in 1684, married Jeanne Marguerite de Brenant de Mauron, of a noble and rich family. This alliance was a great joy to Madame de Sévigné, and it is to the illness of this beloved daughter-in-law that she alludes in the second letter.

son, and that till you married Mademoiselle de Mauron, you were ready to hang yourself; you could not have done better than you have done: but now for the sequel.

All those amiable qualities of her youth, which made Madame de la Fayette say she would not have her for a daughter-in-law if she could bring millions to her son, were happily directed to the service of religion : God was her lover, the only object of her affection, all her desires centered in this single passion; but as every thing was in extremes with her, her poor head could not bear the excess of zeal and fervent devotion with which it was filled; and, to satisfy the overflowings of her Magdalen heart, she resolved to profit by good examples, by reading the Lives of the Holy Fathers of the Desert, and of Female Penitents. She wished to become herself the heroine of such admirable histories, and, full of this idea, left her house and family about a fortnight ago, and, taking with her only five or six pistoles, and a little foot-boy, set out at four o'clock in the morning, and, taking a post-chaise at the skirts of the town, drove to Rouen, fatigued and covered with mud. When she got there, she bargained for a passage in a ship bound for the Indies: it was there, it seems, God had called her; it was there she was to lead a life of penitence and humiliation; it was there the map had pointed out to her an abode, which invited her to pass the rest of her days in sackcloth and ashes; it was there the Abbé Zosimus* was to visit her, and administer to her the last holy rites before she expired. Satisfied with this resolution, and convinced that Heaven inspired her with it, she discharged her foot-boy, and sent him home to his own country, while she waited with great impatience the departure of the ship: her good angel consoled her for the delay; she piously forgot husband, daughter, father, and relations, exclaiming:

---

* A famous hermit of the sixth century, who came on the eve of every Good Friday to give the sacrament to St. Mary the Egyptian, in a desert cave on the banks of the river Jordan. See the Lives of the Fathers of the Desert.

> Ça! courage, mon cœur, point de faiblesse humaine.*

And now the moment arrived in which her prayers are heard; the happy moment that was to separate her for ever from her native land; she follows the law of the Gospel; she leaves all to follow Christ.

In the mean time, however, her family missed her, and finding she did not return to dinner, sent to all the churches in the neighborhood; she was not there. They supposed she would return at night; no tidings were heard of her. They now begin to be uneasy, the servants are all questioned, they can give no account of her further than that she had taken her foot-boy with her. "She must certainly be at her country-house." No. "Where can she possibly be?" A messenger is dispatched to the Curé of St. Jacques-du-Haut-Pas; the curé says he has not had the direction of her conscience for a considerable time; for, being a simple, honest man, and having observed her full of strange chimerical ideas of religion, he would have nothing to do with her. Every one was now at a loss what to think; two, three, four days, a week passed, still no news of her; at length her friends thought of sending to some of the sea-ports, and, by mere accident, found her at Rouen, on the point of setting out for Dieppe, and from thence to the other extremity of the globe. They secure her, and bring her back, a little disconcerted at being disappointed of her journey:

> J'allais, j'étais, l'amour a sur moi tant d'empire.†

A lady to whom she had imparted her design, revealed the whole to her family, who, in despair at her folly, would fain have concealed it from her husband, who happened to be absent from Paris at that time, and who would have been better pleased at an exploit of gallantry in his amiable consort, than such a ridiculous expedition as this. The husband's mother

---

* Courage, my heart! disdain all human weakness.

† I went, I came, impelled by mighty Love.

came to Madame de Lavardin, and, bathed in tears, related the whole story, while the latter could scarcely refrain from laughing in her face; and the next time she saw my daughter, asked her if she could forgive her for having been the instrument of preventing her brother from marrying this pretty creature. Madame de la Fayette was also, in her turn, informed of this tragical story, and repeated it to me with great glee. She desires me to ask you if you are still angry with her; she maintains that no one can ever repent he did not marry a mad woman.

We dare not mention a syllable of this to Mademoiselle de Grignan,* her friend, who for some time past, has been ruminating upon a pilgrimage, and, as a preparative, has lately observed a profound silence toward us all. What think you of this curious narration? Has it tired you? Are you satisfied now? Adieu, my son. Marshal de Schomberg is marching to Germany at the head of twenty-five thousand men, to hasten the emperor's signing.† The gazette will inform you of the rest. Adieu.

LETTER II.

Grignan, September 20, 1695.

And so you are at our poor Rocks, my dear children, experiencing there the sweets of tranquillity, exempt from all duties and all fatigues, and our dear little marchioness can breathe again! Good heavens! how well you describe to me her situation, and her extreme delicacy! I am so affected at it, and I enter so affectionately into your ideas, that my heart is oppressed, and tears rush into my eyes. It is to be hoped that you will only have the merit of bearing your sorrows with re-

* Sister of Count de Grignan.
† This relates to the truce which was on the point of being concluded at Ratisbon, and was published at Paris on the 5th of October following.

signation and submission; but if God should appoint otherwise, like all unforeseen events, it would turn out differently from your expectations; I will believe, however, that this dear being will last, with care, as long as any one; we have a thousand examples of recovery. Has not Mademoiselle de la Trousse suffered from almost every kind of disorder? In the mean time, my dear child, I enter into your feelings with infinite affection, and from the bottom of my heart. You do me justice when you say you are afraid of affecting me too much by relating to me the state of your mind; it does indeed affect me, be assured I feel for you keenly. I hope this letter will find you calmer and happier. Paris seems to be quite out of your thoughts, on account of our marchioness. You are thinking only of Bourbon and the spring. Continue to inform me of your plans, and do not leave me in ignorance of any thing that concerns you.

Give me some account of the letters of the 23d and 30th of August. There was also a note for Galois, which I desired M. Braujon to pay. Give me an answer upon this subject. The good Branjon is married; he has written me a very charming letter upon the occasion. Let me know whether the match is as good as he represents it to be. The lady is related to all the parliament, and to M. d'Arouys. Explain this to me, my child. I also addressed a letter to you for our Abbé Charrier. He will be sorry not to see you again; and M. de Toulon! you express yourself well respecting this ox; it is for him to tame him, and for you to stand firm where you are. Return the abbé's letter to Quimperlé.

With regard to your poor sister's health, it is not at all good. It is no longer her loss of blood that alarms us, for that is over; but she does not recover her strength; she is still so much altered that you would scarcely know her, because her stomach does not regain its tone, and no food seems to nourish her; this arises from the bad state of her liver, of which you know she has long complained. It is so serious an evil that I am really alarmed at it. Remedies might be used for her liver, but they are unfavorable to the loss of blood, which we are in continual apprehension may return, and which has produced a bad effect upon the afflicted part. These two maladies, which require opposite medicines, reduce her to a truly pitiable situation. Time, we hope, will repair this devastation; I sincerely wish it; and if we enjoy this blessing, we shall go to Paris with all expedition. This is the point to which we are arrived, and which must be cleared up; I will be very faithful in my communications.

This languor makes us say little yet of the return of the warriors. I do not doubt, however, that the business will be concluded; it is too far advanced: but it will be without any great joy; and even if we go to Paris, they would set out two days after, to avoid the air of a wedding, and visits, which they wish not to receive; *a burnt child, etc.*

As to M. de St. Amant's grief, of which such a parade has been made at Paris, it was founded upon my daughter's having really proved by memorandums, which she has showed to us all, that she had paid her son nine thousand francs out of ten she had promised him; and having in consequence sent him only a thousand, M. de St. Amant said he was cheated, that they wanted to take advantage of him, and that he would give no more, having already given the fifteen thousand francs of his daughter's portion (which he laid out at Paris in stock, and for which he has the estates that were given up to him here,) and that the marquis must seek for assistance in that quarter. You may suppose that when *that quarter* has paid, it may occasion some little chagrin; but it is at an end. M. de St. Amant thought in himself that it would not be advisable to quarrel with my daughter; so he came here as gentle as a lamb, wishing for nothing but to please and to take his daughter back with him to Paris; which he has done, though, in good truth, she ought to have waited for us; but the advantage of being in the same house with her husband, in that beautiful mansion of M. de St. Amant; of being handsomely lodged, and living sumptuously at no expense; made my daughter consent without hesitation to accept all these comforts. But we did not see her depart without tears, for she is very amiable; and was so much affected at bidding us adieu, that it could scarcely have been supposed she was going to lead a life of pleasure in the midst of plenty. She had become very fond of our society. She set out with her father on the first of this month.

Be assured, my son, that no Grignan intends you harm; that you are beloved by all; and that if this trifle had been a serious thing, they would have felt that you would have taken as much interest in it as you have done.

M. de Grignan is still at Versailles; we expect him shortly, for the sea is clear, and Admiral Russel, who is no longer to be seen, will give him leave to come here.

I shall seek for the two little writings you mention. I rely much upon your taste. The letters to M. de la Trape are books we can not send, though in manuscript. You shall read them at Paris, where I still hope to see you, for I love you in a much greater degree than you can love me. It is the order of nature, and I do not complain.

I inclose you a letter from Madame de Chaulnes, which I send to you entire, from confidence in your prudence. You will justify yourself in things to which you well know what answer to make, and will pay no attention to those that may offend you. I have said for myself all I had to say, waiting for your answer respecting what I did not know; and I added that I would inform you of what the duchess told me. Write to her, therefore, candidly, as having learned from me what she writes respecting you. After all, you should preserve this connection; they love you, and have rendered you service; you must not wound gratitude. I have said that you owed obligations to the intendant. But to you, my child, I say, is this friendship incompatible with your ancient leagues with the first president and the attorney-general? Is it necessary that you should break with your old friends for the sake of securing an intendant! M. de Pommereuil did not exact such conduct. I have also said that you ought to be heard, and that it was impossible you should have neglected to congratulate the attorney-general upon the marriage of his daughter. In short, my child, defend yourself, and tell me what you say, that I may second you.

15

LETTERS TO THE COUNT DE GRIGNAN.*

FROM 1670 TO 1696.

LETTER I.

Paris, Wednesday, 23d June, 1670.

You have written me the most charming letter in the world. I should have answered it much sooner, had I not known that you were traversing your province. I should likewise have sent you the music you desired, but have not yet been able to procure it: in the mean time let me tell you that I love you most affectionately, and if that is capable of giving you the satisfaction you assure me it does, you ought to be the most contented man in the world. You must certainly be so in the correspondence you carry on with my daughter; it appears to me very animated on her part, and I do not think any one can love another more than she does you. I hope to

* Count de Grignan was of an ancient and noble Provençal family. He was rich, and held a high office, that of Lieutenant-General of the Government of Provence; and as the governor, Vendôme, was rarely in his place, M. de Grignan was virtually the governor. He had been twice married before his union with Madame de Sévigné's daughter, and it seems likely, considering the fashion of those times, and indeed of French marriages now, the mother was influenced by ambition. She found it did not confer happiness. The count was extravagant and fond of play, though he seems to have been a kind husband; still it is evident that Madame de Sévigné was constrained in her letters to him. She compliments him, professes much affection, and was always on friendly terms with him, because he was the husband of her darling daughter. But her letters to him never go beyond this

return her to you safe and sound, with a little one the same, or I will burn my books. I am not very skillful indeed myself; but I can ask advice, and follow it, and my daughter on her side takes all possible care of herself.

LETTER II.

PARIS, Wednesday, Aug. 6, 1670.

Is it not true that I have given you the prettiest wife in the world? and can any one be more prudent, more regular in her conduct? Can any one love you more, have more Christian sentiments, long more ardently to be with you, or attend more strictly to the duties of her station? It is ridiculous enough to say all this of my own daughter; but I admire her as other people do, and perhaps more, as I am more an eye-witness of her behavior; and to own the truth to you, whatever good opinion I had of her as to the principal points, I never thought she would have been so exact as she is in all the minuter ones. I assure you, every body does her justice, and she loses none of the praises which are so much her due.

LETTER III.

PARIS, Friday, August 15, 1670.

When I write to you so frequently, you must remember that it is on condition that you do not answer me. Relying on this, I shall proceed to tell you that I am heartily rejoiced at the many honors that are conferred on you. It appears to me that the commandant has less share in them than M. de Grignan himself; and I think I see a partiality for you that another would not experience.

I find there is so brisk a correspondence kept up between a certain lady and you, that it would be ridiculous to give you any news. I have not so much as a hope of acquainting you that she loves you: her every action, her whole conduct, with all her little anxieties and cares about you, tell it plain enough. I am very delicate in the point of friendship, and pretend to know something about it, and I own to you that I am perfectly satisfied with what I see, and could not wish it to be greater. Enjoy this pleasure to the utmost, and never be ungrateful. If there is any little vacant place in your heart, allow me the pleasure of occupying it; for, I assure you, you hold a very considerable one in mine.

LETTER IV.

Paris, Wednesday, December 10, 1670.

Madame de Coulanges has told me several times that you love me sincerely, that you talk of me, that you wish me with you. As I made the first advances toward this friendship, and loved first, you may judge how happy I am to find that you return the partiality I have so long had for you. All that you write of your daughter is admirable, and I had no doubt that the good health of the mother would comfort you for your disappointment. The joy I should have had in acquainting you with the birth of a son would have been too great—it would have been showering too many blessings at once; and the pleasure I naturally take in being the messenger of good news, would have been carried to excess. I shall soon be in the same condition you saw me in last year. I must love you extremely to send my daughter to you at this inclement season of the year. How foolish it is to leave a good mother, with whom you assure me she is very well satisfied, to run after a man at the furthest end of France! I give you my word, nothing can be more indecorous than such behavior. I do believe you were greatly concerned at the death of the amiable duchess. I was so afflicted myself that I stood in need of comfort while I was writing to you about it.

My daughter desires me to acquaint you with the marriage of Monsieur de Nevers;* that Monsieur de Nevers who was so difficult to be caught, who used to slip so unexpectedly through the hands of the fair, is at length going to wed. And whom think you? Not Mademoiselle de Houdancourt, nor yet Mademoiselle de Grancei, but the young, the handsome, the modest Mademoiselle de Thianges,† who was brought up at the Abbaye aux Bois. Madame de Montespan‡ has the wedding solemnized at her house next Sunday; she acts as mother on the occasion, and receives the honors as such. The king restored Monsieur de Nevers to all his posts, so that this *belle*, though she does not bring him a penny of fortune, will be worth more to him than the richest heiress in France. Madame de Montespan does wonders in every thing.

I forbid you to write to me. Write to my daughter, and leave me to the freedom of writing to you, without embarking you in a train of answers which would rob me of the pleasure I have in acquainting you with every little trifle. Continue to love me, my dear count. I dispense with your honoring my motherly dignity, but you must love me, and assure yourself that there is not a place in the world where you are so dearly beloved as you are here.

LETTER V.

PARIS, Friday, January 16, 1671.

Alas! the poor dear child is still with me, for it was utterly impossible for her, do what she would, to have set out the 10th of this month, as she all along hoped and intended to do. The rains have been, and are still, so very violent that it

---

* Philip Julian Mazarini Mancini, Duke of Nevers.

† Diana Gabriel de Damas, daughter of Claud Leonor, Marquis de Thianges, and Gabriel de Rochechouart Mortemar, sister to Madame de Montespan.

‡ Then mistress to Louis XIV.

would have been downright folly to have attempted it. The rivers are overflowed, the roads are all under water, and the carriage-tracks so covered that she would have run the risk of being overturned in every ford. In short, things are in such a state that Madame de Rochefort, who is at her country-seat, and is absolutely wild to be in Paris, where she is expected with the greatest impatience by her husband and mother, does not dare to venture till the roads are a little safer. Indeed, the winter is perfectly dreadful. We have not had an hour's frost, but there has been a continual deluge of rain every day. Not a boat can pass under any of the bridges; the arches of the Pont Neuf are in a manner choked up. In short, it is something more than common. I own to you, that seeing the season so very inclement, I warmly opposed her setting out. I would not stop her for the cold, the dirt, or the fatigues of the journey, but methinks I would not have her drowned. Yet, strong as the reasons are for her stay, nothing could have prevailed on her had not the coadjutor, who is to go with her, been engaged to perform the marriage ceremony of his cousin De Harcourt,* which is to be solemnized at the Louvre. Monsieur de Leonne is to stand proxy. The king has spoken to the coadjutor upon this subject, but the affair has been put off day after day, and may not be finished this week. My poor daughter is in such extreme impatience to be gone that the time she now passes with us can not be called living; and if the coadjutor does not disengage himself from this same wedding, I think I see her ready to commit an act of folly by setting out without him. It would be so extraordinary to go by herself, and so happy on the contrary to have a brother-in-law to accompany her, that I shall do all in my power to prevent their separation. In the mean time the waters may be a little drained off. But I can assure you that I have no sort of pleasure in her

* Mary Angelica Henrietta of Lorraine, married the 7th February, 1671, to Nugno Alvares Pereira de Mello, Duke of Cadaval in Portugal.

company. I know that she must leave us. All that passes now is mere ceremony and preparation. We make no parties, we take no amusement; our hearts are heavy, and we talk of nothing but rains, bad roads, and dreadful stories of persons who have lost their lives in attempting to pass them.

LETTER VI.

The Rocks, Sunday, August 9, 1671.

You alone, my dear count, could have prevailed on me to give my daughter to a Provençal; this is truth, as Caderousse and Merrinville will witness for me; for if I had liked the latter as well as you, I should not have found so many expedients to prevent a conclusion, and she had been his. Do not entertain the least doubt of my having the highest opinion of you; a moment's reflection will convince you I am sincere. I am not at all surprised that my daughter does not mention me to you; she served me just the same by you last year; believe, therefore, whether she tells you so or not, that I never forget you. I think I hear her scold, and say, "Ah! this is a pretense of yours to excuse your own laziness." I shall leave you to dispute this among yourselves, and assure you that, though you are perhaps the most happily formed for general love and esteem of any man in the world, yet you never were, and never will be, more sincerely loved by any one than by me. I wish for you every day in my mall; but you are proud; I see that you expect me to visit you first; you may think yourself very happy that I am not an old woman, but am resolved to enjoy the remains of life and health in taking that journey: our abbé seems to have as strong an inclination to go there as myself; that is one good thing. Adieu, my dear Grignan, love me always; treat me with a sight of you, and you shall see my woods.

LETTER VII.

Paris, June 20, 1673.

Come hither, my son-in-law. So, then, you are resolved to send my daughter back to me in the first coach; you are displeased with her, and quite angry that she admires your castle, and think that she takes too great a liberty in pretending to reside there and command in every thing. As you say you hate every thing that is worthy of hatred, you certainly must hate her. I enter into all your displeasure; you could not have addressed yourself to one who feels the force of it better than myself. But do you know, after what you have said, that you make me tremble to hear you talk of wishing me at Grignan, and I am quite inconsolable for that reason; for there is nothing in futurity so dear to me as the hope of seeing you there; and whatever I may say, I am persuaded that you will be very glad of it too, and that you love me; it is impossible it should be otherwise; I love you so well, that the same sentiments must necessarily pass from me to you, and from you to me. I commend the care of my daughter's health to you above all earthly things; watch over it, be absolute master in all that regards it; do not behave as you did at the bridge of Avignon; keep your authority in this one point, and in every thing else leave her to her own way; she is more skillful than you. Ah, how I pity you for having lost the pleasure of receiving her letters! You were much happier a year ago; would to God you had that pleasure now, and I had the mortification of seeing and embracing her! Adieu, my dearest count, though I believe you are as much beloved as any man in the world, yet I do not think that any of your mothers-in-law* ever loved you so well as I do.

* Madame de Sévigné was the third.

LETTER VIII.

The Rocks, July, 1674.

You flatter me too much, my dear count; I shall accept of but one part of your fine speeches, and that is the thanks you return me for having given you a wife, that constitutes all your happiness; for, indeed, I think I contributed a little toward it: but the authority you have acquired over her in Provence, has been wholly owing to yourself, to your merit, your birth, and your conduct; all this I have nothing to do with. Ah! how much you lose by my heart not being at ease! Le Camus is delighted with me; he tells me I sing his airs extremely well: he certainly composes divinely; but I am so dull and woebegone, that I can learn nothing. You would sing them like an angel; I assure you Le Camus has a high opinion both of your voice and judgment. I regret the loss of these little accomplishments which we are too apt to neglect. Why should we lose them? I have always said that we ought not to part with them, and that they can never be an incumbrance; but what is to be done with a rope round the neck? You have given my daughter one of the most delightful journeys in the world; she is quite enchanted with it; but then you have dragged her over hills and dales, and exposed her to the dangers of the Alps, and to the uncivil waves of the Mediterranean; in short, I have a month's mind to chide you for it; but let me first embrace you most affectionately.

LETTER IX.

The Rocks, November 6, 1675.

Count, I am delighted to hear that my daughter is satisfied with you. Allow me to thank you by reason of the great interest I take in your affairs, and which I entreat you to preserve. You can not fail of this without ingratitude, and without doing injustice to the blood of the Adhémars. I have read, in the Crusades, of one of these who was an illustrious personage six hundred years ago. He was beloved as you are, and would never have given a moment's uneasiness to such a wife as yours. His death was lamented by an army of three hundred thousand men, and mourned by all the princes in Christendom. Not many pages after I find a castellane, not altogether so ancient; he is, indeed, a mere modern; it was but five hundred and twenty years since he made a great figure. I conjure you, therefore, by these two noble ancestors, who are my particular friends, to be guided by Madame de Grignan, and consider how much you will consult your own interest in doing so.

LETTERS TO THE PRESIDENT DE MOULCEAU.*

FROM 1681 TO 1682.

LETTER I.

PARIS, Friday, January 8, 1681.

I SHOULD be very sorry, sir, if our correspondence were to end with the temple of Montpellier; and all you say to this effect, in doing the honors of your letters, by supposing the assurance of their continuance to contain a threat to me, is so ungenerous that I should be disposed to scold you; nor would the pretty turn you have given to this guarantee you from my reproaches, were it not that the letter you have written to my son makes me eager to tell you how much it has delighted me. The neatness of the beginning has reminded me of our merry stories, and the beauty of the verses has made me regret that you have not continued them in good earnest. If you have done so, let us share the pleasure of reading them. The two Latin verses you explain are very just. In short, we esteem your verse, your prose, and all your productions. My son is still your adorer; my daughter

---

* M. de Moulceau was Président of the Chamber of Accounts of Montpellier. It appears that Madame de Sévigné, at the time of her journey into Provence, had found him on terms of strict friendship with M. and Madame de Grignan, and M. de Vardes and Corbinelli, and that she was so sensible of his worth and the charms of his mind as to enter into a correspondence with him. But we remark with astonishment that no mention is made of this interesting man in any of the preceding letters.

admires and esteems you in the highest degree. I presume you know my own sentiments for you, and that you see plainly there is not a family in the world who so justly appreciates your merit. You do the same in regard to M. de Carcasonne, by praising him as you do. The poor chevalier has been here for these six weeks, laid up with the rheumatism. He receives visits from persons almost as lame as himself. Those who are left-handed show at least that their taste is right. You have returned M. de Noailles to us in a very ill state of health. He has so violent a diarrhœa that it seems as if he had eaten to his own share all that he has expended at Montpellier; in short, he has been obliged to resign the staff, the staff that was the object of his love, the staff he went so far to assume, the staff which was the reward of all his other services. It is natural to suppose that he must be very ill, when he gives it himself to M. de Luxembourg. You say much in his favor when you speak of the distinction and expansion of heart he showed you. I wish his generosity had gone so far as to have induced him to return our mortified friend's visit.* Have I not heard you say that we ought to respect the unfortunate? It can not be doubted that this has increased the mortification. I pity him for having suffered this feeling to take possession of

---

* Anne Jules, Duke de Noailles, had been nominated to the command in Languedoc, of which the Duke du Maine, then too young to take it upon himself, had just been appointed governor. Preparations were making for the destruction of Calvinism. In conjunction with the intendant d'Aguesseau, father of the celebrated chancellor, Noailles endeavored for a long time to engage the court to employ mild measures; and even in the execution of the most rigorous he at first showed some humanity; but he afterward became one of the most violent persecutors, and his dispatches, concerted with Louvois, did not fail to excite the king to rigors of which he too late repented.

It appears that he thought he could not, with propriety, in the situation he held, return the visit of M. de Vardes, then an exile, and whom Madame de Sévigné designates by the title of the mortified friend.

him, and to have surmounted even his Christian philosophy; but I pity him still more if your heart be yet closed against him. A friend like you would be a true consolation in all his afflictions. Our *friend* (Corbinelli) is entirely occupied here with his affairs. He does wonders. He is become the best lawyer in Paris; and this qualification came to him unexpectedly along with his peruke and brandenbourg, so that we should much sooner have taken him for a captain of cavalry than a man of business. It is thus the exterior often deceives us. If M. de Vardes had not thrown him into this employment, his gratitude and inclination would lead him straight to you. His heart is still perfect in all the moral virtues. They will become Christian virtues when it shall please Providence, whom we still adore, and who seems to treat you well, by the sentiments it inspires you with. Adieu, my dear sir. We should have many things to say to each other if we met. Who knows that some day or other we may not? Our friend writes to you separately; so much the worse for him: he will not know that I have the pleasure of assuring you here of my sincere and faithful friendship.

LETTER II.

PARIS, April 17, 1682.

If you are alarmed at the appearance of my neglect, be assured, sir, it is a false alarm, and that appearances are deceitful; you do not suffer yourself to be forgotten; Rochecourbières, Livri, and the days in which we have seen you, are faithful guarantees of what I say; and I am certain you believe it, and that, being so well informed on every other subject, Christian humility does not prevent you from knowing your own worth. It is a truth, therefore; you can not be forgotten. Our *friend* and I have said a thousand times, "Let us write to this poor *reprobate;* but by continually delaying it, we have embarrassed ourselves by our miserable security. It seems to me as if Montpellier has given a great deal to the jubilee. You know what a horror Corbinelli has of this sort of parade, which he calls hypocrisy. I do not know exactly how he has acted upon the occasion, and I have not dared question him; but, considering the extreme respect he has for this holy mystery, and how rigorously he enters into the preparations for it, of which he will not abate a single iota, I have long been tempted to say to him, *basta la meta* (the half is sufficient); for, in fact, if all the faithful were to follow his ideas upon the subject, the ceremonials of religion would be done away. This is the inspiration of God, and whether it be light or dereliction, some great change must happen to alter his opinion. M. de Vardes has put the same question to him, that you put to me on his jubilee; he has answered very honestly, and has given him a *probet autem semetipsum homo*, which may occasion great reflections. This is all I can tell you; you know and love the soil, for, indeed, the more his heart is known, the more it must be admired. I perceive his departure approach, and I perceive it with sorrow; but what may not Providence reserve for M. de Vardes? M. de Bussy is recalled after an exile of eighteen years; he has seen the king, who received him most graciously: these are times of justice and clemency; we not only do what is well, but what is perfectly well; I doubt not, therefore, that this poor exile's turn will come, and every one else believes it so firmly that if any thing can do him injury, it is this general report. You tell me the most agreeable truth I can hear, in assuring me the young people will bring from Languedoc all the politeness which failed them here.* They appear to me like the Germans who are sent to Angers to learn the language; they were Germans in manners, and if they had not learned them out of court, would seem to conduct themselves ridiculously. It is easy to comprehend that, having had so good a master as M. de Vardes for six months, they must have profited more than they had done during their whole life.

* This refers to the daughter and son-in-law of M. de Vardes (M. and Madame de Rohan), who had spent six months with him at Montpellier.

LETTER III.

PARIS, May 26, 1682.

Were you not very much surprised, sir, to see M. de Vardes slip through your fingers, whom you had held so firmly for nineteen years? This is the time Providence had marked out for him; in reality, he was no longer thought of, he appeared forgotten, and sacrificed to example. The king, who reflects and arranges every thing in his head, declared one morning that M. de Vardes would be at court in two or three days; he said he had written to him by the post, that he wished to surprise him, and that for more than six months no one had mentioned his name to him. His majesty was gratified; he wished to create surprise, and every one was surprised; never did intelligence make so great an impression, nor so great a noise, as this. In short, he arrived on Saturday morning, with a head singular in its kind, and an old justaucorps à brevet,* such as was worn in the year 1663. He set one knee to the ground in the king's chamber, M. de Chateauneuf being the only person present. The king told him that while his heart had been wounded he had not recalled him, but that he now recalled him with a whole heart, and that he was glad to see him. M. de Vardes made an admirable reply, with an air of being deeply affected, and the gift of tears, which God has given him, produced no ill effect upon this occasion. After this first interview, the king caused the dauphin to be called, and presented him to him as a young courtier. M. de Vardes recognized, and saluted him; the king said to him, laughing: "Vardes, this is a blunder; you know that no one is saluted in my presence." M. de Vardes replied in the same tone: "Sire, I have forgotten every thing; your majesty must par-

---

* This was a blue great-coat, embroidered with gold and silver, which distinguished the principal courtiers: an especial permission was necessary to wear it. The fashion had passed when Vardes returned to court.

don even thirty blunders." "Well, I will," said the king; "stop at the twenty-ninth." The king afterward laughed at his coat. M. de Vardes said, "Sire, when a man is so wretched as to be banished from your presence, he is not only unfortunate, but he becomes ridiculous." All this was said in a tone of perfect freedom and playfulness. The courtiers performed wonders. He came one day to Paris, and called upon me; I was just gone out to call upon him, but he found my son and daughter at home, and in the evening I found him at his own house: it was a joyful meeting; I mentioned our friend to him. "What, madam! my master! my intimate friend! the man in the world to whom I owe the greatest obligations! can you doubt that I love him with my whole heart?" This pleased me highly. He resides with his daughter at Versailles. The court goes to-day; I suppose he will return, to catch the king again at Auxerre, for it appears to all his friends that he ought to take this journey, in which he will certainly pay his court well, by bestowing the most natural praises on three little things—the troops, the fortifications, and his majesty's conquests. Perhaps our *friend* will tell you all this, and my letter will be only a miserable echo; but, at any rate, I have entered into the minutiæ, because I should like, on such an occasion, to be written to in the same style, and I judge you, my dear sir, by myself; I have often been deceived by others, but never by you. It is said that your worthy and generous friend, M. de Noailles, has rendered very important services to M. de Vardes; he is so generous that it is impossible to doubt this. M. de Calvisson is arrived; this must either break off, or conclude our marriage. In reality, I am weary of this tedious affair, I am not in a humor to talk of any thing but M. de Vardes. M. de Vardes forever; he is the Gospel of the day.

LETTER IV.

PARIS, July 28, 1682

You are going to hear a beautiful and an admirable story; pay great attention to every circumstance attending it. The Prince de Conti having expressed himself dissatisfied with the Chevalier de Lorraine, because he had said the Prince de la Roche-sur-Yon was in love with his wife, found an opportunity of telling him, two days ago, in the gardens of Versailles, that he would do him the honor of fighting him, because he had offended him by his conversation, etc. The Chevalier de Lorraine thanked him for the honor he intended him, and wished to justify himself in what he had said; after which the prince told him that he might have M. de Marsan for his second, who, hearing himself named, stepped forward and accepted the office without hesitation, desiring the Prince de Conti to allow M. de Soissons to be the other second, as he had long been an enemy to their family. The proposal was yielded to, the party was formed, the place appointed, the hour chosen, and secrecy enjoined. Can not you fancy yourself in the times of the late M. de Boutteville? Each went his way; but the Chevalier de Lorraine went straight to Monsieur, to whom he related the whole story, and Monsieur the next moment confided it to the king. You may guess what he said to his son-in-law. He talked to him for more than two hours with more of gayety than anger, but in a tone of authority, which must have caused great repentance. Here the affair ended. The public thinks the Chevalier de Lorraine ought to have refused upon the spot, instead of consenting and then betraying every thing; but people of the trade think that a refusal would have excited some angry words from the prince, and perhaps some menace not very easy of digestion; and then to have such a stigma cast upon him, and from a man who is so much to be dreaded! In this way his conduct has been approved, and the more so because his courage is unquestionable. What say you to this affair? How does it appear to you to be handled? Alas! if that sainted princess were to descend from heaven, and to find her dear son troubled with such impetuosity, do you not think she would retrace her steps from grief and affliction? You will talk this over with M. de Vardes. Would to God that the birth of a Duke of Burgundy, which is hourly expected, could restore him to us!

LETTER V.

June 13, 1684.

Word was sent me from Languedoc that I had a law-suit pending there, that M. de Grignan was prosecuted with rigor, and that the judges were strange people. I cursed them heartily, sir, and have since found that you are one of the principals: it is *you*, therefore, I have loaded with so many imprecations, you, whose protection I have claimed to soften the rigor and to attend to the justice of my cause. It is to M. d'Argouges I am indebted for the information, that this odious judge and this highly-esteemed M. de Moulceau, are one and the same. All the anger kindled against the first, has disappeared at the name of the second, and the weapons have fallen from my hand, like those of Arcabonne, when she recognized Amadis. It is to M. de Moulceau that I address this quotation from the opera; you will suppose, that, in virtue of your title of judge, I shall quote nothing but laws to you. There is one established law in the world, particularly among honest men, which is, never to condemn unheard: in this, sir, consists the favor I have to ask you. The Prince de Conti claims an estate of which we have been in possession for three hundred years. I know, from M. de Corbinelli, that three hundred years is a strong title; we request you, sir, to give us time to collect our proofs, to convince you of the weakness of the Prince de Conti's claim and of the solidity of ours.

LETTER VI.

Paris, November, 24, 1685.

I have received no letter from you for more than fifteen months; I know not whether our enraged and jealous friend* has intercepted any; it is not, however, like him to do so; he would be more inclined to assassinate you with the little sword you once used so pleasantly in the garden of Rambouillet. We shall never forget your wisdom, nor your folly; and I have spent a year with my son in Brittany, where we have often mentioned you with sentiments with which your merit must impress all hearts that are not unworthy of knowing it. We have been twenty times on the point of writing some nonsense to you; we wished to assure you that the *scarcity of the gratification* did not prevent you from being often in our remembrance, and twenty times has the demon which turns aside good intentions perverted the course of this. At length, sir, after having been overturned, drowned, and had a wound in my leg, which has not been healed till within these six weeks, I left my son, and his wife, who is very pretty, and arrived at Baville, at M. de Lamoignon's, on the tenth or twelfth of September, where I found my daughter and all the Grignans, who received me with joy and affection. To complete my happiness, my daughter will not leave me this winter. I have found our dear Corbinelli just as I left him, except a little more philosophical, and dying every day from some cause or other: his freedom excites my envy; in changing his object he would become a saint; he is, however, so kind and charitable to his neighbor, that I really believe the grace of God is concealed under the name of Cartesian. He converts more heritics by his good sense, and by not irritating them by vain disputes, than others by all their controversy. In short, every one now is a missionary, every one thinks he has a mission, and particularly the magistrates and governors of provinces, upheld by the dragoons: this is the greatest and most noble

---

* A jest which refers to Corbinelli.

action that has ever been conceived or performed. Like us, you have been surprised with other news. What an event is the death of the Prince de Conti! after having experienced all the perils of the Hungarian war, he came here to die of a disorder which he scarcely felt! His lovely widow has deeply bewailed him: she has an annuity of a hundred thousand crowns, and has received from the king so many marks of friendship, and of his natural affection for her, that with such assistance no one can doubt that she will in time be comforted.

LETTER VII.

LIVRI, October 25, 1686.

I have received your letter, sir; it presented itself to me as if you wished to make me ashamed of my silence, and to believe I had been ill, for the purpose of entering into conversation with me. It reminds me of a very pretty comedy, in which the person who wishes to come to an explanation with the lady who enters, makes her believe she called him, and thus obtains a hearing. If you have the same intention, sir, I return you a thousand thanks; and I really can not comprehend how, esteeming you as I do, remembering you with so much pleasure, speaking of you so readily, having so high a relish for your understanding and your worth, *to say no more for fear of exciting jealousy*, I can, with so many things to promote a correspondence, have left you seven or eight months without saying a word to you. It is horrible; but what does it signify? let us remain in this freedom, since it is not compatible with the sentiments I have just expressed for you. I have seen M. de la Trousse; we talked of you the moment we had embraced; I think him, by what he told me, highly deserving the esteem you appear to entertain for him. The stroke is at least double. I found him perfectly acquainted with, and as sensible of your worth as you can possibly desire. He must pass through this place on his way to La

Trousse; I shall show him your letter, and I do not think it will induce him to change his opinion. You have now M. de Noailles with you: you are in such favor there that I shall rejoice with you on the pleasure you will receive at seeing a man whom you have inspired with such lively sentiments of esteem for you. I can easily imagine the confusion which the derangement of the states must have occasioned you; but you can not dispense with going to Nîmes. I must say a word to you respecting Mademoiselle de Grignan. You know, I presume, that she has been in the convent of the Carmelites for eight months, and that she took the habit in form, with a zeal too violent to last. In the first three months she found herself so reduced, from the severity of the order, and her stomach so injured by the meagerness of the provision, that she was obliged to eat meat by compulsion. This inability to comply with the rules, even in her noviciate, induced her to quit the convent; but with so true a sentiment of piety, of humiliation at the delicacy of her health, and of such perfect contempt for the world, that the holy nuns have preserved an affectionate friendship for her; and she, who has only changed the habit, and not the sentiment, has no false shame, like those who grow weary of the life, and is now with us as usual, giving us the same edification. Her residence at Paris is fixed at the Feuillantines, where she will board with several others; she will return there at Martinmas, when we do. What attaches her to this house is its vicinity to the Carmelites, where she goes almost daily, and whenever a certain princess is there. She takes from this holy convent all that agrees with her, that is, its devotion and conversation, and leaves the strictness of the order, to which she was by no means equal.

It is thus God has conducted her and gently repulsed her from the high degree of perfection to which she aspired, to support her in another a little inferior to it, which can not but be good, since He gives her grace to love him alone, which is all that can be desired in this world. But Providence has also inspired her with the most noble, just, and praiseworthy thought it was possible to conceive for her family. She was determined that her return to the world should not deprive her father of what she wished to give him by her civil death: and at quitting her convent, she made him a very handsome present of forty thousand crowns, which he owed her; that is, twenty thousand crowns principal, and the rest arrears and sums borrowed. This gift has been duly estimated, not only by those who love M. de Grignan, but by those who knew that all her property becoming personal at the age of five-and-twenty, if she had not disposed of any thing by will, would go almost wholly to her father; and that M. de Grignan would have eighty thousand crowns to pay Mademoiselle d'Alerac, reckoning the principal of the jointure at forty thousand. This is enough in conscience for us not to pity the sister, and to rejoice that the family is relieved from this double payment. I own I have been very much affected at this seasonable and generous action; and I admire the goodness of her disposition, which led her to do, without affectation, the only thing in the world that could render her dear to her family, where she is now received and considered as its benefactress. The understanding alone might have wrought this effect in another, but it is best when produced only by the heart. My daughter has contributed so well to this little maneuvre, that she has received double pleasure from its success. The chevalier has also done wonders; for you may suppose it has been necessary to assist, and give a form to these good intentions. In short, all has gone well: even Mademoiselle d'Alerac has entered into the justice of the sentiment. I pray that God may reward her by a good establishment, of which she still conceals from us every prospect, so that at present there is no appearance of any thing of the kind. Do I not weary you, sir, by this long account? you will have an indigestion of the Grignans. To divert you, let us talk a little of poor Sévigné: I should mention him with grief if I could not tell you that after five months of horrible suffering from medicines which worked him to the very bone, the poor child is at length restored to perfect health. He has spent the whole of August with me in this retreat, which you are now acquainted with. We were alone with the good abbé, we had everlasting conversations, and this long intercourse has renewed our acquaintance with each other, and our acquaintance renewed our friendship. He is returned home with a stock of Christian philosophy, sprinkled with a grain of anchoretism, and particularly with an extreme affection for his wife, by whom he is equally beloved, which makes him altogether the happiest man in the world, because he passes his life agreeably to his own mind. We have talked of you twenty times with friendship and delight, and twenty times have we said, " Let us write to him, I wish it very much ;" and when we have been on the point of giving ourselves this pleasure, a demon has stepped in to distract our attention, and turn aside our good resolutions. What is to be done, my dear sir, in misfortunes like these? Perhaps you know the mortification of forming good resolutions without the power of executing them. I fear our dear jealous friend calculates upon spending the winter with you; you will be very glad: you will laugh, and I shall cry; for I have so perfect a confidence in him, and so true a friendship for him, that I can not lose the society of such a man without feeling it painfully every moment; M. de Vardes, however, whom he is delighted to follow, will restore him to us, as he takes him away from us. I am pleased that this attachment continues; you will act your part well, and I consider the pleasure of seeing you, and of establishing himself again in your heart, as a happy circumstance for our friend. M. de Vardes has not been sufficiently particular in the information you omitted to tell me: the surest way is to write ourselves, as you see. I do not write to you often, but you will own when I do that it is not for nothing.

LETTER VIII.

PARIS, November 26, 1686.

I thought, sir, that in purchasing an office, nothing was necessary but to find money; but I see that the manner of giving and receiving it is also to be considered. You will soon be quit of this embarrassment, from the desire you always have to contribute to your own tranquillity. Good heavens! how rational and how worthy of you is this disposition, and how just too is the choice of your company, when we come to speak and point out its excellence! If we judge from appearances, it is very superior to our parliaments. I can fancy I hear M. and Madame de Vernueil say a thousand kind things to you, and receive yours in return. When this princess mentions me, tell her it is impossible to be more at her service than I am. You have a sister of Madame de la Troche with you, who is very amiable; the eldest will place all the attentions you pay her to her own account. I have presented your compliments to the Chevalier de Grignan, who has received them graciously; he pointed out to the prince* the silence and discretion of your departure; nothing can exceed his concern and zeal for your interest: but we can answer for nothing when we are left-handed. What you told me the other day of a certain discourse he held with a certain person, makes me exhort you to preserve the noble tranquility I have always witnessed in you, on the success of this affair. We only returned from Livri yesterday; the beauty of the weather, and the health of my daughter, which has been nearly established there, made us stay out of gratitude. In the two months we have been there, we have not been able to prevail on our friend to give us his company for

---

* The Prince de Conti. It has been seen in the letter of June 13, 1684, that M. de Moulceau was judge in a law-suit in which M. de Grignan was engaged with this prince, and that he was moreover attached to him for other reasons.

more than ten days. He has a thousand little affairs there, to which he is accustomed: I know nothing of his intentions with respect to his departure, I almost doubt whether the society he meets at M. de Vardes' will not prevent him from setting out soon. I assure you I shall reap the advantage of his inclination to do so with pleasure, but I only contribute toward it by my wishes. Pray inform us how M. de Vardes finds himself in the midst of this troop of Bohemians; I can not get this vision out of my eyes. We shall have a thousand things to tell you of the son-in-law;* in short, it struck us the other day that if Homer had been acquainted with him, he would have chosen him in point of anger for his Achilles. We have a new prince and a new princess here.

LETTER IX.

PARIS, December 15, 1686.

I wrote you a long letter, sir, more than a month ago, full of friendship, secrets, and confidence. I know not what became of it; it lost its way, perhaps, in seeking for you at the States, since you have not answered it: but this will not prevent me from telling you a melancholy, and at the same time a pleasing, piece of intelligence: the death of the prince, which happened the day before yesterday, the 11th instant, at a quarter after seven in the evening, and the return of the Prince de Conti to court, through the kindness of the prince, who asked this favor of the king in his last moments. The king immediately granted it, and the prince had this consolation on his death-bed; but never was joy drowned in so many tears. The Prince de Conti is inconsolable at the loss he has sustained. It could not be greater, particularly as he passed the whole time of his disgrace at Chantilly, where he made an admirable use of the understanding and abilities of

* M. de Rohan, who had married the daughter of the Count de Vardes.

the prince, and drew from the fountain-head all that was to be acquired from so great a master, by whom he was tenderly beloved. The prince flew, with a speed that has cost him his life, from Chantilly to Fontainebleau, where Madame de Bourbon was seized with the small-pox, in order to prevent the duke, who had not had the disorder, from nursing her and being with her; for the duchess, who has always nursed her, would have been sufficient to satisfy him of the care that was taken of her health. He was very ill, and at length died of an oppression with which he was seized, which made him say, as he was on the point of returning to Paris, that he should take a much longer journey. He sent for his confessor, Father Deschamps, and, after lying in a state of insensibility for twenty-four hours, and receiving all the sacraments, he died, regretted and bitterly lamented by his family and his friends. The king was much afflicted at the event, and, in short, the grief of losing so great a man and so great a hero, whose place whole ages will not be able to supply, has been felt by all ranks. A singular circumstance happened three weeks ago, a little before the departure of the prince for Fontainebleau. Vernillon, one of his gentlemen, returning from the chase at three o'clock, saw, as he approached the castle, at one of the windows of the armory, an apparition: that is, a man who had been dead and buried. He dismounted, and came nearer; he still saw it. His valet, who was with him, said, "I see the same, sir, that you see." Vernillon had been silent, that his valet might speak of his own accord. They entered the castle together, and desired the keeper to give them the key of the armory. The keeper went with them; they found all the windows closed, and a silence which had been undisturbed for more than six months. This was told to the prince: he appeared struck with it at first, and afterward laughed at it. Every one heard the story and trembled for the prince. You see what the event has been.

LETTER X.

PARIS, Monday, April 29, 1687.

So you like my letters, sir. I am delighted that you do; this is one which will be worth a hundred. My robust health was slightly attacked, about a month ago, by a little colic, a little rheumatism, a little vexation; consequently, all this might excuse me from writing to you; but I had rather die than another should tell you that the Prince de Conti is at length returned to court. He is this night at Versailles, and the king, like a kind father, has restored him to favor, after having exiled him for a while, to leave him at leisure to make his own reflections. No doubt he has done so, and the court will be very gay and splendid on the occasion. His majesty will make several chevaliers at Whitsuntide, but it will be only a family promotion: M. de Chartres, the Duke de Bourbon, the Prince de Conti, and M. du Maine, but no one else: all the other candidates must be pleased to have patience; but they will not see without mortification the adjournment of their hopes. The Duke de Vieuville is governor to the Duke de Chartres. Madame de Polignac, who is not Mademoiselle d'Alerac, paid a visit yesterday to Madame de Grignan. She was brilliant, lively, elated with the grandeur of the house of Polignac, fond of talking of the name, and all the personages belonging to it. She has taken upon herself the fortune of the two brothers, and has supported, generously and courageously, the frown and disapprobation of the king. She has employed skillful artificers; and instead of deserting the deserted, like women in general, she has made it a point of honor to reinstate them at court. I could answer for it that she will revive and re-establish this family. This is what Providence had in store for them, and which prevented us from being able to read distinctly what it had written for Mademoiselle d'Alerac. Adieu, sir; love me, for indeed you ought. I love your mind, your worth, your wisdom, your folly, your virtue, your humor, your goodness: in short, all that belongs to you, and wish you, and the pretty covey under your wing, which must afford you so much pleasure and comfort, every possible happiness. All here salute you, except our *friend*, who knows nothing of this hasty letter. I shall talk of you a great deal with Bourdaloue. Madame Dangeau, formerly *Bavaria*, is very prudent, very amiable, and makes her husband very happy; she might have made him very ridiculous.

LETTER XI.

Wednesday, March 2, 1689.

What things, sir, may not be said! what a period in the history of our monarch is the manner in which he has received the king of England! the presents with which he has loaded him in setting out from hence for Ireland; vessels at Brest, where he now is, frigates, troops, officers; the Count d'Avaux as embassador extraordinary and adviser, and who is also to have the care of the troops and money; two millions on his departure, and as much afterward as he wants! Beside these great things he has given him his arms, his helmet, his cuirass, which can not fail of bringing good fortune to him. He has given him arms sufficient for ten or twelve thousand men. And as to little conveniences they are innumerable: post-chaises admirably made, calashes, carriage and saddle-horses, services of gold and silver, toilets, linen, camp-beds, magnificent swords of state, swords for service, pistols; in short, every thing of every kind that can be thought of; and in embracing him as he bid him adieu, he said to him, "You can not say that I am not affected at your departure: I own to you, however, that I wish never to see you again; but if, unfortunately, you should return, be assured you will find me as you leave me." Nothing could be better said, nothing more just: generosity, magnificence, magnanimity were never exercised as they have been by his majesty on this occasion.

We hope that the Irish war will be a powerful diversion, and prevent the Prince of Orange from tormenting us by descents upon our coast; and thus our three hundred thousand soldiers, our armies so well stationed every where, will only serve to make the king feared, without any one daring to attack him.

This is a time of political discussion: I should very much like to hear you talk over these great events. I inclose the opinion of a respectable upholsterer on the questions, respecting furniture, of Madame de Moulceau: but whatever he may say of a gold fringe and double taffeties for curtains, and though there are many such here, nothing is so pretty, so suitable, or so cool for the summer, as curtains made of these beautiful taffeties single, and tapestry the same. I have seen them at several houses, and admire them exceedingly: every thing must be looped up, and plaited, as he has directed: for the other kind of furniture, you must have damask or brocade.

LETTER XII.

Grignan, Friday, November 10, 1690.

Where do you think I am, sir? Did you not know I was in Brittany? Our Corbinelli must have told you so. After having been there sixteen months with my son, I thought it would be very pleasant to spend the winter here with my daughter. This plan of a journey of a hundred and fifty leagues at first appeared a castle in the air; but affection rendered it so easy, that in fact I executed it between the 3d and 24th of October, on which day I arrived at Robinet's gate, where I was received by Madame de Grignan with open arms, and with so much joy, affection, and gratitude, that I thought I had not come soon enough, nor from a sufficiently great distance. After this, sir, tell me that friendship is not a fine thing! it makes me often think of you, and wish to see you here once more during my life. We shall be here the whole of this winter, and the next summer; if you do not find a moment to come and see us, I shall think you have forgotten me. You will not know this house again, it is so much improved; but you will find its owners still abounding with esteem for you; and me, sir, possessing a regard for you, capable of driving our *friend* to madness, and worthy of your paying us this visit.

LETTER XIII.

GRIGNAN, June 5, 1695.

I intend, sir, to bring an action against you, and thus I set about it. I wish you to judge it yourself. I have been here for more than a year with my daughter, for whom I have as much love as ever. Since that time you have no doubt heard of the marriage of the Marquis de Grignan to Mademoiselle de Saint-Amand. You have seen her often enough at Montpellier to be acquainted with her person; you have also heard mention of the vast wealth of her father. You are not ignorant that this marriage was solemnized with great pomp in the château which you know. I suppose you can not have forgotten the time when the true esteem we have always preserved for you began. On this subject I measure your sentiments by my own, and I judge that, we not having forgotten you, you can not have forgotten us.

I even include M. de Grignan, whose date is still more ancient than ours. I collect all these things, and I find myself injured on every side; I complain of it here, I complain of it to our friends, I complain of it to our dear Corbinelli, the jealous confidant and witness of all the esteem and friendship we bear you; and at length, sir, I complain of it to yourself. Whence proceeds this silence? is it from forgetfulness? from perfect indifference? I know not which to say: what would you have me think? What does your conduct resemble? Give a name to it, sir; the cause is now ready for your sentence. Pass it: I consent that you should be both party and judge.

LETTER XIV.

GRIGNAN, Saturday, February 4, 1696.

I was right, sir, when I supposed you would be concerned at my anxiety, and would use all the diligence in your power to relieve it. M. Barbeirac's prescription and your letter had wings, as you wished; and it seems that this little fever, which appeared so low, had wings too, for it vanished at the bare mention of M. Barbeirac's name. Seriously, sir, there is something miraculous in this sudden change; and I can not doubt that your wishes and your prayers contributed to produce it. Judge of my gratitude by their effect. My daughter goes halves with me in all I say here; she returns you a thousand thanks, and entreats you to give a great many to M. Barbeirac. We are happy in having no longer any thing to do, but to take patience and rhubarb, which she finds agree well with her. We doubt not that in this quiet state, rhubarb is a medicine which M. Barbeirac must approve, with a regimen, which is sometimes better than all. Thank God, sir, both for yourself and for us; for we are certain that you are interested in this acknowledgment; and then, sir, cast your eyes upon all the inhabitants of this château, and judge of their sentiments for you.

LETTERS TO M. DE COULANGES.*

FROM 1676 TO 1696.

LETTER I.

PARIS, Monday, Dec. 15, 1670.

I am going to tell you a thing the most astonishing, the most surprising, the most marvelous, the most miraculous, the most magnificent, the most confounding, the most unheard of, the most singular, the most extraordinary, the most incredible, the most unforeseen, the greatest, the least, the rarest, the most common, the most public, the most private till to-day, the most brilliant, the most enviable; in short, a thing of which there is but one example in past ages, and that not an exact one either; a thing that we can not believe at Paris; how then will it gain credit at Lyons? a thing which makes everybody cry, "Lord have mercy upon us!" a thing which causes the greatest joy to Madame de Rohan and Madame de Hauterive; a thing, in fine, which is to happen on Sunday next, when those who are present will doubt the evidence of their senses; a thing which, though it is to be done on Sunday, yet perhaps will not be finished on Monday. I can not bring myself to tell it you; guess what it is. I give you three times to do it in. What, not a word to throw at a dog? Well then,

---

* Philip Emanuel de Coulanges, master of the requests, so well known in the gay world for his wit, humor, and the singular talent he had for a jovial song. He was cousin-german to Madame de Sévigné.

I find I must tell you. Monsieur de Lauzun* is to be married next Sunday at the Louvre, to ——— pray guess to whom! I give you four times to do it in, I give you six, I give you a hundred. Says Madame de Coulanges, "It is really very hard to guess; perhaps it is Madame de la Vallière." Indeed, madam, it is not. "It is Mademoiselle de Retz, then." No, nor she neither; you are extremely provincial. "Lord bless me," say you, "what stupid wretches we are! it is Mademoiselle de Colbert all the while." Nay, now you are still further from the mark. "Why then it must certainly be Mademoiselle de Crequy." You have it not yet. Well, I find I must tell you at last. He is to be married next Sunday, at the Louvre, with the king's leave, to Mademoiselle, Mademoiselle de ——— Mademoiselle—guess, pray guess her name; he is to be married to Mademoiselle, the great Mademoiselle; Mademoiselle, daughter to the late Monsieur;† Mademoiselle, grand-daughter of Henry the IVth; Mademoiselle d'Eu, Mademoiselle de Dombes, Mademoiselle de Montpensier, Mademoiselle d'Orleans, Mademoiselle, the king's cousin-german, Mademoiselle, destined to the throne, Mademoiselle, the only match in France that was worthy of Monsieur. What glorious matter for talk! If you should burst forth like a bedlamite, say we have told you a lie, that it is false, that we are making a jest of you, and that a pretty jest it is, without wit or invention; in short, if you abuse us, we shall think you quite in the right; for we have done just the same things ourselves. Farewell, you will find by the letters you receive this post, whether we tell you truth or not.

LETTER II.

PARIS, Friday, Dec. 19, 1670.

What is called "falling from the clouds," happened last night at the Tuilleries; but I must go further back. You have al-

---

* Antonius Nompar de Caumont, Marquis de Puiguilhem, afterward Duke de Lauzun.

† Gaston of France, Duke of Orleans, brother to Louis XIII.

ready shared in the joy, the transport, the ecstacies of the princess and her happy lover. It was just as I told you, the affair was made public on Monday. Tuesday was passed in talking, astonishment, and compliments. Wednesday, mademoiselle made a deed of gift to Monsieur de Lauzun, investing him with certain titles, names, and dignities, necessary to be inserted in the marriage-contract, which was drawn up that day. She gave him then, till she could give him something better, four duchies; the first was that of Count d'Eu, which entitles him to rank as first peer of France; the Dukedom of Montpensier, which title he bore all that day; the Dukedom de Saint Fargeau; and the Dukedom de Châtellerault, the whole valued at twenty-two millions of livres. The contract was then drawn up, and he took the name of Montpensier. Thursday morning, which was yesterday, mademoiselle was in expectation of the king's signing the contract, as he had said that he would do; but, about seven o'clock in the evening, the queen, monsieur, and several old dotards that were about him, had so persuaded his majesty that his reputation would suffer in this affair, that, sending for mademoiselle and Monsieur de Lauzun, he announced to them, before the prince, that he forbade them to think any further of this marriage. Monsieur de Lauzun received the prohibition with all the respect, submission, firmness, and, at the same time, despair, that could be expected in so great a reverse of fortune. As for mademoiselle, she gave a loose to her feelings, and burst into tears, cries, lamentations, and the most violent expressions of grief; she keeps her bed all day long, and takes nothing within her lips but a little broth. What a fine dream is here! what a glorious subject for a tragedy or romance, but especially talking and reasoning eternally! This is what we do day and night, morning and evening, without end, and without intermission; we hope you do the same, *E fra tanto vi bacio le mani:* "and with this I kiss your hand."

LETTER III.

PARIS, Wednesday, Dec. 24, 1670.

You are now perfectly acquainted with the romantic story of mademoiselle and of Monsieur de Lauzun. It is a story well adapted for a tragedy, and in all the rules of the theater; we laid out the acts and scenes the other day. We took four days instead of four and twenty hours, and the piece was complete. Never was such a change seen in so short a time; never was there known so general an emotion. You certainly never received so extraordinary a piece of intelligence before. M. de Lauzun behaved admirably; he supported his misfortune with such courage and intrepidity, and at the same time showed so deep a sorrow, mixed with such profound respect, that he has gained the admiration of every body. His loss is doubtless great, but then the king's favor, which he has by this means preserved, is likewise great; so that, upon the whole, his condition does not seem so very deplorable. Mademoiselle, too, has behaved extremely well on her side. She has wept much and bitterly; but yesterday, for the first time, she returned to pay her duty at the Louvre, after having received the visits of every one there; so the affair is all over. Adieu.

LETTER IV.

PARIS, Wednesday, Dec. 31, 1670.

I have received your answers to my letters. I can easily conceive the astonishment you were in at what passed between the 15th and 20th of this month; the subject called for it all. I admire likewise your penetration and judgment, in imagining so great a machine could never support itself from Monday to Sunday. Modesty prevents my launching out in your praise on this head, because I said and thought exactly as you did. I told my daughter on Monday, "This will never go on as it should do till Sunday; I will wager, notwithstanding this wedding seems to be sure, that it will never come to a conclusion." In effect the sky was overcast on Thursday morning, and about ten o'clock, as I told you, the cloud burst. That very day I went about nine in the morning to pay my respects to mademoiselle, having been informed that she was to go out of town to be married, and that the coadjutor of Rheims* was to perform the ceremony. These were the resolves on Wednesday night, but matters had been determined otherwise at the Louvre ever since Tuesday. Mademoiselle was writing; she made me place myself on my knees at her bed-side; she told me to whom she was writing, and upon what subject, and also of the fine presents she had made the night before, and the titles she had conferred; and as there was no match in any of the courts of Europe for her, she was resolved, she said, to provide for herself. She related to me, word for word, a conversation she had had with the king, and appeared overcome with joy, to think how happy she should make a man of merit. She mentioned, with a great deal of tenderness, the worth and gratitude of M. de Lauzun. To all which I made her this answer: "Upon my word, mademoiselle, your highness seems quite happy! but why was not this affair finished at once last Monday? Do not you perceive that the delay will give time and opportunity to the whole kingdom to talk, and that it is absolutely tempting God, and the king, to protract an affair of so extraordinary a nature as this is to so distant a period?" She allowed me to be in the right, but was so sure of success, that what I said made little or no impression on her at the time. She repeated the many amiable qualities of Monsieur de Lauzun, and the noble house he was descended from. To which I replied in these lines of Corneille's Polyeuctus:

> Du moins on ne la peut blâmer d'un mauvais choix,
> Polyeucte a du nom, et sort du sang des rois.

> Her choice of him no one can surely blame,
> Who springs from kings, and boasts a noble name.

---

* Charles Maurice le Tellier.

Upon which she embraced me tenderly. Our conversation lasted above an hour. It is impossible to repeat all that passed between us, but I may without vanity say that my company was agreeable to her, for her heart was so full that she was glad of any one to unburden it to. At ten o'clock she devoted her time to the nobility, who crowded to pay their compliments to her. She waited all the morning for news from court, but none came. All the afternoon she amused herself with putting M. de Montpensier's apartment in order, which she did with her own hands. You know what happened at night. The next morning, which was Friday, I waited upon her, and found her in bed; her grief redoubled at seeing me; she called me to her, embraced me, and whelmed me with tears.

"Ah!" said she, "you remember what you said to me yesterday? What foresight! what cruel foresight!" In short, she made me weep to see her weep so violently. I have seen her twice since; she still continues in great affliction, but behaves to me as to a person that sympathizes with her in her distress; in which she is not mistaken, for I really feel sentiments for her that are seldom felt for persons of such superior rank. This, however, between us two and Madame de Coulanges; for you are sensible that this chit-chat would appear ridiculous to others.

LETTER V.

THE ROCKS, January 8, 1690.

What a melancholy date, my amiable cousin, compared with yours! It suits a recluse like me, and that of Rome suits one whose fate is to wander uncontrolled, and ".who stalks his idleness from one end of the world to the other." What a happy life! and how mildly has Fortune treated you, as you say, notwithstanding her quarrel with you! Always beloved, always esteemed, always carrying joy and pleasure along with you, always the favorite of, and fascinated with, some friend of consequence—a duke, a prince, or a pope (for I will add the holy father by way of novelty); always in good health, never at the charge of any one, no business, no ambition; but, above all, the advantage of not growing old! This is the height of felicity. You doubt, sometimes, whether you are not advancing, by certain calculations of time and years; but old age is still at a distance. You do not approach it with horror, as some persons I could name. This is reserved for your neighbor, and you have not even the fears that are usually felt at seeing a fire in your neighborhood. In short, after mature reflection, I pronounce you the happiest man in the world. This last journey to Rome is, in my opinion, the most delightful adventure that could have happened to you, with an adorable embassador (the Duke de Chaulnes), on a noble and grand occasion, and a visit to the beautiful mistress of the world, whom, having once seen, we are always longing to see again. I very much like the verses you have made on her. She can not be too highly celebrated. I am sure my daughter will approve them. They are well written and poetical; we sing them. I am delighted with what you tell me of Paulina, whom you saw at Grignan in your way. I have judged most favorably of her from your praises, and the unaffected letter you wrote to Madame de Chaulnes, which she has sent to me. Oh, how much I should like to take a journey to Rome, as you propose! but then it must be with the face and air I had many years ago, and not with those I now have. A woman, particularly, should not move her old bones except to be embassadress. I believe that Madame de Coulanges, though still young, is of the same opinion; but in my youth I should have been in raptures with such an adventure. It is not the same with you. Every thing becomes you. Enjoy, then, your privilege, and the jealousy you excite to know who shall be favored with you. I will not waste my time in arguing with you on the present state of affairs. All the duke's prosperities have given me real joy. You fear precisely what all his friends apprehend, that, being the only one who can fill the place he holds with equal success and reputation, 'he will be kept in it too long. This apartment in your new palace creates new alarms; but let us do better. Let us not anticipate evils; rather let us hope that every thing will happen as we wish, and that we shall all meet again at Paris. I was delighted with your remembrance, your letter, and your songs. Write to me whenever it is agreeable and convenient. I take the liberty of sending this by the embassadress; and I do more, my dear cousin, for under her protection I take the liberty of embracing my dear governor of Brittany, and his excellency the embassador, with real affection, and without offense to respect. These high dignities do not intimidate me. I am sure he still loves me. God bless him and bring him back again. These are my wishes for the new year. Adieu, my dear cousin; I embrace you. Continue to love me. I wish it—it is my whim, and to love you more than you love me. But you are very amiable, and I must not place myself on a par with you.

LETTER VI.

GRIGNAN, April 10, 1691.

We have received a letter dated the 31st of March from our dear embassador. It came in less than a week. This expedition is delightful, but what he tells us is still more so. It is impossible to write in better spirits. My daughter takes upon herself to answer him, and as I desire her to send the Holy Ghost with all diligence, not only to create a pope,* but to put a speedy termination to business, that he may be able to pay us a visit. She assures me that she will send him

---

* Alexander VIII. had been dead for two months and a few days. Before he died, he distributed among his nephews all the money he possessed, which made Pasquin say that it would have been better for the church to have been his niece than his daughter.

word of the conquest of Nice in five days after opening the trenches by M. de Catinet, and that this intelligence will produce the same effect for our bulls. Tell us, my dear cousin, if we judge rightly. We have received M. de Nevers' epistle to the little Le Clerc of the academy. It is accompanied by one of your letters; they always give us great pleasure. The packet came very slowly; we know not why. There is neither rhyme nor reason in the conduct of the post. We think the epistle of M. de Nevers very pretty and very entertaining. In short, all his productions have so peculiar and so excellent a character that after them we can relish no others. The two last verses of the song he made for you, charmed my daughter as a Cartesian. Speaking of the fine wines of Italy, he says :

> Sur la membrane de leur sens
> Font des sillons charmans.*

In short, it all deserves praise. For instance, can any thing be more humorous, in his epistle, than the smallest human string wound up to the highest pitch ; and the other extreme, of a hundred crotchets rolling in bass to the very depth of the abyss ? This picture is complete, and the opera of which he speaks is deservedly ridiculed ; but we can not comprehend why he has given his son's name to this epistle : *cui bono?* and where is the wit of it ? for the style resembles his own as much as one drop of water resembles another. It would be impossible to be deceived, and the subject can give offense to none. If you do not explain this to us, we shall be ill.

But let us talk of your grief at having lost this delightful family,† which has so well celebrated your merit in verse and prose, while you at the same time were so much alive to the charms of its society. It is easy to conceive the painfulness of this separation. M. de Chaulnes will not suffer us to believe that he shares it with you. An embassador must be oc-

---

* They make charming furrows upon the membrane of the senses.
† M. and Madame de Nevers.

cupied only with the business of the king, his master, who on his side has taken Mons, with a hundred thousand men, in a manner truly heroic, going every where, visiting every place, and indeed, exposing himself too much. The policy of the Prince of Orange, who was taking his measures very quietly with the confederate princes for the beginning of May, has found itself a little disconcerted by this promptitude. He threatens to come to the assistance of this great place. A prisoner told this to the king, who replied, coolly, " We came here to wait for him." I defy your imagination to frame a more perfect and more precise answer. I therefore, suppose, my dear cousin, that by sending you the news of this other conquest,* in four days, your Rome will not be sorry to live paternally with her elder son. God knows whether our embassador will ably support *the identity of the greatest king in the world*, as M. de Nevers said.

Let us return to our own country. Our little Marquis de Grignan went to the siege of Nice like an adventurer, *vago di fama* (eager for fame). M. de Catinet gave him the command of the cavalry for several days, that he might not be a volunteer. This did not prevent him from going every where, from exposing himself to the fire, which was at first very brisk, or from bearing fascines, for this is the fashion; but what sort of fascines, my dear cousin? All from orange-

---

* The town of Mons surrendered to the king on the 10th of April, the day on which this letter is dated, after a siege of eighteen days. To Boileau is attributed the following impromptu, addressed to a lady who required him to write some verses upon the occasion:

> Mons était, disait-on, pucelle
> Qu'un roi gardait avec grand soin ;
> Louis-le-Grand en eut besoin,
> Mons se rendit : vous auriez fait comme elle.

> Mons was a virgin, it is said,
> Kept by a king with greatest care ;
> Louis the Great wished for the maid,
> Mons yielded : so would you, my fair.

trees, laurels, and pomegranates! They feared nothing but too great a profusion of perfumes. Never was there so beautiful or so delightful a country seen. You can conceive what it must be from your knowledge of Italy. This is the country M. de Savoie has taken pleasure in losing and destroying. Can we call this good policy? We expect the little colonel (the Marquis de Grignan), who is preparing to set out for Piedmont; for this expedition to Nice is only *throwing the bait in expectation of the game*. He will not be here when you pass; but do you know who will find you here? My son, who is coming to spend the summer with us, and to meet his governor, by following the footsteps of his mother.

By the by, speaking of mother and son, do you know, my dear cousin, that I have been for these ten days or more in a sorrow of heart from which you alone have had the power of relieving me, while I have been employed in writing to you. This has been occasioned by the illness of the dowager Madame de Lavardin, my most intimate and oldest friend; this woman, of such excellent and sound understanding; this illustrious widow, who gathered us all under her wing; this person of such exalted merit, has fallen suddenly into a sort of apoplexy; she is drowsy, paralytic, and feverish; when she is roused, she talks rationally, but she soon relapses; in short, my child, my friendship could not sustain a greater loss; I should feel it keenly. The Duchess de Chaulnes writes to me respecting her, and is very much grieved at her illness; Madame de la Fayette still more so. Indeed, her merit is so well known, that every one is interested as in a public loss; judge, then, what her friends must feel. I am informed that M. de Lavardin is very much affected; I hope it is true; it is an honor to him to grieve for a mother to whom he is in a manner indebted for whatever he is. Adieu, my dear cousin; my heart is full, I can write no more. If I had begun with this melancholy subject I should not have had the courage to chat with you as I have done.

I shall say no more respecting the Temple, I have given my

opinion of it already; but I shall never like or approve it. Not so with regard to you, for I love you, and shall love and approve you always.

LETTER VII.

GRIGNAN, July 24, 1691.

"Short reckonings make long friends:" I have received all your letters, my dear neighbor; that of May 20, that of June 4, about which you were uneasy, and the last of July 4; with the epistle M. de Nevers sent you from Genoa, and, in short, all the works of this duke, who is the true son of Apollo and the Muses. You ask me if I do not treasure all his productions: indeed I do; I have not lost a single one; they have highly amused us, as well as every one who has passed this way whom we have deemed worthy of them. The last epistle is rather above Paulina's capacity; but we have had the pleasure of finding ourselves capable of explaining to her what she did not understand. With respect to the description of the dinner, it is suited to the taste of the best guests; and it made M. de Grignan's, the Chevalier de St. André's, my son's, and all our mouths water. I never saw so excellent a repast. I have just placed it among the other wonders of this duke. To conclude the article of letters: when you have received that of the 25th of June, and this, you will have received all.

Let us now come to yours, the beginning of which had nearly brought me to tears. How can I fancy you confined to your bed, afflicted in every limb and every joint of your poor little body; and your nerves so affected that you can neither stir hand nor foot? This is enough to drive us to despair; but to see that all this produces a song upon your melancholy situation, accompanied by another, the most humorous in the world, on a thing which you see daily; you may suppose, my poor cousin, this is a real comfort to our hearts, as it proves that the vital principle is not attacked. This fit of the gout has only given you the blue devils, and made you look forward to futurity under the most melancholy aspect in which it can present itself to you; but this situation, so violent, and so contrary to your disposition, has not had leisure to make any impression on you.

In spite of St. Peter, which is past, and of the predictions of the physicians, a pope is made, and the cardinals will leave the conclave without the event having cost them their lives; on the contrary, they will recover their health and their liberty. It is not the first time that gentlemen of the faculty have erred in judgment. The Duke de Chaulnes has written us a letter by the courier, dated the 15th, which brings the news of the exaltation: he thinks of nothing now but of coming to see us; he will be with us a fortnight; and though the pope* be a Neapolitan, he maintains that the affair of the bulls is so well disposed of, that it will be the signal gun for saddling horses and setting out for Grignan; this hope gives us great pleasure, and very much abridges the share I wished to take in all your melancholy calendars; it is at an end, however, my dear cousin; you are cured, you are set out, you are on the point of arriving here. I embrace you a thousand times. Let us talk a little of the table in the embassador's closet, of the chaos of letters, of the deep abyss of bags, of the confusion of papers, from which, like the infernal regions, when once a poor letter is thrown into it, it never comes out again. It was a miracle, indeed, that mine was found; but it was my daughter's letter, in which I had written; she had a great inclination to be offended at being thus lost and confounded with the rest; but I appeased her in the best way I could, by assuring her that the embassador read what she wrote to him with the deepest attention, and that it was upon my lines he had not condescended to throw a single glance: and it is the fact; for he said I had not written to him. She replied, "But as it was my letter, why consign it to this chaos?" To this I knew not

---

* Cardinal Pignatelli was elected pope on the 12th of July, and took the name of Innocent XII.

what to answer; the embassador will think of it, if he pleases. It is true that my poor letters have only the value you give to them, by reading them as you do; for they have their tones, and are unbearable when they are brayed out, or spelled word by word: be this as it may, my dear cousin, you give them a thousand times more honor than they deserve.

LETTER VIII.

GRIGNAN, July 26, 1691.

I am so astonished at the news of the sudden death of M. de Louvois,* that I know not how or where to begin the sub-

* The death of Louvois, as it is well known, has been the subject of many discussions. It has been said that he was poisoned. Saint Simon affirms it; and his account charges the king with this crime. Voltaire says, with reason, that this is repugnant to every idea that has been formed of the character of Louis XIV. Of those who felt like him, some said that it was a revenge of the Duke de Savoy's; others, that Louvois poisoned himself. The last opinion deserves to be inquired into. It is agreed on all sides that he was on the eve of disgrace, that he expected harsh treatment, that he spoke of death as preferable to this fall, and that he was a violent and passionate man, whom no scruple restrained. Under all these circumstances, there is nothing very improbable in his suicide. But it appears that this fact was never cleared up; and it is an inconvenience to which we are easily resigned. It is certain, however, that the king made no concealment that the event of his death happened very opportunely to draw him out of difficulties; it is also certain that the death of this man, who had done so much harm, was a great loss. The epitaph of Louvois, which appeared at that time, gave a good idea of the public opinion respecting him:

>Ici gît, sous qui tout pliait,
>Et qui de tout avait connaissance parfaite;
>Louvois que personne n'aimait,
>Et que tout le monde regrette.

>Here lies one to whom all yielded;
> And who knew of all the bent;
>Louvois, who sense with power wielded,
> Whom no one loved, and all lament.

ject to you. This great minister then, this man of consequence, who held so exalted a situation, whose *le moi* (*I*), as M. Nicole says, was so extensive; who was the center of so many things, is dead: how many affairs, designs, projects, secrets, interests to unravel, wars begun, intrigues, and noble moves at chess, had he not to make and to conduct! "O God, grant me a little time; I want to give check to the Duke of Savoy, check-mate to the Prince of Orange." No, no, not a moment, a single moment. Can we reason upon this strange event? indeed we can not; it is in our closet we must reflect upon it. This is the second minister* you have seen expire since you have been at Rome: nothing is more different than the manner of their death; but nothing more similar than their fortunes, and the hundred thousand chains which attached them both to the world.

With regard to the great objects which ought to lead you to God, you say you find your religious sentiments shaken by what is passing at Rome and in the conclave. My poor cousin, you are deceived; I have heard that a man of very excellent understanding drew quite a contrary inference from what he saw in that great city; he concluded that the Christian religion must necessarily be all holy and all miraculous to subsist thus, of itself, in the midst of so many disorders and so much profanation. Do then as he did, draw the same inferences, and believe that this very city was formerly washed with the blood of an infinite number of martyrs; that in the first centuries, all the intrigues of the conclave ended in choosing from among the priests him who appeared to have the greatest zeal and strength to endure martyrdom; that there were thirty-seven popes who suffered, one after the other; and that the certainty of their fate had no influence over them to make them fly from or refuse a situation to which death was attached, and a death of the most horrible nature. You have only to read this history to be convinced that a religion, subsisting by a continual miracle, both in its establishment and its

---

* With M. de Seignelai.

duration, can not be an invention of men. Men do not think thus: read St. Augustin in his *Vérité de la Religion* (Truth of Religion); read Abbadie,* very different indeed from that great saint, but not unworthy of being compared with him when he speaks of the Christian religion. Ask the Abbé de Polignac what he thinks of this book. Collect all these ideas and do not judge so hastily: believe that whatever intrigues may take place in the conclave, it is the Holy Ghost that always makes the pope. God works all, he is the sovereign of all, and this is what we ought to think: I have read this sentiment in a good book: "What evil can happen to a man who knows that God does all things, and who loves whatever God does?" And with this, my dear cousin, I take my leave.

LETTER IX.

GRIGNAN, August 14, 1691.

Come hither, that I may embrace you, caress you, and tell you that my daughter, whose approbation you so highly value, is delighted with your two little couplets on the holy father. Nothing, in my opinion, could be better imagined, or better executed: we have all been in raptures. But, my dear cousin, the Duke de Chaulnes, in his letter of July 20, says not a word respecting M. de Louvois ;† his death seems to me to demand an exclamation or two. His hopes are very sanguine as to the new pope, though not the work of his hands; all our interest is that he will give us our bulls, and that you will come and pay us a visit; that day seems to me to be at our finger's end, so swiftly does time pass. You will find my son at Marseilles, who will be there to meet you; this is an attention he

---

* Author of a book on the Truth of the Christian Religion. He was a Protestant.

† M. de Louvois died on the 16th July, and it is not surprising that the news of this event should not have reached M. de Chaulnes on the 20th.

owes to our governor, by way of amends for not having gone to Rome.

I long to know what you thought of the return of M. de Pomponne to the ministry: it was to us a subject of real joy; M. and Madame de Grignan had no doubt of this event from a truly prophetic spirit; but I wished it too much even to listen to them; and when Madame de Vins sent the news to my daughter, I was so surprised and so transported that I knew not what I heard: at length I comprehended that it was a very agreeable truth, not only to me but to the rest of the world, for you can not form an idea how generally his return is approved. I have paid my compliments to Madame de Chaulnes and our embassador, on the choice of M. de Beauvilliers; this is another strange man with whom the king augments his council; which is now perfect, like every thing his majesty does. He is the cleverest man in his kingdom, he is never idle, and provides for every thing; nothing remains but to pray to God that he may be preserved to us. The dauphin enters into all the councils; do you not also approve this? it is truly associating him with the empire. We have subjects for admiration every where. If your good pope would make peace, it would be an act worthy of himself, and would place us in a situation to praise, with a more tranquil mind, all the wonders we see. Adieu, my dear cousin, you know how I am disposed toward you. M. de Barillon and M. de Jannin are dead; we shall die too.

LETTER X.

PARIS, February 3, 1695.

Madame de Chaulnes sends me word that I am fortunate in being here in the sunshine; she thinks all our days are woven with silk and gold. Alas! my dear cousin, it is a hundred times colder here than at Paris; we are exposed to every wind; it is the south wind, the north-east wind, it is the devil; it is who shall insult us; they fight among themselves which shall have the honor of confining us to our apartments. All our rivers are taken; the Rhone, the furious Rhone, can not resist them. Our writing-desks are frozen, our benumbed fingers can no longer guide our pens. We breathe nothing but snow; our mountains are charming in their excess of horror. I wish every day for a painter who could take a good representation of these frightful beauties; such is our situation. Relate it to our good Duchess de Chaulnes, who fancies us to be in meadows with parasols, walking under the shadow of orange-trees. You have formed an excellent idea of the rural magnificence of our wedding;* every one has shared in the praises you bestow, but we know not what you mean by the wedding-night. Alas, how coarse you are! I was charmed with the manner and modesty of the evening; I informed Madame de Coulanges so: the bride was conducted to her apartment; her toilet, her linen, her night-clothes, were brought; she took off her head-ornaments, was undressed, and went to bed. We knew nothing of who came in or went out of her room; every one retired to his own apartment. We arose the next morning without going to the bride-folks. They also arose, dressed themselves. No foolish questions were asked them: Are you my son-in-law? are you my daughter-in-law? They are what they are. No gay breakfast was prepared; every one ate and did as he pleased; every thing was conducted in silence and with modesty; there were no uncomfortable looks, no confusion, no improper jests; this is what I had never seen before, and what struck me as being the most becoming and the pleasantest thing in the world. The cold freezes me, and makes the pen fall from my hands. Where are you? at St. Martin's, at Meudon, or at Baville? What happy spot contains the youthful and amiable Coulanges? I have just been railing against avarice to Madame de Coulanges. It gives me great joy, from the riches Mad-

* The marriage of the Marquis de Grignan.

ame de Meckelbourg has left, to think I shall die without any ready money, but at the same time without debts; this is all I ask of God, and is enough for a Christian.

LETTER XI.

GRIGNAN, May 28, 1695.

I have received your two letters from Chaulnes, my dear cousin! we found some verses in them that delighted us; we have sung them with extreme pleasure, and more than one person will tell you so, for you must not be ignorant of the good taste we preserve here for every thing you do. With respect to the gayety and charms of your mind, you certainly advance, and go back with respect to your register; this is all that can be wished, and is what naturally lays the foundation of the desire every one has for your society. To whom are you not welcome? with whom do you not accommodate yourself? and then, which is best of all, your conduct in not obtruding yourself, and in allowing room to the wish of seeing you, gives the true relish to your vanity. The proverb must be forcible indeed, if it be true, that you are not a prophet in your own country. I often receive news from Madame de Coulanges; her correspondence is very entertaining, and her health ought no longer to create alarm, especially having the resource which we must have, that when she is tired of medicine, and undeceived with respect to it, the most salutary remedy will be to take no more.

But to return to Chaulnes. I know its beauty, and can discern from hence how dull our good governor is there. It is in vain for you to give the best reasons in the world; he will constantly answer, "I do not know:" and if you go on, he will silence you by saying, "I shall die." This is what will happen, no doubt, till he has acquired a taste for repose, and for the charms of a quiet life. Habits are too strong, and the agitation attached to command and to a high station has made too deep an impression to be easily effaced. I wrote to this duke upon the deputation of my son, and I jested with him, saying things I did not believe respecting his solitude at Chaulnes; I treated him like a true hermit, holding conversations with the beautiful fountain called *the solitary*. I supposed his repasts suited to his situation, and that dates and wild fruits would compose all his banquets; I pitied his house-steward, and in saying all these trifles, I found that I stood in great need of you; and that the braying* I know him to possess, would make strange work with my poor letter. You came to my assistance, as I supposed you would; and you are now in another country, where you feel all the delight of paternal love; what say you? you could not have believed it to be so strong if you had not experienced it; it would have been a great pity if all the good instructions you have given to little children had not been followed by some child of your imagination. The little Count de Nicei is a master-piece,† and the singularity of being invisible makes him superior to the rest. You make so good a use of this story that I scarcely dare recall you; you have immortalized it; nothing can be prettier than these couplets; we sing them with pleasure. We have had a delightful introduction of spring; but, for two days past, the rain, which we do not like here, has been as violent as in Brittany and Paris, so that we have been accused of having brought it into fashion; it interrupts our walks, but it does not silence our nightingales; in short, my dear cousin, our days pass too quickly. We dispense with great bustle, and with the great world; our society, however, would not displease you; and if ever a puff of wind should blow you to this *royal* château—. But this is a chimera, we must hope to see you again elsewhere in a more natural and probable situation; we have yet a summer before us for writing to each other.

* M. de Chaulnes read as ill as M. de Coulanges read well.
† The whole of this pleasantry is explained in some songs of M. de Coulanges to Madame de Louvois, and turns upon a story which had come to them from Provence.

LETTER XII.

GRIGNAN, August 6, 1695.

I shall write you only a very short and poor letter, my dear friend, to thank you for yours, which has given us great pleasure. I shall never change my opinion with respect to long and circumstantial details, while I read yours. We are charmed with Navarre;* the situation, the building, like that of Marly, which I have never seen, the excellent society—all this convinces me that the house ought to rank with yours; as for Choisy, it is made on purpose for you. Your couplets inform all who pass, of the nobility of its origin and its fate; but you deserve to be exalted to the skies by the couplet, in which you humble yourself to the foot of the mount *with the coachman of Verthamont;*† any man who will place himself up to the ears in this mud, and will croak such pretty couplets, deserves the situation M. Tambonneau gives him. The couplet ranks with the best you have ever made; the countess, whose approbation you always ask, entreats you to believe it; it is charming, it surprises; in short, croak on, and communicate your croakings to us.

But, good God, what an effusion of blood at Namur! how many tears! how many widows! and how many afflicted mothers! And they are cruel enough to think this is not sufficient, and they wish that Marshal de Villeroi had also beaten, killed and massacred poor M. de Vaudemont?‡ what madness! I am uneasy respecting your nephew de Sanzei; I pity his mother; it is said that she is coming nearer to wait the event of the siege, which appears to us to be worthy of the fury of the marshal (de Boufflers) who defends it; no opportunity of fighting is lost. Our Germany is very quiet; our principal

---

* A château near Evreux, which belonged to the Duke de Bouillon.

† A famous coachman, who made all the songs of the Pont-neuf.

‡ M. de Vaudemont made a noble retreat before Marshal de Villeroi, who had lost time.

anxiety is for her.* Adieu, my dear cousin; did I not promise you that my letter would be dull? We have sometimes sorrows, and we know why; I speak of them to Madame de Coulanges. My daughter sends you her remembrances; you have highly amused her by your songs and your chat, for your letter is a true conversation. I have scattered your remembrances in every apartment; they have been received, and are returned with zeal. I embrace you, my amiable cousin, and exhort you still to spend your time delightfully in honor of polygamy,† which, instead of being a hanging-case to you, constitutes all the pleasure and happiness of your life.

LETTER XIII.

GRIGNAN, October 15, 1695.

I have just been writing to our Duke and Duchess de Chaulnes; but I excuse you from reading my letters; they are not worth reading. I defy all your emphasis, all your points and commas to produce any good effect, therefore leave them as they are; besides, I have spoken of several little things to our duchess, which are not very entertaining. The best thing you could do for me, my good cousin, would be to send us, by some subtle magic, all the blood, all the vigor, all the health, and all the mirth which you have to spare, to transfuse it into my child's frame. For these three months she has been afflicted with a species of disorder which is said to be not dangerous, and which I think the most distressing and the most alarming of any. I own to you, my dear cousin, that it destroys me, and that I have not fortitude enough to endure all the bad nights she makes me pass; in short, her last state has been so violent that it was necessary to have recourse to

---

* On account of the Marquis de Grignan, who was in the army of Germany.

† A jest on the subject of M. de Coulanges' *second wife*, Madame de Louvois.

bleeding in the arm; strange remedy, which makes blood to be shed when too much has been shed already; it is burning the taper at both ends; she has told me so, for, in the midst of her weakness and change, nothing can exceed her courage and patience. If we could regain strength, we should soon take the road to Paris; it is what we wish, and then we would present the Marchioness of Grignan to you, with whom you must already begin to be acquainted on the word of the Duke de Chaulnes, who has very gallantly forced open her door, and has drawn a very pleasing likeness of her. Preserve your friendship for us, my dear cousin, however unworthy of it our sorrow may make us; we must love our friends with all their faults; it is a great one to be ill: God grant, my dear friend, that you may escape it. I write to Madame de Coulanges in the same plaintive tone, which will not quit me; for how is it possible not to be as ill in mind as this countess, whom I see daily before my eyes, is in body? Madame de Coulanges is very fortunate in being out of the scrape. It seems to me as if mothers ought not to live long enough to see their daughters in such situations; I respectfully complain of it to Providence.

LETTER XIV.

Grignan, March, 1696.

I know not how the affairs of England go on; the Countess de Fiesque is the only one who has a good opinion of them, and is still certain that they will end well. I have taken three meals at the Marsans', which agree very well with me; I shall put their whole family into my basket. M. de Marsan always reminds his wife that she is no longer Madame de Seignelai; and that, being only Madame de Marsan, she must accommodate herself to all his friends, of whatever form or rank, and let every one live after his own way. I am to go on Saturday to Saint Martin's, and to-morrow I shall go to Versailles, to condole with my friend, and pass the day with Mesdames de Villeroi and Mademoiselle de Bouillon, whom I shall find there. Madame de Guise has ordered her funeral to be conducted without ceremony, and has preferred the burial-ground of the Carmelites of the great convent, to all the pomp of Saint Denis, with the kings her ancestors. She was only forty-nine years of age. Father de la Ferté will preach again on Wednesday; and on Friday, without saying a word, he will set off for Canada. If he were not to take his departure in this way, it would cause a tumult, he is so much liked by the populace; the Church of the Jesuits was too small for the multitude which crowded to his sermons.

I have just been dining at the Hôtel de Chaulnes, where I met the Marquis de Grignan; he can tell you that I was not in a very ill humor. Madame (La maréchale) de Villeroi yesterday announced to Madame de Saint-Géran the death of her husband; and the duke has taken upon himself the charge of the funeral this evening. He will probably be the privileged creditor on the inheritance, for he will advance, no doubt, what is necessary for the ceremony. This is all I know, madam; I, therefore, conclude, and take leave of you till my return from Saint Martin's, which will be when it pleases God. Madame de Coulanges is free from the colic; she only complains that she has sometimes the *little colic*, which does not prevent her from eating and drinking, and associating with the young. She is very partial to the Chevalier de Bouillon and Count d'Albret, and she was delighted to meet M. de Marsan again, with whom she has renewed a snuff acquaintance. Winter is come back within these two days: it has snowed and frozen in such a manner, that we must expect no apricots; I fear the peaches also will suffer. Madame de Frontenac has a violent cold and fever; the fashion of dying alarms us for her. Our poor D'Enclos has also a slow fever, which returns slightly every evening, with a sore throat, that makes her friends uneasy; in short, I very much fear that the work of death is not at an end.

LETTER XV.*

GRIGNAN, March 29, 1696.

When I have no other employment I weep and bewail aloud the death of Blanchefort, that amiable, that excellent youth, who was held up to all our young people as a model for imitation. A reputation completely established, valor acknowledged and worthy of his name, a disposition happy for himself (for a bad disposition is a torment to its possessor), for his friends, and for his family; alive to the affection of his mother and his grandmother, loving them, honoring them, appreciating their merit, taking pleasure in proving to them his gratitude, and thereby repaying them for their extreme affection; uniting good sense with a fine person; not vain of his youth, as most young people are, who seem to think themselves paragons of perfection—and this dear boy, with all his perfections, gone in a moment, like a blossom borne away by the wind, without being in battle, without having an opportunity to fight, and without breathing even an unhealthy air! Where, my dear cousin, can we find words to express our ideas of the grief of these two mothers, and to convey to them an adequate sense of what we feel here? We do not think of writing to them, but if at any time you should have an opportunity of mentioning my daughter, and me, and the Grignans, make known our regret at this irreparable misfortune. Madame de Vins has lost every thing, I own;† for when the heart has chosen between two sons, one only is seen. I can talk of nothing else. I bow in reverence to the holy and modest tomb of Madame de Guise, whose renunciation of that of the kings her ancestors, merits an eternal crown. I think M. de Saint-Géran happy indeed, and so I think you, for having to comfort his wife; say to her for us every thing you think

---

* As the death of Madame de Sévigné happened in the beginning of April, it is probable that this letter is the last she wrote. We consider its recovery as a fortunate circumstance.

† Madame de Vins had lost an only son.

proper. And as for Madame de Miramion, that mother of the church, she will be a public loss. Adieu, my dear cousin, I can not change my tone. You have finished your jubilee. The delightful trip to Saint Martin's has closely followed the sackcloth and ashes you mentioned to me. The happiness M. and Madame de Marsan are now enjoying well deserves that you should sometimes see them, and put them into your basket; and I deserve a place in that in which you put those who love you; but I fear that for them you have no basket.

SELECTIONS FROM VARIOUS LETTERS.*

A Supper.—We supped again yesterday with Madame de Scarron and the Abbé Têtu, at Madame de Coulanges'. We had a great deal of chat, in which you had your share. We took it into our heads to conduct Madame de Scarron home, at midnight to the very furthest end of the Faubourg St. Germain, a great way beyond Madame de la Fayette's, almost as far as Vaugirard, and quite in the country, where she lives in a large handsome house—the entrance of which is forbidden to every one—with a large garden, and beautiful and spacious apartments; she has an equipage, servants, and a genteel table: dresses neatly, but elegantly, in the style of a woman who associates with people of rank; she is amiable, handsome, good, free from affectation, and, in a word, an excellent companion. We returned very merrily, in the midst of a number of flambeaux. and in full security from thieves.

* These selections from letters necessarily omitted in our plan, comprise nearly, if not quite all, that is of literary or moral value in the whole series. We are thus able to give a more distinct impression of Madame de Sévigné's character as a mother and a Christian. Besides the many amusing anecdotes here collected, her sentiments on important duties of life are of much value; and her religious feelings are deserving distinct recognition. It will be seen that she studied her Bible, and strove to follow its divine teachings; like Fénélon, though nominally a Romanist, or rather Jansenist, she had in her heart and mind protested against the corruptions of that Church. Her clear insight, just principles, and heart-piety are remarkably displayed in these extracts.

PORT ROYAL.—That Port Royal is a perfect Thebais, a very paradise; a desert where all that is left of true Christian devotion is retired. The whole country for a league round breathes the air of virtue and holiness. The nuns are angels upon earth. Mademoiselle de Vertus is wearing out the remains of a miserable life there, in the most excruciating pain, but with inconceivable resignation. The very meanest of the inhabitants have a virtuous serenity in their countenances, and a modesty of deportment to be met with in no other place. I own to you I was delighted to see this divine solitude of which I have heard so much; it is a frightful valley, calculated to inspire a taste for religion.

HINTS ABOUT CHILDREN.—A word about the little Marquis (de Grignan);* I beseech you not to be under any apprehension about his timidity. Remember that the charming Marquis (de la Châtre) used to tremble and quake till he was twelve years old, and that La Troche, when young, was so terrified at the least thing, that his mother could not bear to have him in her sight; and yet you see how much they have distinguished themselves since: let that comfort you. Fears of this kind are the mere effect of childhood, and when childhood is surmounted, instead of being afraid of raw-head and bloody bones, these personages are afraid only of being thought fearful, are afraid of being less esteemed than others, and that is sufficient to make them brave, and kill their thousands and ten thousands: let me then again beg you to make yourself easy on that score. As to his shape, it is another matter: I would advise you to put him into breeches, and then you will see better how his legs go on, and whether they are straightened as he grows. You must let him have room to stir himself, and unfold his little limbs: but you must put on him a pretty tight vest, which will confine his shape. I shall receive some further instructions, however, on this subject, which I will not fail to transmit to you. It would be a fine thing in-

* Grandson of Madame de Sévigné.

deed to see a Grignan with a bad shape! Do you not remember how pretty he was in his swaddling-clothes? I am no less uneasy than yourself at this alteration.

REFLECTIONS.—What you say of death taking the liberty of interrupting fortune is admirable; this ought to comfort those who are not in the number of her favorites, and to diminish the bitterness of death. You ask me if I am religious: alas! my dear, I am not sufficiently so, for which I am very sorry; but yet I think I am somewhat detached from what is called the world. Age and sickness give us leisure enough for serious reflection; but what I retrench from the rest of the world I bestow upon you, so that I make but small advances in the path of detachment; and you know that the law of the game is to begin by effacing a little what is dearest to our heart.

VERSAILLES IN 1676.—I was on Saturday at Versailles with the Villars. You know the ceremony of attending on the queen at her toilet, at mass, and at dinner; but there is now no necessity of being stifled with the heat, and with the crowd, while their majesties dine: for at three, the king and queen, monsieur, madame, mademoiselle, the princes and princesses, Madame de Montespan, and her train, the courtiers, and the ladies, in short the whole court of France, retire to that fine apartment of the king's which you know. It is furnished with the utmost magnificence; they know not there what it is to be incommoded with heat; and pass from one room to another without being crowded. A game at reversis gives a form to the assembly, and fixes every thing. The king and Madame de Montespan keep a bank together. Monsieur, the queen, and Madame de Soubize, Dangeau, and Langlé, with their companies, are at different tables. The baize is covered with a thousand louis-d'ors; they use no other counters. I saw Dangeau play, and could not help observing how awkward others appeared in comparison of him. He thinks of nothing but his game, though he scarcely seems to attend to it; he gains where others lose; takes every advantage; nothing escapes or distracts him; in short, his good conduct defies fortune. Thus, two hundred thousand francs in ten days, a hundred thousand crowns in a month, are added to his account-book under the head *received*. He had the complaisance to say I was a partner with him in the bank, by which means I was seated very commodiously. I bowed to the king in the way you taught me; and he returned my salutation, as if I had been young and handsome. The queen talked to me of my illness, nor did she leave you unmentioned. The duke paid me a thousand of those unmeaning compliments which he bestows so liberally. M. de Lorges attacked me in the name of the Chevalier de Grignan; and, in short, *tutti quanti* (all the rest). You know what it is to receive a word from every one who passes you. Madame de Montespan talked to me of Bourbon, and desired me to tell her how I liked Vichi, and whether I had found any benefit there. She said that Bourbon, instead of removing the pain from her knee, had given her the tooth-ache. Her beauty and her shape are really surprising; she is much thinner than she was; and yet neither her eyes, her lips, nor her complexion are injured. She was dressed in French point; her hair in a thousand curls, and the two from her temples very low upon her cheeks; she wore on her head black ribbons, intermixed with the pearls which once belonged to the Maréchale de l'Hôpital, diamond pendants of great value, and three or four bodkins. In a word, she appeared a triumphant beauty, calculated to raise the admiration of all the foreign embassadors. She has heard that complaints were made of her having prevented all France from seeing the king; she has restored him, as you see, and you can not imagine the delight this has occasioned, nor the splendor it has given to the court. This agreeable confusion, without confusion, of all the most select persons in the kingdom, lasts from three o'clock till six. If any couriers arrive, the king retires to read his letters, and returns to the assembly. There is always music, to which he sometimes listens, and which has an admirable effect: in the mean time, he chats with the ladies who are accustomed to have that honor. They leave off their game at the hour I mentioned, without the trouble of reckoning, because they use no marks or counters. The pools are of five, six, or seven hundred, and sometimes of a thousand or twelve hundred louis-d'ors.

At six they take the air in calèshes; the king and Madame de Montespan, the prince and Madame de Thianges, and Mademoiselle d'Heudicourt, upon the little seat before, which seems to her a seat in paradise. You know how these calèshes are made; they do not sit face to face in them, but all look the same way. The queen was in another with the princesses: the whole court followed in different equipages, according to their different fancies. They went afterward in gondolas upon the canal, where there was music: at ten the comedy began, and at twelve they concluded the day with the Spanish entertainment of *media noche*; thus we passed the Saturday.

THE TELESCOPE.—Apropos, did I mention to you an excellent telescope that amused us exceedingly in the boat? It is really a master-piece of its kind; it is a still better one than that which the abbé left with you at Grignan. This glass brings objects quite home that are at three leagues' distance; alas! that it would bring those which are two hundred! You may easily guess the use we made of it on the banks of the Loire, but I have found a new method of using it, which is this: you know that one end brings objects nearer to you, and the other throws them to a great distance; now this end I turn toward Mademoiselle du Plessis, and in a moment I see her three leagues from me. I tried this experiment the other day on her, and the rest of my neighbors; this was amusing, but nobody knew what I meant by it; if there had been any one to whom I could have given the hint, the pleasure would have been greater. When tired with disagreeable company, it is only to send for the glass, and look through it at the end that distances the objects. Ask Montgobert, if she would not have laughed heartily. This is a pretty subject to talk nonsense upon. If you have Corbinelli with you, let me recommend the use of the glass to you.

Adieu, my dear; we are not mountains, as you say, so I hope to embrace you a little nearer than two hundred leagues: but you are going still further off; I have a great mind to set out for Brest. It is very hard, in my opinion, that the grand-duchess should not have the good Rarai as her lady of honor; the Guisardes have appointed La Sainte-Même to the office. I hear that La Trousse's good fortune is doubled, and that he will have De Froulai's situation.

Rules of Living.—I am never in bed more than seven hours, and I eat sparingly: I add to your precepts walking a great deal, but the worst is, that I can not prevent somber thoughts from intruding into my long gloomy avenues. Sadness is poison to us, and the source of the vapors. You are right in thinking this disorder is imaginary; you have admirably defined it; it is sorrow that gives birth to, and fear that nourishes it.

Work.—I was employed yesterday on a piece of work as tedious as the company I had: I never work but when I have company; when I am alone, I walk, I read, or write. La Plessis incommodes me no more than Maria; I am so happy as to have no inclination to listen to any thing she says, and find as little interruption from her presence, as you do from some whom you have the same kind of regard for. In other respects she has the best sentiments in the world; I admire how all her good qualities are spoiled by her impertinent and ridiculous manners. It is quite laughable to hear what she says of my patience in bearing with her; how she explains it; and the obligations she fancies it lays her under to attach herself to me; and how I serve her for an excuse for not visiting her friends at Vitré. It would make you smile, to observe her little arts to satisfy her vanity (for vanity is the growth of every soil); and her affected fears that I am growing jealous of a nun of Vitré, for whom she has a partiality. All this would make an excellent farce.

***

EVENING EMPLOYMENTS.—I was perfectly rejoiced to return here; I am making a new walk, which employs me wholly. I pay my workmen in corn; and find nothing so profitable as to amuse one's self, and forget, if possible, the evils of life. Neither do my evenings, my child, about which you are so much in pain, hang more heavily on my hands: I am almost always writing, or reading, and midnight overtakes me before I know where I am. Our abbé (her uncle) takes his leave of me at ten, and the two hours that I am alone, are no more irksome to me than the rest. In the day I am either employed with the abbé, or among my dear laborers, or in my favorite work. In short, my dear, life flies away so swiftly, and we are always drawing so near our end, that I can not conceive how people can make themselves so unhappy about worldly affairs. I have here sufficient time for reflection, and it is my fault, and not that of the place, if I do not indulge it. I am quite well; all my people obey you admirably: they are ridiculously careful of me; they come to guard me home in the evening armed cap-à-pie, and it is against a squirrel they draw their swords.

***

AN IMPROMPTU MARRIAGE.—M. de Chaulnes concluded a marriage the other day, which gave me pleasure, between the little Du Guesclin, and a very pretty girl with a large fortune; when he had with great difficulty settled the articles, he said, "Let us draw up the contract;" the parties consented, and he immediately resumed, saying, "What prevents their being married to-morrow?" Every one exclaimed, "There must be wedding-clothes, a toilet, and linen."—He laughed at this. M. de Rennes gave a dispensation of two banns, and the next day being Sunday, one was published in the morning, and they were married at noon; after dinner the little bride danced like an angel; she had learned at Paris of the duchess' master, and had caught her air; the next day she was Madame du Guesclin, and had saved 20,000 livres that would otherwise have been spent in the wedding. It is consistent with good sense to rise superior sometimes to trifles and customs.

A BRIDE.—Madame de Coulanges informs me that the new Madame de la Fayette was reclined upon a magnificent bed in a noble house; the room hung with beautiful tapestry belonging to the Keeper of the Seals; the bed decorated with an ancient mantle of the order, and the room hung with fine tapestry, having the arms ornamented with the staves of the Marshal of France, and the collar of the order; looking-glasses, chandeliers, glass plates, and crystals, according to the present fashion, out of number; a great many servants, and valets-de-chambre in livery; the bride in an elegant dress. In short, such taste reigns in the house of the new-married couple and in their family, that our Madame de la Fayette ought to be perfectly satisfied at her son's having formed so great and honorable an alliance.

BLEEDING.—You tell me you have found it necessary to be bled; the trembling hand of your young surgeon makes me tremble. The prince said one day to a new surgeon, "Does not the idea of bleeding me make you tremble?"—"Faith sir," replied the man, "your highness has most reason to tremble." He was in the right.

COMPANY.—I have for a long time adopted your opinion, that bad company is preferable to good: how dismal it is to part with the good! and what a pleasure it is to get rid of the bad! Do you remember how we were tormented at Fouesnel, and how overjoyed we were when the company thought proper to take their leave? I think we may then establish it as a maxim, that nothing is more desirable than bad company, and nothing more to be dreaded than good. Let whoever is puzzled with this enigma call upon us for the solution of it.

———

QUARRELS IN HIGH LIFE.—I think I mentioned to you the quarrel between the Duke de Ventadour and the Duke d'Aumont; the latter was returning from Bourbon with his wife, and the Duchess de Ventadour and the Chevalier de Tilladet. The Duke de Ventadour was at an estate he has in the same county, called La Motte. He had desired his wife to come to him there, and sent, at the same time, to invite the whole company, but was refused; he then came himself, but was ill received, because, following the company about from dinner-time till bed-time, his conversation was mixed continually with menaces and reproaches; in short, he was like Don Quixotte, pistol in hand, threatening and challenging the gentlemen. The chevalier treated him as a person fit only for Bedlam. At length the ladies arrived in great fear at Paris, where the king, being informed of what had happened, sent a guard to take care of Madame Ventadour, so that she is now under the protection of his majesty. What think you the monster did? he went to the king, attended by his neighbors, that is, the Princes de Condé, de Conti, Messieurs de Luxembourg, Duras, Schomberg, Bellefond; and, with incredible assurance, told the king that the Chevalier de Tilladet had not paid him the *respect due to his rank;* mark the expression: he places the dukedom where it was formerly. "Sire," said he, "I want to know why I am refused the company of my wife! what has happened to my person of late? Am I uglier, or more ill made than formerly, when I was as much courted as I am now avoided? If I am ugly, sire, is it my fault? Had I been my own maker, I would have been like your majesty; but these are things that are not in our own disposal." In short, partly owing to this natural and proper, and at the same time unexpected, flattery, and partly to the justice of his argument, the king was pleased with him, as well as the whole court. However, they are to be separated; the difficulty is, that he insists that his wife shall be shut up in a convent, which is a sad affair. M. de la Rochefoucault is employed to accommodate this business, and settle matters between the gentlemen.

EXTRAVAGANCE OF M. DE SÉVIGNÉ.—I have been ready to weep to see the desolation of this estate; there were the finest trees in the world upon it, and my son, in his last journey, gave the finishing stroke to the last. He would even have sold a little copse, which was the greatest ornament of the place. Is not this lamentable? He scraped together four hundred pistoles by this plunder, of which he had not a single penny left in a month. It is impossible to think with patience how he acts, and what his Brittany journey cost him, notwithstanding he discharged his coachman and footman at Paris, and took nobody but Larmechin with him. He has found out the art of spending an immense deal of money, without making any show for it, of losing without playing, and of paying without discharging his debts. War or peace, he is forever crying out for money; in short, he is a perpetual drain, and what he does with his money I can not conceive, for he appears to have no particular passion. I really think his hand is a crucible, which melts money the instant it is put into it. * * * * * * * * *

My son writes me word that he is going to play at reversis with his young master:* this makes my blood run cold within me; two, three, or four hundred pistoles are lost before we can look around us. "This is nothing for Admetus, but a great deal for him." If people, before they play, would think that they may possibly lose a great deal, and that debts of honor must be paid immediately, they would not be so ready to engage in such parties; but the misfortune is, that every one thinks he shall win, and this leads him on to destruction. If

* The Dauphin.

Dangeau is one of the party, he will carry off every thing; for he is a perfect harpy at play. However, it will all turn out as it shall please God, and so it will be with the 6,000 francs which I expected to receive from Nantes, and which a demon has interfered in the shape of a point of law, that throws us as far back as ever.

———

GAMING.—They play extravagantly high at Versailles: the *hoca** is forbidden at Paris under pain of death, and yet it is played at court: five or six thousand pistoles of a morning is nothing to lose. This is no better than picking of pockets. I beseech you to banish this game from among you.

* * * * * * *

The other day the queen missed going to mass, and lost twenty thousand crowns in one morning. The king said to her, "Let us calculate, madam, how much this is a year." And M. de Montausier asked her the next day, if she intended staying away from mass for the *hoca* again; upon which she was in a great passion. I have heard these stories from persons who have come from Versailles, and who collect them for me. * * * * * * *

But now about this *breland*,* what a folly is it to lose so much money at such a rascally game! It has been banished from us for a downright cut-throat. We do things in a more serious manner. You play against all chance: you lose forever: take my advice, and do not continue it: consider it is throwing money away without having any amusement for it: on the contrary, you have paid 5,000 or 6,000 francs to be the mere dupe of fortune. But I am rather too warm, my dear, and must say with Tartuffe, "'tis through excess of zeal."

* * * * * * *

I will tell you, my dear child, a thought that has occurred to me on the frequent losses you and M. de Griguan sustain at cards. I would have you both be cautious. It is not pleas-

---

* A game at cards.

ant to be made a dupe of; and be assured that it is not natural to be perpetually the winner or the loser. It is not long since I was led into the tricks of the Hôtel de la Vieuville. You remember, I suppose, how our pockets were picked there. You are not to imagine every body plays as fairly as you do yourself. The concern I have for your interest makes me say so much; and as it comes from a heart entirely devoted to you, I am persuaded you will not be displeased at it.

PROVIDENCE.—You say you never mention Providence but when you have a disorder on your lungs, whereas that subject always exhausts mine, for I can find none that furnishes so large a field for discussion, observation and inquiry; and why may we not discourse as well on this as on natural philosophy? Why did you not still say, as you did last year, that our fears, our reasonings, our decisions, our wills, our desires, are only so many means employed by God for the execution of his purposes? Is not this an inexhaustible subject, fraught with the most entertaining variety? * * * * *
Believe me there is no experiment in natural philosophy more interesting than the investigation of the connection and diversity of our several sentiments; so that you see, *It is God's will* may be paraphrased in a thousand different ways.

FREE WILL.—I have no other answer to make you upon what St. Augustin says, except that I hear and understand him, when he tells me, and repeats to me five hundred times in the same book, that all things depend, as the apostle says, " not on him that willeth, nor on him that runneth, but on God, that showeth mercy to whom it pleaseth him; that it is not for any merit in man, that God bestows his grace, but according to his own good pleasure; that man may not glory in his own strength, seeing he receives all things from God." His whole book is in this strain, filled with passages from Scripture, the writings of the Apostle Paul, and the Homilies of the Church. He calls our free will, a deliverance, and an aptitude to love God, because we are no longer under the dominion of the devil, and are chosen from all eternity, according to the decrees of the Almighty before all ages. When I read in this book the following passage, "How could God call men to judgment, if they were not free agents?" I confess I am at a loss to understand it, and am disposed to think it a mystery: but as free will can not put our salvation in our own power, and as we must always be dependent on God, I have no desire to understand it better, and will endeavor, as much as possible, to remain in a state of humility and dependence.

DEVICES.—As to devices, my dear child, my poor brain is in a very bad condition for thinking of any, much less for inventing them; however, as there are twelve hours in the day, and above fifty in the night, my memory has furnished me with a rocket raised to a great height in the air, with these words; *Che peri, pur che s'innalzi.** I am afraid I have seen this somewhere in the late tournaments, though I can not exactly say where or when; for I think it too pretty to be my own. I remember also having seen in some book, a rocket on the subject of a lover who had been bold enough to declare himself to his mistress, with these words, *Da l'ardore l'ardire,*† which is pretty but does not apply in this instance. I am not quite sure whether the first I have mentioned is in strict conformity to the rules of devices: for I do not perfectly understand them; all I know is, that it pleased me, and whether it was in a tournament, or on a seal, is a matter of no great importance; it is scarcely possible to invent new ones for every occasion. You have heard me a thousand times repeat that part of a line in Tasso, *L'alte non temo:*‡ I used to repeat this so often, that the Count de Chapelles had a seal engraved, with an eagle flying toward the sun, and

---

* Let it perish, so it be exalted.
† My boldness arises from my **ardor**.
‡ I rise without fear.

L'alte non temo for the motto: a very happy device. * *
* * M. de Montmoron came hither post: among other things we were talking about devices: he assures me he does not remember to have seen any where the one I proposed: he knew the one with these words, *Da l'ardore l'ardire,* but that is not the thing: the other, he says, is much more complete, *Che peri, pur che s'innalzi*. And whether it is my own, or borrowed, he thinks it excellent. * * * * *
I have seen a device which suits me exactly; it is a leafless tree, apparently dead, with this inscription round it, *Fin che sol ritorni.** What think you of it, my child?

THE USE OF REASON.—I am still alone, my dear child, without being dull: my health is good; I have plenty of books, work, and fine weather; these, with a little reason, go a great way.

PECUNIARY EMBARRASSMENTS.—You ask, why am I not with you? Alas! I could easily answer you, if I were inclined to debase my letter with a detail of the reasons that obliged me to quit you, of the misery of this country, the sums that are owing me here, the delays in the payment of them, what I owe elsewhere, and the ruin my affairs must have sustained had I not taken this resolution in time. You well know that I put it off for two years with pleasure; but there are extremes, my dear child, in which we should destoy every thing in attempting to wrestle with necessity; the property I possess is no longer my own; I must preserve the same honor and the same probity I have all my life professed. This, this, my child is the cruel cause that tears me from you; and is this a subject to entertain you with?

AN OBSTINATE SON.—In regard to my son, I find I have courage enough to tell him my sentiments without disguise. I wrote him a letter which I think unanswerable; but the

* Till the sun returns.

more I enforce my reasons, the more he urges his arguments, and he appears so determined, that I now perfectly understand what is meant by an unconquerable wish. There is a degree of ardor in the desire which animates him, that no prudence can withstand. I can not accuse myself of having preferred my own interest to his. I wish for nothing but to see him walk in the path I have traced out for him. He is wrong in all his arguments, and far beside the mark; I have endeavored to set him right by incontestible arguments, corroborated by the opinion of all our friends; and ask him if he has not some doubts, seeing he is alone in an opinion which every one else disapproves? He answers me always by an obstinate perseverance; so that I am reduced to the last expedient, that of keeping him from making a rash or injurious bargain.

A Forgiving Mother.—As I was returning from my walk yesterday, I met the poor *frater*,* at the end of the mall, who immediately fell upon his knees, so conscious of having done wrong in having been three weeks under ground, singing matins, that he thought he dared not approach me otherwise. I had resolved to scold him heartily, but I was so glad to see him, that I could not find an angry word to use. You know how entertaining he is; he embraced me a thousand times, and gave me the worst reasons in the world; which, however, I received as sterling; we chat, we read, we walk, and we wear away the year; or rather, what is left of it.

Love—its symptoms.—You want to know the symptoms of this love, of which I spoke to you the other day. *Imprimis*, To be the first on all occasions to deny it: to affect an air of great indifference, which is a sure mark of the contrary: the opinion of those who can judge from being near: the public voice: an entire suspension of all motion in the globular machine: a neglect of ordinary concerns to attend to a single

---

* Her son.

one: a continual satirizing old people who are so foolish as to be in love. "Such nonsense! they must be idiots! fools! And with a young woman too! Very pretty indeed! it would become me mighty well! I had rather break both my arms and legs." And then we make answer internally: "Indeed what you say is very true; but, for all that you are in love: you tell us all these fine things: your reflections are doubtless very just, very true, very tormenting; but for all that you are in love; reason is on your side, but love is stronger than reason; at the same time you are sick, you weep, you are out of humor, and you are in love."

CHESS.—You tell me of chess what I have often thought before. In my opinion, there could not have been contrived a better expedient to humble pride than this game, which at once sets before our view the narrowness and insignificance of the human mind. I think it would be of real utility to any one fond of such reflections. But then, on the other hand, the foresight, the penetration, the address in defending ourselves, as in attacking our adversary, the success attending the right management of the game, is so pleasing, and affords so much inward satisfaction, that it may at the same time nourish our pride and swell our self-sufficiency. I am still far from being cured of this passion, and therefore want to be further convinced of my own weakness.

ALONE.—I am delighted to be alone; I walk out, I amuse myself with reading and work, and I go to church; in short I ask pardon of the company I expect, but I own I do wondrous well without them.

A COURTIER.—The other day the dauphin was shooting at a mark, and shot very wide of it: M. de Montausier rallied him upon it; and told the Marquis de Crequi, who is very skillful to fire, saying to the dauphin, "See how well he will hit the mark. The arch youth had the complaisance to shoot a foot further from it than the dauphin, which turned the laugh on M. de Montausier: "Ah! little wretch," said he, "you deserve to be hanged."

THE KING.—The king, in reality, is well served: neither life nor fortune is considered when his pleasure is the question. If we were as well disposed toward God, we should be saints indeed.

CHRISTIAN HUMILITY.—I know very well that Jesus Christ, St. Paul, and St. Augustine, preached and exhorted, it was their business; this latter gives good reason for doing so. But a poor sinner, recovered only three days from a worse state than ours, should keep silence, penetrated with the mercy of God toward him, occupied only with his happiness, and the true gratitude he owes to his Saviour, for having selected and distinguished him from so many others, without any merit, through free grace: such should be the sentiments of his heart, and if charity should make him interest himself for his neighbor, it should display itself in lamentations before God, and in supplicating the same grace for others that has so plentifully been poured upon him. Such was that penitent and holy princess, Madame de Longueville; she did not forget her situation nor the abyss from which God had saved her; she preserved the remembrance as a foundation for her penitence and her lively acknowledgment to the Almighty. Thus is Christian humility preserved and the grace of Jesus Christ honored. This does not preclude reflection and Christian conversation with our friends; but no sermons, no scolding; these revolt, and make us recollect and refer persons to their past life, because we find they have forgotten it. I am astonished that people of good sense should fall into this injustice; but we ought to be astonished at nothing; for what do we not meet with in our journey through life?

HOME LIFE.—We lead so regular a life that it is scarcely possible to be ill. We rise at eight, and I often walk till nine, when the bell rings for mass, to breathe the fresh air in the woods; after mass we dress, bid each other good-day, return and gather orange-flowers, dine, and work or read till five. Since my son's absence, I read to save his little wife's lungs; I leave her at five, and return to those delightful groves, with a servant who follows me: I take books with me, change my route, and vary my walks; from a book of devotion I turn to one of history, this creates a little change; I think of God, and his over-ruling providence possesses my soul, and reflect on futurity; at length, about eight o'clock I hear a bell. This is the summous to supper. I prefer this life infinitely to that of Rennes; is it not a fit solitude for a person who should think of her salvation, and who either is or would be a Christian? In short, my dearest child, there is nothing but you that I prefer to the tranquil repose I enjoy here; for I own with pleasure, that I would willingly pass some more time with you if it pleased God.

LIBERTY AT HOME.—What do you say my child? would you not suffer me to have two or three hours to myself, after having been at mass, to dinner, and till five o'clock working, or talking with my daughter-in-law? she would, I believe, be as much vexed at this as myself: she is a good little woman, and we agree wonderfully well together; but we have a great taste for the liberty of parting and meeting again afterward. When I am with you, my child, I own I never leave you but with regret and consideration for you; with every other person, it is from consideration for myself. Nothing can be more just or more natural: it is impossible to feel for two persons what I feel for you; leave us, therefore, a little to our sacred freedom; it agrees with me, and by the help of books the time passes in this way as quickly as it does at your brilliant castle.

READINGS.—Our readings are delightful. We have Abbadie* and the History of the Church; this is marrying the lute to the voice. You are not fond of wagers; I know not how we could captivate you a whole winter here. You skim lightly, and are not fond of history; and we have no pleasure but when we are attached to our subject and make it a business. Sometimes, by way of change, we read *Les petites Lettres* of Pascal; good heavens! how delightful they are, and how well my son reads them! I constantly think of my daughter, and how worthy of her this extreme propriety of reasoning would be: but your brother says you find that it is always the same thing: ah! so much the better; can there be a more perfect style, more finely wrought, more delicate unaffected raillery, or more nearly allied to the dialogues of Plato, which are so very beautiful! And when, after the first ten letters, he addresses himself to the R. P.s, what seriousness! what solidity! what force! what eloquence! what a way of supporting it and of making it understood! All this is to be found in the last eight letters, which are very different from the former. I am persuaded you never did more than glance over them, selecting the most beautiful passages; but they should be read leisurely. * * * *

You ask me what books we are reading. When we have company reading is laid aside; but before the meeting of the states, we read some little books that scarcely took us up a moment:—Mohammed II., who took Constantinople from the last emperor of the East; this is a great event, so singular, brilliant, and extraordinary, that we are carried away with it; and it happened but two hundred and thirty-six years ago:— the Conspiracy of Portugal, which is very fine: the Variations of M. de Maux: a volume of the History of the Church, the second is too full of the detail of the councils, and therefore might be tedious: *Les Iconoclastes* and the Arianism of Maimbourg; this author is detestable, his style disagreeable; he is always desirous of being satirical, and compares Arius, a

* Author of *La Vérité de la Religion Chrétienne.*

princess and a courtier, to M. Arnauld, Madame de Longueville, and Treville; but setting aside these fooleries, the historical passages are so very fine, the Council of Nice so admirable, that it is read with pleasure; and as he brings us down to Theodosius, we shall find consolation for all our evils in the elegant style of M. de Flechier.*

ARIANISM.—I am at present reading the history of Arianism; I neither like the author† nor his style: but the history itself is admirable; it is indeed that of the whole world: it has a share in every thing, and seems to have springs that move all the powers of the earth. The genius of Arius was astonishing; as it likewise is, to see how his heresy spread itself over the world; almost all the bishops join in the error; St. Athanasius alone stands forth to defend the divinity of Jesus. These great events are truly worthy of admiration. When I wish to feast my understanding and my soul, I retire into my closet; I listen to *our fathers*, and their glorious morality, which makes us so well acquainted with our own hearts.

* * * * * * *

I am employed in reading my Arianism: it is a strange history, in which nothing displeases me but the author and the style; but I have a pencil, and am revenged on him, by marking some passages which I think highly diverting from the earnest desire he shows of drawing parallels between the Arians and the Jansenists, and the perplexity he is under to reconcile the conduct of the Church in the first ages of Christianity with that of the Church at present. Instead of passing slightly over them, he says, that the Church for *good reasons* does not act now as it did then.

ADORATION.—I find communion is frequent in Provence; to my shame be it spoken, I neglected the immaculate concep-

---

* Esprit Flechier, Bishop of Nimes, author of the Life of Theodosius.
† Louis Maimbourg.

tion of the Mother, to reserve myself wholly for the nativity of the Son; for this we can not be too well prepared.

JEALOUSY.—You are doubtless convinced that my sentiments and yours are the same; but I want to teach you jealousy, at least in theory, and assure you, *credi a me pur che l'ho provato*,* that we often say things we do not think; and even if we did think them, would that be a sign of not loving? Quite the contrary; for if we were to analyze these speeches, so full of anger and resentment, we should find a great deal of affection and attachment at the bottom. Some hearts are remarkably delicate; when these happen to meet with a cool or indifferent disposition, a very considerable progress is made in the region of jealousy. This I have thought myself obliged in conscience to say to you; make your own reflections upon it, for I can not pretend to enter into particulars at the distance of two hundred leagues.

FOLLY.—A young man came to visit me the other day, who is the son of a gentleman of Anjou, with whom I was formerly intimately acquainted. At his entrance I beheld a fine, graceful, handsome figure, which struck me with pleasure; but, alas! as soon as he opened his mouth, he laughed at every word he spoke, which made *me* almost ready to cry. He has a smattering of Paris and the opera; he sings; is familiar and airy; and repeats with great gravity, "Quand on n'a point ce qu'on aime, qu'importe, qu'importe, à quel prix?† instead of *to obtain what we love*, which you know are the words of the opera. I recommend this charming alteration to M. de Grignan, to set it to music.

THE LOT OF MANKIND.—I wish to write in my prayer-book what M. de Comines says of the cross purposes of human life. It is pleasant to see that, even in his time, tribulation and

* Believe me for I have proved it.
† To obtain what we do not love, what price is too great?

misery were the lot of mankind. His style gives peculiar grace to the solidity of his argument. For my part, I am determined to be more than ever convinced of the impossibility of being happy in this world, since God keeps *loyally* to what he has promised.*

EXPENSES, RETRENCHMENTS, ETC.—I readily conceive that you are fearful of looking into the expense you have incurred: it is a machine that must not be touched, lest it fall and crush you with its weight. There is something of enchantment in the magnificence of your castle, and the elegance of your table. The dilapidation must be ruinous, and I can not conceive what you mean by saying that it is not considerable. It is a kind of black art, like that among courtiers, who, though they have not a penny in their pockets, undertake the most expensive journeys both by land and water, follow every fashion, are at every ball, masquerade, and ring, in every lottery, and still go the same round, though overwhelmed in debts. I forgot to mention gaming, which is another curious article. Their estates dwindle away; but no matter, they still go on. Just so it is with you.

* * * * * * *

I fancy that by this time you are somewhat cured of your Grignan economy, where you were to live for little or nothing; for it was nothing, it seems, nothing at all, to have four or five tables, to keep open house, and furnish entertainment for man and horse; a thing that no one in the world now thinks of doing: in short, say what you please, that famous caravansera of yours appears to me to teem with ruin; this concourse of people seems to me like the flood which carries all before it. In short, my child, I dare not think of this vortex; Paris will prove your resting-place: stay here at least till you have confronted your expenses, and can look your return in the face.

* * * * * * *

---

* This is the passage from Comines.
"No creature is exempt from suffering. All eat their bread in pain."

There are many things yet to settle, which concern you as much as myself, and I might as well not have made this journey at all, as to make it too short; so that I must resolve to drain the bitter cup to the bottom. Besides, as I observed to you in a former letter, the money I save by being here, serves to pay off a part of my debts elsewhere; without this expedient, what could I have done? You well know what I mean; it has cost me many an uneasy moment: and, indeed, what could you yourself have done, but for the assistance you received? At present, I fancy, you have made matters up tolerably well.

Baptism.—What you said the other day, as to humor and memory, was perfectly just; they are certainly things which are not sufficiently known. I also intend to convict you of heresy, my child; and, be as angry as you please, I insist, that the death of Jesus Christ is not alone sufficient, without baptism: he requires the water, the spirit, and the blood, and it is on these conditions alone that his death can be of service to us. No part of the old man can enter into heaven, but by regeneration through Jesus Christ. If you ask me my reasons, I shall reply with St. Augustine, that I can give none, any more than I can tell why, having come into the world to save all men, he saves so very few; or why he concealed himself during his life-time, and would not let any one know or follow him. I can give no reason for all these things; but of this I am certain, that since he thought fit they should be so, they must be right and proper, seeing that his will is truth and justice.

Order.—If Providence delights in order, and order is no other than the will of God, there must be many things contrary to his will. The persecutions against St. Athanasius, and other orthodox divines, and the calm prosperity of tyrants, are all contrary to order, and consequently to the will of God therefore, with leave of Father Malebranche,* would it not be as well to confine ourselves to what St. Augustine says, that God permits all things that come to pass, that he may derive glory from them to himself, by ways unknown to man? St. Augustine acknowledges no rule or order but the will of God, and if we do not follow his doctrine, we shall have the mortification of finding, that, as scarcely any thing in this world is agreeable to order, every thing must pass contrary to his will who made all things; which, in my mind, is a shocking supposition.

MARY BLANCHE.†—You give me an excellent idea of your eldest daughter; I see her before me; pray embrace her for me; I rejoice that she is happy. For your son, you may love him as much as you please; he deserves it; every one speaks highly of him, and praises him in a way that would give you pleasure; we expect him this week. I have felt all the force of the phrase he made use of to gain esteem, " which must come, or tell the reason why:" it brought tears into my eyes at the moment; but esteem is come already, and will not have to say why it staid away. The reputation of this child is already commenced, and will now only increase.

THE YOUNG MARQUIS DE GRIGNAN.‡—Your son was last night at the Duke de Chartres' ball; he was very handsome, and will inform you of his success. You must not, however, calculate upon his studying much; he owned to us yesterday, very sincerely, that he is at present incapable of paying proper attention; his youth hurries him away, and he does not understand what he reads. We grieve that he has not, at least, a taste for reading, and that he wants inclination more than

* Father Malebranche says, that "all that is done in nature is done from the nature of order."

† Mary Blanche, eldest daughter of Madame de Grignan. She was a nun at St. Mary at Aix.

‡ Grandson of Madame the Sévigné.

time. His frankness prevented our scolding him; I know not what we did not say to him; I mean the chevalier, myself and Corbinelli, who was rather warm upon the occasion. But we must not fatigue or force him; this taste will come in time, my dear; for it is not possible, that, with so much spirit, good sense, and love for his profession, he should have no desire to be made acquainted with the exploits of the heroes of antiquity, and particularly *Cæsar at the head of his Commentaries.* Have patience, and do not fret: he would be too perfect were he fond of reading. * * * * *

I am also of opinion, that by reading we learn to write; I know some officers of rank, whose style is vulgar; it is, however, a delightful thing to be able to communicate our thoughts; but it also often happens that these people write as they think, and as they speak; every thing is in unison.

PAULINA.*—I am pleased with Coulanges' praise of Paulina; it is well applied, and makes me understand what sort of charms she possesses, curbed however by persons who have not given her the best nose† in the world. If the count had

---

* Paulina de Grignan, born in 1674, and married in 1695, to the Marquis de Simiane, was noticed at five or six years of age, for the agreeableness of her wit, as well as the beauty of her person. Her letters were already looked upon as performances in which the pleasing and the natural were equally combined. She had scarcely entered her fourth year, when she would occasionally utter repartees full of wit and pleasantry. She was not more than thirteen when she wrote, at Madame de Grignan's request, a small piece of devotion which the brightest genius might have been proud of. It is easy to guess how a person thus favored by nature must turn out, educated under the eyes of a mother and grandmother whose good sense seemed as it were transfused into her. She excelled not only in the epistolary style, but also in the poetic, though she never wrote but for amusement. The solid principles of true religion, in which she was brought up, shone forth in her, amid the bustle of courts and secular affairs; and never with so much splendor as in the last year of her life, which she employed wholly in the exercise of the most sublime virtues of Christianity.

† Paulina's nose resembled her grandmother's.

given her his fine eyes and fine person, and left the rest to you, Paulina would have set the world on fire; she would have been irresistible; this pretty mixture is a thousand times better, and must certainly form a very pretty personage. Her sprightliness resembles yours; your wit always bore away the palm, as you say of hers; I like this panegyric. She will soon learn Italian, with the assistance of a better mistress than you had. You deserve as excellent a daughter as mine has been. I told you that you might do what you wished with yours, from her disposition to please you; she appears to me worthy of your love. * * * * * * *

Paulina then is not perfect; I could never have supposed that her chief imperfection would have been ignorance of religion. You must instruct her in this, which you are very capable of doing; it is your duty, and you have good books to assist you: in return, your sister-in-law, the abbess, will teach her the world. * * * * *

You astonish me by what you say of Paulina; pray, pray, my dear child, keep her with you; think not that a convent can repair the errors of education, whether as to religion, with which the sisterhood are very little acquainted, or as to any thing else. You will do much better at Grignan, when you have time for application. You will make her read good authors; you will converse with her, and M. de la Garde will assist you: I am convinced that this is preferable to a convent.

FAITH IN CHRIST.—So then, you read St. Paul and St. Augustine; two excellent laborers to establish the absolute will of God. They never scruple to assert, that God disposes of his creatures as the potter does of his clay; some he chooses, some he rejects. They are no loss to apologize for his justice, since there is no other justice but his will. It is justice itself, it is the rule of right; and, after all, what does he owe to man? Is he in any way dependent on him? Not at all. He, therefore, does them justice in rejecting them, on account of the stain of original sin, which is communicated to all; and he selects a few, whom he saves by his son Jesus Christ, who himself says, "I know my sheep, and am known of mine: I will lead them forth to the pasture, and not one shall be lost." "I have chosen you," saith he in another place to his apostles, "and you have not chosen me." There are numberless passages of this nature; I meet with them continually, and understand them all; and when I find others that seem to contradict them, I say to myself, This is to be understood figuratively, as when we read that "God was in wrath," that "God repented him," and the like: and I always abide by that first and great truth, which represents God to me as he is, the sovereign master, the supreme creator and author of the universe; in a word, as a being infinitely perfect, agreeably to Descartes' idea. Such are my humble and reverential thoughts, from which, however, I deduce no ridiculous consequences, nor do they deprive me of the hope of being of the number of the elect of God, after the mercies he has bestowed on me, which are so many foundations upon which to ground my confidence.

THE FIRE-EATER.—Yesterday a young man came here from Vitré, whom I knew to have lived formerly as footman with M. Coulanges. M. de Grignan has seen him at Aix. He showed me a printed list of the feats he performed with fire; he has the secret of the man you have heard spoken of at Paris. Among a thousand wonderful things that he did, and which I am astonished the government permits, on account of the consequences, I was struck with one in particular, which is soon done; this was the letting fall from his hand into his mouth ten or twelve drops of flaming sealing-wax, with which he appeared to be no more affected than if it had been so much cold water; he did not make the least grimace, or sign of uneasiness, and his tongue looked as fair and unhurt after the operation as before. I have often heard of these fire-eaters; but I must confess, that to see the thing performed in my own room, and under my very eye, struck me with astonishment.

Books.—We pass our time here very quietly; this you can not doubt; but very swiftly, which will surprise you: work, walking, conversation, reading, all these are called in to our assistance. Speaking of books, you tell me wonders of M. Nicole's last production; I have read some passages that appeared to me very fine; the author's style enlightens, as you say, and makes us enter into ourselves, in such a way as discovers the beauty of his mind and the goodness of his heart; for he never scolds out of season, which is the worst thing in the world, and never produces the desired effect. I did not purchase the book at the time, which was in Lent: I contented myself with the good Le Tourneux.* We are reading a treatise of the pious man of Port-Royal upon continual prayer, which is a sequel to certain pious works that are very fine; but this, which is much larger, is so spiritual, so luminous, and so holy, that though it be a thousand degrees above our understandings, it does not fail to please and charm us. We are delighted to find that there have been, and still are, people in the world, to whom God has communicated his Holy Spirit and grace in such abundance; but, good heavens! when shall we be possessed of one little spark, of one single degree? How sad it is to find ourselves so far behind here, and so near in other things! fie, fie, let us not name this misfortune! we ought to humble ourselves at it a hundred times a day.

Liberty of Mind.—There are certain periods of life in which we attend to nothing but ourselves. You indeed have never been much occupied in that way; but when we came down this river together, we were more engaged in disputing about the Count des Chapelles than in admiring the beauties of the rural scenes that surrounded us. Now, the case is exactly the reverse: we observe a profound silence, are perfectly at our ease, reading, musing, admiring, out of the way

* Nicholas de Tourneux, confessor of Port-Royal, so well-known by his excellent work, entitled "The Christian Year," and by a great number of other important works.

of all sorts of news, and living upon our own reflections. The good abbé (her uncle), is always praying: I listen attentively to his pious ejaculations; but when he has got to his beads I beg to be excused, finding that I can meditate much better without them. In short, we manage to pass twelve or fourteen hours without being very unhappy; such a fine thing is liberty.

The Nuns of Saint-Marie.—My greatest satisfaction is in visiting the nuns of Saint-Marie; they are truly amiable women; they still retain the remembrance of you, of which they do not fail to make a merit with me: they are neither silly nor conceited, like some you know; they do not believe the present Pope* to be a heretic; they understand the religion they profess, and will never reject the Holy Scriptures because they have been translated by worthy men; they pay all due honor to the saving grace of Christ; they acknowledge the power of providence; they educate the young girls committed to their care very properly, and neither teach them to lie nor to dissemble; no chimeras, no idolatry is to be found among them. In short, I have a great regard for them. M. de Grignan would think them Jansenists; for my part, I think them Christians: there are two of them who have an infinite deal of wit. I shall go to their house to-morrow to write, and I shall dine with them on Saturday: they are all the comfort I have here.

Moral Essays.—Do you not intend to read the Moral Essays, and to give me your opinion of them? For my part, I am charmed with them; and so I am with the funeral oration on M. de Turenne; there are passages in it which must have affected all that were present. I do not doubt but it has been sent you; tell me if you do not think it very fine. Do you not intend to finish Josephus? We read a great deal of serious as well as lighter subjects; fable and history. We

---

* Innocent XI., who passed for favoring the Jansenists, merely because he took no steps against them.

are so deeply engaged with these, that we have scarcely leisure for any other employments. They pity us at Paris; they think us confined to a fire-side by the inclemency of the season, and languishing under a dearth of amusement; but, my dear, I walk; I find a thousand diversions; the woods are neither wild nor inhospitable. It is not for passing my time here instead of at Paris that I am to be pitied.

HISTORY OF THE BIBLE.—I am, moreover, reading the emblems of the Holy Scriptures,* which begin from Adam. I have begun with the creation of the world, which you are so fond of, and shall end with the death of our Saviour, which you know is an admirable series. We find in it every circumstance, though related concisely; the style is fine; it is done by an eminent hand: the history is interspersed throughout with excellent reflections, taken from the fathers, and is very entertaining. For my own part, I go much further than the Jesuits; and when I see the reproaches of ingratitude, and the dreadful punishments with which God afflicted his people, I can not help concluding, that we, who are freed from the yoke to which they were subjected, are, in consequence, highly culpable, and justly deserve those scourges of fire and water which the Almighty employs when he thinks fit. The Jesuits do not say enough on this subject, and others give cause to murmur against the justice of the Deity, in weakening the supports of our spiritual liberty, as they do. You see what fruit I derive from my reading. I fancy my confessor will enjoin me to read the philosophy of Descartes.

AFFECTION.—I fancy myself qualified to write a treatise on affection; there are a thousand things depending on it, a thousand things to be shunned, in order to prevent those we

---

* History of the Old and New Testament, by M. de Saci, Sieur de Royaumont. He composed this book in the Bastile. It is, they say, filled with allusions to the vicissitudes of Jansenism in that age. M. de Saci was president of the nuns at Port-Royal.

love from smarting for it: there are innumerable instances where we give them pain, and in which we might alleviate their feelings, were we to reflect and to turn things in all the points of view we ought, out of regard to the object of our love. In short, I could make it appear in my book, that there are a thousand different ways of proving our regard without talking of it; as well as of saying by actions that we have no real regard, even while the treacherous tongue is making protestations to the contrary. I mean no one in particular, but what I have written, I have written.

SUBMISSION.—I beg you will read the second part of the second treatise in the first volume of *Moral Essays;* I am sure you know it, but you may not perhaps have observed it particularly; it is on the subject of *submission to the will of God.* You will there see how clearly it is demonstrated that Providence governs all things; that is my creed, by that I abide: and though a contrary doctrine may be advanced elsewhere, to keep fair with all sides, I shall consider such conduct only in the light of a political stratagem, and follow the example of those who believe as I do, though they may change their note.

PHILOSOPHY.—You say that I make God the author of every thing that happens; read, read, I say, that part of the treatise I have pointed out to you, and you will find that we are to look to Him for every thing, but with reverence and humility, and consider man only as the executor of his orders, from whose agency he can draw what effects he thinks proper. It is thus we reason, when our eyes are lifted up to heaven, but, in general, we are apt to confine our views to the poor contemptible second causes that strike our bodily senses, and bear with impatience what we ought to receive with submission; and such, alas! is my present wretched situation. I join with you in believing that philosophy is good for little, except to those who do not stand in need of it. You desire me to love you more and more: indeed, you embarrass me; I know not where to find that degree of comparison; it is beyond my conception: but this I am certain of, that I never can, in thought, word, or deed, evince the thousandth part of the affection I bear you; and this is that sometimes distracts me.

OLD AGE.—So then you were struck with an expression of Madame de la Fayette's ("you are old,") blended with so much friendship. Though I say to myself that this is a truth which should not be forgotten, I confess I was all astonishment at it; for I yet feel no sort of decay that puts me in mind of it. I can not, however refrain from calculating and reflecting, and I find that the conditions of life are very hard. It seems to me that I have been dragged against my will to the fatal period, when *old age* must be endured; I see it, I have attained it; and I would, at least, contrive not to go beyond it, not to advance in the road of infirmities, pain, loss of memory, *disfigurements* which are ready to lay hold of me; and I hear a voice which says, You must go on in spite of yourself; or, if you will not, you must die, an alternative at which nature recoils. Such, however, is the fate of those who have reached a certain period. * * * * *
I contemplate this evil, which has not yet proved itself so, with heroic courage; I prepare myself for its consequences with peace and tranquillity; and seeing there is no way of escape, and that I am not the strongest, I think of the obligation I owe to God, for conducting me so gently to the grave. I thank him for the desire he daily gives me to prepare for death, and the wish of not draining my life to the dregs. Extreme old age is frightful and humiliating: the good Corbinelli and I see a painful instance of this truth hourly, in the poor Abbé de Coulanges, whose helplessness and infirmities make us wish never to reach this period

SERMONS.—When I am as good as M. de la Garde, if ever God grants me this grace, I shall like all sermons; in the mean while I content myself with the Gospels as explained by M. le Tourneux; these are real sermons, and nothing but the vanity of man could load modern discourses with their present contents. We sometimes read the Homilies of St. John Chrysostom; these are divine, and please us so highly, that I persist in not going to Rennes till passion week, to avoid being exposed to the eloquence of the preachers who hold forth in behalf of the parliament. * * * * * *
The Marshal de Grammont was so transported the other day, at a sermon of Bourdaloue's, that he cried out, in the middle of a passage that struck him, "By ——, he is right." Madame burst out a laughing, and the sermon was interrupted so long that nobody knew what would be the consequence. If your preachers are as you represent them, I am apt to think they will be in no great danger of their being interrupted by such praises.

JOSEPHUS.—I am glad you like Josephus, Herod, and Aristobulus. I beg you to go on, and see the end of the siege of Jerusalem, and the fate of Josaphat. Take courage; every thing is beautiful in this historian, every thing is grand, every thing is magnificent, every thing is worthy of you; let not an idle fancy prevail with you to lay him aside. I am in the History of France; that of the Crusades has occasioned my looking into it, but it is not to be compared to a single leaf of Josephus. Alas! with what pleasure we weep over the misfortunes of Aristobulus and Mariamne:

HOPE EVER.—We should never despair of our good fortune. I thought my son's situation quite hopeless, after so many storms and shipwrecks, without employments, and out of the way of fortune; and while I was indulging these melancholy reflections, Providence destined, or had destined, us to so advantageous a marriage, that I could not have wished for a better alliance, even at the time when my son had the greatest reason to expect it. It is thus we grope in the dark, not knowing our way, taking good for evil, and evil for good, in entire ignorance.

Twilight.—I hate twilight when I have nobody to chat with; and I had rather be alone in the woods, than alone in a room. This is like plunging up to the neck in water to save one's self from the rain: but any thing rather than an arm-chair.

A Presentiment.—Good Heavens! my dear child, what fools your women are, both living and dead! your top-knots* shock me! What a profanation! it smells of paganism; foh! It would make me shudder at the thoughts of dying in Provence; I would, at least, be assured that the milliner and undertaker were not sent for at the same time. Fie, fie, indeed! but no more of this.†

* It was the custom in Provence to bury the dead with their faces uncovered; and the women who wore ribbons as a head-dress, retained them in their coffins.

† This passage might deserve the name of presentiment. All she feared came to pass. She died in Provence, and the very head-dress which was so repugnant to her mind, adorned her in her coffin.

LETTERS ON THE DEATH OF MADAME DE SÉVIGNÉ.

LETTER I.

FROM THE COUNTESS DE GRIGNAN TO THE PRESIDENT DE MOULCEAU.

PARIS, April 18, 1696.

YOUR politeness, sir, need not lead you to fear the renewal of my grief,* in speaking to me of the afflicting loss I have sustained. This is an object which my mind bears constantly in view, and which is so deeply engraven in my heart that nothing has power to increase or diminish it. I am convinced, sir, that you could not have heard the dreadful misfortune which has happened to me without shedding tears; I can answer for your heart: you lose a friend of incomparable merit and fidelity; nothing is more worthy of your regret; and what, sir, do not I lose? what perfections were not united in her to me, by different characters, most dear and most precious? A loss so complete and so irreparable, leads me to seek for consolation only in the bitterness of tears and groans. I have not strength to raise my eyes to the place whence comfort flows; I can yet only cast them around me, and I no longer see the dear being who has loaded me with blessings, whose attention from day to day has been occupied in adding fresh proofs of her love to the charms of her society. It is too true, sir, that it requires more than human fortitude to bear so

* Madame de Sévigné, as it appears, died early in April.

cruel a disunion and so much privation. I was far from being prepared for it: the perfect health I saw her enjoy, and a year's illness, which a hundred times endangered my own life, had taken from me the idea that the order of nature could be fulfilled by her dying first. I flattered myself that I should never have this great evil to endure: it is come upon me, and I feel it in all its severity. I deserve your pity, sir; and some share in the honor of your friendship, if sincere esteem and high veneration for your virtue can deserve it. My sentiments have been the same toward you since I had the pleasure of knowing you; and I believe I have more than once told you that it is impossible for any one to respect you more than I do.

LETTER II.

FROM M. DE COULANGES TO MADAME DE SIMIANE.*

PARIS, May 25, 1696.

Far from taking it unkindly, madam, that you did not write to me with your own hand, I am very much surprised that you even thought of me at a time so cruel and so fatal as the present. I did not doubt your sensibility at the loss we have sustained; and I could easily conceive what it would cost your excellent heart. God of heaven, what a blow is this to us all! For myself, I am lost in the thought that I shall no longer see the dear cousin to whom I have been from infancy so affectionately attached, and who returned this attachment so tenderly and so faithfully. If you could see, madam, all that passes here, you would be still better acquainted with the merit of your grandmother, for never was worth more truly acknowledged than hers; and the public renders her, with pious regret, all the honor which is due to her. Madame de Coulanges is grieved to an excess that it is impossible to de-

* The dear *Pauline*, the favorite grand-daughter of Madame de Sé- vigné. See page 418.

scribe, and I tremble for its effect upon her own health. From the day that announced to us the fatal illness, which in the end took our friend from us forever, we have lost all peace of mind. The Duchess de Chaulnes is almost dead, and poor Madame de la Troche—.* In short, we meet together to weep, and to regret what we have lost; and in the midst of our grief, we are not without anxiety for the health of your mother. Do not write to me; order one of your meanest attendants to inform us how you are: I entreat you to believe that your mother's health and your own are very precious to me, for more reasons than one; for I think I owe it to the memory of Madame de Sévigné, to be more attached to you and Madame de Grignan than before, from knowing so well the sentiments she entertained for her and for you. I shall not write to your mother for a long time, for fear of increasing her grief by my letters; but omit me not, whenever an opportunity offers; make mention of my name; be assured that of all your servants, relations, friends, no one is more deeply afflicted than I am, no one feels a greater interest in all that concerns you. I shall not show your letter immediately to Madame de Coulanges; but I shall not fail to tell her that you do not forget her. I can assure you that you owe her this justice on account of her love for you. Allow me to pay my sad compliments to M. de Simiane, the Chevalier de Grignan, and M. de la Garde. Heavens, what a scene in this royal château! Poor Mademoiselle de Marsillac too, who has so well discharged all the duties of friendship, how I feel for her!

LETTER III.

FROM MADAME DE COULANGES TO MADAME DE SIMIANE.

PARIS, May 2, 1696.

I am truly obliged to you, madame, for still thinking of me. I knew all your excellences; but the affection of your

* This phrase is incomplete.

heart, and the regard you have felt for a person so worthy of being beloved as she whom you regret, appear to me to be above all praise. Ah! madam, how much reason have you to believe me to be deeply affected! I can think of no other subject; I can talk of nothing else. I am ignorant of the particulars of this fatal illness, and the eagerness with which I seek for them shows that I have little power over myself. I spent the whole of yesterday with the prior of St. Catharine's. You may guess upon what our conversation turned. I showed him the letter you have done me the honor to write to me. It gave him real pleasure, for persons of his turn of mind are so convinced that this life ought only to serve as a passport to the other, that the dispositions in which we leave the world are to them the only ones that are worthy of attention. But we think of what we have lost, and we lament it. For myself, I have no female friend left. My turn will soon come; it is reasonable to expect it; but to hear a person of your age entertain such serious and melancholy thoughts is rare indeed. Your understanding, madam, makes me forget your youth; and this, added to the natural partiality I feel for you, seems to authorize me to address you as I do.

LETTER IV.

FROM THE COUNT DE GRIGNAN TO M. DE COULANGES.

GRIGNAN, May 23, 1696.

You, sir, can understand better than any one the magnitude of the loss we have sustained, and my just grief. Madame de Sévigné's distinguished merit was perfectly known to you. It is not merely a mother-in-law that I regret; this name does not always command esteem; it is an amiable and excellent friend, and a delightful companion. But it is a circumstance more worthy of our admiration than our regret, that this noble-minded woman contemplated the approach of death, which she expected from the moment of her attack, with astonishing firmness and submission. She, who was so tender and so timid respecting those she loved, displayed the utmost fortitude and piety when she believed that she ought to think only of herself; and we can not but remark how useful and important it is to fill the mind with good things and sacred subjects, for which Madame de Sévigné appears to have had a peculiar taste, not to say a surprising avidity, by the use she made of these excellent provisions in the last moments of her life. I relate these particulars to you, sir, because they accord with your sentiments, and will be gratifying to the friendship you have borne for her whom we lament; and at the same time my mind is so full of them that it is a relief to me to find a man so well disposed as you are to listen to the recital, and take pleasure in hearing it. I hope, sir, that the memory of a friend who highly esteemed you will contribute to preserve to me the regard with which you have long honored me. I prize it too highly, and wish it too much, not to deserve it a little.

INDEX.

	PAGE
Adhemar, Count (see note)	30
Adoration	413
Affection	423
Alone	409
Apparition, An	362
Arianism	413
Baptism	416
Bellefond, Marshal	75, 152
Blanchfort	392
Bleeding, An anecdote	401
Books	421
Bouillon, Duchess de	189, 191
Bourdaloüe	91, 111
Broncas	43
Bride, A	401
Brinon, Madame de	260, 270
Brinvilliers, Madame de	154, 155
Brittany, Disturbances in	124, 238
Bussy, Count de (see note)	19, 350
Bussy, Count de, Letters to	19–28
Calprenedre, La	62
Chantal, Baroness de	15
Charles II. of England	245, 246
Chaulnes, Madame de	66
Chatelet, Magdalen de (see note)	56
Chaulnes, Madame de	66
Chaulnes, Duke de	386
Chess	409
Children, Hints about	395
Christian Humility	410

	PAGE
Colbert	178
Company	401
Condé, Prince de	87
Conti, Prince de	353, 356, 361
Corbinelli	181, 217, 355
Coulanges, M. de, Letters to	368–393
Coulanges, M. de, Letters from	425
Coulanges, Madame de	187, 212, 223, 426
Court News	38
Courtier, A	409
Dauphiness	208, 216
Death	79
Death of Madame de Sévigné	428
Departure of Madame de Sévigné	28
Descartes (termed *Father* in the Letters)	238
Devices, Several	406
Dreux, Madame de	214
Dubois	220
Dullness	134
Elopement	331
Esther, Tragedy of	283
Evening employments	400
Expenses	415
Faith in Christ	419
Fayette, Madame de La	211, 212, 294
Feuillade, M. de	129
Fire-eater, The	420
Flechier, (see note)	217
Folly	414
Forgiving Mother, A	408
Fortune, Calculation of her	51
Fouquet, M.	205, 208, 297–329
Fouquet, Madame de	300, 303
Free will	405
Gaming	404
General Preface	7
Geneviève	121
Grammont, Countess de	**182**

INDEX. 435

	PAGE
Grammont, Marshal de	91, 422
Grignan, Count de	26, 27
Grignan, Count de, Letter from	427
Grignan, Count de, Letters to	338–346
Grignan, Madame or Countess, Letters to	28–296
Grignan, Countess de, Letters from	424
Grignan, Mademoiselle	357
Grignan, the young Marquis	417
Granville, M.	17
Guiche, Count de	91, 92
Harcourt, Countess de	63
History of the Bible	423
Home Life	411
Hope ever	426
Jealousy	414
Jews, their religion	147
Joli, Claude	29
Josephus	426
King, The (see note 197)	410
King of England	265, 269, 271, 280, 282
King of France, Anecdote of	308
King of France, Generosity of	364
La Marans	76, 89, 107
La Trousse	129
Launoi, Mademoiselle de	112
Lauzun, Duke de, Marriage of	369
Lavardin, M. de	228, 234, 378
La Voisin, The prisoner	184, 190, 200
Liberty at Home	411
Liberty of Mind	421
Living, Rules of	399
Longueville, Madame de	89, 210, 211
Lot of Mankind, The	414
Louvois, M. de	381, 383
Love, its symptoms	408
Luxembourg, M. de	185, 188, 192, 215
Mainbourg, Father (see note)	148

	PAGE
Maine, Duke of	102
Mademoiselle de Montpensier, Marriage of	368–373
Maintenon, Madame (see note)	181, 182, 223
Marriage, The impromptu	400
Mary Blanche	417
Mary Stuart (see note)	253
Maxims	57, 67
Meri, Chevalier de	181
Montespan, Madame de	118, 119, 160, 396, 397
Montmort, Abbé	40
Moonlight Walk	230
Moral Essays	422
Moulceau, President de, Letters to	347–367
Namur	388
Nicole	61, 70, 72
Ninon de l'Enclos	16, 39
Noailles, Duke de (see note)	348
Nuns of St. Marie	422
Obstinate Son	407
Old age	425
Order	56, 416
Order de la St. Esprit	255
Pain	81
Paulina	162, 164, 279, 289, 291, 418
Pecuniary embarrassments	407
Philipsburg	252
Philosophy	424
Plessis, Mademoiselle du	49, 51, 60, 225
Polignac, Madame de	363
Pomponne, M. de, his dismissal	177, 187, 193
Pomponne, M. de, Letters to	297–329
Port Royal	395
Potable Gold (see note)	167
Preface, General	7
Presentiment	427
Providence	405
Puissort (see note)	302
Quarrels in High Life	402

	PAGE
Queen of England.............................. 267, 271,	273
Queen of France, Illness of........................	312
Queen of Spain poisoned (see note).................	277
Rabutin-Chantal, Marie de.........................	15
Racine.. 75,	80
Readings...	412
Reason, Use of...................................	405
Reflections......................................	396
Regrets..	32
Reproaches......................................	161
Retz, Cardinal de........................ 114, 117,	120
Rheims, Archbishop of............................	111
Rheumatism.....................................	151
Richelieu, Cardinal (see note)......................	229
Robbery (see note)..............................	109
Rochefoucault, M. de la 42, 82, 202,	204
Rocks, The (Madame de Sévigné's estate).............	48
Roquette, Gabriel de (see note).....................	210
Saint Simon, Duke of.............................	109
Scarron, Madame de........................... 74,	394
Schomberg, Count de.............................	253
Schomberg, Madame de (see note).................	102
Selections from various letters.....................	394
Sermons...	426
Sévigné, Madame de, and her time..................	13
Sévigné, Marguerite de (see note)...................	28
Sévigné, Marquis de..................... 172, 183,	198
Sévigné, Marquis de, Letters to...............	330–337
Sévigné, Madame de, Death of.....................	428
Sévigné, Marquis de, Extravagance of..............	403
Sobieski, John (see note)..........................	95
Soissons, Countess de........................ 186,	190
St. Augustine............................... 157,	414
St. Cyr..	275
Submission......................................	424
Supper at Madame Coulanges.....................	394
Telescope, The...................................	398
Termes, M. de............................... 168,	169
Thianges, Madame de............................	100
Thianges, Mademoiselle de.........................	341

	PAGE
Transparencies	159
Trappe, La	37
Turenne, Marshall de (see note)	64, 126–135
Twilight	427
Vallière, Duchess de la	33, 104, 114
Vardes, M. de	54, 351
Vatel	44, 45
Vendome, Chevalier	93, 94
Ventadour, M. de	38
Versailles in 1676	396
Villars, Abbé (see note)	68
Villeroi, Marshal de	189
Vivonne, M. de	93, 94, 110
Whims	123
Words, The use of	139
Work	399

www.ingramcontent.com/pod-product-compliance
Lightning Source LLC
Chambersburg PA
CBHW051734300426
44115CB00007B/557